FOLLOW ME AND DIE

Also by Cecil B. Currey:

Self-Destruction: The Disintegration and Decay of the United States Army During the Vietnam Era.
Reason and Revelation: John Duns Scotus on Natural Theology.
The Craft and Crafting of History.
Code Number 72: Ben Franklin, Patriot or Spy?
Road to Revolution: Benjamin Franklin in England, 1765–1775.
Puritan Churches in the Golden Age.
Guide to Images of America.

and other writings.

FOLLOW ME AND DIE

The Destruction of an American Division in World War II

Cecil B. Currey

MILITARY HERITAGE PRESS
New York

Publisher's Note: German terms and German military units are printed in *italics*.

This edition published by Military Heritage Press,
a division of Marboro Books Corporation,
by arrangement with
Stein and Day/Publishers
1988 Military Heritage Press

ISBN 0-88029-285-7
(formerly ISBN 0-8128-2842-5)

Printed in the United States of America

M 9 8 7 6 5 4 3 2 1

For

Earl Fuller, Jr.

who cared enough to help and who believed that if war and battle could be shown in proper perspective, other and younger men might not have to suffer as did those of his generation.

CONTENTS

PHOTOGRAPHS

MAPS

High above the Chattahoochee
Near the Upatoy
Stands an old abandoned brick house
Benning School for Boys

Onward ever, backward never
Follow me and die
To the Port of Embarkation
Next of kin goodbye.

Sung to the tune of
"High Above Cayuga's Waters,"
this was the unofficial song
of young officer candidates
training during World War II
at the U.S. Army
Infantry School at Ft. Benning,
Georgia

PREFACE

I first learned of this battle in August 1975, when I arrived at the United States Army Command and General Staff College at Fort Leavenworth, Kansas, and received my initial issue of text material for courses that all students would study during coming months. Among those piles of printed manuals was one for a course in "fundamentals of combined arms warfare"; it dealt with the calamitous attack by the 28th Infantry Division on the little German crossroads town of Schmidt in November 1944. Classes and assigned readings on this battle fascinated me, and the saga of that division continued to haunt me long after I graduated from the school. I taught it to my own students and continued to learn as much about it as I could. It was a story that needed retelling.

I rode in the front passenger seat of the Volkswagen van beside the driver, my friend and former student, Michael Depuhl, who is a German national. His wife and three children rode in the rear. We turned east on one of the roads leading out of Germeter, a village that nestles in the high Eifel country. The countryside flowed by that August day in 1979 as we passed tiny checkerboard fields. Soon we slowed for the houses of Vossenack, and then we were at the crossroads where stands the old church, now rebuilt but still bearing on its outer walls ravages from the pox of war. Inside remains no sign of the combat that once raged through the sanctuary, and a new steeple again points its finger toward God. In the quiet, well-tended cemetery at the rear, a caretaker pointed out the grave of *Generalfeldmarschall* Walther Model, who shot himself on 21 April 1945, leaving a request to be buried here where so many of his soldiers had fallen.

We drove south from the church, the tarmac soon ending, leaving only a dirt trail much as it must have looked in 1944. We traveled toward the tree line running along the southern edge of the Vossenack ridge, the woods there a remnant of the once-feared Hürtgen Forest barrier faced by American troops as they thrust their way across the borders of Germany. As the trail ended at a fence line, Michael pulled the van into a meadow rank with grass. We parked near a bench someone had placed at the head of the trail that winds down into the Kall River gorge. It is a beautiful spot for weary travelers to sit and rest under a large maple tree. Nearby a fire tower stands guard.

Among the thick trees in the Kall Valley, pines and firs still predominate as they did in those November days of battle. The meadows are peaceful now, and fat Jersey cows grazed nearby. Overhead flew an occasional stork or crane. Wild flowers bloomed in profusion.

Michael and I left his family picnicking in the shade and set forth down the trail. We could see as we walked the concave reminders of foxholes and trenches once dug by desperate men. I thought of young panic-stricken soldiers trembling in the bitterly cold weather—men who fled their positions to run with heaving chests from Schmidt to Kommerscheidt, across the stone arch over the river, up the steep Kall trail to Vossenack, Germeter, and safety. The old rifle pits touched by a scattering of pine straw bore mute testimony to that old war.

We strolled out of the trail's darkness onto the meadow, and I thought of that battle. The commanding general flung three regiments into combat in as many directions. The 109th, sent toward Hürtgen, north of Germeter, blundered into a minefield and became trapped by explosions and wooded ambushes. Booby traps and deadly enfilade fire from fortifications of the Siegfried Line south of Germeter butchered men of the 110th. The 112th divided its battalions. One invested Vossenack, while the other two marched south down the trail into the gorge, across the river, and up the other side into Kommerscheidt and Schmidt. All three battalions—and all three regiments—succumbed to an abattoir of bloodshed caused by fierce and unexpected German resistance. What before I had studied only on maps and from printed pages now actually spread out before my eyes.

I could see plainly the various high ridges circling Vossenack. To the northeast were the towns of Brandenberg and Bergstein, both close set on a ridge overlooking Vossenack. Toward the south I could see the half-moon-shaped hamlet of Kommerscheidt, and beyond it was Schmidt, once the battle objective of an American division.

My friend wondered aloud if perhaps those who died had a moment to think before they perished. Did they believe their sacrifice to be worthwhile? Did they think of their families? Did they mourn themselves and the years that might have stretched before them but now were cut short? Did they worry who would win the battle, the war? Or did they just scream in pain as their spirits fled their broken clay?

The peaceful silence of the Vossenack ridge was shattered by thunderous roars from airplanes passing overhead, fighters operating out of nearby airbases. One jet soared low, its shadow streaking across woods and meadow, then flickering from sight. We two stood there—an American, a German—and wondered if mankind in the years since that battle may have learned too much. I recalled a survivor of the battle with whom I corresponded. Interested in helping me with my research, he expended great energy on my project even while suffering from throat cancer; he hoped that his efforts might spare other men the misery and anguish he endured on these high ridges of Germany.

Michael called out to *Frau* Dupuhl and their children and we climbed back into the van to return to Vossenack. I glanced at my North Eifel Nature Park map as we bounced over the rough dirt road. That map shows a military cemetery just south of nearby Hürtgen, where lie bodies of some of those

Germans who died when Americans were tied down on the west side of the road we traveled and their enemies were dug in to the east.

Almost all of Vossenack dates since 1945. Of the old buildings, only the strongest managed to withstand utter devastation from bombs, TNT, tank blasts, bazooka shells, mortar rounds, and artillery barrages. On the main east–west street still stands a Bavarian-style wayside crucifix that survived. Bullet pocks scar the form of the *Christus,* as if doubting Thomas were dissatisfied with but five wounds in the body of his Lord. A house six feet behind the cruciform was totally destroyed.

Across that thoroughfare to the north is the home of the village *burgomeister, Herr* Baptiste Palme. A kindly man, he invited us to visit with him and we sat on his porch drinking lemonade. He informed us that during the struggle for the *Hürtgenwald,* some 56,000 people—both soldiers and civilians—died in the vicinity of Vossenack, Germeter, Kommerscheidt, and Schmidt. Not all those bodies have even yet been recovered. In the fourth decade after the battle, farmers toil at their work. Laborers build fences, dig wells, or repair roads. They uncover perhaps ten to fifteen ancient and decayed corpses each year, reluctantly surrendered by the earth.

Such rotted remains can no longer be identified by nationality. Wearing U.S. Army khaki or *Wehrmacht* gray, they fell in clinging wet snow and cloying mud. Martial strife churned on and war's detritus covered them. Having fought one another, they lay stiffly together, united in death as they never were in life. All arguments ceased, all differences vanished as their earthen tomb embraced them.

Palme called that great battle the Verdun of Germany and told us that he fought in it as a *Feldwebel*—a sergeant—in the *Wehrmacht's 116th Panzer Division.* He saw Vossenack, his own hometown, shatter and burn, leaving only piles of unrecognizable rubble. Now he was mayor of a town risen from ashes. He recalled for me the hatred he felt at the time. Then he told of his pleasure when American survivors of that battle came back many years later as a tour group to visit those scenes and to refresh their memories. They visited Vossenack at the same time that German veterans of that action held their own reunion. Palme recounted how old adversaries laughed and drank and regaled new and former friends with oft-told war stories.

Before time obscures and blurs completely their story; before the Final Victor encompasses them, this account sets forth the ensanguined record of the Khaki and the Gray as they heeded the call of their leaders.

The chances of men in the 28th Infantry Division surviving the raging conflict in the Hürtgen Forest, 2–16 November 1944, were slim. In 1st Battalion, 110th Regiment, for example, 871 men went into battle. Two hundred additional replacements were assigned to the unit before the action ended. When the outfit was withdrawn, just 25 men were still considered fit enough to be listed as "combat effective." Many other units suffered in similar fashion.

In a real sense, then, the sources for this story were accidental in two ways. First, few lived through the combat to tell about it. Second, the combat interviews that recorded the action were initially planned to illustrate a successful battle operation. When the outcome at Schmidt was so much different than was originally hoped for, authorities classified the interviews. These stories remained buried for the most part thereafter except for a few publications by the Center for Military History of the Department of Army, few of which were available to the general reading public.

This work is not only an explanation and reenactment of the battle but also a testament to those who survived it. For this reason, I have often allowed individuals to speak at length in their own words. It seemed important to me to allow them at last to have the opportunity to describe what they saw and endured. Many of the names of those who appear herein could have been omitted, for they are important only to their descendants. But that was enough to persuade me to include them.

The names of other men were central to the story, and they reappear with regularity during the action: Major General Norman Cota, Brigadier General George Davis, Lieutenant Colonel Sam Mays, Captain George Rumbaugh, PFC Nathaniel Quentin, PFC Joseph Perll, Technical Sergeant Tony Kudiak, Captain John Pruden, First Sergeant Frank Ripperdam, First Lieutenant Ray Fleig, and many others. Those men and their companies belonged to dozens of different units—squads, platoons, companies, battalions, regiments, and divisions—each with their own distinctive designation, such as 3rd Squad, 2nd Platoon, Able Company, 1st Battalion, 109th Infantry Regiment, 28th Infantry Division. I have minimized use of such designations within the text, giving them in full only in the Notes, at the end of the book. For the most part, it seemed more important to identify individuals as engineers, tankers, infantrymen, medical personnel, or tank destroyer crewmen than to repeat endlessly the units to which they were assigned.

I have diverged from this practice primarily when writing about infantrymen. To identify a man as assigned to Able Company or 1st Battalion was not enough, for each regiment had a 1st, 2nd, and 3rd Battalion. Each battalion was composed of companies A, B, C, and D. Each company had a 1st, 2nd, 3rd, and 4th Platoon. All platoons had a 1st, 2nd, 3rd, and 4th Squad. To avoid confusion, infantrymen are given—where necessary—more complete unit identifications.

It gives me great pleasure to note here the names of several persons who have helped me as I worked on this story. My thanks to students in my classes and seminars in which I have taught the events of this November 1944 conflict for their help in clarifying my thinking on certain aspects of this battle; to my student and graduate assistant Anita Bradley Eastman for locating illustrations and for valuable suggestions, including my choice of publisher; to Brigadier General (Ret.) Uzal W. Ent, Pennsylvania Army National Guard, for his help in sharing documents and valuable ideas with me; to Sergeant First Class Jim Melzark, Department of Tactics, Command and General Staff College, Fort Leavenworth, Kansas, for his aid in procuring large-scale maps of the battlefield; to Bejay Huening for creating the maps that accompany this text; to Major John Spencer, Florida Army National Guard on duty with the National Guard Bureau, the Pentagon, for his aid in securing photos from Signal Corps archives; to Raymond George Carpenter, Albert G. Kuhn, Fred Cope, Harry Geary, Jr., and Ed Guthrie for sharing their thoughts with me; to Professor Russell F. Weigley, Temple University, and to Colonel George W. Porter, Deputy Brigade Commander, 53rd Infantry Brigade, for their reading of this manuscript and for their helpful suggestions; and to Laura Gene Currey, with whom I have discussed every aspect of this project. Most of all, I offer my thanks to Earl Fuller, Jr., who gave more of himself in supporting this project than any author should have the right to expect.

Lutz, Florida — Cecil B. Currey
May 1983

FOLLOW ME AND DIE

1

"Jerry seemed to know exactly where we were at all times"

Headquarters
109th Regimental Combat Team
30 October 1944

Field Order Number 14

The enemy has manned the West Wall with the battered remnants of his western armies. . . .

In the zone of action of this Combat Team, the defenses consist of a series of field fortifications rather than deliberate defenses. . . .

It is estimated that the strength of enemy forces to the immediate front of the [28th Infantry] Division is approximately 3360 troops . . . : Immediately to the North about 1970 and to the South approximately 1390.

It is believed that the line in the GERMETER-HURTGEN area is thinly held. . . .

2 November-7 November 1944

In the still hours of dark, men huddled in blankets and ponchos, trying to hang on a little longer to their troubled sleep. They shivered in the cold, bodies trembling inside rain-damp shelters, crouched down for the night wherever they could find cover—in foxholes and dugouts, under shelter halves and in two-man pup tents, in captured bunkers and pillboxes. Their rest was fitful, punctuated by the pain of frostbitten toes and fingers and their knowledge that at dawn they would be rousted to prepare for an attack.

As blackness in the eastern sky gave way to predawn grayness, noncommissioned officers (NCOs) moved among the squads and platoons of tired, half-sick men, touching some, calling the names of others, awakening them all. Across the entire war front occupied by the American 28th Infantry Division, ripples of movement grew as soldiers stretched their aching frames into wakefulness. Infantrymen, crews of tanks and tank destroyers, engineers, medics, cooks and ammunition haulers, Army Air Corps pilots and mechanics, battalion, regimental, and divisional staffs, generals and privates—all readied themselves for battle.

Miles behind the front line, cannon cockers readied their gun positions. Land lines connecting telephone sets buzzed with activity as men in fire direction centers gave target coordinates to far-flung gun batteries. Ammunition carriers hauled 155mm and 105mm rounds and powder sacks up to tubes dug into the muddy earth.

At 0728 hours, 2 November 1944, the first rays of the morning sun broke through the pines and firs of the Hürtgen Forest, illuminating their shattered tops and glinting off puddles of water. From Rott to Zweifall, from Struffelt to Kitzenhaus, in this narrow salient near the western border of Germany, metal cannon snouts rose skyward beside mountainous stacks of ammunition.[1]

At precisely 0800, artillery crews launched the first shells of an hour-long barrage against German defensive positions. This was a customary prelude to attack, the "prep fire" or preparatory shelling of enemy hiding places—foxholes, log bunkers, reinforced concrete pillboxes—to soften up gray-clad German soldiers and to "prepare" them for killing or capture by American infantrymen who would later advance into their midst.

Concussive waves swept around those artillerymen as they ejected spent rounds and slammed new shells into steel breeches. Shells followed a parabolic curve high above shattered trees of the *Hürtgenwald*, over checkerboard fields and winding roads, and then downward toward predetermined targets.

Along the left flank of the 28th Infantry Division, crouching men of the 109th Infantry Regiment waited at the line of departure (LD), alert to shells screaming above them that lighted the distance with savage explosions.

Lieutenant Colonel Daniel B. Strickler, a lawyer from Lancaster, Pennsylvania, knew the problems he and his men faced. He was commander of the 109th Infantry Regiment, one of the 28th Infantry Division's three combat regiments. Weather conditions were less than ideal. According to General Dwight David Eisenhower, Supreme Commander of Allied forces in Europe, recent rains were "the worst known on the Continent in many years and created flood conditions along our whole front, reducing the lesser roads to quagmires and impeding tank operations and vehicular movements."[2]

Strickler may also have worried about his lack of knowledge of enemy defenses to his front. Maps supplied to the regiment were woefully inaccurate, and there is no record of patrols scouting in the 109th's path of advance prior to the attack.

The regimental order of battle worked out by Colonel Strickler and his S-3 operations officer, Major William Moraney, called for two battalions—the 1st on the left and the 3rd on the right—to move toward the two objectives of the regiment. One target was a woods line to the west of the little town of

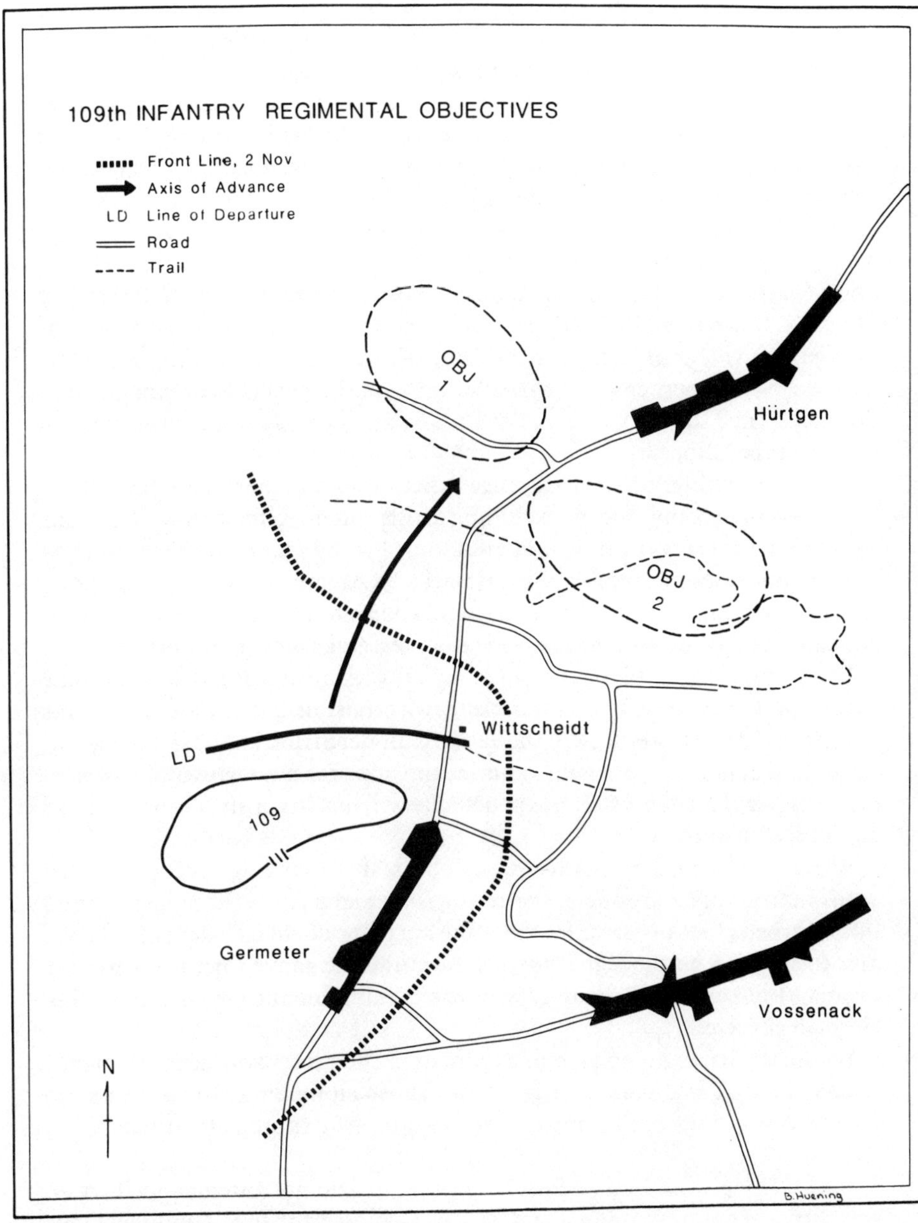
109th INFANTRY REGIMENTAL OBJECTIVES
Front Line, 2 Nov
Axis of Advance
LD Line of Departure
Road
Trail
OBJ 1
OBJ 2
Hürtgen
Wittscheidt
LD
109
III
Germeter
Vossenack
N
B. Huening

Hürtgen to their front. This target was assigned to the 1st Battalion. The second objective, assigned to the 3rd Battalion, was another woods line, this one on high ground south of Hürtgen. 2nd Battalion was to advance to the west of and behind 1st Battalion, protecting the regiment's left rear flank and assisting assault battalions as needed. It was a customary formation for infantry assaults: two up and one back.

Each rifle company was strengthened by attachment of a heavy-machine-gun section, and 81mm mortar units were already dug in, waiting to provide supporting mortar fire for advancing troops as needed. Engineers stood by to clear any mines located on routes of advance.

Strickler and his staff had done as well as they could in the limited time available. The regiment had moved into the front lines only five days earlier, on 28 October, to relieve exhausted and battered elements of the 9th Infantry Division. Since then the 109th had remained in an assembly area just west of the German village of Germeter, awaiting orders. A directive to attack at 0900 hours, 2 November, came to Strickler only on the previous evening. It was not much time to ready a regiment for an assault, and he spent the night in frantic preparations.

Colonel Strickler's S-2 intelligence officer told him there were fewer than two thousand enemy troops, excluding artillerymen, to their front. Germans held this entire sector thinly and could not bring in large numbers of reinforcements, or even supplies, due primarily to American air operations. Any enemy reinforcements, the S-2 assured Strickler, would be walking wounded, civilian reserves, or administrative staffs pressed into combat duty.[3]

Even weather seemed to favor an attack. It was the first decent day for some time. The morning was cool and clear, with fair visibility, although it was damp and a faint haze cloaked the earth. Colonel Strickler hoped the light of the brightly shining sun would vaporize the mist, for if it endured, its wraithful veils would conceal German defenders from his men as they moved anxiously forward.

Strickler observed bursts from exploding shells landing several hundred yards in front of his troopers, shattering trees and beating the winter ground into churned clods of earth. He knew the big guns would fall silent in an hour, and this would be the signal for his battalions to move forward, carefully probing the ruined forest until they made initial contact with the waiting German survivors.

Before the barrage ended, clouds obscured the sun's rays and transformed the day into a customary cold grayness. Those along the LD tried to ignore the increasing cold and aching numbness spreading through their hands and feet.

Strickler visualized no real problems that he had not anticipated. Terrain was difficult but not impossible. German soldiers were tough and tenacious but not invincible. It would all work out.[4]

Men of the 109th Infantry Regiment waited in their assembly area just behind the LD north of Germeter village and spread west from the north-south Germeter–Hürtgen road, which sliced through the trees of the *Hürtgenwald.* One author described that terrain in these words:

> Looking east from the little German border villages southeast of Aachen, the Huertgen Forest is a seemingly impenetrable mass, a vast, undulating, blackish-green ocean stretching as far as the eye can see. Upon entering the forest, you want to drop things behind to mark your path, as Hansel and Gretel did with their bread crumbs.[5]

Man-made detritus gave this area an even more alarming aspect. This was ground fought over in October by soldiers of the 9th Infantry Division, who conquered only 3,000 yards of forest at a cost of 4,500 casualties. Military flotsam and jetsam lay everywhere around men of the 109th Infantry Regiment: helmets, gas masks, empty ration cans, field jackets splotched with blood, loose mines, and grotesquely stilled bodies of Germans and Americans killed in that October combat and unretrieved by graves registration units. Constant rainfall turned roads and trails into troughs of mud. Shell holes dotted the landscape. It was a gloomy sight and lay heavily upon men of the 109th.

They faced danger the moment they came into this thick barrier of trees, the western fringe of the German homeland. First Lieutenant Edward Peer, L Company, 3rd Battalion, described how easily disaster could strike. "We could not move past the CP [command post] as the enemy was shelling open ground to our front. . . . We were only about 200 yards away" and "lost several men even before the attack due to enemy patrols and artillery. . . . We knew the enemy was digging in, as we could hear them. We had two-man foxholes. One man had to be awake at all times, constantly on the alert."[6] Casualties struck at their morale, and many men already knew too well the face of battle.

Divisional artillery batteries fired 7,313 rounds during the hour-long barrage. Crews from V and VII corps also blasted shells from their tubes at German positions. One artillery liaison officer reported 34,000 rounds expended during that hour in support of the 28th Infantry Division. Terrain made it difficult for artillery forward observers to adjust fire on objectives. In many instances, they brought rounds on target by sound rather than sight.*[7]

Captain Max Whitetree, commander of A Company, 1st Battalion, gave his men their orders. From the LD to the enemy lines was only 200 yards, some 50 of which were open ground. "At 0900 each man," he said, "is to fire a full clip from his M-1 and then keep firing as he moves forward."[8]

The minute hand swept across 0900 hours. Shells ceased bursting as the

---

*During the first two weeks of combat, the 109th Artillery, its batteries located southwest of Zweifall, fired 3,832 missions and 23,521 rounds of ammunition in support of the regiment. Gun crews suffered no deaths and only four injuries.

bombardment lifted. Whistles shrilled and commands were shouted. GIs scrambled to their feet and moved forward. Some companies advanced in squad columns; others in lateral skirmish lines with men about six yards apart. When the first wave was 75 yards out, the second group advanced, then the third. They received only light small-arms fire from German positions at first. Then mortar and artillery rounds fired from behind enemy lines began to drop among them; German forward observers could watch them every step of the way.

1st Battalion moved forward on the west, the left side of the advance, with 3rd Battalion on the east, its right flank. Soldiers in 1st Battalion crossed an open area, hastened down a slope to the bottom of a draw, and then bunched there, fearful of nearby German machine guns hammering at them from adjacent cover in the forest. Able Company troops hunkered down, hiding from deadly staccato bursts fired by well-camouflaged enemy automatic weapons emplaced within hidden log bunkers.

Second Lieutenant Samuel Leo saw his men huddled in the draw, unable to move. Scrambling to his feet, he ran up the slope, firing his carbine. It jammed. He continued on toward the enemy bunker and threw a grenade inside. He wounded five Germans, and the machine gun fell silent. He yelled at his men to start moving forward. "We kept on going," said one. They went through exploding shells from German 105mm artillery and 81mm mortars, and Leo charged a second bunker, ordering those inside to surrender. When they refused, he threw two grenades inside and the surviving Germans came out with hands held high.

American casualties fell writhing on the damp ground. Technical Sergeant Robert Pavlowski, an Able Company squad leader, was shot in the face by one of those machine guns. As a medic went to his aid, he also was wounded. Pavlowski died before he could be evacuated.[9]

Everywhere GIs encountered stiff German resistance from survivors of the artillery preparatory barrage hidden in machine-gun nests, rifle pits, open foxholes, and log bunkers. That hour-long bombardment blew out treetops, dropping branches over many German foxholes, sometimes hiding their positions and enabling them to wait until American troops plodded past and then shoot GIs in the back.[10] Frantic pleas for 81mm mortar crews to place rounds on such targets seemed to have little effect on German defenses.

Efforts to find their way through the thick forest provided another kind of difficulty. Second Lieutenant Thomas Whitney, B Company, 1st Battalion, angrily complained about his map, which "was so inaccurate that it showed woods where there was a clearing. . . . We thought we were coming close to our objective, but the map was so bad that we weren't sure of our location, so we dug in. Later we found we were in Company A's area. The woods were so thick it was impossible to see any distance or recognize any terrain features."[11]

Major James Clark Ford, Jr., commander of 1st Battalion, agreed with Whitney. Ford stormed, "If anyone, from private right on up to me, says he knows where he is at any one time, he's a damned liar."*[12] So confused soldiers stumbled ahead through dense growth, along paths cluttered with splintered branches while enemy mortar shells exploded at every open turn along the way. Their feet squelched into the earth as they moved ever deeper into the dark forest.

3rd Battalion, on the right, was caught up in its own troubles. It also crossed open fields as it moved out from the LD, protected by clouds of smoke from bursting chemical rounds just ahead of its advancing troops, fired by mortars of the regimental heavy-weapons H Company. The Germans retaliated even before 3rd Battalion could cross the LD. Heavy German counterbarrage fire landed right in the holes of some men who were waiting to start forward, while to their front was an enemy crossfire of machine guns and 81mm mortars fired from the north and east.

Trying to make use of protective smoke rounds falling ahead of them, First Lieutenant Edward Peer started his men across open ground one at a time. After several reached protective cover, Peer said, Germans "put tracers in their guns to see why our men could run across in front of their fire. They got the sixth man in the leg. . . . The Jerries had a lot of snipers and good observation. Every time a man would move he would draw a lot of mortar and sniper fire." Peer tried using available machine guns to provide protection for his men "but their fields of fire were very limited."[13]

While Peer's L Company received heavy enemy fire, K Company initially fared only a little better. Its men advanced across open ground for 200 yards amid shattering explosions. Then Staff Sergeant William Herman, of 2nd Platoon, was blown off his feet and wounded. His men picked him up and pressed forward hoping to get out of range but came up against a roll of concertina wire extending completely across K Company's front.

Rifle and machine-gun fire from German emplacements pinned them down, causing heavy casualties. Second Lieutenant Edmund Tropp, a platoon leader in 3rd Battalion's heavy-weapons M Company, tried to knock out enemy machine guns with salvos of mortar shells but was unsuccessful. Men of King Company were in a real predicament. Unknowingly they had advanced through a minefield, and it was an exploding mine that had injured Sergeant Herman. Now they were caught between a wire barrier to their front and a minefield to their rear and were pinned down by enemy bullets.[14]

---

*Born 4 August 1916, Major Ford graduated from Monongahela High School, enlisted in the Pennsylvania National Guard in 1934, and was inducted into federal service with A Company, 1st Battalion, 110th Infantry Regiment in February 1941. He received a direct commission to second lieutenant in 1942. By 1944 he was a major, assigned as S-3 operations officer for the 110th Regiment. A friend described him as a "total" leader, able to lead rather than push his men into actions they were reluctant to undertake. Shortly before this battle, he took command of 1st Battalion, 109th Regiment, and was killed, 8 November, while on a reconnaissance survey near Vossenack. See Charles Chattaway, "Gentlemen from Hell: The History of the 110th Infantry Regiment, 28th Division" (privately printed pamphlet, March 1979), p. 33.

Casualties mounted so high that soon Staff Sergeant Aiken Still was the only NCO left in the platoon. He ordered his men to save themselves, to move back out of the minefield if they could. Over 40 men in King Company were by now wounded. Soldiers crawled carefully toward safety, when possible dragging injured buddies with them. Evacuation of those with wounds was difficult. One man encountered "three German medics who could speak a little French. They had two of our men and three of theirs . . . the lines were so mixed up no one knew where his own lines were. One of the German medics carried one of our men back and gave himself up at the same time."[15]

With both King and Love companies in trouble, heavy-weapons H Company tried to lend all possible support. Set up at a sawmill a little distance beyond the LD, its machine-gun crews fired enfilade fire into Hürtgen to the north and swept the ground in front of advancing GIs. During that day, machine-gun crews used up over 140,000 rounds, or four boxes of ammunition every six hours. It still was not enough. Mortarmen fired patterns on suspected enemy routes of approach and onto targets of opportunity called in by infantrymen. By day's end, mortar crews chalked up nearly 900 salvos of high explosives. They also suffered casualties. One battery of Howe Company was wiped out by a treetop burst from an enemy artillery piece. Two officers were also evacuated—one from combat exhaustion, the other from wounds.[16]

L Company desperately tried to get through the minefield. "We sent out patrols," said Lieutenant Peer, "to probe the minefields to see if we could find an opening. The Germans had about one hundred yards of firebreak full of scrub pine under observation. Everytime one of our men would move through it the artillery and mortars would start. A four-man patrol went out walking and crawling. When they got to the wire, they cut as much as they could, but they lost two men and had to return. . . . Then they started picking up logs and throwing them . . . to set off the mines." Such actions were not all that helpful. Mines and concertina wire were such barriers that Love Company men could move forward only a few feet at a time. "Even the Germans became entangled and some were killed," Peer related, "as they tried to move toward us."

Trapped and terrified GIs found themselves struck by continuing barrages of German artillery and mortar fire. "No one was dug in at this time," Peer stated, "and we were having a good many casualties." Sergeants took command from fallen lieutenants, corporals gave orders when sergeants died, and privates first class (PFCs) became acting sergeants and sometimes received battlefield commissions as their comrades were wounded or died all around them. "Medics were taking men out as fast as they could," commented Lieutenant Peer, "but there were too many for them." At 1530 that afternoon, L Company survivors pulled back and dug in for the night.[17]

With both K and L companies immobilized, Major Howard Topping, 3rd Battalion commander, determined to commit his reserve force, I Company. Thrown into the fray, it moved forward only about 400 yards before it, too, became entangled in the minefield.[18]

Item Company's Technical Sergeant Thomas Blair recalled that as they worked their way forward "men took what cover they could and started looking for some place to cross." Four men got through the minefield "before Jerry put down machine-gun and mortar fire." The four men pulled back in the face of machine gun, mortar, and small-arms fire and snipers hidden in trees. As they pressed forward to attack, Blair said, "we didn't know about the minefield covered with barb wire."[19]

Another member of Item Company, Staff Sergeant Frank Stunar, spoke German. He talked with some prisoners of war. Their news was not good. "They said . . . there was another minefield further on."[20]

First Lieutenant Bruce Paul, I Company commander, felt the hopelessness of his men's plight. No one had any idea how far the minefield stretched. Neither of his leading platoons could advance, and I Company casualty figures mounted. "In 1st Platoon," Paul lamented, "there were now only 12 men left."

As if conditions were not bad enough, German tanks now rolled south down the road out of Hürtgen toward American positions. They pulled to a stop several hundred yards away and opened fire with their turret guns. Behind them, on high ground at Hürtgen, German 105mm artillery and 81mm mortars launched withering barrages every 10 to 15 minutes. To Americans trapped in the woods and minefields, it seemed that if hell existed, they had found it.[21]

It was easy for inexperienced men to make mistakes under such pressure. Hit by fire from all sides, in the midst of a forest "so thick it was impossible . . . to move or see any distance," terrified of triggering booby traps and mines, some officers led their men to their deaths. Second Lieutenant George Vance, E Company, 2nd Battalion, was one officer who unknowingly led his 2d Platoon into a deathtrap. His entire group, with the exception of four men, were killed or wounded by mines, booby traps, and machine-gun fire. German gunners kept their weapons trained on the site where those bodies lay, preventing evacuation of the corpses.*[22]

Captain Max Whitetree, commander of Able Company, could not believe how thickly Germans infested the woods. Tree boles often prevented effective rifle fire, so Whitetree and his men used hand grenades. It seemed very one-sided to him: grenades against burp guns. "As soon as Jerry knew we were there," deplored Whitetree, "all hell would break loose." In his view, their single gravest problem was that "Jerry seemed to know exactly where we were at all times."[23]

German resistance continued to prevent troops of the 109th from achieving their objectives. First Lieutenant Charles Potter, S-2 intelligence officer for

---

*Engineers tried to clear a path through the minefield to the bodies, but each time German mortar fire drove them back to cover. Some corpses lay where they fell until they were finally evacuated on 15 November.

1st Battalion,* complained of the uncanny ability of Germans "to follow advancing units with their artillery and mortar fire."[24] Whitetree agreed. Platoons of his Able Company were so depleted he combined two, giving them a total strength of fewer than twenty-five men.[25]

Few American soldiers still continued to press their attack. They hoped instead to survive for the rest of the day. "We improved our positions and tried to improvise shelters to protect us from the tree bursts," Staff Sergeant William Horan recalled, as Germans "continued to pound the living hell out of us." Not far from Horan was an enemy log bunker. GIs and Germans exchanged occasional shots as both groups worked at digging entrenchments. Every time Horan and his men bent to their shovels, "the noise would bring enemy fire" down on them.[26]

Only in the area of Whitetree's depleted A Company did the war proceed in ways Americans found satisfactory. Their first success began at around 1400 hours. Lieutenant Leo, having wiped out two enemy machine-gun bunkers earlier in the day, saw a column of Germans marching through the woods in a column of twos. Leo signaled his men to hold their fire until their foes were well within killing range. They opened fire when their targets were 25 yards away. Machine gunners fired a full belt, and each American armed with a Browning Automatic Rifle (BAR) snapped through an entire clip of ammunition. When sounds of gunfire ceased, every enemy soldier save one was dead. The survivor, a Polish-German, was taken prisoner and shunted to the rear. Forty bodies lay on the ground.[27]

From then on Able Company troops reacted as if they were participants in a turkey shoot. Since even Germans were confused by the fluid lines within the forest, it was not surprising that an enemy messenger came riding a bicycle south down the Germeter–Hürtgen highway, expecting to pedal right up to his destination. He had no indication Americans were nearby until the moment a rifleman from A Company drew a bead on him and killed him.

A horse-drawn "chow wagon" carrying cabbage and tea for German soldiers next came south down the road. GIs cheerfully surrounded it, forcing a surprised driver to surrender. They were glad for such unexpected refreshments, for no one expected hot food from their own rear area to be sent forward.

Able Company troops then observed a horse-drawn ammunition wagon moving slowly along the road toward them. Having already hidden the captured chow wagon, they allowed this new driver to draw quite close before they opened fire, killing both him and his horse. Twenty minutes later, a platoon of German soldiers moved along this much-used route. Technical Sergeant Charles Frawley griped disgustedly that "one of our men fired too soon, giving them a chance to get away. They lost only two men."[28]

* Only Potter, of the entire 1st Battalion staff, lasted out the battle. All others were wounded or killed in action.

Despite difficulties of terrain and stiff German resistance, some soldiers of the 109th Infantry Regiment made progress toward those assigned objectives. As early as 1400 hours, while men in Able Company were beginning their target practice, two 1st Battalion companies reached their goal: a woods line to the left of the Germeter–Hürtgen road. Yet consolidation of even small gains was not easy, for they were harassed by artillery and mortar bombardments and by German soldiers infiltrating behind them. Rear areas became as much a battlefield as the "front."

These rifle companies of 1st Battalion were now as far north as they could get. Their sister units in 3rd Battalion, however, were hopelessly ensnarled within the minefield along the Germeter–Hürtgen road, having moved little more than 300 yards north of the LD since 0900 hours. During the day Colonel Strickler committed two rifle companies of his reserve 2nd Battalion in an effort to pierce through German resistance. It was to no avail. First Battalion now sat on part of its objective, the woods line above Hürtgen, but Third Battalion was stymied.

As night closed in, no further advance was likely, so men of the 109th began to seek cover for themselves. Cool all day, the air grew gradually colder until men were shivering helplessly, trying to bring circulation to their hands and feet and wondering what the next day would bring. The night was quiet, with only an occasional German artillery shell bursting within American lines.[29]

28th Infantry Division G-3 Periodic Report
020001 November to 022400 November 1944

Weather: Cool and clear; visibility fair

109th attacked at 0900; 1 BN advanced about 2300 meters meeting light enemy resistance. 3 BN advanced about 1300 meters, meeting heavy enemy resistance.

Result of Operation: 109th Infantry advanced to its objective on the left, encountering light enemy resistance. Progress on the right was slow due to heavy artillery, mortar, machine gun and small arms fire. . . . Division operation was successful and placed units in position for future action.

Combat Efficiency: Excellent.

THOMAS E. BRIGGS
Assistant Chief of Staff
G-3

At 0500 on 3 November, men of the 109th Infantry Regiment solemnly chewed K rations for their morning meal as they prepared once again to carry battle to their German foes. As on the previous day, visibility through the trees was limited by a cold and clammy morning mist. The sky was clear for a time after sunrise at 0730 hours, although clouds soon formed.

1st Battalion sat partially on its objective. This day 3rd Battalion was also assigned to complete its mission to seize high ground south of Hürtgen. The unit was in poor condition for renewed combat. Its companies were split, with elements on both sides of the Germeter–Hürtgen road, and all of them were tangled in the minefield barrier. Its objective was roughly 500 yards south of Hürtgen and 900 yards beyond the previous day's initial LD.

Major Topping, commander of 3rd Battalion, gave his company officers their orders. King Company was to remain in position south of the minefield, thereby protecting the regimental right flank. Love Company and one platoon of Item Company were to withdraw to the south, cross over to the west side of the Germeter–Hürtgen road, advance north, then swing east onto the objective. Despite the fact that this complicated maneuver would violate the long-standing military principle of simplicity, if successful it would allow 3rd Battalion soldiers not only to pass around the minefield, but also that barrier itself would then serve to protect the force's right flank as it moved north. 2nd Battalion would assist when needed.[30]

Once again, artillery batteries laid down a preparatory barrage on German positions. As the big guns ceased firing, GIs moved forward, staying close together to keep in contact with one another. By this time most trees in the forest no longer wore crowns. Their tops, blown out by artillery, piled up on the ground, hampering infantry movement. The brush from severed branches was so dense men could only push their way through, shoving limbs aside by main force. So difficult was it to move that 3rd Battalion was late beginning its advance. Designated departure time was 0900 hours; it was 0930 before the unit was actually on its way.[31]

At 1030 hours a message from regimental headquarters stopped the fumbling forward motion of 3rd Battalion. Its troops had wondered about the sounds of an early-morning artillery barrage in the west. Now they knew. Those resonating reports were explosions from German guns. At about 0730 hours, the enemy launched a counterattack on 1st Battalion preceded by an artillery preparation.[32]

Colonel Strickler ordered 3rd Battalion "to continue its attack to the west" to reinforce 1st Battalion, now faced with a German offensive. Captain Bill Rogers, at 3rd Battalion's command post, was confused: "This mixed up everyone as the battalion was attacking east."[33] The intent, however, was plain, even if the words were not. This German attack on 1st Battalion had to be stopped. So 3rd Battalion shifted direction, causing even greater confusion among its men who stumbled blindly through the dark, threatening forest. Sergeant Alexander Zaltsburg wondered as they moved west from the road what he was going to do with the bangalore torpedoes received just that morning for use against the minefield. He abandoned them among the broken tree trunks. They were of no use against German small arms.[34]

The German offensive against 1st Battalion came in two thrusts, each involving more than 200 men, who pushed south, generally following the course of a little meandering north–south stream, the Weisser Weh, which lay west of the Germeter–Hürtgen road. Following hard upon their artillery barrage, German infantrymen met with much initial success, sliding through and around American forward elements of 1st Battalion, reaching and capturing the headquarters command post. They even took Major James Ford, battalion commander, prisoner for a time, although he managed to escape later in the day.[35]

Able Company's commander, Max Whitetree, remembered the ferocity of the enemy barrage. It began at 0654, he said, and the "Jerries shelled us for forty-five minutes." At about 0730 hours came the first German attack wave, following their own bombardment so closely "they were taking casualties among their own men."[36]

1st Battalion soldiers put up stiff resistance. Lieutenant Potter recalled how their "machine guns did not fire until the Germans were right on top of them. By this method they killed many more than usual, as the Germans were unable to see our positions and walked right into the face of the guns. Some fell within six feet of our positions and gun crews had to move the bodies in order to continue firing." It was, he said, a frightening time inasmuch as enemy troops were to their front, their rear, and along both flanks. Their numbers "made it impossible to tell just where they would attack."[37]

Five German tanks, about 1,500 yards away on high ground above Hürtgen, fired on 1st Battalion troops. They were joined by enemy self-propelled assault guns. American artillery finally knocked out three of the five tanks, and the other vehicles withdrew under protective cover before continuing their shelling.[38]

1st Battalion's Baker Company received an initial heavy barrage lasting two and one-half hours, and intermittent bombardments much of the rest of the day. Despite such shell bursts, NCOs and platoon leaders moved out of their protective foxholes, collecting ammunition from the dead and wounded for redistribution to those still capable of fighting. Such actions took courage, for enemy infantry fired at them from no more than 40 yards away.[39]

As 3rd Battalion's Love Company neared the site of the German counter-offensive, its men ran into sniper fire, mines, and explosions from a continuing mortar barrage. Most company NCOs were already evacuated, dead, or wounded, and its riflemen tried hard to cope with that loss. At one point they allowed a German probe to get within 25 yards before opening fire. Moving on, nearing 1st Battalion, L Company troopers came up in back of 200 Germans and took nearly 150 prisoners.[40]

Lieutenant Bruce Paul took command that morning of 3rd Battalion's Item Company and led it west through the trees to aid 1st Battalion. There was, he said, continuous "fighting all the way." As they trekked toward 1st Battalion, Lieutenant Paul related, "We got a few PWs but shot the most of them." Reaching his destination about noon, he found 1st Battalion drawn up in a protective half circle with an open side to the south. "We tied in with them," he stated, "for an all-round defense."[41] Those companies of 3rd Battalion traveled more than 600 yards under heavy small-arms fire to reach their threatened sister units.[42]

Fighting slowed down as the afternoon dwindled away. Late in the day, men in Able Company noticed a Volkswagen, headlights burning, moving toward them. They seemed to control the market on ambushes. "We opened up with heavy machine guns, light machine guns, rifles. The car turned over and two men ran away." Captain Whitetree sent out a six-man patrol to search for the car's occupants. Sergeants Louis Schwieger and Leo Balleger found a wounded artillery captain and his messenger in an open field. The officer died a short while later, but the two NCOs found on his body "an overlay of the entire German positions, locations of guns, battalion and regimental CPs." Whitetree sent the map back to regiment. Its information, distilled and relayed to higher headquarters, served as the basis for a later air strike.[43]

As darkness grew closer, Colonel Strickler ordered his battalions to dig in for the night. A drizzling rain began that lasted for several hours, punctuated by periodic German artillery and mortar fire into American positions. Enemy planes could be seen directly overhead from 1800 to 1815 hours. It had not been a good day for the 109th Infantry Regiment.[44]

American forces now occupied a narrow salient extending toward Hürtgen east of the Weisser Weh creek and along the Germeter–Hürtgen road. Their position was perilous, however. Although they stopped the forward progress of the German counterattack, the enemy controlled a comparable counter-salient along the Weisser Weh that extended dangerously along the left flank of the 109th Regiment. German soldiers infiltrated American lines almost at will, making life very hazardous.

3rd Battalion failed to penetrate or outflank the minefield to its front; its energies had been expended in moving west through the woods to aid 1st Battalion. Colonel Strickler's reserve battalion, the 2nd, was tied up in efforts to stop or slow German infiltration into the regimental rear area. Every American effort seemed only to add to the number of casualties. Soldiers in the woods and the minefield remained within easy range of German artillery and mortar fire.[45]

Cloudy skies and rain prevented GIs from receiving helpful air support. A gloomy performance log and summaries of IX Tactical Air Support Group show, time and again, entries such as "missions cancelled due to WX," or "aborted WX," or "WX poor," or "WX not flyable," or "WX infavorable." Pilots did, however, fly sorties. The 366th Fighter Group sent 12 P-47s over the combat area of the 109th Infantry Regiment. They claimed destruction of three armored vehicles and damage to three more. They further knocked out five trucks and three motorcycles northwest of Hürtgen; hit a radio tower at Kleinhau, a small settlement northeast of Hürtgen, and strafed a German barracks there. Such activities, while perhaps helpful, were not what desperate men fighting within the *Hürtgenwald* needed.[46]

28th Infantry Division Summary of Activity
from Regiments, 030001 November to
032400 November 1944, G-2 Section

> *109th Infantry Regiment:* 1st Battalion received counterattack this morning supported by 12 assault guns and 2 tanks. 2d Battalion was thrown in on line to the west of 1st Battalion and is holding the shoulder of the penetration. 2d Battalion didn't make much progress since they ran into concertina wire—two rolls on the ground, a third placed on them, booby-trapped and mined. 2d Battalion attack didn't get too far but their preliminary attack in the 109th area sucked the Germans in. The big artillery barrage foiled them, too. So the Germans committed their local reserves, drawing troops from other towns nearby. The overall attack was a fine success, a tribute to prior planning and the opportunity of letting every man know what he is supposed to do. Things were generally quiet in this regimental area today. The weather was clear, cool most of the day.

Such daily summaries from 28th Infantry Division headquarters might have confused riflemen in the battalions of the 109th Infantry Regiment. They did not feel they had "sucked in" the German counterattack or "foiled" their enemies. As they stumbled blindly through the battle area following inadequate maps, they might have marveled to know that divisional headquarters prided itself on "letting every man know what he is supposed to do."

It rained during the night of 3/4 November. Roads, trails, and forest, already wet, dissolved into thick, clinging mud. The sun occasionally tried to break through low, overhanging clouds, but for the most part, visibility remained poor throughout the day of 4 November. The air was relatively warm, so GIs without overcoats suffered less than on previous days.

Regimental units achieved no more success on 4 November than on earlier days. Just as it was getting light, at about 0700, Germans once again attacked southward in force. They pressed against American lines for nearly an hour before drawing back a few yards. "We stopped them," Lieutenant Peer believed, "only because we stayed in our holes, letting German infantry get to about twenty-five yards before opening fire, killing many, causing the rest to withdraw."[47] He and his men stayed in their foxholes all day, hiding from bursting shells, unwilling to advance into the heavily defended, rain-saturated forest stretching in front of them.

Lieutenant Tom Whitney believed he saw a pattern emerging: "We came to expect daily attacks at 0730 and 1630."[48] Between enemy probes they endured constant artillery and mortar barrages.[49] Lieutenant Potter feared they might be cut off and encircled, for German troops "were still infiltrating into our rear area, giving us a lot of trouble."[50] Carrying parties bringing ammunition and supplies forward from rear depots could only do so after nightfall. When they did so during daylight hours, too many of them died.[51] Some men could not wait for nightfall. Signal Corps wiremen, such as Sergeant Louis Brooks and PFC Jewel Latham, swallowed their fears and slogged repeatedly across the battlefield, busy stringing telephone ground wire so front-line units might talk with battalion command posts to the rear. Even during heavy barrages they left their foxholes to seek out and repair damaged communication lines severed by artillery blasts.[52]

Casualties mounted. First Lieutenant William Purdy, 1st Battalion S-2, died while carrying orders to unit commanders from regimental headquarters.[53] Sergeant Joseph McMichael stepped on a booby trap and lost his foot.[54] Soldiers' nerves stretched toward a breaking point. Shell bursts exploded and sniper rounds snapped through the trees. Men got hung up on concertina wire or triggered mines. Army tables of organization called for rifle companies to number six officers and 187 enlisted personnel.[55] By late afternoon, 1st Battalion's Baker Company numbered only two officers and 72 enlisted men. It began the battle on 2 November at full strength.[56]

Even nightfall brought no lessening of danger. "It was so dark I couldn't see a thing," lamented Lieutenant Paul, "and men were throwing hand grenades at every noise."[57] Some few GIs still retained their sense of humor. Lieutenant Don Clark of Easy Company, 2nd Battalion, ordered Private Elbert Parrish and others to set up an outpost to cover a nearby German machine-gun nest. It was almost dark when the men set to work, so close to the enemy weapons crew they "called us names as we were working." It was too close for Parrish, who commented cynically that he "even borrowed a pick from a Jerry" to use as he dug.[58]

28th Infantry Division G-3 Periodic Report
040001 November to 042400 November 1944

Weather: Cool and cloudy.

Result of Operations: 109th Infantry Regiment advanced across Hurtgen–Germeter road and occupied northwest edge of objective; made preparations to continue attack 050700.

Combat Efficiency: Excellent.

THOMAS E. BRIGGS
Assistant Chief of Staff
G-3

28th Infantry Division Summary of Activity from Regiments, 040001 November to 042400 November 1944, G-2 Section

> *109th Infantry Regiment:* The 2d Battalion continued to press forward on the right, jumping off at about 0700–0730 to take the 3d Battalions original objective. . . . They ran into the same booby traps and mines the 3d Battalion had. The road to Hurtgen was very heavily mined. . . . The rest of the day things were relatively quiet in this area.

Daylight on 5 November 1944 filtered through foggy, low-hanging clouds, bringing no cheer at all to sodden, cold infantrymen of the 109th. The precise moment of sunrise was 0734. Almost simultaneously, Captain Max Whitetree discovered a German patrol in his Able Company area. "A Jerry sergeant came over to Sergeant N. Felker and said 'Hands up.' Felker fell back in his hole, put a grenade on his rifle, pointed it up and pulled the trigger. It hit a tree, bounced back, wounding the Jerry. This shot alerted the company and as the Jerries started to run they were killed."[59]

Things were little better in Baker Company. Seventeen replacements arrived early that morning; only moments later a German 81mm mortar treeburst exploded, killing two of them as well as an artillery liaison officer, and an officer and two enlisted men from Charley Company. Then came a barrage so intense men could only huddle stricken in their holes. "Yet during the worst," Lieutenant Whitney said, he saw Major Ford and Major Owens, the battalion commander and his executive officer, "standing up and walking around talking to men and encouraging them."[60]

Many small German patrols probed American lines, looking for an opening, covered in their movements by heavy artillery and mortar fire.[61] In 3rd Battalion area, Love Company suffered heavy casualties beating back a German attack at about 0900 hours. During that same onslaught, Item Company lost 15 men, and the remainder scattered, losing contact with one another. Lieutenant Paul's helmet was blown off by an exploding round.

When the barrage lifted, Paul's men tried to return to their old area. Gone only about 45 minutes, they now found Germans occupying their positions. "We formed on a skirmish line and went in on them. . . . Jerry dropped back, so we didn't have much trouble, but within ten minutes an artillery barrage came that blew trees all over the place."[62]

Germans also stormed 2nd Battalion at dawn, moving in a skirmish line toward American troops as if "they didn't even know we were there." Aided by two tanks, they assailed GIs for an hour before withdrawing. As if taking out their frustrations, enemy gun batteries then dropped mortar and artillery fire on men in 2nd Battalion.[63]

Opposing armies were so close that day they threw hand grenades at one another. "Germans would throw grenades at us and we would throw some back at them. Jerry could not move in on us," said Lieutenant Don Clark, "and we could not move against him."[64]

The day ended, as had previous ones, with no improvement or advance in American positions. It had been a strange way for soldiers of the 109th Infantry Regiment to spend a Sunday.

28th Infantry Division G-3 Periodic Report
050001 November to 052400 November 1944

Weather: Cool, visibility limited.

Result of Operations: 109th Infantry Regiment exerted pressure against the enemy.

Combat Efficiency: Excellent.

THOMAS E. BRIGGS
Assistant Chief of Staff
G-3

The *Hürtgenwald* was beautiful under bright moonlight during the night of 5/6 November. There were few to appreciate it. American soldiers were too tired and battered to pay attention to the silvery moonrays reflecting from dark branches of fir trees above them. Struggling to wakefulness with the coming of daylight, they once again faced orders to punch northward through tight German defenses, their objective almost 1,200 yards away. They were to cut the road leading south from Hürtgen.

Following hard upon their own artillery preparation, men of 3rd Battalion stalked forward at 0900 hours. Within five minutes, a German counterbarrage stopped them cold after an advance of less than 150 yards. "While we were gone," Lieutenant Peer related, "the Jerries moved into our old positions, so we had to turn around and route them out of our own holes." It was noon before men were again secure in their foxholes.[65]

As 3rd Battalion tried to advance on the regimental right, Germans thrust at 2nd Battalion from the south and west. In George Company, Private William Shores saw an enemy machine-gun crew trying to set up their weapon. He picked off the ammunition carrier and the assistant gunner, and as the gunner turned to wave his two assistants forward, Shores shot him as well. German artillery responded with a solid rain of shell bursts. When the din of battle lessened, G Company had only 19 men left in its 2nd Platoon, nine in its 3rd Platoon, and 22 in its 1st Platoon.[66] At full strength, 36 men were assigned to each platoon.[67]

Divisional headquarters was not yet through. It ordered regiment to continue its mission. At 1600 hours, Colonel Strickler decreed that his men must strike toward the northwest. Major Howard Topping, commander of 3rd Battalion, was appalled. His casualties were already staggering, and he feared for his few remaining survivors. He sought out Colonel Strickler at regimental headquarters. It was impossible, he said, for his companies to carry out such orders. His argument succeeded. Strickler relayed Topping's plea to divisional headquarters at Rott. At 1700 hours, Division notified the regimental commander of good news: His unit would be relieved sometime that night or the next morning by fresh troops from the 12th Infantry Regiment, 4th Infantry Division.[68]

28th Infantry Division G-3 Periodic Report
060001 November to 062400 November 1944

Weather: Cool and clear.

Result of Operations: 109th Infantry Regiment continued pressure against the enemy, improved positions with 1st and 2d Battalions.

Combat Efficiency: Excellent.

THOMAS E. BRIGGS
Assistant Chief of Staff
G-3

Darkness on 6 November brought little rest for exhausted GIs of the 109th. The moon shone briefly, but clouds rolled across its face. In the night blackness, men crouching among the trees could literally see nothing at all. The temperature dropped rapidly and heavy rain began to fall, turning to sleet and then snow. Soldiers were soaked to the skin, and damp cold gripped their bones. Miserable, they lay sleepless in their foxholes, aching hands grasping weapons, a few dozing fitfully. As morning light crept through the forest, they were too exhausted and sick even to feel gratitude as fresh troops from the 12th Infantry Regiment moved in to replace them. More like zombies than men, these disheveled warriors of the 109th Infantry Regiment shuffled rearward toward an assembly area west of Germeter.

Rifle companies normally contained six officers and 187 men. Able Company, 1st Battalion, needed 60 replacements. B Company was down to 74 officers and men. Only one officer remained out of the entire staff of 1st Battalion. 2nd Battalion's Easy Company arrived at the assembly area with four officers and 47 enlisted men. Fox Company lost 20 men on its final day in position; one rifle squad consisted of three men rather than the normal complement of 12. Only 72 men in the company survived. King Company, 3rd

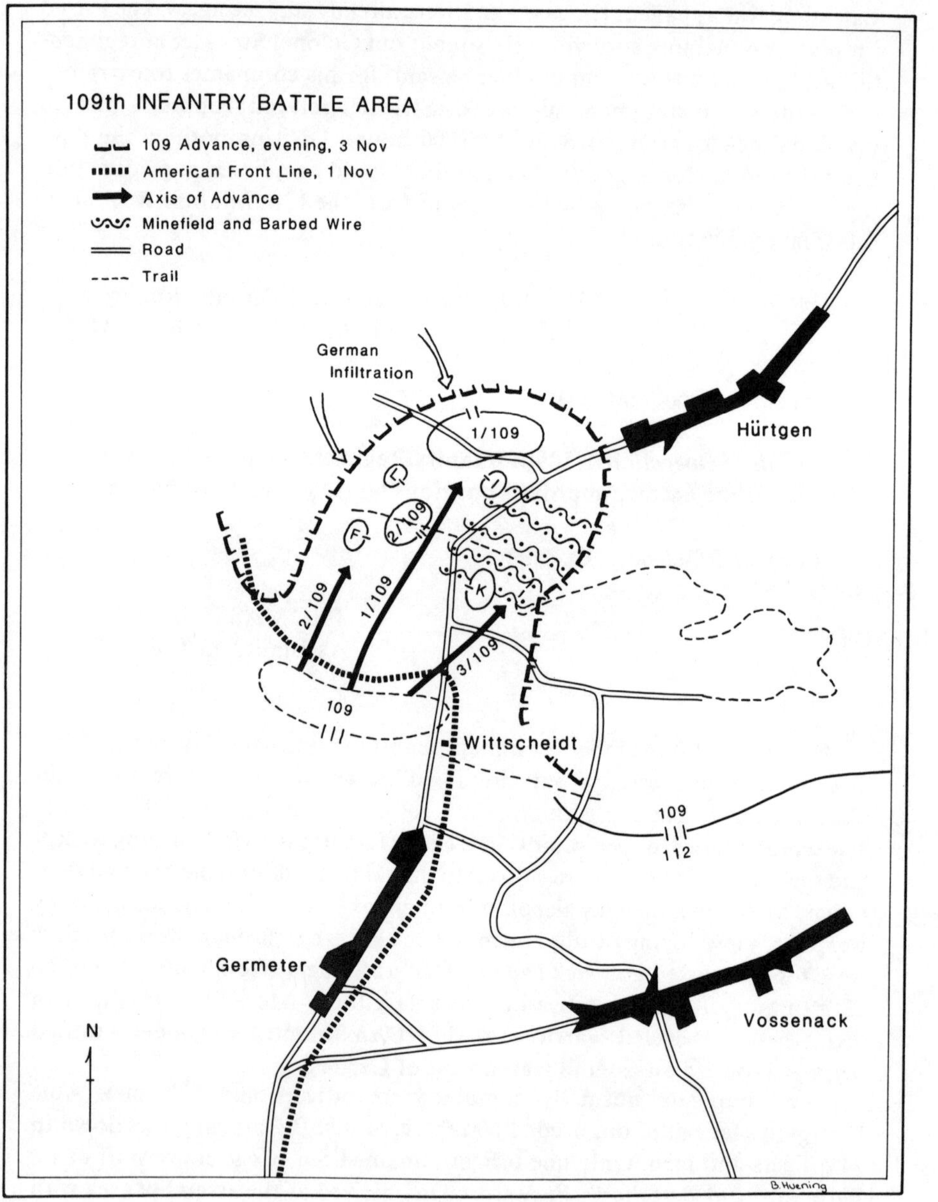
109th INFANTRY BATTLE AREA
109 Advance, evening, 3 Nov
American Front Line, 1 Nov
Axis of Advance
Minefield and Barbed Wire
Road
Trail
German
Infiltration
1/109
2/109
1/109
2/109
3/109
109
F
L
I
K
Hürtgen
Wittscheidt
109
112
Germeter
Vossenack
N
B. Huening

Battalion, lost upward of 65 men killed or wounded. Regimental casualties exceeded a 50 percent rate, a high price exacted from its troops.[69]

What had their sacrifice accomplished? 1st Battalion seized part of its objective but failed to secure the crossroads to the northwest. This allowed the Germans to maintain an important part of their supply lines in the sector. 2nd Battalion arrived at the bend in the Germeter–Hürtgen road but then could not secure necessary high ground south of Hürtgen. 3rd Battalion never got close to its objective, becoming entrapped in a minefield of which regimental headquarters was not even aware prior to its offensive on 2 November.[70]

At the Germeter assembly area, men of the regiment received a meal of cold K rations, an issue of newly arrived overcoats, and a fresh supply of ammunition. Some slept, while others talked over possibilities of a real break in front-line duty. They were wrong. It was not rest these men were facing, only a change in mission. Within a few hours they received orders to provide aid to their two sister regiments of the division. Those other units, the 110th and 112th had, if possible, found themselves in peril even more deadly than that experienced by the 109th.

2

"A bloody finger pointing into Germany"

Roll On, 28th

by
Sergeant Emil Raab

We're the 28th Men, and we're out to fight again
For the Good Old U.S.A. We're the Guys who know
Where to strike the blow, And you'll know just why
After we say:

Roll on, 28th, roll on, set the pace,
Hold the banners high, and raise the cry,
"We're off to Victory!"

Let the Keystone shine, right down the line
For all the world to see. When we meet the foe
We'll let them know, We're Iron Infantry, So
Roll On, 28th, Roll on!"*

17 February 1941-31 October 1944

By fall of 1944, encouraged by several weeks of unremitting combat success against their German foes, morale among American GIs in western Europe was at an all-time high. Many men, veterans of continued campaigning against *Wehrmacht* armies, believed Germany might surrender by Christmas.

In late July, Allied armies finally struggled out of the Normandy beachhead area. In following weeks, German forces retreated everywhere. Almost encircled at Falaise, barely avoiding disaster at the Seine, driven from Paris, pushed back against its famed and feared Westwall—or "Siegfried Line," as GIs called it—German armies failed to live up to their reputation. They no

---

*Brigadier General (Ret.) Uzal W. Ent, Pennsylvania Army National Guard, sent a copy of this poem along with the following comment: "This was written in World War II, set to march music and, at times since, played *ad nauseam.*"

longer seemed quite so formidable, having suffered losses of some 500,000 men, well over 2,000 tanks and self-propelled guns, and mountains of supplies.

Supreme Headquarters, Allied Expeditionary Forces, Europe (SHAEF), however, was not as sanguine as were its line troops. Careful observers believed German resistance would stiffen the nearer its soldiers retreated to the borders of the Third Reich itself. Resupplying front-line defenders from still vast reservoirs of materiel from deep inside Germany became ever easier. Allied logistics lines—already extended thousands of miles across dangerous Atlantic waters—grew ever lengthier and more tenuous, and the flow at the end of the pipeline thinned to a trickle.

Allied goals remained the same: to pursue German forces into their own heartland without faltering or slowing; to break through the redoubtable Siegfried Line defenses; and to press on quickly to seize bridges over the Rhine River, clearing the way for a final thrust against the German nation. Strangely enough, the gravest problem faced by planners at SHAEF was their own success. It cast doubt on the ability of Allied armies to continue that race for the Rhine.

American forces gained a toehold within the German border some 233 days ahead of the schedule established in England prior to the Normandy invasion. As early as September, American advances outpaced their own logistics capabilities. Filler replacements for depleted fighting units—mittens; galoshes; jackets; overcoats; gasoline and antifreeze for wheeled and tracked vehicles; spare parts; ammunition; even food—all were in short supply. Quantities on hand were not sufficient for minimal front-line needs. None of these logistics difficulties could be readily corrected. Only time and exhaustive transportation efforts could produce levels of support necessary for continued pressure against retreating German forces.

General Dwight David Eisenhower, Supreme Allied Commander, was not even certain his armies could reach the Rhine with available supply levels. Better, he believed, to press forward more slowly on a broad front, rationing all his forces, than to parcel out significant amounts of materiel to any one army, thus giving it the capability of forging ahead too quickly, pushing a narrow and unstable salient into some part of the German lines. Such a thrust could all too easily be cut off. Eisenhower determined that all his armies would advance concurrently toward the Rhine. Only at that river's banks would they regroup, receive appropriate resupply, and then, fully prepared, storm powerfully eastward.

Only once did General Eisenhower diverge from this approach, and that at the entreaty of Field Marshal Sir Bernard Law Montgomery, commander of 21st Army Group, who convinced "Ike" that with sufficient men and supplies, his forces could punch through to Berlin and end the war in 1944. The disastrous Operation Market-Garden action in and around Arnhem, Holland, during September was the result, and Eisenhower chose not to risk such a venture again. He thus bears ultimate responsibility for those desperate days in November 1944 when an American division was ground into mincemeat. Battles were planned by "Ike's" subordinates, but his was always the final voice declaring strategic courses of the war. Plans executed by three of his generals tell us much about a time of waste, misuse, and destruction of literally thousands of United States soldiers in futile and unnecessary assaults against several lonely rural ridges in German's *Hürtgenwald.*

The first of those three men was Lieutenant General Courtney H. Hodges, commander of First United States Army. Fifty-seven years old in 1944, Hodges entered West Point in 1904. Its rigorous mathematics program was too much for him and he dropped out to enlist as a private in the regular army. He received his commission as a second lieutenant in 1909, only one year behind his comrades on the Hudson. He made for himself a distinguished record in World War I, and in the years of peace between the wars Hodges' contemporaries often regarded him highly. Subordinates believed him to be thoughtful and considerate toward them. For a time Hodges served as commandant of the Infantry School at Fort Benning, Georgia. In many ways he seemed, according to one analyst, much like a "rumpled, unassertive, small-town banker."

Hodges was not a strong commander of First Army, delegating much authority and responsibility to his chief of staff, Major General William B. Kean. Kean was a hard, less than amiable taskmaster much resented by those who worked for him, and consequently staff headquarters at First Army was not always a smooth-running operation. Hodges, who affected a cigarette holder after the style of his commander-in-chief, was intemperate, unforgiving, and brittle, caught between leading First Army himself and allowing Kean to do so in his name. Rumor mills sniped that, full of impatient intolerance, his reach far exceeded his grasp. Some believed him to be unable to cope with responsibilities of continued command and to be in a state of near collapse by the time of the German Ardennes offensive.[1]

The squads, companies and batteries, battalions, regiments, divisions, and corps comprising the 250,000 men of First Army pushed through the Siegfried Line in two places by the end of September 1944: at Aachen* and near Roetgen. The left flank of First Army rested at Aachen. The three corps of Hodges' army—VII on the left, V Corps at the center, and VIII Corps on the right—covered a front extending southward nearly 100 miles.

The front faced by those three corps was overlain by a rugged barrier, a large and thick mass of trees consisting of the Meroder, Wenau, Roetgen, Hürtgen, and others, all known collectively to GIs as the Hürtgen Forest.[2] These woods rose steeply to heights of 1,000 feet and were threaded with

---

*Called Aix-la-Chapelle by the French, the city lies some 40 miles southwest of Cologne and north of the Eifel Mountains, only a few miles from the point where the boundaries of Germany, Belgium, and The Netherlands meet. Here Charlemagne was crowned, as were no fewer than 28 later emperors of the Holy Roman Empire.

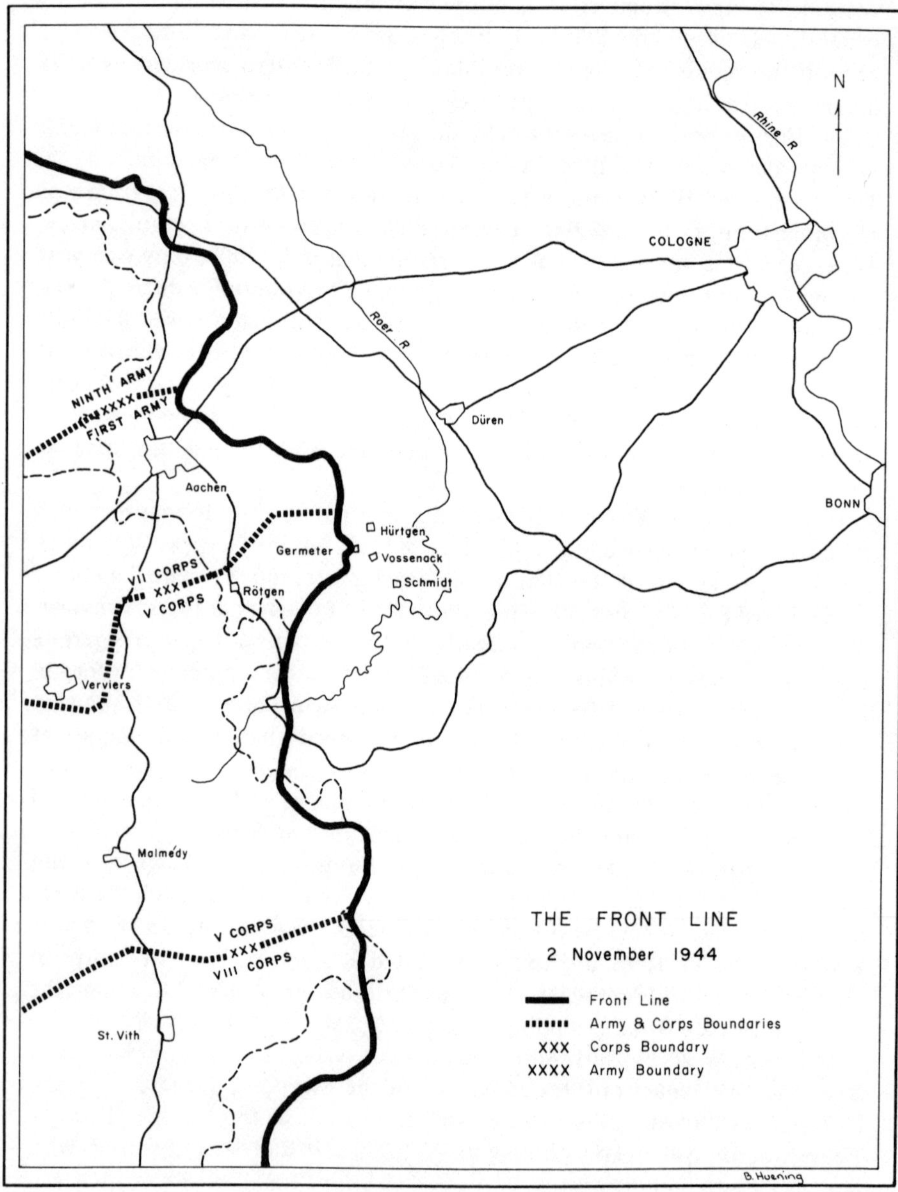
N
Rhine R
COLOGNE
Roer R
Düren
BONN
NINTH ARMY
XXXX
FIRST ARMY
Aachen
Hürtgen
Germeter
Vossenack
Schmidt
VII CORPS
XXX
V CORPS
Rötgen
Verviers
Malmedy
V CORPS
XXX
VIII CORPS
St. Vith
THE FRONT LINE
2 November 1944
Front Line
Army & Corps Boundaries
XXX Corps Boundary
XXXX Army Boundary
B. Huening

precipitous gorges through which ran small torrents and streams, the smaller emptying into larger ones until they became rivers.

Beginning about five miles southeast of Aachen, the Hürtgen Forest covered some 200 square miles, extending south to the village of Steckenborn. In its midst astride high plateaus cut by gorges of the Kall and Rur rivers lay open farming country. Three high ridges dominated the sector of Germany faced by First Army; the more southerly contained the villages of Kommerscheidt, Schmidt, Froitscheidt, and Harscheidt and rose in places to heights of 500 meters. To the immediate north lay a second ridge, on which sat the towns of Germeter, Vossenack, Hürtgen, Kleinhau, and Grosshau. To the northeast lay a third ridge, some 400 meters high, holding the little settlements of Brandenberg and Bergstein. All those hamlets, filled with brightly painted woodwork-and-plaster houses with pointed roofs and shuttered windows, were shielded by the lush growth of the *Hürtgenwald*, a tangled mass of firs and other evergreens, stiff and unyielding. The closely spaced trees, like sentinels, guarded the entrances to Germany and covered with their branches fortifications of the West Wall.

The entire eastern side of the Hürtgen Forest was faced by a chain of fortifications stretching in a double line through the trees. Running parallel to one another, these defenses consisted of concrete pillboxes with interlocking fields of fire, camouflaged log and earth bunkers, reinforced concrete command posts, hidden machine-gun nests, and tall concrete pylons or "dragon's teeth" rearing up from the ground to prevent armored vehicles from penetrating its defenses. Minefields shielded these bulwarks, themselves protected by single, double, and sometimes triple rolls of booby-trapped concertina wire to hamper infantry movement. The entire line of the West Wall was well within reach of well-emplaced artillery batteries.

It was a formidable defense, made more so by the fact that each pillbox had its own cluster of outposts and was self-contained, making it necessary for an invader to attack each one separately, capturing it before moving on to the next. Each pillbox was large, often containing several rooms, and their builders tried to blend them into the forest. General James Gavin would later write that "usually they were so well covered by leaves and pine needles that they were hardly visible. I was startled when I first realized that I was looking right at one only a short distance away and hadn't realized it was a pillbox." They would, he knew, reduce "fighting to its most primitive form: man against man at grenade distance."[3]

It was into such territory, at the end of September 1944, that the 60th Infantry Regiment, a part of Major General Louis Craig's 9th Infantry Division, penetrated. Its objective was the Hürtgen–Kleinhau road network. A resolute German defense forced the regiment to break off its attack and retreat.

With Hodges' approval, General Craig tried again in October. His objective was the little village of Schmidt, a crossroads town, which sat on the

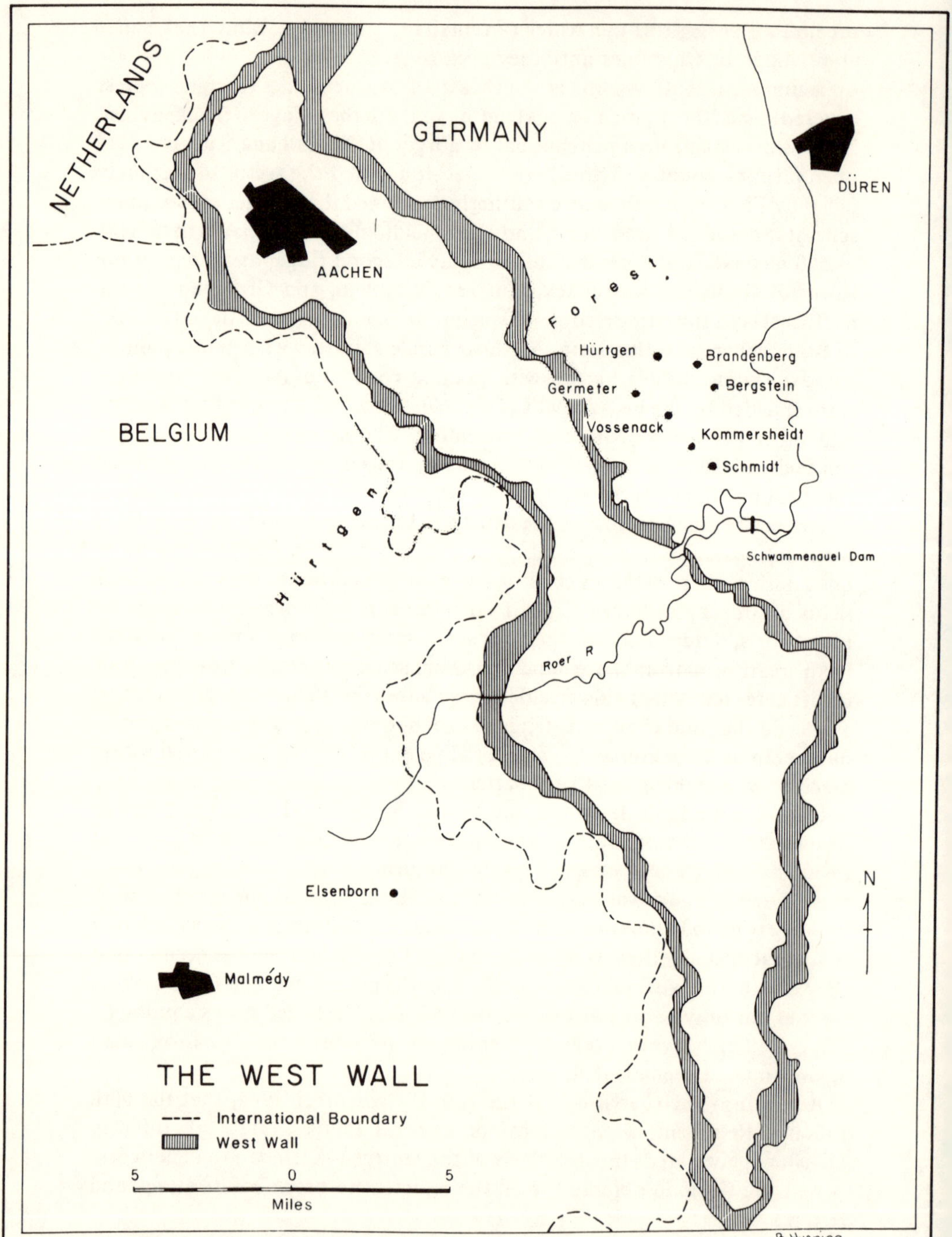
NETHERLANDS
GERMANY
DÜREN
AACHEN
Hürtgen Forest
Hürtgen
Brandenberg
Bergstein
Germeter
Vossenack
Kommersheidt
Schmidt
BELGIUM
Schwammenauel Dam
Roer R
Elsenborn
N
Malmédy
THE WEST WALL
International Boundary
West Wall
5
0
5
Miles
B. Huening

southernmost of those three high ridges amid the Hürtgen Forest. Schmidt overlooked the important Schwammenauel Dam, located to the south along the Rur River.* To its north, land fell away sharply into a deep gorge through which flowed the little Kall River. To its west, along the Rollesbroich–Strauch–Steckenborn line, was a road net that American forces would need if they were to penetrate farther into Germany in that sector.

At 1130 hours, 6 October 1944, Craig's 9th Infantry Division attacked toward Schmidt. For 10 days the division tried to overrun German defenders protected by their minefields, pillboxes, bunkers, and wire. German soldiers resisted with fierce tenacity. At the end of those deadly days, 9th Division held only 3,000 additional yards of forest, captured at a casualty rate of more than one man per yard. A total of 4,500 men died. Survivors were pulled out of the front line and sent to the rear to rebuild the division.

General Hodges knew his First Army would soon be called upon to fight its way to the Rhine, slogging its way along the traditional invasion route through Köln and onto the Köln plain toward Berlin. Directly athwart his path lay a smaller river, the Rur, with passage to it blocked by the gray-green Hürtgen Forest barrier and the Siegfried Line. Hodges decided that VII Corps, commanded by Major General J. Lawton "Lightning Joe" Collins—perhaps the best operational and tactical commander among senior American generals in Europe in World War II, and a man with a great deal of influence with Hodges—would spearhead First Army's main drive eastward. That unit's battle for Aachen was nearly complete; soon it would be in position to move on once again.

During the last days of October, General Hodges decided upon 5 November as the date on which VII Corps would strike for the Rur and beyond, toward the Rhine. He was heartened by filler replacements arriving for depleted units and grateful that crucially low stockpiles were being replenished.[4]

Hodges and Collins planned for their coming offensive. Both men were troubled by the Hürtgen Forest, unwilling to bypass such a stronghold. An officer veteran of World War I but with no combat experience during that conflict, Collins was still greatly influenced by his memories of that war. He was deeply suspicious that Germans might use the *Hürtgenwald* as an assembly area for a drive into his right flank, just as they used the Argonne to threaten the left flank of American troops during the Meuse-Argonne campaign in the previous war. It was important, Collins believed, to secure all ridges on the eastern edges of the Hürtgen Forest, thus neutralizing it as a possible staging ground for an enemy counteroffensive. This view was both a misperception of the dangers to be expected from Germans in the forest and a major cause of the consequent disaster to the 28th Infantry Division, made all

---

*Usually translated as "Roer," this river is shown as "Rur" on German maps and is so used throughout this story.

the more certain because of Collins' influence over Hodges. Perhaps more than any single individual, Collins was responsible for the American fascination with the Hürtgen.

Collins did not, however, wish to lessen his corps' combat strength by diverting any part of it into the Schmidt sector. He needed all his forces concentrated upon their main task. General Hodges concurred with Collins' reasoning; VII Corps would be safe only if its right flank was protected. Such a security cushion should extend along the Rur River from Monschau in the southwest to Schmidt. Acquisition of Schmidt and its environs would also provide First Army with a line of departure within the forest from which to wrest the Hürtgen–Kleinhau road net, a natural avenue down which U.S. forces could move in a later attack upon Düren, a major communications and transportation hub.

Alert to Collins' ideas, Hodges ordered an adjustment in First Army's corps boundaries. Collins' VII Corps would be freed from responsibility for the Schmidt sector. On 25 October, Hodges reassigned the zone to V Corps, commanded by Lieutenant General Leonard T. Gerow. Since VII Corps was to attack on 5 November, Hodges further decreed that General Gerow must launch a diversionary attack by 1 November. He did allow a little leeway; if Gerow was unable to move by the first, he could delay until 2 November. That would be the latest possible date.[5]

Hodges was the first. Gerow was the second of those three generals directly responsible for the disaster in the Hürtgen Forest during early November 1944. Gerow did not like his corps boundaries juggled in such fashion and exchanged "harsh words" with Hodges, angered because it seemed Hodges was responsive only to Collins. Other corps commanders went begging. During the German retreat through France, Hodges felt a seldom-surfaced confidence; now with enemy resistance stiffening, it seemed to erode and Hodges turned ever more of his responsibilities over to his ubiquitous chief of staff, General Kean. Those who knew Hodges as commander of Third Army prior to its overseas deployment felt uncomfortable about the changes they saw in him.

It is highly questionable whether Collins' fears, shared by Hodges, of a German strike out of the Hürtgen Forest against the right flank of VII Corps were justified. Collins' comparison of the Hürtgen and the Argonne needed to be received with scepticism, but no one that fall was in a position to provide it. Those trees were not a present menace, but they could become one. American soldiers received no particular training in combat in wooded areas. Thrust into dark forests suppurating with water, they would face injury and death from explosive artillery tree bursts and possible capture if they lost their sense of direction.

Germans manning defensive units within the forest were battered remnants from dozens of units, wretched refuse tossed up by the tides of war. Like rats, they would be a menace only if attacked within their own lair. Should they venture forth, they could be swiftly and savagely destroyed by American firepower. Sought out in their labyrinthine corridors of firs and pines, they might well exact a terrible toll from invaders. Someone needed to tell Hodges—and Collins—that the best plan would be to bypass that wooded fastness and use American superiority in "mobility, firepower and technology" where it would serve best.[6]

Gerow might grumble but he was not one to pit himself against such as Kean and Hodges. His superiors made plans based on their fears, and that, one analyst insists, is among the worst possible forms of generalship.[7] Those enemy units needed to be hit by American troops from the flank along the Rollesbroich–Strauch–Steckenborn–Schmidt axis, and Gerow may well have known it. James Gavin believed such an approach route to be obvious.[8] Hodges' fears were primarily responsible for the "long nightmare" in November,[9] and Gerow acceded with only minimal resistance, concerned more with having to reshuffle his divisions and boundaries than with basic inadequacies in Hodges' thinking.

When war began in 1941, Gerow was in his element as head of the General Staff's War Plans Division. His deputy was a man named Dwight Eisenhower. Cold and unresponsive, with little personality, Gerow was a careful organizer. He should have been; he had spent his years in the Army as a staff officer for other men. With the outbreak of war, many believed the habits of his career unsuited him for command. He overcame such resistance and by D Day headed a corps.[10] He was now as hard on his own staff as he once was on himself. Always careful to control movements of his subordinate divisions, he made no exception this time. If Hodges wanted one of his units to provide a diversionary attack, then that division would do it precisely according to Gerow's instructions. Unable to trust himself fully, neither could he rely on others. Maintenance of control at all times was of the utmost importance for Gerow. This insistence doomed thousands of soldiers in the November campaign.

Gerow rode his staff at V Corps headquarters to work out details for the diversionary attack, insistent that his divisional commander have sufficient corps operational planning so that there would be little need for him to exercise his own skill and initiative. Gerow decided that a newly arrived division would bear the brunt of the attack: the 28th Infantry Division.

Prayer of the 28th Infantry Division

Our Father, Creator of beauty and life,
Spare this earth from wanton strife.
28th men, who through history long,
To thy Kingdom now belong,
Bless and abide with them there.

God in Heaven, Eternal Love,
Protect their homes with Grace from above;
Their loved ones, who Thy will endure,
Comfort their hearts, keep them secure,
Bless and abide with them here.

We, on earth, who await Thy call,
Help us to keep the Faith with all,
With banners high and hearts in line,
In Thy holy light may the Keystone shine,
Bless and abide with us all.

Amen.*

For that which we are about to receive,
Make us properly grateful.

Amen.†

The heritage of the 28th Infantry Division was rich. A Pennsylvania Army National Guard outfit, many of its component units were fighting their second war, and some had histories dating back two centuries. Three batteries of its 109th Field Artillery fought with General George Washington's Continental Army. The first militia force within the United States to adopt the name "National Guard" was its 109th Field Artillery, anglicized from Lafayette's *Garde Nationale.* Battle streamers on unit color standards indicated the part they played during the American Revolution, the War of 1812, the Mexican War, the Civil War, the Spanish-American War, the Philippine Insurrection, and World War I.

Organized as the 28th Infantry Division on 11 October 1917 at Camp Hancock, Georgia, its "Doughboys" arrived in Europe in the spring of 1918 to play their part in the "Great War." Attached to the French Army, the 28th fought on the Marne River near Château-Thierry from 28 June to 14 July. In the Aisne–Marne offensive that year, the 28th made a difficult advance during the Oise–Aisne offensive that began 18 August. This division helped rescue the famous "Lost Battalion" of the 77th Infantry Division during the Meuse-Argonne fighting. General John J. "Black Jack" Pershing gave the unit its first nickname—it was an "Iron Division."

After the Armistice with Germany on 11 November 1918, men of this

*A copy of this prayer was supplied to the author by Brigadier General (Ret.) Uzal W. Ent, Pennsylvania Army National Guard.

†This is a traditional prayer within the British military forces, uttered just prior to going into combat.

Pennsylvania Army National Guard "Keystone" Division boarded troop transports for a long ocean voyage home. There they received celebrations and congratulations from their neighbors. Those men who remained active in the National Guard in the years of peace that followed saw no more divisional-level training. Summer after summer, for two decades, they met for military training in company, battery, battalion, and—occasionally—in regimental-sized units, where they drilled over and again in basic principles of fire and movement.

Those were lonely years for Guardsmen. The nation no longer wanted to think of war and combat but of Harding's "Normalcy" and Coolidge's "Prosperity." Then came the Great Depression of the 1930s, and funds to pay National Guard salaries and provide its equipment dwindled to a trickle. Promotions for enlisted men and officers alike came slowly. Those who remained in the National Guard of Pennsylvania—or of any other state—were dedicated men.

During Franklin Delano Roosevelt's third term as President of the United States, American citizens became increasingly troubled about a new conflict as war raged once again both in Europe and in Asia. To increase the nation's readiness, the U.S. government federalized several National Guard units, including, on 17 February 1941, the 28th Infantry Division.

When they fought in Europe during World War I, American divisions were large and powerful organizations, consisting of four regiments and two brigades, numbering about 22,000 men. They were almost twice as large as divisions of other nations. In 1940, their structure shifted from its earlier "square" configuration to a "triangular" system with only three regiments and 15,514 officers and men.*[11]

For weeks following their February mobilization, units of the 28th Infantry Division assembled at divisional headquarters endeavored to cope with the new triangular structure. During following months, the division conducted three separate field maneuvers in the Carolinas, and, after Japan's attack on Pearl Harbor, the division was ordered to Camp Livingston, Louisiana, to begin more intensive combat training. In those early months, the War Department did this division no service, stripping its ranks of cadremen to use in building other units, nearly wrecking it by such reassignments.

Throughout 1941, during 1942, and into 1943, the 28th Infantry Division received additional tactical instruction in Virginia, Texas, and Florida. Guard outfits, at least initially, were different from Regular Army ones. When mobilized into federal service, Guardsmen were not a congeries of disparate, unfamiliar strangers. They knew one another. Many officers and

*By mid-1943, an American infantry division consisted of 14,253 officers and men. In the change from "square" to "triangular" divisions, the 28th lost the 111th Infantry Regiment, which was later reconstituted as a separate regimental combat team. The regiment served in the Pacific Theater of Operations.

noncoms had served on active duty during the Great War. Following their release from service, they found there were elements of military life that appealed to them but not sufficiently to make the army a career. So they remained in the National Guard, going to their local armory for evening meetings each week and training together every summer. Over the years they worked their way up through the ranks to positions as senior noncom or field-grade officers.

Periodic reorganizations of their units by the War Department caused them recurrent confusion but also gave them broad experience. A light truck company might be reorganized into a Signal Corps outfit. A 105mm howitzer (towed) battalion might have its tubes taken from it and replaced with eight-inch howitzers or 155mm cannon. A support company might be phased out to reappear as an infantry organization. Officers and men often shouted in dismay at what was expected of them, but they coped.

They operated with old radios that worked barely if at all. Tankers drove antiquated tracks. Supplies were inevitably short and equipment was often of the "field utility"—that is, homemade—variety. Invariably those dedicated men found a way to make things work or to do without, and units survived as men remained in them year after year, unappreciated, underpaid, undersupplied.

They were an interesting breed. In small towns throughout Pennsylvania and other states, they were butchers and bakers, farmers and laborers, truck drivers and postmen. Towns nearly shut down once a year as they donned their uniforms and went off to their "encampments." In larger towns, professional men—teachers and professors, doctors and ministers, lawyers and college presidents, opticians and musicians and druggists—joined with others holding like interests to provide an ongoing life for National Guard units struggling to survive.

Strangely enough, morale in those units was usually high. Guard members liked what they did. As the 1930s came to a close, they trained even harder to prepare for any mobilization that might occur. It is not that they wanted to go to war, although some probably did. Rather they were willing to do so if called upon by their country. Few actually wanted to fight, but thousands were ready to do so if necessary, interrupting the tenor of their lives and civilian occupations because they believed in what they did as part-time soldiers. What in peacetime was a hobby would become in wartime a means of expressing their devotion to their country.

Service in World War I or tales from older comrades taught them what combat was like. They were not professional soldiers, and so if a private or corporal or sergeant or lieutenant received a "chewing out" at an armory meeting, it was too bad but would not change the entire pattern of his life. He wore the uniform only once a week and at the summer encampments, and Sergeant Johnson or Captain Collins were actually Fred and Tim, the town mailman and the manager of the local Woolworth five and dime.

After federalization, such attitudes continued at training camps and during various maneuvers. Difficulties were to be overcome; they were not disasters. Rebukes irked, but Guardsmen took them with different spirits than did draftees or their active-duty counterparts. Who really cared? They came only to fight a war, to get it over with, and to get back to their civilian jobs and their real lives.

In two or three years the war would be over. Then they could resume their weekly evening meetings and, during quiet times at the armory, reminisce about their experiences when they "answered the call of their country." They were not only fellow soldiers, but also friends and neighbors from all over the Keystone State who had known one another for years. Those who manned the component companies, batteries, battalions, and regiments of the 28th Infantry Division really *knew* one another, and this knowledge made them a better fighting unit.[12]

Orders came finally for the 28th Infantry to proceed to its overseas staging area. On 5 October 1943, its men set sail across the Atlantic aboard crowded troop transports. Debarking in South Wales in mid-October, the 28th underwent intensive preinvasion training—six months in Wales, another three months in England. By then it was July 1944. The massive Allied invasion of *Festung Europa*—Hitler's European fortress—shoved ashore earlier, 6 June, onto beaches of the French Normandy peninsula. The "Iron Division" followed on 22 July. Assembling northwest of the French town of St.-Lô, the 28th Infantry Division pushed into battle in that nation's hedgerow country.

Farmland in Normandy was separated into small squares by a checkerboard pattern of hedgerows. Germans defended viciously from these hard-packed, earthen, root-filled mounds, each one overgrown and topped with thick, nearly impenetrable rows of hedges and trees. They fired from hidden positions, showering GIs with murderous automatic-weapons crossfire. Battering through hedgerows was difficult, but American troops prevailed, and German defenders retreated, slowly at first but then—as more Allied soldiers and equipment poured into France—at an ever-increasing rate.

The 28th Infantry Division entered combat near Percy, then struck into the forests of St.-Sever and St.-Sever de Calvados. On it moved to Gathemo, Sourdeval, and toward the Egrenne River.

German soldiers called the unit the *Blutiger Eimer* division. They were men of the "Bloody Bucket." Such a name not only described the blazing red of the keystone-shaped patch worn on left shoulders of shirts and jackets but also was a recognition of the courage and intensity with which men of the 28th fought.

Hedgerows fell behind. The pace of battle quickened. No longer did men of the 28th's three regiments—the 109th, 110th, and 112th—mark their advance in yards conquered. By 21 August, they moved forward as much as 17 miles a day through Verneuill, Breteuil, Damville, Nogent-le-Sec, Bonneville, Conches, Cleville, Boquipuis, and Le Neubourg; the latter was captured on 24

August. At Elbeuf, on the banks of the Seine River, "Bloody Bucket" soldiers seized a key escape route from the Germans. On 29 August, the 28th Infantry Division marched through thronging streets and under the Arc de Triomphe, part of a victory parade through Paris in celebration of the capture of that famed "City of Lights" only four days earlier.

Its men were not, however, allowed to remain in Paris. Marched through its streets, they moved east without pause into combat once again. They pursued German soldiers toward Compiègne along the Aisne River, through Chantilly, Creil, Pont-St.-Maxence, Senlis, Montpilloy, Brasseuse, Ravoy, Villeneuve-sur-Verberies, and across the Oise River. On 6 September, elements of the 28th Infantry Division crossed the Meuse River, then fought at Ham, St.-Quentin, and Soissons. The division crossed the Belgian border, swept into Luxembourg, and then on to liberate Martelange, Ravigne, Wiltz, Bastogne, Longvilly, and Arlon.

Finally they reached Germany's border and from their positions could look into a country that had not suffered the heel of an invader in wartime since legions of Napoleon marched eastward nearly 150 years earlier. Men from Philadelphia, Carlisle, York, Washington, and Lancaster gazed into the homeland of the enemy they had fought for so long. Dairy cattle switched their tails and chewed cuds in pastoral meadows. Grain shocks stood drying in the sunlight, heads ripe with golden kernels waiting for the coming harvest. Storybook villages, house gables rich with *Fachwerk* of wood and white plaster slumbered quietly.

There were ominous notes. American officers and NCOs who crept stealthily forward on reconnaissance missions observed carefully hidden pillboxes, exposed portions camouflaged with streaks of green and yellow paint, covered elsewhere with thick coats of earth and grass. They finally faced obstacles long rumored and much discussed that barred their way into Germany—the massive fortifications of the Westwall.

Regiments of the 28th Infantry Division sent patrols across the Our River. Those men entered Germany at 2100 hours on 11 September 1944. The following morning, 1st Battalion, 109th Infantry Regiment, seized an intact bridge over the Our across which rushed the 1st and 2nd battalions, 110th Infantry Regiment. The next day, 13 September, the remainder of the division marched into Germany; it was the first American unit to enter the German heartland in force.

American soldiers soon learned what it was like to attack a pillbox and found they did not like it. GIs finally devised a technique of mounting a bulldozer blade on a tank, which then pushed dirt over a "box," trapping its soldiers inside and neutralizing its defenses. Elsewhere they used flame throwers, or poured small-arms fire into apertures and doorway areas, allowing them to creep close enough to throw grenades into the interior. Then they blew up the structure with TNT. It was never easy.

One particularly stubborn "box" resisted all efforts. One GI twice braved a

25-yard gauntlet of murderous fire, dragging with him two 35-pound TNT pole charges. It was discouraging enough when he found the first to be defective; it was with chilling dismay that he found the second also to be unworkable. Without avail he threw hand grenades and antitank grenades at the apertures. Finally he exploded his pole charges by lighting their fuzes with a kitchen match!

Men of the 28th became skilled in neutralizing such fortifications. In one day, troops of the 110th Infantry Regiment captured 27. In 10 days they destroyed 143 pillboxes. Once again the tempo of fighting changed. In Normandy, advances were measured in yards. Through eastern France, Belgium, and Luxembourg, they were calculated by miles. Now movement slowed to inches as American soldiers slogged doggedly from one "box" to the next in battle areas around Trois Verges, Grosskampenburg, Heckhuscheid, and Elsenborn.

On 1 October, worn out, badly in need of supplies and replacements, the division was relieved from front-line duty and sent to Camp D'Elsenborn, Belgium to recuperate. This rotation to the rear gave commanders and officers opportunity to allow some men to go on leave to Paris and other now safe areas; to send others to special military training schools; to receive and integrate filler replacements into newly assigned units; and, through training, to rehone the 28th's fighting edge. Only one regiment remained on front-line duty at a time in this quiet sector, allowing the other two to receive rest, rehabilitation, and training. Each regiment in line rotated its battalions every three days, a commonly accepted method of providing replacements with some slight combat experience. New fillers arriving for duty with the 28th certainly needed such experience, for many of them had little or no infantry training.[13]

The U.S. Army chief of staff, General George Catlett Marshall, visited the divisional CP on 11 October. For America's top soldier, this visit was a return to the past. In 1906 and 1907, as a young lieutenant, Marshall served in one of the 28th's units. He praised the division's combat record. "You are doing excellent work over here and people back home are aware of it."[14]

Pennsylvanians were aware of the 28th's combat record, kept informed through dispatches written by men such as Ivan H. "Cy" Peterman, war correspondent for *The Philadelphia Inquirer*. Those back home were less aware of the extent of battle injuries and deaths suffered by the 28th Infantry Division. Whatever else it was, by October 1944 the Keystone Division no longer bore many hallmarks of a National Guard unit. War's attrition in the months since men of the "Bloody Bucket" landed in Normandy steadily thinned out many of those native Pennsylvanians. Now most of those who came into federal service at Indiantown Gap in 1941 were gone, casualties of war—dead, wounded, or reassigned to other duties. Although still "home" to a number of men from Pennsylvania, it would take a close look at NCOs and officers to determine that the "Iron Division" began the war as a National

Guard outfit. From privates to successive commanders, rapid transfers and sudden death brought men in and out of the 28th with dispatch. Many of those assigned to it could no longer trace their relationships back to some small Middle Atlantic stateside town. Lone replacements found themselves among groups of strangers with little chance to get acquainted before being flung into battle. Many arrived at night and were dead before the following sunset. Such newly assigned men made buddies quickly or not at all.*

Even commanders of the 28th Infantry Division moved rapidly in and out of office. Major General Omar N. Bradley,† who commanded the unit from June 1942 to February 1943 during its training in the United States, was replaced by Major General Lloyd Brown when Bradley was reassigned to take command of II Corps in Tunisia in early 1943. Brown headed the division from mid-February 1943 until August 1944, when he was relieved from command because of dissatisfaction with the performance of the 28th Infantry Division; he was replaced by Brigadier General James E. Wharton. Only a few hours after taking over, Wharton was fatally wounded while visiting one of his regiments, shot through the head by a sniper. He was followed by a New Englander, Brigadier General Norman D. "Dutch" Cota, assigned on 13 August 1944. A veteran of North African fighting, he was a former assistant divisional commander of the 29th Infantry Division. Landing in France on D Day, Cota personally did much to help the 29th get off that exposed beachhead. Later wounded at St.-Lô, he was now back in action and in command of his own division.‡[15]

The trio of Eisenhower's generals is now complete—those men who must bear much responsibility for the debacle in the Hürtgen. The first was Courtney Hodges, commander of First Army. The second was Leonard Gerow, V Corps commander. "Dutch" Cota was the third. Their mistakes led to the death of a division.

While men of the Keystone rested at Camp D'Elsenborn, Belgium, Courtney Hodges sent Major General Louis Craig's 9th Infantry Division on its

*One wonders how disruptive was the impact of change from a "square" to a "triangular" division and how much the War Department's system of individual filler replacements contributed to the changing nature of the 28th Infantry Division and its subsequent trauma in the Hürtgen Forest.

†If Bradley's memoirs are to be believed, the 28th was in a deplorable state until he took command and turned a floundering division and training program around. He approved the rape of its cadres, reassigned as individual replacements and to initiate formation of other units. What sort of influence did Bradley really have? How much truth is there in Bradley's accounts? The matter is of some consequence because his descriptions of the allegedly deplorable state of the 28th until he improved it are implicitly condemnations of the whole structure of the National Guard. Might the breakup of Guard units, the system of filler replacements, and the loss of the peacetime National Guard structure with all the local associations of Guardsmen have injured the division greatly and helped account for its troubles in the Hürtgen in November 1944?

‡For a time, combat leadership problems of the 28th Infantry Division came to an end with the appointment of General Cota.

abortive attack into the Siegfried Line and the Hürtgen Forest near Schmidt, Germany. When that battered and decimated division reeled back out of line on 26 October, the now-rested 28th Infantry Division replaced it.

When higher headquarters ordered units of the "Bloody Bucket" into line, they held positions in the forward Westwall near the right flank of V Corps. The attack that Hodges and Gerow wished to make necessitated shifting the 28th from V Corps' right flank to its extreme left, into part of VII Corps' zone of operations taken over temporarily for the assault on Schmidt.[16] One member of the 28th's artillery remembered the move: ". . . we packed and headed for the Hürtgen Forest. . . We camped inside the Siegfried Line at this point, and most of our command posts and sleeping quarters were down under ground in the pillboxes. We connected a system of telephones from pillbox to pillbox, put in electric lights by way of truck batteries and wire, and slept in the German beds hanging on the sidewalls of the pillboxes."[17] Men of other divisional elements, less fortunate in securing such quarters, slept wherever they could find a reasonably dry spot.

Cota, now a major general, quickly became involved in planning for the attack on Schmidt. Gerow supervised his progress carefully, even visiting Cota's newly established command post at Rott, Germany. Accompanied by General Collins, Gerow arrived at the 28th's war room on 31 October to spend over two hours talking with Cota and visiting his regimental command posts.[18]

In discussions with his own staff, Cota may well have used words like those he later spoke to an army interviewer. Their mission, he said, was that of "clearing the road center of Schmidt preparatory to a southeast drive by elements of the 5th Armored Division with which the 28th was to establish contact." By securing that road net through Schmidt–Steckenborn–Strauch–Kesternich–Rollesbroich, said Cota, his division would provide additional supply routes for the main First Army attack by VII Corps toward the Rhine, which would begin several days after the fall of Schmidt. Simultaneously, he noted, the 28th's assault would deny roads to Germans who needed them to resupply their Siegfried Line fortifications in the main V Corps area. This might, Cota believed, cause the enemy to withdraw or weaken his defenses in front of V Corps, thus allowing a more rapid eastward advance by American troops.[19]

In Cota's mind that was the "big plan." Gerow warned him that General Collins' VII Corps would launch the main drive for the Rhine on 5 November. Therefore it would be necessary for Cota's 28th Infantry Division to strike out by the end of October or early November. All evidence indicates Cota believed his forces could accomplish their task of securing Schmidt and its road net in time to "provide additional lateral supply routes for VII Corps" by 5 November. It was not only wishful thinking to believe his mission could be accomplished in such a short time; it also was folly.

Long after the battle, Cota spoke of his "grave misgivings" at the time.

Perhaps he should have spoken out before he wrote orders launching his troops into an absolutely impossible situation. Cota admitted the "main consideration" was the terrain over which his troops would fight—high ground on each succeeding hill dominating that of the preceding one in such a way that Germans had a decided advantage along the entire avenue of approach to Schmidt.[20]

Terrain is always important in combat operations. In the contest for Schmidt it would be vital. At all times high ground may be used to control the course of battle. An attacking force must therefore secure it with infantry and armor. If that is not possible, it must do so with artillery fire. If ground is rough and broken—"crosscompartmentalized" is the term used by military planners—infantry must be used to conquer it. If it is more open and rolling, tracked armor vehicles can cross and acquire it. Forward movement by either infantry or armor is channeled—"canalized"—by contour lines of ridges and valleys. Rivers, dams, and lakes, depending upon conditions of their banks, swiftness of their currents, and their depth and width, can make formidable obstacles. Weather effects can be devastating, defeating the plans of well-trained, well-equipped, and well-led forces. *All* these factors screamed out for careful consideration by Cota, Gerow, and Hodges. Those three generals chose instead, for the most part, to ignore them.

Wise and observant military commanders carefully study terrain across which their men will attack. They consider what such ground can do to and for both them and their enemies. They try to understand what effect terrain features will have on tactical troop movements. They use this hard-won knowledge to enhance operations of their troops.[21] Cota may have known these principles, but there is little evidence that he looked at the countryside stretching away before him and appreciated how difficult it would be. We know only that he protested to his superiors, Hodges and Gerow, of the dangers of attacking at a point where Germans "looked right down the throat" of the assaulting force. When Hodges and Gerow were unresponsive to his complaint, he swallowed his objections and went ahead with plans for battle.[22]

The "big plan" was simple. On 5 November, VII Corps would drive east, cross the Rur River, capture an important communications center at Düren, and move on for the Rhine. As a preliminary, the 28th Infantry Division would launch itself toward and capture Schmidt. It would then attack south and southwest, acquiring the towns of Strauch and Steckenborn. Meanwhile, 5th Armored Division would push out from near Lammersdorf and move northeast to link up with elements of the 28th as they thrust southward. So important did Hodges believe this action to be that he credentialed 36 reporters to cover its story.[23]

Hodges of First Army, Gerow of V Corps, and Cota of the 28th Infantry Division expected to achieve three—perhaps four—tactical advantages by this diversionary attack. (1) By this action in V Corps' area, VII Corps would gain additional supply routes and maneuvering space for its main attack in the north. (2) The 28th Infantry Division would protect VII Corps' southern flank from possible counterattack by German armies striking out of the *Hürtgenwald.* (3) Such an American onslaught would pull enemy reserves away from VII Corps' area of operations, preventing their use against General Collins' troops as they pressed for the Rur River. Both local and mobile German reserves would move against the Keystone troops, thus thinning any enemy defense in front of VII Corps. That planners expected to achieve those three advantages is clear. Less certain is whether Hodges or Gerow were aware that successful acquisition of Schmidt would put American troops in position to seize several large dams in the area of the Rur River.[24]

Seven dams sat near Schmidt, four on the Rur River and three on its tributaries—the Dreiländerbach, the Paulushof, the Heimbach, the Obermaubach; the Kall Valley; and the two most important ones, the Urft and the Schwammanauel, the latter laying just to the south of the Schmidt ridge. They became known collectively as the Rur dams, even though all did not set along that river.

The Urft and Schwammanauel in particular harnessed waters of the Rur and generated hydroelectric power for Düren and other more northerly population centers. Staffs of First Army and V Corps seemed generally unaware of the awesome power the Germans could unleash should they decide to open floodgates on those dams. Any effort to cross the Rur in VII Corps' area of operations could be thwarted by a sudden flood of monstrous proportions, and if Collins' troops were already across the Rur, such rampaging waters could cut them off, leaving them to be destroyed piecemeal and in isolation by the Germans. If they had not yet crossed the river, floods from opened dam spillways could prevent their doing so for weeks.

Comments by American commanders long after the Schmidt operation in November indicate some awareness of the dams' value. Following the war, General Omar Bradley stated, "It might not show in the record, but we did plenty of talking about the dams."[25] A First Army report written after February 1945 described the attack on Schmidt as "a preliminary phase of a plan by V Corps to seize the two large dams on the Roer River. . . ."[26] Major Jack A. Houston, G-2 intelligence officer of the 9th Infantry Division, knew of the destructive possibilities posed by those dammed waters. His report, written prior to his division's attack on Schmidt, spoke of "Bank overflows and destructive flood waves" which could be produced on the Rur "by regulating the discharge from the various dams. By demolition of some of them great destructive waves can be produced which would destroy everything in the populated industrial valley [along the Rur] as far as the Meuse and into Holland."[27] On 8 October, the XIX Corps engineer officer wrote his commander, "If one or all dams were blown, a flood would occur in the channel of the Roer River that would reach approximately 1,500 feet in width and 3 feet or more deep across the entire corps front. . . . The flooding would probably last from one to three weeks."[28]

Perhaps a more commonly expressed view was that of First Army's G-2 intelligence section, which belittled any real danger Germans might cause by releasing the dammed water. On 3 October this report stated that if "all of the dams" in First Army's area of operations were destroyed by the Germans, "they would cause at the most local floodings for about 5 days counted from the moment the dam was blown until all the water had receded."[29]

That sanguine view prevailed despite warnings received at levels as high as SHAEF headquarters. V Corps forwarded to SHAEF a summary of an interview with a German PW who reported civil defense measures then in effect at Düren. Citizens there were warned that continued ringing of town church bells was a signal that upstream dams had been destroyed and they should immediately evacuate the city inasmuch as flood waters there would be nearly 20 feet deep.[30] SHAEF knew of this report by 20 October yet took no action other than making it available to anyone who might wish to read it. Throughout October, General Omar Bradley's 12th Army Group headquarters remained unconcerned about the dams, believing them to be "an Air Force matter."[31]

Such a dismissal is difficult to understand in light of continued warnings. As late as 27 October, a V Corps engineer officer described how hazardous it would be for American forces to cross the Rur below the Schwammenauel as long as it remained in German hands.[32] Such warnings went unheeded. If staffs of Corps or Army discussed those dams, lower echelons most certainly did not. Colonel Carl L. Peterson, commander of the "Bloody Bucket's" 112th Infantry Regiment, later commented that the dams "never entered the [planning] picture."[33]

Only long after the start of the Schmidt operation did anyone finally become thoroughly interested in the problem of those dams. On 7 November, five days after the 28th Infantry Division jumped off from its line of departure, Major General William Kean, Hodges' irascible chief of staff at First Army headquarters, ordered V Corps staff members to prepare contingency plans for use "in the event First Army is ordered to capture and secure the [Schwammenauel] dam."[34] It was apparent from this message that General Hodges still had no well-developed plan for acquiring the Rur dams, nor any notion of their strategic importance. He was not alone. The day before Kean's message went down to V Corps, a division commander in VII Corps indicated his own belief that the Germans would not flood the Rur Valley because such action would hinder movements of their own troops.[35]

In February 1945, retreating Germans did indeed flood that valley. Partial destruction of *only* the Schwammenauel Dam south of Schmidt caused a flood lasting *13* days.[36]

This American lack of interest in the dams was certainly not shared by the

Germans. Their high command assumed without question that the attack by the Iron Division was a direct thrust toward the Rur dams. Their violent and tenacious defense of the Schmidt sector grew directly from German unwillingness to lose them. *Generalmajor** Rudolf Freiherr von Gersdorff, chief of staff of the German *Seventh Army,* well knew the value of the Schwammenauel—an immense concrete and earth structure 188 feet high and 1,000 feet thick at the base, topped by a 40-foot roadway, which held back 20 trillion gallons of potentially deadly water.

"We took it for granted," Gersdorff wrote,† "that it was of primary importance for the American command to capture the commanding heights of Bergstein and Schmidt via Vossenack, in order from there to cross the Rur to the East, capturing the dams of the Rur valley at the same time. . . . The deep penetration in the direction of Hurtgen and Voosenack assured us that the attack was headed for the roads to Duren, the Rur, and the dams. . . . In view of the Ardennes Offensive,‡ which was already planned at that time, this enemy intention had to be prevented at all costs."[37]

American planning was not as shrewd as Gersdorff and other German military officers believed at the time. It continued with no appreciation for the strategic importance of the Rur dams, nor knowledge of the already planned German counteroffensive in the Ardennes.

Impervious as he may have been to the importance of the Rur dams, V Corps commander, General Leonard Gerow, at least knew he was assigning a difficult mission to the Keystone Division. He consequently ordered a significant strengthening of the unit by attaching other forces to it. Attached organizations included the 707th Tank Battalion (medium), the 893rd Tank Destroyer Battalion (self-propelled), the 630th Tank Destroyer Battalion (towed), the 86th Chemical Battalion (4.2-inch mortars), the 1171st Engineer Combat Group, the 447th Anti-Aircraft Artillery Automatic Weapons Battalion, Battery A of the 987th Field Artillery Battalion (155mm howitzers, self-propelled), and the 76th Field Artillery Battalion (105mm howitzers).

---

*German general ranks did not parallel those in use within the U.S. Army. *Generalfeldmarschall* was equivalent to our five-star general of the army. *Generaloberst* corresponded to an American full general. *General der Infanterie (Artillerie, Kavallerie, Panzertruppen, Pioniere, Luftwaffe, Flieger, Flakartillerie,* etc.) referred to an officer of a particular branch of service and was comparable to an American lieutenant general. *Generalleutnant* was equivalent to major general and *Generalmajor* was the same as a brigadier general.

†German-speaking readers will note that many of these quotes from German sources are, upon occasion, technically incorrect with incorrect plurals, lacking umlauts, and so forth. They are taken from translations made at the end of the war by members of the Historical Office, United States Forces, European Theater, who occasionally made mistakes in their work. The original documents were unavailable to me, so I have cited them as they are given in translation.

‡The German army planned to drive out of the Ardennes, splitting Hodges' First Army and Patton's Third Army, capture Liège's huge supply dumps, take Antwerp's key port, and prolong the war to such lengths that the Allies would ask for a negotiated compromise peace rather than continue to insist upon "unconditional" surrender.

Gerow also ordered attachment of the 12th Regimental Combat Team of the 4th Infantry Division.

Gerow ordered other units to support the 28th Infantry Division: Headquarters, V Corps Artillery; the 17th Field Artillery Observation Battalion; and seven battalions of the 187th, 188th, and 190th Field Artillery groups. Gerow further arranged for six battalions of VII Corps artillery to take part in the preattack preparatory bombardment on German positions. He also assigned to the division 47 new vehicles only recently come into the army inventory: M-29 cargo carriers, tracked, known to GIs as "Weasels." Finally, he directed IX Tactical Air Command to use five fighter-bomber groups and a night fighter group to provide battlefield air support for the assault.[38]

The Bloody Bucket Division was now a force to be reckoned with, but there remained certain seemingly insoluble problems. To its front the Brandenberg–Bergstein ridgeline overlooked the towns of Vossenack, Kommerscheidt, and Schmidt. As men of the 28th pushed forward they would be under observation by spotters there and subject to constant artillery barrages. Yet General Cota did not have sufficient troops—nor were any available from other units—to launch an attack against Brandenberg and Bergstein.

Enemy artillery on that ridge's reverse slope, corps planners decided, would be counteracted by "blinding" it—that is, by covering a five-mile-long ridge with constant barrages of smoke rounds, blanketing American movements from observers there. That was an impossible requirement even had sufficient shells been available, for even a heavy pall of smoke would not stop enemy artillery forward observers from telephoning coordinates back to hidden gun batteries already preregistered on every foot of ground over which American troops might cross. The Brandenberg–Bergstein ridge would remain a threat.

A second, even more serious problem was that neither map studies nor aerial reconnaissance photos verified whether the little trail that ran south out of Vossenack to the divisional front, and that then dropped down into dank pine forest lining the gorge of the Kall River, actually continued on to that stream. If it did, was a bridge in existence there? No one could tell. Maps and photos showed a road of sorts rising south out of the gorge toward Kommerscheidt, through that half-moon shaped settlement, and on into Schmidt. Were the trail from Vossenack and the road through Kommerscheidt connected? They did not know. If so, in what condition was the trail? How wide was it? How firm was its surface? How much had recent rains affected it? How much traffic could it bear? How well was it defended? Maps and photos supplied no solutions to these questions, and General Cota ordered no patrols sent out on reconnaissance missions to provide firsthand information and real answers.

Patrols are dangerous missions and suffer disproportionate casualties. Germans in the Germeter–Hürtgen area were exceedingly sensitive to such American probes. Such assignments, however, are essential if a commander needs information about the enemy he faces. Cota was negligent in not insisting upon thorough and regular patrols that could have supplied much of the knowledge he needed. His reticence to do so ultimately cost his division far more lives than would have been lost on patrol duty.[39]

In an incredible move, General Cota designated the inadequate path of the Kall River trail as the main supply route (MSR) for the resupply, movement, and maneuver of an entire infantry *division.* Inadequate in good weather, it was nearly impassable in bad even for tracked vehicles, yet it now became the lifeline for men of the Keystone. Cota's decision would play a major role in the coming disaster.

Because of the trail's shortcomings, once GIs started down the precipitous slope of the Vossenack ridge, the battle for Schmidt would become primarily an infantry conflict. Riflemen could not count on tank support in their assault on Kommerscheidt and Schmidt. It therefore became even more imperative that Ninth Air Force assume responsibility for protection of the 28th's infantrymen south of the Kall. Its IX Tactical Air Command would have to interdict any German armored counterattack. Planes would have to isolate the battlefield.

That, in turn, would depend upon the vagaries of weather. Recent forecasts called for more of the same: cold, damp, rainy days interspersed with snow. The Schmidt sector sat in a weather trough, and unless conditions changed rapidly, IX TAC Air would fly very few sorties on behalf of the 28th Infantry Division.

Weather would affect more than flying. It was a trial to infantrymen as well. Roads were muddy mires, and foxholes filled with seeping water. Soldiers, wet to the knees, stamped their feet, flapped their arms, and huddled inside woolen blankets in efforts to keep warm. The division was short some 9,000 pairs of overshoes for its troops. Already by the hundreds, men suffered from trench foot, called "foot immersion" by medics. Antifreeze was in short supply, forcing tanks and self-propelled guns to idle their engines even when not in operation to prevent freezing up. This caused wear on batteries, engines, and consumed vast quantities of fuel, which also was in short supply. If General Superiority led American forces, Generals Winter and Logistics smiled upon German defenders.

With Cota's acquiescence, General Gerow pounded the last nails into the coffin for the 28th Infantry Division. Fearful of a counterattack such as had hit the 9th Infantry Division in its October assault in the Hürtgen, Gerow ordered Cota to divide his forces. One regiment would strike north toward the town of Hürtgen to prevent an enemy countermove down the Grosshau–Kleinhau–Hürtgen corridor, to protect the divisional left flank, and to secure a line of departure to use in a later thrust against Hürtgen itself. That assignment fell to Cota's 109th Infantry Regiment.[40]

Gerow was not through meddling. Another of Cota's regiments, the 110th, was to attack south from Germeter through dense forest containing strong German defenses in order to seize the Rollesbroich–Strauch–Steckenborn road network. This would provide a more reliable MSR into Schmidt than could the tiny, inadequate Kall trail from Vossenack to Schmidt.[41]

This stripped two thirds of Cota's infantry strength from him, leaving him with but one regiment, the 112th, to make the main divisional assault on Schmidt. To compound matters, even that final regiment would first have to strike directly east from Germeter to capture Vossenack. Only then could it wheel 90 degrees south for the second phase of its drive, leaving one of its three battalions behind occupying conquered ground.[42]

The 110th Infantry Regiment, if it succeeded in capturing the Rollesbroich–Strauch–Steckenborn road net, would then have to turn back toward the northeast to drive on to Schmidt. Both the 110th and 112th regiments were thus forced to violate a cardinal principle of war—that of simplicity in maneuver.

Perhaps the generals were so sanguine because of weak German troop dispositions arrayed before them. Cota later wrote that at the start of the attack, his division faced "an estimated hostile force of 3,000 Infantry and Engineers, 5 Light and 3 Medium Artillery Batteries, but no Armor."[43] His G-2 intelligence officer estimated that some 1,970 enemy troops were in position facing the route of the 109th Infantry Regiment. Another 1,390 opposed the 110th Infantry Regiment in the south. Between those enemy soldiers were perhaps 1,700 more men, "the battered remnants" of *Wehrmacht* western armies. One field order summed up the situation: "It is believed that the line in the GERMETER–HURTGEN area is thinly held."[44]

Cota believed he could accomplish his mission. After 15 July 1943, army tables of organization called for divisions to consist of 14,253 officers and men. Even that was three times the estimated strength of German defenders. To add a preponderance of power, General Gerow attached other units to the 28th and supported it with still additional forces.

His troops might no longer be as well trained as they had once been, but at least replacements filled out manpower slots in Cota's division. Was Cota aware that many of his new officers and particularly noncommissioned officers were drawn from antitank companies, antiaircraft units, air forces ground personnel, and other noninfantry sources? Did he know how few of them acquired needed training and experience to function efficiently in infantry units while the division rested in Belgium?*[45] Was he sufficiently aware that over the next several days along a 170-mile Allied front, his would be the only division engaging the Germans?

There were formidable obstacles of men, weather, and terrain in his way.

---

*As a result, wrote combat interviewer Captain John S. Howe, when the attack began and casualties mounted, loss of the few remaining well-trained infantrymen showed immediately. Continued attrition of companies and loss of ever more remaining experienced officers and noncoms, coupled with a complete lack of trained infantry filler replacements, virtually ensured failure for the 28th Infantry Division.

Cota reckoned he had, however, "a gambler's chance" of success.[46] He was willing to do whatever was necessary, stating at one point that his division would take Schmidt even if he "had to use every medic in the division" to do so.[47] Some who talked to his men at the time found them less hopeful. "None of the officers . . . was in the least bit optimistic. Many were almost certain that if the operation succeeded it would be a miracle."[48] Few if any officers at regimental, battalion, and company levels were aware of the place in the overall plan that their particular actions were to play. Consequently, morale of men and officers in the division took a distinct drop. "I saw it happen," one officer reported.[49]

Gerow's iron control over his subordinates and Cota's acquiescence sealed the fate of thousands of Bloody Bucket soldiers. Once again, the rule for those men would simply be "follow me and die." It was not likely that generals would suffer any harm in the coming action. It was far more difficult for those who expected wounds or death as they sat poised and waiting "on a bloody finger pointing into Germany, surrounded by the enemy on three sides."[50]

Prayer of an NCO

Dear Lord,

Give me strength to bear

ignorance with understanding,
stupidity with toleration,
boorishness with forgiveness,
personal insults with patience.

Let me remember that

being enlisted, I am mindless, common, unquestioning.
My views do not count.

Impress upon me that

I am only a tool of my officers
to use to hammer my subordinates into line;
their loudspeaker to use to blast my soldiers'
ears with beliefs of the greenest lieutenant;
their broom to sweep up and gather up all the loose
ends.

Constantly remind me that

jocularity is an affront to authority,
wit in lesser creatures such as I always borders on
impertinence.
Lack of enthusiasm is a cardinal sin
since it implies disagreement.
Personal pride is the property only of those with
commissions.

Grant me these things, O Lord, that I may be a fitting and
successful NCO.

Amen.

(A composition from World War II.
Author unknown.)

3

"Battered remnants"

The Horst Wessel Song

Raise high the flag, close tightly the ranks.
SA [Sturmabteilung] marches with firm stride and step.
Comrades who have been shot and killed by Red Front and
Reaction forces
March with us in spirit.

Fall 1944

During planning sessions before the battle began, the G-2 divisional intelligence staff section briefed General Norman Cota on enemy units facing them. They were, his staff told him, parts of two divisions, both of which could be brought to bear against soldiers of the 28th: the German *275th Infantry Division* and the German *89th Infantry Division*. The *275th* lay directly athwart their path, stationed in and around such towns as Hürtgen, Vossenack, Schmidt, Kommerscheidt, Brandenberg, and Bergstein. The *89th Division* waited along the Monschau–Schmidt corridor, just south of the Schwammenauel Dam and the Rur River.

The 28th Infantry Division, Cota's staff stated knowledgeably, would come into contact with only parts of those enemy forces before reaching its objectives. German units should not prove to be an insuperable obstacle for the three American regiments even now forming for attack on the line of departure. Cota should have known better. More caution was urgently needed, yet devils of his own pursued Cota. He was under great pressure. He bore responsibility for diverting enemy troops away from the path of General Collins' VII Corps later assault. Both terrain and weather were bad. His division needed more time to integrate new replacements. Both Hodges and Gerow would watch his performance carefully, and they were unforgiving men. So General Cota remembered how armies of the *Reich* crumbled and retreated out of France at a record pace. Perhaps there was no reason to believe they would react any differently now. With some trepidation, he approved the plan of battle.

By the time of the Normandy invasion, the once superb German military organization was already showing signs of decline. A two-front war slowly ground it down. Yet despite heavy losses, the quality of individual German soldiers remained high, and small units and their leaders performed well.

Three different military commands governed Germany's fading ground forces: the *Wehrmacht,* the *Waffen-SS,* and, strangely enough, the *Luftwaffe.* Jealousy, competition, and lack of coordination among these commands did little to heighten desperately needed fighting efficiency. The German *Wehrmacht,* or regular army, continued to experiment with reorganization of its units so they could retain their deadly fighting competence despite growing numbers of casualties.

In the fall of 1943, *Oberkommando des Heeres (OKH),* Army High Command, restructured its divisions. To cope with the nation's dwindling manpower pool, the number of support personnel was ruthlessly pared from divisional configurations as they had been organized since 1939, while still maintaining most of their existing firepower. Prior to restructure, each division contained three infantry regiments. The 1944 division operated with one less battalion in each regiment and one less platoon in each rifle company. This reduced manpower needs by nearly one quarter with little other change in combat strength.

Massive losses on both fronts during the summer of 1944 required the Army High Command to make another change. Whereas the 1944 division contained roughly 12,300 men, this new model called for only 10,000 troops. In the fall of 1944, *Volksgrenadier* divisions found their reconnaissance battalions replaced by companies. Other variations reduced manpower by about 20 percent. Combat service support units within divisions were so reduced that divisional fighting proficiency also declined. Army units simultaneously faced a problem in integrating replacements who had little training. This was the point where corrosion bit most deeply into *Wehrmacht* combat efficiency.

Small units at infantry platoon and company levels continued to operate in superior fashion. They were competent, often well trained, sufficiently equipped, and continued to do well against Allied armies. Their performance was assuredly not the reason for Germany's defeat.

Throughout October 1944, bemonocled *Generalfeldmarschall* Walther Model, *Kommandant* both of *Heeresgruppe B* in the northern sector of the western front and of *Oberbefehlshaber West (OB West),** carefully studied situation maps lining walls of his headquarters. Model was 54, a decade younger than most others of his rank. A tough, uncompromising officer, Model bore the nickname of Hitler's *Feuerwehrmann*—his fireman—because

*In English translation, Model's title was Field Marshall, Commander of Army Group B and of Headquarters, Western Front.

of his abilities. He repeatedly demonstrated his capability to stabilize front lines and to stem enemy penetrations.

When Germany struck at Poland in late summer of 1939, Model served as chief of staff for *IV Corps* and later in the same capacity for *Sixteenth Army* during its assault on France. Promoted to commander of *3d Panzer Division,* Model was in the forefront of the attack on Russia and Germany's race to the Dnieper River. He soon headed a panzer corps and, by winter 1941, commanded *Ninth Army.* After fall 1943, Model successively led *Army Group North, South,* and *Center* on the Russian Front. After the 20 July 1944 assassination attempt on the life of Germany's leader, Model's was the first message of loyalty and support Hitler received from the Eastern Front. It was no wonder Model was high in Hitler's regard.

Because of his favored position and obvious loyalty to the *Führer*, Model could occasionally act on his own judgment and disregard Hitler's wishes in ways others could not. At times he even refused to carry out direct orders that seemed unwise to him. Almost alone among Germany's generals, Model even stood up to Hitler when he believed his leader to be wrong.*

As October 1944 ended, Model knew that every foot his enemies advanced strained their fragile resources ever nearer a breaking point. He understood that every mile his own troops fell back meant they could be resupplied ever more easily, their positions better consolidated. He was also aware that his *Führer* was absolutely insistent that not one additional inch of German soil should be surrendered. Further retreat would mean dishonor and also threaten planning for and execution of the *Vaterland's* massive December blow against the Allies, scheduled to thrust out of the Ardennes sector in a matter of mere weeks. Nothing must interfere with that offensive, which would allow Germany to hammer its way to victory.

Aachen might fall. There might even be some adjustment in front lines south of that city, but the broad front facing Model's *Fifth Panzer Army,* whose left flank ran along the Düren–Aachen line, and his *Seventh Army,* which lay just to the south, must remain fixed or the carefully conceived route for the Ardennes *Blitzkrieg* through Luxembourg, into Belgium, and on to the Channel would be sorely endangered.

There came a moment when Model's finger traced the location on his wall maps of *LXXIV* and *LXVI Corps,* located on the right flank and in the center of *Seventh Army.* Model knew those corps had a great natural ally in the 200 square miles of the *Hürtgenwald* in which, only some days earlier, his *275th Infantry Division* had thrown back an attack by the U.S. Army's 9th Infantry

---

*After the Allied crossing of the Rhine, Model found himself encircled in the Ruhr pocket. He shot himself on 21 April 1945 because "a field-marshal does not become a prisoner." He left behind a request for burial in Vossenack's churchyard cemetery, where so many of his soldiers had died.

Division, decimating it in the process. The *Generalfeldmarschall* was proud of the valor with which his soldiers had fought their enemy. He may have managed a thin smile as he recalled the bravery of his men, now defending their own homes and the sacred soil of their nation. *Ein Volk, ein Reich, ein Führer* (One People, One Nation, One Leader) was still a phrase to evoke emotions in the heart of this German officer.

Model was fully aware that Americans might soon mount a drive for the Rhine River. That would require an attack across the Rur, probably at Düren. The Rur formed the southern and eastern limits of the *Hürtgenwald* and any Allied push would have to force its way through the tangled mass of trees clogging the rolling hills of western Germany. Conflict in the Hürtgen Forest, Model knew, would be won or lost by the Queen of Battle—lonely infantrymen of Germany and America. Model relied on *General der Panzertruppen* Hasso von Manteuffel of *Fifth Panzer Army* and *General der Panzertruppen* Erich Brandenberger of *Seventh Army* to resist any such attack with every weapon and man at their disposal. And so Model's staff at *OB West* briefed western army commanders time and again as all worked to ready themselves for the next Allied incursion.

Brandenberger's Chief of Staff, *Generalmajor* Rudolf Freiherr von Gersdorff, was deeply involved with efforts to prepare front lines for defense. Although divisions waiting behind Germany's western fortifications were up to full strength, Gersdorff did not believe they were manned by satisfactory soldiers. Many were *Halbsoldaten,* half soldiers, overage or inferior in other ways, formerly assigned to housekeeping duties within the borders of the *Vaterland.* Consequently they possessed little or no field experience. In Gersdorff's view, their officers and NCOs also left much to be desired. He described the state of his troops in language nearly identical to that used by Cota's staff: ". . . when the German Armed Forces in the West during their withdrawal through France—Belgium approached the German frontier, the bulk of those formations could be designated only as remnants."

Oberkommando des Heeres (OKH), Army High Command, *Oberkommando der Wehrmacht (OKW),* Armed Forces High Command, and *OB West,* Headquarters, Western Front, all cooperated to round up sufficient troops to man Germany's western defenses. The result produced a conglomeration of Ukrainian and Polish soldiers, cadres from training camps, barely trained recruits, overage men, those recovering from minor war wounds, and weary veterans of earlier campaigns. Such men, Gersdorff said, came from "a variety of units of every branch of arms."

Seventh Army, Gersdorff recalled, collected thousands of stragglers, assembled and fitted them out, and assigned them to new units. It integrated former artillery and antitank crews into infantry outfits, absorbed training battalions, twelve *Luftwaffe* battalions, dozens of *Festung* battalions, some police battalions and, he noted sourly, "one battalion of men with gastric complaints."

All units now received such soldiers, but army, corps, divisional, regimental, and battalion organizations still contained many good men who provided experienced cadres able to leaven the new lumps they encountered. These more seasoned soldiers struggled continuously to train new assignees.

"It was only by such means," said Gersdorff, "that the German command succeeded in keeping troops under efficient control and, even if with very weak troops, in offering effective resistance to the pursuing enemy. . . . This very difficult work was successful. . . . Thus the divisions were gradually brought up to full strength."

Just as it was difficult for *Seventh Army* to procure enough soldiers, so also was it a problem to arm them. Its chief of staff sent forward successive reports in which he described his troops as "inadequately armed and equipped." Neither weapons waiting in stockpiles at the West Wall nor new deliveries were sufficient for his needs. "In part by communicating directly with the war industry and by driving search campaigns in the home country, we succeeded in improving the armament and equipment." Gersdorff knew how crucial such efforts were, for his *Seventh Army* was critically short of equipment.

At one point, Gersdorff stated, "the *I SS Pz Corps* had at its disposal only one tank fit for action and the *LXXIV Army Corps* possessed only one gun which was in full fighting order. Weapons were unsatisfactory and not uniform. Artillery regiments were composed of guns of German, Russian, Italian, and French origin. For some of these foreign guns there was an insufficient supply of ammunition, i.e., the 12.2 Russian howitzer." Except for *Panzerfäuste* (a bazookalike hand-held, shoulder-fired weapon), "there were also very few anti-tank weapons. . . . Especially distressing was the personal clothing of the soldiers. This was especially felt when the weather became cold and wet and we incurred a large number of non-battle casualties."

Because of a consistent lack of artillery caliber rounds, German batteries were restricted to firing only about one fourth to one fifth as many shells as their American counterparts. Not only were the Germans short of ammunition, but of guns as well. An army reserve battalion normally had about 30 artillery pieces, but in *Seventh Army,* lamented Gersdorff, such units made do with 12 to 15 self-propelled guns, and even these "were not in satisfactory condition." German industry labored around the clock to produce needed weapons and ammunition.

Even the Westwall itself, built in 1939, was no longer up to date. Many bunkers were flooded. Others were looted of their equipment. Even where technical furnishings, such as air-clearing machinery and radios, still remained in place, much of it was no longer in working order. "In addition," Gersdorff remembered, "the foremost elements of the *Wehrmacht* flowing back from France—in most cases these were supply and *Luftwaffe* units and individual stragglers—reaching the Westwall unorganized and uncontrolled, took unauthorized possession of the shelters, using them for quartering purposes. These people stole and destroyed more than the weak engineer troops had built up previously.

"In many places," the chief of staff of *Seventh Army* continued, "fields of fire were covered with grown up bushes, wire obstacles were removed, and even embrasures were buried under rubble." *Festung Deutschland* needed a great many repairs.

On 20 August 1944, Hitler ordered fortifications of the Westwall restored to improve Germany's western frontier defenses. He entrusted supervision of this work to his Nazi Party. Gersdorff criticized that decision. "As the party organs had no special knowledge of these things and even the military home officers were not able to judge the requirements of a modern large-scale war, a lot of nonsense was done prior to the arrival of the troop staffs in mid-September." The Party mobilized civilian repair crews. "Thousands of old men, women and children dug out antitank ditches and built positions, which, owing to their tactically meaningless locations, were never used."

Changes for the better came only when field armies took over direction of the work. While troops were still fighting rearguard actions along the Maas [Meuse] River, *OB WEST* ordered its subordinate units to reconnoiter the Westwall to establish contact with troops and workers employed there and to improve its defenses. During the short time available to them, army divisions were unable to repair years of damage to the Siegfried Line or to make it completely adequate for future defense efforts, but troops worked feverishly in the effort.

One difficulty they encountered arose because when the Westwall antiaircraft bunkers were originally constructed they were tailored exclusively for 37mm weapons. Newer guns, with air-cooled fixtures and higher firing speeds, could not be handled in those shelters. *OB WEST* reluctantly recognized that problem and agreed that pillboxes could be used primarily for housing troops who could defend their positions from nearby reinforced log bunkers and machine-gun nests protected by booby traps, mines, and concertina wire.

"Ultimately," wrote Gersdorff, "the system was rendered considerably more effective. By steadily making use of improvisations and resorting to every kind of makeshift method, we succeeded in building up a connected defensive front on the western border. Divisions were again at full strength and in spite of their mixed composition and varying fighting qualities of their units, despite shortcomings resulting from improvisations and insufficiencies in replacement of personnel and equipment, we felt this work would make an impression on the enemy. The units seemed to be capable of defense. The West Wall had a reputation of being an 'unconquerable' fortress line, which was in fact never justified, but this bluffing had been successful in 1939, and we knew that this mythical reputation of the West Wall as a reversed 'Maginot Line' would be a further advantage to us."

The Hürtgen Forest was the southern cornerstone of German defenses against an American breach of the West Wall in the large Aachen sector. Armies of the *Reich* knew they must prevent any additional crumbling of their fortification line. So also did Hitler. According to his orders, every pillbox was to be defended to the utmost. A detailed investigation would be held into the reasons for each loss of a pillbox. "For this reason alone," suggested *Generalmajor* Gersdorff, "a voluntary withdrawal could never be contemplated."

OB WEST also realized a forest defense would be most favorable to them. Enemy supremacy in tanks would be neutralized among closely spaced trees. Hidden defensive positions dug into the earth under overhanging pine branches would not be susceptible to destruction by overwhelming Allied air superiority. Infantry attacks upon them could be beaten off by well-emplaced defenders capable of inflicting savage casualties upon any invader.

For such forest bastions to remain effective, however, it was also essential to retain all commanding heights—ranging from 380 to 500 meters in elevation—of those ridges on which sat Hürtgen, Vossenack, Kommerscheidt, Schmidt, Brandenberg, and Bergstein.

During the coming winter, when weather conditions turned forest roads almost impassable, the Düren–Hürtgen road would be an important supply route for the entire right wing of *Seventh Army*. From those ridges Germans could also protect against any enemy advance toward Düren and the Rur.

Despite the final loss of Aachen to the Americans on 20 October, *OB WEST* believed further enemy gains could be prevented. *OKW* and *OKH* intelligence reports made clear that American forces would strike next for Cologne and Düsseldorf and the industrial complex of the Ruhr valley. German observers felt the British, in a coordinated action, would also drive for the Ruhr, sweeping down from the north. The staffs of *Seventh Army* and *Fifth Panzer Army*, as they considered those probabilities, "came to believe that the right flank of the American attack would be just north of Monschau. We felt their main effort would be directed at the Hurtgen–Monschau–Duren road for the purpose of (1) capturing Duren and (2) seizing the Rur Dams." As a precaution, Germans prepared the dams and their generating machinery for demolition.

Seventh Army tested its defenses in October when it threw back soldiers of the 9th Infantry Division from the Schmidt sector. Gersdorff observed the costly nature of that abortive attack. "In addition to the natural difficulties of fighting in a forest, there were the added complications" for the Americans "of poor communication, poor observation, and danger from flank attacks. The terrain was difficult, especially bad in the wooded area. The mud became worse with the frequent snow and rains. Differences in elevation and the condition of the ground soil due to inclement weather made it extremely difficult to commit tanks."

So men and officers of German units were fully aware of the importance of this zone of operation, availed themselves of its natural advantages, and were ready to do their best in its defense. However, *Seventh Army* labored under another burden. Many of its *panzer* and *Schutzstaffel (SS)* units were already earmarked for the coming December Ardennes offensive and under control of the armies that would launch that strike. Even *Volksgrenadier* outfits could only be committed in inactive sectors of the front. "Even our Siegfried Line divisions, which possessed secondary troops and poor weapons, were likewise ill-qualified for commitment in the difficult Hurtgen fighting. But we could do nothing else, for had the American forces crossed the Rur, the Ardennes Offensive would not have been possible to execute in its original plan."

Seventh Army did what it could with what was available. *LXXIV Corps* occupied its right flank. *LXVI Corps* held in the center. *1st SS Panzer Corps* controlled the left flank. "In addition," said Gersdorff, "we had some badly mauled formations of numerous Kampfgruppen assigned to various divisional headquarters." Within the area of *LXXIV Corps,* scattered along the Hürtgen–Vossenack–Schmidt sector, were the *983rd, 984th,* and *985th Kampfgruppen regiments* of the *275th Infantry Division.* To the south near the Schwammenauel dam, in the middle of the corps area, were the *1055th* and *1056th regiments* of the *89th Infantry Division.* Each battalion of those regiments had a strength of about 750 men.

General Cota's staff informed him about the location and size of both the *275th Division* and the *89th Division.* What those briefers did not know, and never learned until too late, was that the *89th Division* would soon be relieved of its front line duties by the *272nd Volksgrenadier Division.* They were consequently unaware that this third division could quickly be thrown against them.

Those intelligence officers confidently informed Cota about the nature of German units they faced. They knew that on 30 November 1943, elements of the German army reserve, primarily from the Luneburg recruiting district, were formed into *Reserve Grenadier Regiment 1023* and, on 13 January 1944, transferred to duty in Norway. Only two days later, along with other reserve elements, they were incorporated into the *89th Infantry Division* at the Bergen troop training area. Shortly after D Day, this new unit was rushed to France. In late June, the *189th Füsilier Battalion* was formed and made a part of the division. The unit fought near Amiens, in the Lille sector, and at Le Havre. Badly mauled at Falaise, said to have been destroyed in the Mons pocket on 8 September, its divisional headquarters and surviving troops were pulled out of line and moved back into the Siegfried Line. As early as 10 October intelligence reports located it in the area west of Gemund, where it was rebuilding its component units: the *1055th,* the *1056th Infantry regiments,* and the *189th Fusilier Regiment.* Under orders from *OKH* received on 27 September, it incorporated the *5th, 9th,* and *14th Luftwaffe Field battalions,* the *1403 Festung Infantry Battalion,* and other reserve battalions to fill its ranks once again. Its original commander, *Generalmajor* Heinrichs, had been killed at Liège. It was now commanded by *Generalmajor* Bruns, known affectionately to his soldiers as "Papa."

General Cota knew that the *275th Infantry Division,* like the *89th,* was made up of extremely heterogeneous troops from all parts of the German army, navy, and air force. He knew it was commanded by *Generalleutnant* Hans Schmidt. How ironic that the town that was Cota's major objective and one of the generals sworn to defend it bore the same name.[2]

German planners could not understand the fixation of Hodges and Gerow on the Hürtgen, particularly after the 9th Infantry Division learned how effectively it would be defended. There was no danger of a large-scale German operation pushing north through the wooded area to relieve the Aachen sector. "We could not employ our tanks in this territory," Gersdorff admitted. "We had no forces available for such a purpose. Such an operation was never planned by us." Even months after the war, Gersdorff remained amazed at how unnecessarily his American enemies had scarred themselves in the Hürtgen Forest.

"It would have been more favorable," said *Seventh Army's* chief of staff, "to secure the area in a sufficient manner and to mine [its approaches] effectively. In my opinion, had the Americans the intention of breaking through [toward the east], it would have been more favorable to strike forward north of the large wooded area toward Duren. In fact, *later* American troops succeeded in breaking through there comparatively easily."

Gersdorff continued, "By fighting in this area, American troops were denied the advantage offered them by their air and armored forces, the superiority of which had been decisive in all battles waged hitherto. The fighting caused them heavy losses, without bringing them any tactical or strategical success of decisive importance."

So the Germans waited for their American enemies to spring the jaws of a trap set for them. The attack by the 28th Infantry Division was no surprise. German observers watching American troop movements, reports received from agents, increasing patterns of preplanned artillery fires—all served to warn Germans that an assault was imminent. When it began on the morning of 2 November 1944, Hitler's armies were ready.

"There was," Gersdorff saw, "bitter fighting for every foot of ground. The strength and bitterness of the fighting, the conditions of the ground, the weather, the constantly increasing artillery barrages on both sides along a narrow front resulted in fighting of such intensity that those who had taken part in the First World War compared it with the heavy barrages of 1918. The similarity was noticeable." Gersdorff was neither a novice nor impressionable. "I have engaged in long campaigns in Russia as well as other fronts, in addition to the time I spent on the Western front, and I believe the fighting west of the Rur, and especially in the Hurtgen, was the heaviest I have ever witnessed."

In Gersdorff's view, there was one salutary benefit for American forces in their November attack into the *Hürtgenwald.* Fighting there gradually wore down German divisions so they could not be reconditioned prior to the Ardennes offensive. The very fact of massed American forces moving in the Hürtgen constituted a threat. Had that forest been clear of Americans and under complete German control, they could have started their December offensive with a quite different emphasis. As it was, this American infantry threat tied up strong German forces, thereby weakening the striking power of *Sixth Panzer Army* from the outset. "In my opinion," judged Gersdorff, "this was one of the primary reasons for the failure during the Offensive by the German right wing.

"On the other hand," he continued, "the advantage to the Americans of binding strong German forces and preventing the reconditioning of divisions to be used in the Ardennes Offensive was cancelled out by the fact that even for the Americans, the Hurtgen Forest had become a 'death-mill.'"

Fighting was extremely costly for both sides. Bitter, close combat and continuous bad weather subjected troops to terrible strains. Most German casualties came from American mortar fire, particularly effective in the woods. Other losses occurred because of cold weather and numerous frostbite cases. More than once, German troops found dead comrades lying stiffly in their foxholes, killed by sheer exhaustion and below-freezing temperatures.

Generalmajor Rudolf Freiherr von Gersdorff did not have a high opinion of the tactical or strategic skills of Lieutenant General Courtney Hodges of First Army or Lieutenant General Leonard T. Gerow of V Corps or Major General Norman D. Cota of the 28th Infantry Division. The thrust into the West Wall, said Gersdorff, "was neither planned nor executed skillfully. It would have been necessary to use stronger forces. The execution of this attack was weak and inefficient, and, therefore, we were able to contain and later eliminate it by comparatively weak German forces. This enterprise caused the Americans heavy losses and greatly improved the morale of German troops, who had suffered a previous series of defeats. For the first time it had been possible to defeat American troops. The steadily increasing feeling of inferiority, on the German side, was reduced substantially by this fighting. Thus this operation was disadvantageous to the American command in every respect, even if it was meant to be only a scouting raid or a [diversionary] attempt."[3]

The battle for Schmidt began at 0800, 2 November 1944, with an intense artillery barrage. For an hour thunder from exploding shells sounded on target areas. At 0900, soldiers of the 28th Infantry Division's 109th Infantry Regiment crawled from their foxholes in woods west of Germeter to storm toward their objectives on the north. They were disappointed as they looked upward. Thick clouds scudded through the gray sky as if they too were hurrying off to war. Such cloud cover meant that all air-support missions on their behalf would be delayed or called off.

To the rear of the 109th, a second unit, the 112th Infantry Regiment, left the relative safety of the tree line west of Germeter to sally east along the bald Germeter–Vossenack ridge to capture the village of Vossenack. After occupying it, they were to dig in on the exposed northeast nose of that ridge facing the Brandenberg–Bergstein heights across an intervening valley. Leaving one battalion in control of Vossenack, the other two combat battalions of the 112th were to wheel 90 degrees to the right, move down into the Kall gorge, up its southern slope, and drive on through the hamlet of Kommerscheidt to their objective, the small town of Schmidt.

Holding its position for three hours after its sister regiments launched their operations, the 110th Infantry Regiment was to strike south from Germeter directly into the heart of the Siegfried Line pillboxes toward the town of Simonskall and a fortified strongpoint named Raffelsbrand. These soldiers were to gain control of a road network that would provide the 28th Infantry Division with a secure main supply route into Schmidt. One battalion of the 110th would remain at Germeter to serve as a small divisional reserve.

Those, at least, were the plans worked out by staff officers at corps and division. Their design did not stand up to the test of combat. Erwin Rommel may have said it best. He allegedly once commented that the best plan of battle lasted only until the first shot was fired.

In an ironic twist of fate, a group of German officers convened that same morning at Schlenderhan castle near Quadrath, west of Cologne. Their staff cars, pennants fluttering, which brought them to that gathering arrived at almost the precise moment when artillery tubes of VII and V corps and 28th Infantry began their preattack fire preparations. Officers who strode through vaulted corridors of *Schloss* Schlenderhan toward a large meeting hall represented commanders and staff officers of crucially important German military units.

General der Panzertruppen Hasso von Manteuffel, commander of *Fifth Panzer Army*; his chief of staff, *Oberst* Kahlden; and *Oberstleutnants* von Neckelmann and von Zastrow were there and greeted *Generalmajor* Hans Krebs, chief of staff for *Heeresgruppe B,* and a subordinate, *Oberstleutnant* Michael. Present also were *General der Panzertruppen* Erich Brandenberger, commander of *Seventh Army*; his chief of staff, *Generalmajor* Rudolf Freiherr von Gersdorff; and Brandenberger's senior artillery officer, *Generalmajor* Heuke. Others who waited for the meeting to begin included *General der Infanterie* Friedrich J. M. Koeching, commander of *LXXXI Corps; General der Infanterie* Friedrich Wiese, chief of staff of *LXXXI Corps; General der Panzertruppen* Heinrich Freiherr von Luettwitz, commander of

XXXXVII Panzer Corps; General der Infanterie Erich Straube, commander of *LXXIV Corps;* and *Generalmajor* Siegfried von Waldenburg, commander of *116th Panzer Division.*

These men stood stiffly at attention as their host, the ranking officer present, called them to order. He was *Generalfeldmarschall* Walther Model, and the purpose of this meeting was to conduct a war game—a map exercise—the subject of which was a defense by *Fifth Panzer Army* and *Seventh Army* in the area of the *Hürtgenwald* against a theoretical attack by an American force.

Shortly after play began a frantic telephone call from *Seventh Army* headquarters called Gersdorff away from the map maneuver. He listened carefully as an excited voice told him that the 28th Infantry Division had thrust north toward Hürtgen and east toward Vossenack. The situation, the voice warned, was critical. Gersdorff must inform his superior, *General der Panzertruppen* Erich Brandenberger, commanding general of *Seventh Army,* and *General der Infanterie* Erich Straube, commander of *LXXIV Corps.* The attack was in Straube's sector, driving straight against the *983rd, 984th,* and *985th Kampfgruppen regiments* of *Generalleutnant* Hans Schmidt's *275th Infantry Division.* The regiments might be unable to hold. *LXXIV Corps* lacked sufficient reserves for effective reinforcement of those troops. It would need help from *Seventh Army.* What should be done?

Gersdorff returned to the meeting. On walls of the room hung large maps marked with color-coded pins and military symbols grease-penciled onto acetate overlays, showing actual and indicated positions of German and American army units. Gersdorff reported news of the developing situation to Model and Brandenberger. Model immediately ordered Straube to return to *LXXIV Corps* headquarters.

With some equanimity, Model told his assembled officers to continue the map exercise. His only stipulation was that they use the actual situation on the battlefield to the south as the basis for their war game.

As the morning progressed, Gersdorff spent much time on the telephone, listening to reports of the battle's progress from *LXXIV Corps* and from *Oberstleutnant* Vogt-Ruschewey at *Seventh Army's* command post at Muenstereifel. Other officers at Schlenderhan Castle, commanders of key forces that already were, or would soon be, involved in the battle, had to form conclusions and react appropriately from information supplied them—all under Model's watchful gaze.

First indications, both actual and from map maneuvers, suggested the American attack was more than a simple probe. It seemed as if those enemy soldiers were striking for a strategic objective—Düren, the Rur, and the dams seemed most likely. The American attack toward the north was evaluated as a lateral cover for a main thrust east into Vossenack and south toward Schmidt. German commanders assumed it was of primary importance for American forces to capture the heights at Vossenack, Brandenberg–Bergstein, and Kommerscheidt–Schmidt. From there they would cross the Rur to the east, capturing dams along the Rur Valley at the same time. In view of the planned Ardennes offensive, this must be prevented at all costs.

Model studied the situation map. To the north of Düren along the Rur River was the town of Jülich, in *Fifth Panzer Army's* sector. Bivouaced near Jülich was the *116th Panzer Division.* Its commander, *Generalmajor* Siegfried von Waldenburg, was in the room with Model, present for the map exercise. Model spoke with von Manteuffel, Brandenberger, and von Waldenburg. They agreed it would be best to launch a counterattack against the enemy's northern flank to disintegrate his force and to reestablish the old front line in forests west of Germeter.

Such a counterattack, after shattering the enemy's northward thrust, could then push forward, penetrating his rear area. Strung out as Americans were along the Germeter–Vossenack ridge, cutting their rear not only would prevent further foward movement of men and supplies but also would make retreat impossible. Such encircled troops could then be destroyed at will.

At least a move like this was possible. A German counterthrust from the east would have to contend with inadequate roads and the heavily wooded terrain of the Hürtgen Forest. A move from the southeast would be little better. It would face the same problems of road and forest. In either case, however, roads available to Germans were better than those their adversaries had to rely on.

Satisfied with the discussion, Model ordered one *Kampfgruppe* of the *116th Panzer Division* to move down the Grosshau–Kleinhau–Hürtgen road to counterattack the 109th Infantry Regiment, which had become pinned down short of its objective by a minefield. Model then instructed von Waldenburg to move the remainder of his division forward into the Düren region to protect the boundary between *Fifth Panzer Army* and *Seventh Army.* Later, when Model learned that the counterattack against the 109th Infantry Regiment had been ineffective, he ordered forward a complete regimental combat team from the *116th* and ordered the remainder of that division to close with American forces as rapidly as possible.

Model also ordered *Generalmajor* Walther Bruns, commander of the *89th Infantry Division,* to ready his *1055th Infantry Regiment* for a counterattack against any American troops gaining a foothold in Schmidt.

When *General der Panzertruppen* Erich Brandenberger asked for permission to return to his command headquarters at *Seventh Army,* Model agreed. It was about noon. He informed others present that the map exercise would be discontinued. They could all return to their posts.

There can simply be no doubt that the map exercise at Schlenderhan Castle, which brought together crucial German commanders at an opportune moment, gave them a chance to react to the 28th Infantry Division assault on

Schmidt more rapidly and efficiently than would otherwise have been possible. There would be no respite from the calamity facing men of the Bloody Bucket.

Deutschland, Deutschland über alles

Germany, Germany above all, above all in the world,
May she always, for protection and defiance, hold together as brothers,
From the Maas to the Memel, from the Etsch to the Belt,
Germany, Germany above all, above all in the world.

4

"We left a hell of a lot of our best men up there"

2 November-5 November 1944

Nearly 40 years after the battle, one wonders what men of the 110th Infantry Regiment would have done had they known how many casualties they would suffer and how few would survive. They remained unaware of the awesome carnage entrenched enemy soldiers would inflict upon them.

By 13 November, when the 13th Infantry Regiment of the 8th Infantry Division began relieving men of the 110th from their front-line positions, it seemed as though a scythe had sliced through their ranks. As *Philadelphia Inquirer* war correspondent Ivan H. "Cy" Peterman wrote in a dispatch: "Survivors sat silently staring straight ahead, and if there were heroics to recount, someone else had to talk for them. The men . . . would not."[1]

The motto of the 110th emblazoned on its regimental shield was *Cuiusque Devotio est vis Regiment*—"The devotion of each is the strength of the regiment." Both devotion and strength were tested by the hell of enemy fire that rained on its men. Their casualties were appalling.

All regiments were composed of squads, platoons, companies, and battalions. At normal strength, each squad consisted of 12 men; 10 were armed with M-1 rifles, one with a BAR, and one with an M-1903 Springfield bolt rifle (itself an adaptation of the earlier Krag-Jorgenson standard-issue weapon used during the Spanish-American War). Three such rifle squads formed a rifle platoon. Three rifle platoons plus a weapons platoon (armed with one .50-caliber machine gun, two .30-caliber machine guns, three bazookas, and three 60mm mortars) made up a rifle company of six officers and 187 men. Three rifle companies and a heavy-weapons company made up an infantry battalion of 871 men. Three battalions plus a headquarters and support unit constituted an infantry regiment of 153 officers and 3,049 men.[2] It was a group like this that entered combat in the Hürtgen Forest.

Captain Gerald Harwell, regimental S-3 operations officer, later totaled the unit's losses for 1–30 November 1944. Ten casualties occurred after the regiment was withdrawn from the Schmidt sector and transferred into a quiet area to the south, in Luxembourg. All others happened during the battle that began on 2 November.

Table 1[3]

Battle Casualties, 110th Infantry Regiment

Category	*Officers*	*Enlisted Men*
Killed in action (KIA)	9	56
Wounded in action (WIA)	40	809 (1,412) [1,584]
Missing in action (MIA)	5	283
Captured in action (PW)	0	3
Nonbattle casualties (NBC)	23	861 (258) [86]

Even disregarding bracketed figures above, this report lists total casualties as *2,089* for only *one* regiment within *sixteen* days. Those statistics are too low and are also misleading in other ways.

The regiment listed only three PWs captured by Germans. Despite inherent difficulties in using enemy statistics, it is still worth noting that the German *89th Infantry Division* claimed on 9 November to have captured 535 PWs during heavy fighting south of the Kall.[4] Although that enemy unit also engaged the 1st and 3rd battalions of the 112th Infantry Regiment, elements of it struck at American forces at Mestrenger Muehle and Simonskall, the very area then held by the 110th, which still faced several more days of battle before it would be relieved. The truth lies somewhere between the American figure of three PWs and the German claim of 535.

Another factor makes Captain Harwell's regimental figures suspect. During the action itself, American military officials changed the category of foot immersion (trench foot) injuries from "battle" to "nonbattle" casualties.[5] Since over 70 percent of the 861 "nonbattle" casualties were caused by trench foot, the figure of 809 WIAs could be increased by a minimum of 603, to 1,412.

If one further accepts that mental injuries can be as real and hurtful as physical ones, and since some 20 percent of other "nonbattle" cases were relieved for combat exhaustion caused by pressures men could no longer bear, then the number of WIAs could be increased from 1,412 to 1,584.[6] Most remaining "nonbattle" casualties were evacuated suffering from colds, influenza, and pneumonia contracted by prolonged exposure to winter weather. "Nonbattle" perhaps, but those men would not have become sick had they not been required to participate in the fighting. Very few of the 86 casualties remaining in the "nonbattle" category were disabled away from the combat zone when a jeep in a rear area ran over their foot or when hurt by injuring their backs falling from a truck bed.

There is a more graphic way of looking at injuries suffered by men of the 110th. On 2 November when they struck south from their line of departure, 2nd and 3rd battalions led the way. 1st Battalion remained behind in reserve. At H Hour, all three battalions were at full table of organization strength.

When relieved on 16 November, 3rd Battalion had lost its commanding officer, its executive officer, its S-2 intelligence officer and S-3 operations officer, its surgeon, and its medical assistance officer. Companies I, K, and L each had but one surviving officer. M Company fared best. Four of its officers still lived. Already wracked from battle action, 3rd Battalion started out at 0600 hours on 6 November to relieve an encircled body of troops. A total of 316 men moved forward. Only about 200 returned, of whom all but 75 were evacuated—and this despite having received some 200 replacements since 2 November. When relieved from line duty, 3rd Battalion was commanded by a captain![7] Of 871 men who began the action, 75 were still capable of fighting at the end, a survival rate of less than 10 percent.

The other unit to lead off at H Hour on 2 November was 2nd Battalion. It also suffered severe losses. Company E lost all but two NCOs and two officers. On 9 November it could count but six or seven men left in the entire company. F Company lost its commander, its executive officer, platoon leaders of 2nd, 3rd, and 4th platoons, platoon sergeants of 1st, 3rd, and 4th platoons, all NCOs in 2nd Platoon save for the platoon sergeant and platoon guide, and five NCOs in 3rd Platoon. All but two privates in the machine-gun section were lost. Only two squad leaders and two privates in the mortar section survived in 4th Platoon. Despite such horrendous casualties, on 11 November, Fox Company was ordered to "protect the division right flank." It had one surviving sergeant and 25 men!

In G Company, all NCOs and officers were casualties except for one second lieutenant, who was not assigned to the unit until 11 November. Joseph K. Paczesna began as a private and ended as a staff sergeant. William M. Pennington started as a private and was promoted to platoon sergeant. Between 2-10 November, George Company had *five* different company commanders.[8]

Strangely enough, 1st Battalion, which initially remained in reserve, fared worst of all. By 13 November, *all* officers in A, B, and C rifle companies were listed as KIA, MIA, WIA, or evacuated with trench foot or combat exhaustion. Not only did Able Company have no remaining officers, neither were any NCOs left. Baker Company consisted of only four men: three privates and a sergeant. Charlie Company had 23 men but only one NCO. In Dog

Company, only two officers and six privates were still carried on the roster. Their MIA statistics were high. Able company lost 38; Baker lost 44; Charlie counted 39; Dog suffered eight.

These figures become even more poignant in light of the fact that 1st Battalion began with 871 men and received nearly 100 replacements during the fighting. When its remnants returned to the battalion assembly area on 13 November, only *57* men stood there. Medics immediately evacuated 37 of those because of trench foot, wounds, combat exhaustion, or a combination of all three. Only *25* out of nearly 1,000 men could still function as infantry. In the next two days, perhaps 50 more men straggled back from the front. Most of them also were evacuated because of trench foot.*[9]

As Captain James Burns, 1st Battalion S-3 operations officer, bitterly stated during the action: "We left a hell of a lot of our best men up there. . . ."[10] They certainly did. After the battle, divisional headquarters queried the 110th Regiment's headquarters, asking why so few recommendations for combat heroism awards had been forwarded. The answer was simple: Few company commanders or platoon leaders survived to initiate the paperwork.[11]

As they prepared to attack, regimental officers of the 110th expressed concern as to whether the area road network would be capable of handling their resupply needs. To forestall that problem, division attached two companies of the 1340th Engineer Combat Battalion to the regiment. Their sole mission was to construct an adequate system of roads behind advancing American troops. Divisional headquarters also attached 15 M-29 cargo carriers, tracked ("Weasels") for regimental use in hauling provisions over the difficult terrain. As late as 1 November, these vehicles—new both to their drivers and to regiment—were still being tested to learn what type and weight of loads they could successfully transport along muddy trails and firebreaks. Late that afternoon two of them broke down and were deadlined for repairs.[12]

Despite having been in the sector for some days, Lieutenant Colonel Theodore Seely, commander of the 110th Infantry Regiment, knew very little about his enemy's positions in the woods south of Germeter. The 60th Infantry Regiment, 9th Infantry Division, turned over to Seely very little information about enemy strengths, defenses, and positions when it pulled out of the forest. Nor was divisional headquarters much more helpful. Even its few aerial reconnaissance photos that came to Seely were unhelpful. And Seely worried. So did his men.

They looked around and shuddered. Bob Craff told how as he came into

---

*Captain John S. Howe, one of the combat interviewers, believed 1st Battalion was plagued with bad luck. "The final command Captain Fox and I heard on the morning of December 17th while we were at the Regimental CP trying to obtain information as to routes out of Clerveaux—the Germans were fighting furiously at the start of this [Ardennes] counteroffensive [which began on 16 December]—was from the Regimental CO to the 1st Bn CO: 'Get out as best you can. You are cut off.'"

line "another guy took me back in the woods to a blanket, pulled it back, and showed me a man laying there with a hole in his back, already mouldering. I thought of this guy's family with him still layin' there. That was my first contact with what combat was all about."[13]

Many of the dead scattered over the area had no covering blankets, save those provided by nature. Earl Fuller, Jr., a 22-year-old platoon sergeant, didn't like what he saw. "Graves registration needed to remove the dead from the 9th Division, many truckloads of them. There was about a foot of snow, and you could see bumps in it made by dead men. The temperature was just below freezing in the woods and those frozen dead men were loaded into trucks like cord wood."[14]

Another man's reaction was similar. "Red" Guthrie thought of the forest as "them damn woods." Like Fuller, Guthrie saw "stiff and frozen bodies from the Germans and 9th Division lying around. Many were booby-trapped." He said to himself, "What the hell am I in? If this is what the jungle in the South Pacific is like, I don't want to be in the jungle."[15]

Neither did Fred Cope. "The Hurtgen was a real rough deal. They called it the 'Green Hell' in there, but it wasn't so green when we were there. From start to finish it was a 'lot of fun.'" They suffered casualties from the moment of their arrival there. On a day prior to the attack, Cope sat in a four-wall tent talking to a lieutenant, "an Indiana boy named Lynn." German mortar fire bracketed them, splinters striking Cope in the arm and slicing off three of the officer's fingers.[16]

Sergeant M. C. Schreffler, an acting platoon leader in 3rd Platoon of King Company, was 22 years old when he was wounded. His unit was holding its positions prior to the attack. No one was close to Schreffler, for the thin ranks of King Company were spread across their front. They heard German artillery rounds whistling toward them. "We were scared when we heard them coming in, but we didn't want to run. Everybody's scared out there, so we just went on layin' there." A shell burst overhead in the pine trees, spraying wood and steel splinters. Sergeant Schreffler felt a blow on his arm and threw up his rifle to protect his face as he fell forward. As he lifted his arms he felt another punch in his armpit. "At first I got up and walked, but then couldn't get my breath. I was gasping for air and then just fell over." It seemed like a long time to him before medics came and carried him away on a stretcher. The first splinter took a piece of bone from his arm; the second entered his chest at his armpit, hit his lung, and came to rest alongside his heart.[17]

There was no place, Cope knew, to hide from such tree bursts. "They'd get you among the trees, in the open, even in our foxholes."[18] Private Geary rightly complained about their foxholes. "They were useless in the Hurtgen. They'd fill immediately with water."[19] And it was cold. "It was tough, tough going," Cope recalled. "There was no place to get warm, so we burned those little Sterno heat blocks. We'd stand on 'em and we wouldn't even feel 'em when they'd burn up through the soles of our shoes."[20]

Such men quickly learned what would happen to their feet if they did not care for them. Comrades everywhere were evacuated with trench foot. "So," said Harry Geary, "I began a nightly ritual of bathing my feet in my helmet, rinsing the wet socks and placing them between my shirt and underwear where they would remain drying until the next night."[21]

They continued to receive German harassing fire. One night one soldier hung his overcoat between two branches of a tree. In the morning he counted "at least forty holes" torn through it by shrapnel from tree bursts.[22] For more security than foxholes offered, some men built large log bunkers and piled dirt on top. Inside they measured about 10 feet square, with six-foot-high ceilings. They heated them with small gasoline stoves, issued two per squad. Most logs came from trees blown down by German shelling. "They gave men a place to get in out of the cold and have a hot cup of coffee. Building them kept us all busy and gave us less time to think."[23]

Like soldiers everywhere, these men alleviated their tension and stress with humor. One new lieutenant asked a Keystone soldier how he kept his teeth so clean and white. "I said it wasn't that," replied Private Dan DeFail. "My face was just so goddam dirty they looked clean."[24]

Humor could even be found amid the strain of artillery barrages. German shelling settled into a pattern. They laid bombardments down at breakfast and again at suppertime. Occasionally, as an act of bravado and to signal an insult to their enemies, a GI would clamber out of his foxhole as shells burst nearby. "Here we were, pinned down by shellfire and you see some guy going out in the middle of a field to take a crap. It broke the tension and brought a laugh to most everyone."

As those daily barrages began, men of the 110th ran for their holes. In the distance they could hear mortars going off. "Tchungk. Tchungk. Tchungk." Usually Germans would fire about 18 rounds. A moment or two later those shells would land. "BOOM. BOOM. BOOM." As debris from explosions settled, someone would lift his head out of his hole and ask if anyone was hit. Soon Germans found out that GIs were counting the shell rounds, so while the 18 expected ones were landing, they dropped three more rounds in their tubes. "Tchungk. Tchungk. Tchungk." Bob Wells said "those last three rounds blew the ass off more than one of our guys because we weren't expecting them." He refused to be cowed by such German efforts. As noises faded from bursting rounds, "I would always look out of my hole and call out, in imitation of President Roosevelt: 'I hate wah. Eleanor hates wah. Even Fala hates wah. Your sons will never step foot on foreign soil.' And here we were, sitting just inside Germany. It helped to keep up the guys' spirits."[25]

Another favorite comment was to call out to one's buddies: "Alright. I want to take a poll. All you confirmed atheists sound off. I want to see how many of you are left."[26]

No matter how good their humor, GIs could not hold back the hands on the inexorable clock that moved toward H Hour. Colonel Seely still had no firm notion of what German defenses were like in those thick forests to the south.

He ordered patrols sent out. They were not much help. Until 1 November, none went out at night due to the complete blackness men on reconnaissance encountered once they entered the closely packed trees of the forest. Nor was it much easier to penetrate them during daytime hours. Any American movement in the forward area during daylight drew intense German responses from small-arms, automatic weapons, and mortar fire.

American soldiers reacted with equal ferocity to German patrols. Instead of remaining quiet while holding their positions, doing little firing in order not to divulge their locations, troops of the 110th opened up with their weapons at the slightest sign of enemy patrol activity. At times their firing was so heavy that 3rd Battalion intelligence sergeant, Staff Sergeant Martin J. Joyce, claimed that at the battalion command post it sounded as if a major German attack was in progress against their forward positions.[27]

Only one man seemed to like patrolling. He was Staff Sergeant Abraham Kumukau, from Hawaii. "He went out for every patrol he could volunteer for. He had this 1903 Springfield rifle and I don't know how many Germans he picked off. With him it was like a duck shoot. He was out for revenge."[28]

Seely met with his three battalion commanders: Lieutenant Colonel William S. Tait of 3rd Battalion; Lieutenant Colonel Floyd A. Davison of 1st Battalion; and Lieutenant Colonel James R. Hughes of 2nd Battalion. They discussed the battle facing them. They knew their initial task was to take and secure two very limited objectives on the right flank of 28th Infantry Division. In the divisional operation plan they were listed as objectives 3 and 4. Number 4 was the tiny hamlet of Simonskall; number 3 was hill 396—a horseshoe loop in the road that came into Simonskall from the east. Having acquired these objectives, the 110th was to prepare to advance in conjunction with the 112th to the east, southeast, south, or southwest; the latter direction seemed most likely, for that would take them toward the towns of Strauch and Steckenborn, where they could secure the main east–west road into Schmidt.[29]

Seely, Tait, Hughes, and Davison believed that between their units and Schmidt were perhaps five enemy battalions, part of the *89th Infantry Division,* plus some engineers and other attached troops. Enemy infantry were calculated to number perhaps 1,500. Divisional objective number 4, the town of Simonskall, was reputed to be in wreckage, leveled by previous American artillery fire and army air forces bombings.*

To approach Simonskall, GIs would cross a heavily wooded, downward slope into the Kall gorge and thence into the town. This route was thought to be covered by only three German pillboxes—two on high ground south of town covering its western approaches, and one on high ground north of the hamlet, protecting it from the north and northwest. A reinforced concrete

*When men of 1st Battalion later captured Simonskall, they found only very slight damage there, another example of the poor state of American information about the enemy prior to the attack.

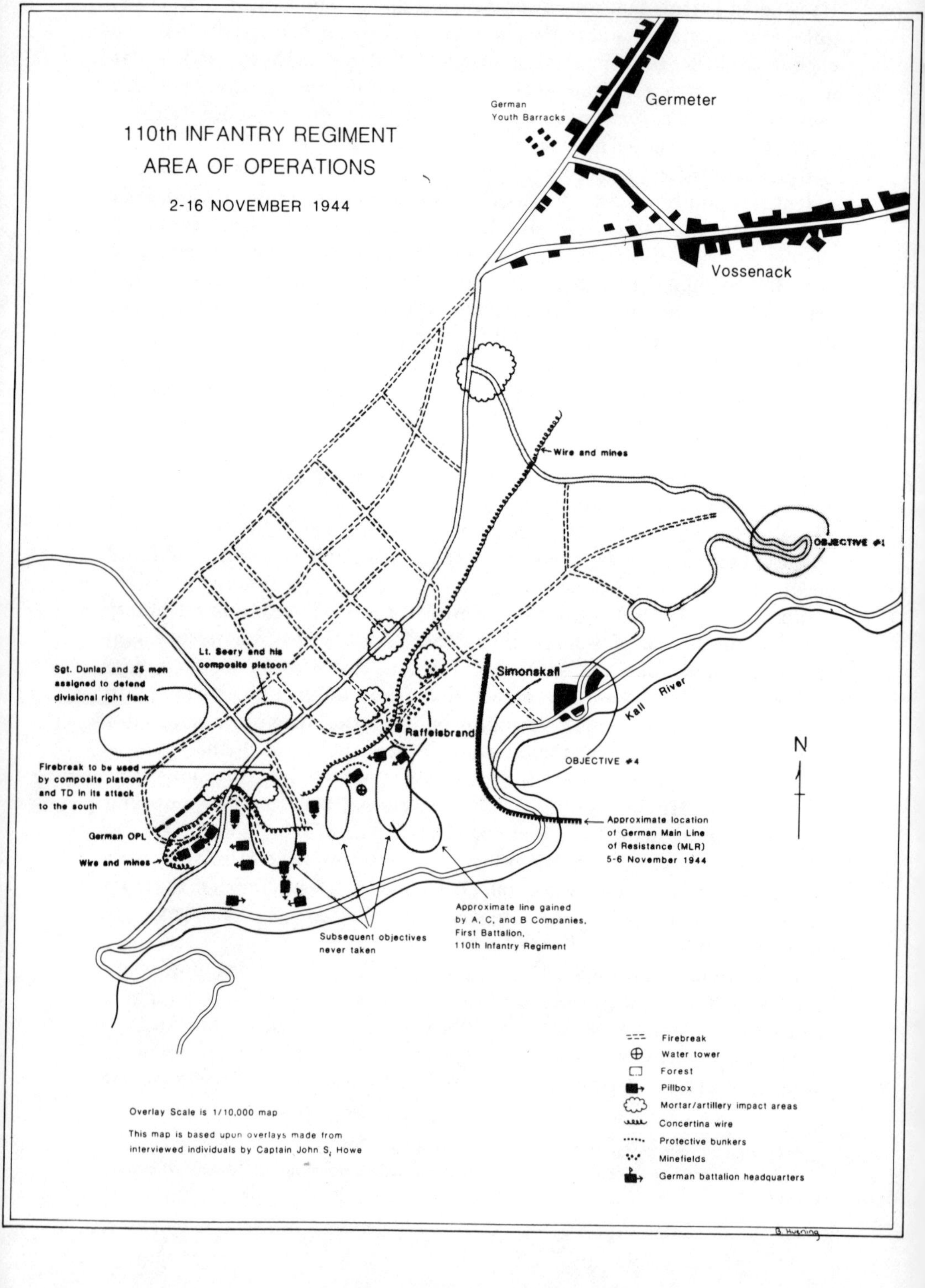
110th INFANTRY REGIMENT
AREA OF OPERATIONS
2-16 NOVEMBER 1944
German Youth Barracks
Germeter
Vossenack
Wire and mines
OBJECTIVE #1
Lt. Seery and his composite platoon
Sgt. Dunlap and 25 men assigned to defend divisional right flank
Simonskall
Kall River
Raffelsbrand
OBJECTIVE #4
N
Firebreak to be used by composite platoon and TD in its attack to the south
German OPL
Wire and mines
Approximate location of German Main Line of Resistance (MLR) 5-6 November 1944
Approximate line gained by A, C, and B Companies, First Battalion, 110th Infantry Regiment
Subsequent objectives never taken
Firebreak
Water tower
Forest
Pillbox
Mortar/artillery impact areas
Concertina wire
Protective bunkers
Minefields
German battalion headquarters
Overlay Scale is 1/10,000 map
This map is based upon overlays made from interviewed individuals by Captain John S. Howe

house, Raffelsbrand, a former German forestry station near Simonskall, was believed to be an enemy command post serving as a firing point to repel any American attack toward Simonskall from the west.

Captain William S. Linning, regimental S-2 intelligence officer, told Tait, Hughes, and Davison that the terrain was so unsuitable for tank operations that GIs would encounter very few antitank mines. He did believe they might chance upon a profusion of antipersonnel mines. He was correct. Linning also learned from a German PW, captured the night of 1/2 November, that all enemy defenses were wired in and that much of any German resistance would be done from emplacements or bunkers outside pillboxes rather than from within their depths. Neither Linning nor his intelligence sergeant, Staff Sergeant Martin Joyce, believed the PW's information to be complete, so they did not pass it on to the three battalion commanders.[30]

The morning of the "jump-off" against the Germans, a patrol from K Company, 3rd Battalion, moved a little way south into the forest and discovered a German defensive line made from concertina wire: two rolls stretched side by side through the trees, with a third placed on top of them, creating a six-foot-tall barrier. In front of the wire, German troops had dug a shallow ditch, varying in width from four to six feet. "This barrier area," lamented Joyce, "was not located until just an hour or two prior to the start of the attack and it is doubtful that all the men in the company knew what obstacles confronted them." Worse than the barrier itself was the fact that it was capable of being covered with low, grazing, enfilade fire from several machine-gun emplacements dug in along it.[31]

This then was the extent of information known about German defenses prior to the attack. It was woefully inadequate.

Seely gave his orders. Tait's 3rd Battalion was ordered to secure divisional objectives 3 and 4; Simonskall and the horseshoe bend in the road to the east. Hughes' 2nd Battalion was to move south, clean out all known pillboxes, and secure the regimental right flank in preparation for the later divisional attack on Strauch and Steckenborn. Davison's 1st Battalion was to hold in position as a reserve, for later commitment on divisional order.[32]

Tait planned to employ two of his companies in the attack. King Company would advance on the right and seize Simonskall. Love Company on the left was to penetrate enemy defenses and capture the road loop east of the hamlet.[33] In 2nd Battalion, Hughes ordered Fox Company ahead on the right, with George Company on the left.[34] And so during the morning of 2 November, aware of the 109th Infantry Regiment attacking north to their rear and the 112th Infantry Regiment pushing eastward, the men of the 110th waited along their line of departure until 1200 hours and the signal to attack. When the time came they moved bravely south into the forest against German defenses.

Love Company came under fire almost immediately as German weapons screeched and hammered, forcing GIs to fling themselves behind broken tree trunks or grovel in shell holes filled with icy water. Mortar shells blew gaping craters in the forest floor, and men of the 'Bloody Bucket' hugged the clinging, sodden earth. Rivulets streamed from wooded slopes, washing slurries of oozing slime onto nearby debris. Platoons of men slithered forward through clinging, broken leaves and stinking mud. Young Earl Fuller saw his first sergeant die. "He had been a lieutenant in World War I but had stayed in as an NCO. All summer he had said the war would end in November. It did for him but I still remember the twinkle in his eyes when he put us on details."[35]

Love Company soldiers continued forward until they reached the ditch and triple roll of wire. Fire from machine-gun emplacements they could not locate stopped them in their tracks. King Company also got as far as the ditch, where 12 of its men were either killed or wounded from heavy German machine-gun fire. Most injuries were from the hips down because of low, grazing fire. A very few men crawled through the barrier and got perhaps 25 yards farther before they were stopped. They could go no farther. For four hours these men suffered under enemy bullets before Colonel Tait recalled them to the line of departure, at about 1600 hours. They would try again the next day.[36]

Wounded men were treated at the 110th's aid station, known for some obscure reason as "Honeymoon" aid station. Sergeant Schreffler received treatment there for his shrapnel wounds, as did Fred Cope. Albert Kuhn, a medic, recalled how busy they were. "It was not unusual," he said, "to treat fifty to seventy-five wounded per day."[37] Medical personnel worked with equal fervor on both American and German soldiers who suffered injury. Near the aid station was a collecting point for German prisoners, and Harry Geary, one of the medics, remembered a young enemy soldier shot through the foot on whom he worked. "He told me he was twelve years old and should be in school."[38]

In 2nd Battalion sector at noon on 2 November, Fox Company moved out. Second Lieutenant Fred Huto, leader of its 2nd Platoon, confused by the thick woods—or unwilling to commit suicide in the face of determined enemy resistance—somehow guided his men along a trail away from their objective, ending up along a firebreak considerably to the *north* of his starting point.[39]

The other two platoons of F Company managed to push their way a little more than 100 yards south from their line of departure. There they were pinned down by enemy bunkers from which poured withering fire from burp guns, rifles, and machine guns. Those bunkers protected a pillbox. Forty-five minutes after leaving the LD, an assault team from Fox managed to crawl within 25 yards of barbed wire stretched around the perimeter of the "box." Then a sudden mortar shell landed in their midst, killing three and wounding four others. Those still able to do so dragged their injured comrades back toward shelter.

Neither 1st nor 3rd Platoons could advance, caught in the beaten zone of a well-placed mortar barrage. If they crawled forward to escape from tree bursts of exploding mortar shells, they came under fire from machine guns nested in log bunkers around the pillboxes to their front. Fallen tops from blasted pine trees effectively screened enemy positions from view. The best those terrified GIs could do was to fire an occasional round from their rifles in the general direction of the Germans. At 1630 hours they were ordered to fall back to their original positions. Their attack had failed.[40]

George Company's assignment was to neutralize two pillboxes as it moved forward. Between the pillboxes was a water tower that men in G Company could guide on to locate their objectives among the tall trees. Three separate wire obstacles guarded their line of approach. As they drew closer to the pillboxes they saw first a two-strand barbed-wire fence nailed to tree trunks. Passing through that, they confronted a single roll of concertina wire about three feet high protected by mines and booby traps. Less than ten yards out from the pillboxes was another roll of concertina wire.

American soldiers moved carefully forward in squads, with scouts leading the way, followed by BAR teams and bangalore torpedomen. Last of all came men carrying demolitions that would be used to blow up those "boxes" when captured. As they closed on their target, Staff Sergeant Manuel C. Suarez, armed with a 1903 Springfield rifle equipped with a launcher, fired grenades at the embrasures of the closest pillbox. Alongside him, a BAR team emptied clip after clip at those same openings. Private Frank Owczarsak, an assistant gunner, was seriously wounded by the explosion of an enemy antitank grenade. In spite of his pain, he stuck to his job, loading magazines into his gunner's BAR. Despite all efforts, those men were unable to close on the "box."

A few yards away, Private George Nikola, a scout in 1st Platoon, ran along a firebreak toward a shallow dip in the ground he thought might serve as a good field of fire for use against the pillboxes. He carried a light machine gun. As he reached the hollow, he dropped to the ground and set the gun down beside him. As it touched the earth it depressed a hidden plunger on a buried mine that then exploded, destroying the barrel of the machine gun and wounding Nickola in the face. Thrashing with pain, his right foot struck a booby trap, setting it off and injuring his foot. Refusing to crawl back to safety, Nickola remained where he was for over an hour in order to shout warnings to his buddies not to venture into the area of mines and booby traps.*

G Company received notice to withdraw at about 1320 hours. 1st Platoon alone carried back 11 casualties, including two men who had fallen prey to combat exhaustion. One of the battle fatigue cases, Private Trybus, a recent replacement from an antiaircraft artillery unit, had been thrown that day into battle without any infantry training. When his buddies found him he was trying to dig a foxhole into the moist earth with his bare hands. They forcibly

---

*Taken back that afternoon to Honeymoon aid station, Nickola was evacuated later that day. He was subsequently recommended for the Silver Star.

lifted him from the ground and carried him to the rear. Men in George Company retreated, one or two at a time, in a movement that took two hours. They reached their positions behind the line of departure at about 1600 hours, having been unable to achieve their mission.[41]

The combined efforts of Love and King companies, 3rd Battalion, and Fox and George companies, 2nd Battalion, came to naught that first day of battle. Those shaken men, had they been aware, might have marveled to know that 2nd Battalion's Easy Company was not committed to battle that day because regimental headquarters thought the operation would be easy. After all, the objective was a "limited" one only "a short space of ground away," guarded by just a "few" pillboxes.[42]

Men of the 110th were grateful to be out of combat, if even for only a few hours. They talked about their fears to one another. Charles Hubner remembered such conversations. "At first we were petrified, really scared. But if we were lucky enough to live through a few skirmishes we weren't so much scared of a fight as of getting maimed. Most of us said we would rather be dead than go home a cripple."[43]

Some men achieved a fatalistic measure of peace. Bob Craff recalled his experiences. "The Germans called in mortar fire on us. I ran to get out of it and got half way up this two hundred meter hill. Even though I was only 20 years old, I couldn't go any further. So I laid there and shuddered and clawed ground and then for some reason a calm came all over me and I wasn't afraid anymore. I said to myself, 'If God's willing, I'll make it to the top of this hill'—and I did. From that time on I had no fear of death."[44]

That night as those lonely infantrymen huddled behind their line of departure, fearing for what the morrow might bring, some watched the dark skies, listening to the sound of Royal Air Force planes on their nightly flight toward targets in Germany. The drone of planes continued uninterrupted for some time. At about 2200 hours, a German interceptor group closed in on those British bombers. A young artilleryman, Jack Colbaugh, had just finished delivering ammunition to firing batteries and was preparing for a few hours' sleep when the fight in the skies began. "It was definitely a very weird and frightening feeling to see the tracer bullets fly around at all angles and listen to that terrifying noise of machine gun clatter in the darkness. Two balls of flame came down into the Hurtgen Forest that night."

Two British aviators parachuted through the velvet blackness toward an unknown fate below: Pilot Officer Walter MacKay and Pilot Officer Albert Howe, who bailed out of their burning aircraft. In the darkness they were unsure if they were in friendly or enemy territory, but it seemed wise to make their way westward. At about dawn they stumbled into outposts of B Company, 707th Tank Battalion. Private James "Spike" Malloy, from Brooklyn, first spotted the two men. He asked them for the password, which obviously neither knew. The British pilots did indicate they would be pleased to drop in for tea. None of this made good sense to Malloy, who roughly pushed them around for a while and then called his company command post. "Dere are a coupla guys here speakin broken English. We tink dere Germans." Finally succeeding in establishing their identity, the two pilots were sent to the rear, arriving at the divisional command post in Rott at 0856 hours.[45]

By the time those British fliers reached safety, men of the 110th Infantry Regiment were once again fighting for their lives. At 0700 hours, 3 November, men of Fox and George companies, 2nd Battalion, moved south to renew their attack on German defenses. Visibility was limited not only by fallen treetops scattered across the forest floor but also by a heavy morning mist. It was impossible to see more than a few feet in any direction. Once again they faced slaughter. Those in F Company were hit each time they attempted to close on their enemies. When they slid backward out of range of machine guns and rifle grenades, mortar shells exploded in their midst.

Two soldiers, Private John Fabrizio and Private George C. Cutchis, wormed their way forward to the wire barrier that had blocked them the previous day. As they crawled through it, both were wounded and left hanging on the wire's vicious barbs. Other men tried to squirm close enough to evacuate them but were driven off by heavy fire. One rifleman—a brave soldier named Private Harold Sheffer—took a white hankerchief from his pocket and stood up, waving it. German defenders ceased firing.

With his heart in his throat, Sheffer walked slowly up to the wire. A German officer met him and permitted him to remove the two wounded men and carry them to safety.* Taking advantage of the lull, German soldiers stood up in their foxholes and bunkers, holding their rifles at port arms, to stretch and relieve cramped muscles. Men of Fox Company were startled to see many more enemy soldiers there than they expected. In that one small area, they counted 90 Germans. It wasn't official, but it was a soldiers' truce—and a very temporary one.

When Sheffer dragged the two men to safety, soldiers resumed their firing positions and began shooting once again. By 1400 hours it was obvious no gains would be made that day. Fox Company commander, Captain Lake W. Coleman, ordered his platoons to pull back. "It took," he said, "about two hours before the last men [got back] one at a time. Each one would crawl about fifty yards to the rear, then jump to his feet and run like hell. Some of the men did a combination of rushing and crawling; the remainder provided a constant covering fire on the barely visible German positions. A sergeant and I and the BAR gunners remained until all the others who could make it had withdrawn. Then we took off. Only one of the several BARs remained operational at the end. Their barrels were shot." Fox Company suffered 30 casualties that day.[46]

George Company was also in trouble. Its commander, Captain James Kitchens, led off the attack side by side with Fox Company at 0700 hours.

---

*Private Harold F. Sheffer was killed in action the following day.

Skirmishers rushed forward, using folds in the ground and tree trunks as cover until they were within 15 yards of the pillbox that had so frustrated them the preceding day. As they lay there, seeking what cover they could find, snipers on top of the "box" fired at the rearmost GIs, moving their aim closer as they scored on one man after another. Near the front of the group lay Sergeant Suarez. When he realized what was happening, he fired rifle grenades and threw hand grenades at the snipers in efforts to dislodge them. At one point an enemy "egg" grenade bounced off Suarez' foot, hit another sergeant on the helmet, and fell to earth without exploding.

One man, unwilling to lay waiting any longer for a sniper's bullet, crawled forward dragging a pole charge with him, trying to get close enough to blow the door on the pillbox. Ten yards from the fortification, he swore at the clumsiness of the charge he was dragging, stood up, and walked toward the concrete bunker. He was only four yards from the door when a sniper shot him in the face.

For forty minutes those GIs endured the remorseless sniper fire. At 0800 hours, Captain Kitchens ordered them to pull back to their original positions.[47]

3rd Battalion also resumed its attack at 0700 that morning. King Company men twice tried to capture their objective. Both times they suffered so many casualties they had to fall back. At 1515 hours, Colonel Seely ordered Item Company, 3rd Battalion, to join the fray. Those men made no more progress than did members of their sister companies. Seely thought the regiment was met by heavier fire on 3 November than on the preceding day; perhaps as many as 200 more riflemen and several added machine guns strengthened German defenses.[48]

By 1600 hours, all men in the regiment capable of doing so had dragged themselves behind the line of departure once more. There would be no other attempts that day to breach German lines.

That afternoon General Cota informed Seely that he wanted 1st Battalion, 110th Infantry Regiment, to mount a flanking attack against German positions the following day. If frontal assaults would not work, then an end run might allow them to achieve their objectives. Cota told Seely that 3rd and 2nd battalions would hold in place, exerting pressure on enemy lines. 1st Battalion would hit unsuspecting German defenders on their right flank.

Colonel Seely passed the word to Lieutenant Colonel Floyd A. Davison. He must move his men into Vossenack during the night. They would move out at 0700 hours, on 4 November, move on, and capture divisional objective 3, the horseshoe bend in the road to Simonskall. There they would leave one company to consolidate and hold that position. Other companies would resume the attack and seize objective number 4, the town of Simonskall.

Seely promised Davison that his infantrymen would have tank support as they moved south out of Vossenack. One armor platoon south of town would fire from hull defilade in front of advancing GIs until they gained the woods at the edge of the ridge. The tanks would then lift fire and rejoin their own company.

Also, said Seely, a heavy machine-gun platoon from 1st Battalion's Dog Company would place long-range overhead fire on target areas. Nearby, another heavy-weapons platoon would fire across the front of advancing infantrymen until they reached the woods south of Vossenack.

It was 2000 hours on 3 November, before Seely and Davison completed plans for the next day's attack. Onset of darkness meant none of 1st Battalion's platoon leaders could make a ground reconnaissance prior to attacking. It was not a comfortable night. Continuing rain from black skies shut off most ambient light. Platoon leaders ordered their men fed at 0200 hours. They were in formation and ready to move out by 0430.

They started forward in a column of companies, one file walking on each side of the Germeter–Hürtgen road, then east through a clearing in a friendly minefield outside Germeter. They reached the western edge of Vossenack and waited. At 0630 hours Germans laid a heavy concentration of artillery shells on them, estimated at 1,000 rounds from 105mm, 155mm, and 170mm guns. Men of 1st Battalion scattered for cover, leaving behind four dead and 35 wounded.

The barrage lifted just prior to 0700 hours as the tank platoon moved into position and opened fire on its assigned targets. Infantry officers rounded up their scattered men, who by this time were used to living from minute to minute. "Whoever thought of the phrase SNAFU knew what he was talking about," said Charles Hubner. "We rarely knew what was going on and all we ever heard was 'O.K. men, let's move out.'"[49] This time they were more than ready to leave the artillery impact area.

Able Company moved south, followed by Charley and Baker companies. Riflemen crossed the meadows so rapidly it was not even necessary for supporting artillery batteries to shoot all their planned concentrations. Able Company moved down the slope of the Kall gorge, through the trees, and onto the hill and horseshoe bend of the Simonskall road. Except for a few scattered rifle shots they encountered almost no enemy resistance. Objective 3 was seized by 0820 hours.

Baker Company remained there to guard the road bend while Able and Charley companies marched west down the road toward Simonskall. Charley Company dropped off squads along the way to hold the road. By 0900 Able Company entered the little settlement, capturing it with only superficial German resistance. Within an hour, however, GIs found themselves targets for snipers on high ground outside town. Mortar shells dropped into the hamlet whenever they ventured along its street. Troops of Able Company found it wise to remain under cover except when absolutely necessary. They were in a precarious situation at best, for high ground virtually surrounded the town, and Germans on those elevated heights could easily see them. They were in danger, yet the flanking effort by 1st Battalion, 110th Infantry, had worked. They had captured divisional objectives 3 and 4: the horseshoe bend in the road and the hamlet of Simonskall. It had been far more effective to make this flanking attack than to continue thrusting south from Germeter into minefields and fortifications of the Siegfried Line. Yet all around them were their enemies. 1st Battalion may have achieved its goals, but it was in grave danger.

Slightly northeast of Simonskall were three pillboxes. When A Company moved into town those "boxes" were quiet, supposedly empty. Fearing they might be reoccupied, the company commander ordered First Lieutenant Edward McKee, 2nd Platoon leader, to take one rifle squad and a bazooka team to reconnoiter and, if necessary, attack those positions. As McKee and his men closed on the first "box," the bazooka team fired at its embrasures. The others rushed the entrance and found seven Germans, who surrendered without a fight. One PW volunteered that "an officer and some 20 men" were in the next pillbox some 100 yards away.

The small task force moved on and cautiously approached its next target. Its men charged in through an open doorway and found the huge structure empty except for a smashed radio. A little after 1600 hours, they entered the third "box" and learned it also had been vacated. They requested an engineer squad to come up and dynamite the pillboxes. Just after dark 15 men and an officer from the 1340th Engineer Combat Battalion arrived but brought no demolitions. It was not until the next morning that carrying parties were able to pack in enough TNT to blow up the structures.*

Early on 5 November, men of A Company awakened to noises made by Germans digging in across their front to the south of Simonskall. Captain James Burns, only 100 yards away, watched them work. He tried to call for an artillery barrage, but his radio batteries were so weak it took over an hour to make contact and arrange for a shelling. Soon high explosives began to burst among the Germans. "At each concentration," Burns observed, "the Germans would scream and holler and begin to run out of the fire [zone]. Then they would be shot down by [our] small arms fire. When we lifted the artillery and

---

*In the initial operation plan, regimental staff officers planned to use Weasels to carry supplies forward to the Simonskall area on a firebreak trail through trees lining the Kall gorge's northern slope. When a group of M-29s loaded with rations, ammunition, and demolitions arrived at the trail at about 1200 hours, 4 November, their drivers found it much steeper than indicated on their maps. The slope was so great it was simply impassable even for their tracked carriers. From then on all supplies had to be hand-carried to units along the river and in Simonskall.

Nor was medical evacuation from Simonskall easy. Medics who worked all of 4 November on patients at the horseshoe bend in the road finally completed their treatment of patients and walked on into Simonskall accompanied by extra litter teams attached to the 28th Division by V Corps. Those teams evacuated injured men from Simonskall, hand-carrying them east along the road to objective 3 and thence uphill through the trees to open ground south of Vosenack. Captured German riflemen were assigned to carry litters in this difficult and exhausting evacuation route, and some German medics volunteered to assist in caring for American wounded.

mortar fire, they would come back into their positions."[50] It was troubling to Burns and his men to watch the tenacity of their enemies.

When Colonel Seely pulled his 1st Battalion out of line on the night of 3/4 November to make its flanking attack on objectives 3 and 4, he plugged the gap it left with a special unit named Task Force Lacy. This group was composed of the regimental intelligence and reconnaissance platoon, the antitank platoon, and a provisional raider platoon, all under the command of First Lieutenant Virgil R. Lacy. His 66 men thus filled a battalion-sized hole in American lines. For a time on the afternoon of 4 November, Easy Company, 2nd Battalion, held down the line on Task Force Lacy's flank, arriving at about 1430 and remaining until 2100 hours.[51]

Captain William Dobbs, commander of Easy Company, received orders that night from Lieutenant Colonel James Hughes, 2nd Battalion commander, to pull back out of line and, under cover of darkness, move to an assembly point in the west end of Vossenack. At 0700, on 5 November, Dobbs and his company were to move down into the Kall gorge and attack still active pillboxes there. As Easy Company moved up the Germeter–Hürtgen road, its men marched past tanks and tank destroyers parked almost bumper to bumper. Filing past those tracked vehicles, riflemen of East Company turned east toward Vossenack, reaching their assembly point at 0640 hours. They formed into position for the move south.

At 0700 hours, with no artillery preparation, E Company crossed the Vossenack line of departure and went rapidly across country and down the wooded slope to the river road, which ran parallel to the Kall River along its north bank. There they made contact with Charlie Company.

Captain Sidney Dini, commander of Charlie Company, joined forces with Dobbs for a joint attack on nearby pillboxes. They advanced so rapidly through thick undergrowth and they were on top of defending German soldiers so quickly there was no time for them to fight back. They captured 30 enemy troops. Engineers blew up two pillboxes by 0915 hours.

At 0930 Easy and Charlie Companies moved on. An artillery barrage struck them at 1030. As shells landed, men everywhere scrambled pell-mell into the woods seeking cover, straight into enemy trip wires and booby traps. Crying and shouting from pain and fear, men scrabbled for hiding places, only to find themselves under enemy small-arms fire. Hours of disorganized confusion and separate struggles ensued. Just before dark, Captain Dobbs sent a three-man patrol forward to find a way out of the wires and mines. All three were wounded. One of them, Private Meley Lukich, stepped on a mine that nearly severed his leg. His team members managed to drag him back to company medics, who saved his life.

It was now dark. Dobbs decided his company would remain exactly where it was, without venturing through those dark and forbidding woods in the midst of an enemy minefield. Easy Company had suffered 30 casualties that day.[52] Charlie Company was in no better condition. For those men it was a night of endless horror.

Earlier that afternoon, Lieutenant Colonel William S. Tait, commander of 2rd Battalion, received word from Colonel Seely that his companies were to be prepared to move out on a new assignment by 1600 hours. Those new orders would require the life of Colonel Tait and would take men of the 110th Infantry Regiment even farther into the valley of death.[53]

5

"Into the Valley of Death"

2 November–3 November 1944

Lieutenant Colonel Samuel E. Mays commanded the 893rd Tank Destroyer Battalion, part of the 3rd Tank Destroyer Group, which was attached to the 4th Infantry Division. That division was one of the more successful units of the regular army. Landing in Normandy, fighting its way across France, few U.S. Army units saw more war than did the 4th. Repeated combat actions provided both Colonel Mays and his men with invaluable experience and continued training in the use of their M-10 tank destroyers.

M-10s, built on a Sherman tank chassis, were fully tracked vehicles mounting a three-inch, flat-trajectory, high-velocity 75mm artillery piece. Thinly armored with open, boxlike turrets, they were much like German assault guns used in breaching permanent fortifications such as gun positions in the Maginot Line during the 1940 invasion of France. American M-10s employed the "shoot and scoot" method of fire and maneuver, and their primary mission was to provide antitank support and protection. Tank destroyers provided bases of fire from which tank formations could maneuver, and they proved their worth in the open and wide-ranging terrain of North Africa. No one at the Tank Destroyer Desert Training Center taught how M-10s could be used in wooded terrain or in fighting for built-up areas, for both forests and cities were believed to be unsuited for tank operations. Little thought was given to the possibility that M-10s might be called on for close-in antitank support in the Hürtgen Forest.

North African "wadis" were deep, but visibility and fields of fire were clear of forest, buildings, and fog, unlike the area of the Hürtgen. The terrain there would limit combat to small-unit actions, and use of M-10 tank destroyers in built up and forested areas was not what Headquarters, Army Ground Forces, had in mind when in 1942 it authorized the organization of 53 antitank battalions.[1]

On the afternoon of 28 October 1944, General Gerow's staff at V Corps notified Colonel Mays that his 893rd Tank Destroyer Battalion would be attached to the 28th Infantry Division. It would provide indirect fire support during an attack in the Hürtgen. The next morning Mays reported to his commander at 3rd Tank Destroyer Group headquarters. From the beginning, Mays was displeased with his orders. He reminded his commander tht he had only two companies, Baker and Charlie, available to support the 28th Division. Able Company was already attached to the 102nd Cavalry Group.

Mays also contacted the commanding officer of the 899th Tank Destroyer Battalion, which had supported the earlier attack of the 9th Infantry Division in the Hürtgen. Mays did not wish to relearn those bitter lessons. They discussed positions used by the 899th and problems caused by terrain. "We knew," Mays stated, "that the terrain was very unsuited to Tank Destroyer operation. It would put the guns out where they would be like a fly in a saucer."[2]

Mays plotted on his map possible sites his M-10s could use so their crews might repel German armored counterattacks on the 28th from the north or northeast. Then he alerted his companies for movement and relocation forward. As the battalion moved into positions near Germeter, Mays worried about the weather. His men were unable to register their guns prior to the attack because of clouds, haze, and poor visibility.

Then Mays received orders changing the role of his M-10 crews from one of providing indirect fire to one of attack and close-in support. He didn't like this new plan, which "came with great abruptness." Concerned about what he believed to be a gross lack of information, on 1 November Mays "challenged our own [3rd Tank Destroyer Group] Headquarters as well as [28th] division [headquarters] for the big picture." It was an unusual move for a subordinate commander to make. "As we envisaged this operation, it was to be a 1-2 punch; a short, quick action by the 28th Division and supporting units, followed by a strong attack to the north by VII Corps." The change from indirect to direct support now meant Mays would be required to send his crews forward as infantrymen and tanks attacked their German enemies. His M-10s would be within easy reach of enemy shells, very much like "a fly in a saucer."

As the opening barrage against German lines began on 2 November, Mays' crews fired their guns in accordance with divisional requirements. After firing those initial rounds, one M-10 broke down from a leaking recoil mechanism on its tube. It was evacuated to the rear for maintenance. Already without a third of his battalion firepower due to A Company's attachment to the 102nd Cavalry Group, Colonel Mays' unit began the action with only 24 tank destroyers (TDs). One of those was already out of action.*[3]

At 0900 hours, 2 November, American barrage guns fell silent. Tense and frightened infantrymen moved up to the line of departure. In his divisional command post at Rott, Major General Norman D. Cota knew assaults by two of his regiments—the 109th and 110th—were secondary and in support of V Corps' primary goal, the capture of Schmidt. The 112th Infantry Regiment bore responsibility for achieving the Bloody Bucket's main effort. It would first attack and subdue the village of Vossenack and the ridge on which it sat. That task belonged to its 2nd Battalion, which, if successful, could protect the regimental north flank as the other two battalions moved forward. They would advance along the tree line at the south side of the ridge, wheel southeast, plunge down into the Kall gorge, cross the river, move into Kommerscheidt, and then forge on to their final objective of Schmidt.[4] It was chancy, but General Cota said it could be done. His prestige rode on results to be achieved by his infantry battalions.

As American guns ceased firing their artillery barrage, Germans responded in kind, aiming for massed ranks of infantry and vehicles at the line of departure. GIs were glad for the massive tanks hulking beside them, which waited to move forward through friendly minefields in front of them, and stretching eastward from Germeter. Those tanks belonged to the 707th Tank Battalion commanded by Lieutenant Colonel Richard W. Ripple, whose wife and children lived in Bethesda, Maryland.

Colonel Ripple's men no longer operated "General Grant" tanks. Those 29-ton vehicles with their 37mm turret guns and 57mm armor plate were gone. Even upgrading them by positioning 75mm guns in their sponsons had not made them fit competitors for German armor. Ripple's men now used "General Sherman" M-4s weighing 35 tons, protected by 81mm armor and mounting a 75mm turret gun.

Ripple's operation plan called for his C Company to support the 112th's 2nd Battalion as it moved on Vossenack. One tank platoon would operate with an infantry company as it moved east on the south side of the Germeter--Vossenack road. A second platoon would support another infantry company on the north side of the road. These two leading tank platoons were to advance as rapidly as possible, consolidating the western edge of Vossenack before moving on east, shooting toward the Bergstein ridge to give Germans the impression that the major American thrust was aimed there. The third tank platoon would accompany the reserve rifle company, assisting it in mopping up any remaining German resistance in Vossenack.[5] Ripple would

---

*Of the 23 remaining tank destroyers, 17 were lost in the combat actions which followed.

monitor his unit's progress, moving as needed between his rear command post at Jagerhaus and his forward command post near Germeter.

Tanker crews each fired four rounds at the exposed and burning church steeple in Vossenack and then engaged clutches on their M-4s and rolled forward. They were completely exposed to, and for the first 500 yards the targets of heavy German artillery and mortar fire.

One tank moved south and became lost in a draw below Vossenack, where it was destroyed by a German *Panzerfaust.* Another struck a mine while crossing the minefield and was knocked out. A third mired down in soft, muddy earth and could not pull free. A fourth tank, 800 yards out from the LD, lost use of all its weapons. Its crew could not loosen a jammed round in its 75mm turret gun. Both its coaxial machine guns and bow guns had stoppages. Its antiaircraft gun broke down last when its bolt jammed from overheating.[6]

Tanks stayed closer than planned to infantrymen in the advance on Vossenack. M-4 crews wanted close-in support, and GIs wanted to huddle behind those tanks for protection. One infantry officer kept his hand on the lead tank's rear fender for the first 500 yards. As M-4s clanked into Vossenack their crews could see German soldiers retreating north, east, and southeast. A large group ran into a draw southeast of town, while still others fled over high ground north of Kommerscheidt, some two kilometers away. Tankers fired their machine guns and turret cannons at those enemy soldiers as they ran for safety.[7] Leading tanks reached the eastern end of the Vossenack ridge by 1030 hours and moved back and forth on its forward nose firing at the Brandenberg–Bergstein ridge.[8]

Two assault companies of 2nd Battalion trudged toward Vossenack with G Company on the left and F Company on the right. Every one of those men knew the war would not soon be over, and some left behind hastily written onion skin V-mail letters cynically inquiring of loved ones at home how plans for Victory Day parades were developing.[9] Vossenack would soon be the hottest spot in American front lines this side of the Rhine.

George Company, although hit by fairly heavy artillery fire and some small-arms fire, moved forward quickly. Its men were on their objective on the forward slope of Vossenack ridge in only one hour and five minutes. They began digging in there, surprised that enemy soldiers almost ignored their activities save for an occasional burst of small-arms fire.[10]

Fortune was not so gentle with men in Fox Company. They left positions on a former German rifle range in a draw west of Germeter, past 2nd Battalion's command post, which occupied a captured pillbox, and up to the LD. The men were nervous, aware that enemy soldiers still held ground just east of the Germeter–Hürtgen road and in former German youth barracks just to their right front.[11]

Enemy shelling disrupted men in Fox Company. They were so slow moving forward that the tail of the unit did not clear the LD until 1030 hours.[12]

Private John Allard thought German resistance unbelievable. The minute Fox Company left its protected rear area, its men were plunged into a storm of "grenades, artillery, burp guns, small arms fire, rain, fog, mortar fire, booby traps, mines, snipers, screaming friends, continued prayers . . . and constant fear."[13] Another soldier, Jack Colbaugh, called the drive on Vossenack a "suicide mission." No one, he said, could fight against such odds and expect to be among the living at the end of battle.[14]

Men in F Company found themselves targeted by a deadly hail of 8cm shells. 2nd Battalion's .50-caliber machine-gun platoon tried to neutralize some of this enemy activity by firing into trees on the left of Vossenack in front of Fox. It was still slow going. Disorganized movement by men in Fox brought troubles to their buddies in Easy Company, who were already formed at the LD waiting to move out. No one suspected F Company might be delayed and so, while waiting for it to pass, three men in Easy Company became casualties.[15]

Followed closely by Easy Company, soldiers of Fox edged along past the youth barracks, keeping pretty much to the ditch on the right side of the Germeter–Vossenack road. German troops holed up in the barracks resisted for a time but then gave way and retreated. As they fled, a nearby enemy machine-gun nest opened fire on F and E companies. Artillery bursts continued to explode.

Private Joseph Kuirter, E Company, was hit in the arm by shell splinters. PFC Thomas Shelbelski died from an exploding round. Staff Sergeant Edward Peck collapsed on the ground, badly wounded. Easy Company was only 300 yards out from its line of departure.

A private first class staggered toward the rear, supporting a wounded buddy. He blurted out to Lieutenant Jim Condon, commander of E Company, that most of those in his platoon were dead. Condon saw other casualties moving rearward. Then Sergeant Henry Bart told Condon that he was now the senior NCO in 1st Platoon and that only a few others still survived. It was essential to take out defending German machine-gun nests. At Condon's urging, Sergeant Bart and PFC Clyde Wallace crept forward and knocked out two enemy gun crews with hand grenades.*[16] Easy Company slowly worked its way east.

First Lieutenant John Wine, a Fox Company platoon leader, led his men only 200 yards from the LD when they were forced into cover from an artillery barrage and fire from a machine gun. Creeping through a rain of bullets while shells burst around him, Wine moved to within 25 yards of the enemy weapon. Throwing a grenade at it, he killed or wounded its crew. Wine signaled his men to move up.[17]

F Company troopers struggled into the edge of Vossenack. A burp-gun

---

*PFC Wallace was killed later that day when he was hit in the chest by an 88 shell with a delayed fuze that exploded on contact.

sniper near the main crossroads effectively halted their advance. The German soldier killed a platoon leader and wounded two NCOs. First Lieutenant Eldeen Kauffman, Fox's company commander, contacted a nearby tank, requesting it to fire on the house where the sniper was barricaded. It threw in two rounds of high explosives and white phosphorus. As the smoke settled, Kauffman and his runner, PFC Bud Kern, ran into the shattered building. They saw two German officers and seven enlisted men. One officer brought up his weapon, and Kauffman shot him. The other officer, already wounded, and his men surrendered.[18]

Kauffman and Kern ran to the next house where "for luck" they threw grenades into the basement. They heard shouts of "*Kamerad,*" and several German officers climbed out with hands held high. Questioning them, Kauffman learned he had captured an entire enemy battalion command post. One prisoner was *Oberleutnant* Vennemer, a *Wehrmacht* captain whose unit was responsible for Vossenack's defense. "I got tough with him," said Kauffman, "and stuck a .45 in his stomach and he quickly showed me his positions on a map." Vennemer told Kauffman there were five 30-man companies in town ready to launch a counterattack. Kauffman spread the word.

"From then on," Kauffman recalled, "it was just a question of searching out each building. Our method was to have the tanks shoot a hole in them and then to follow with a rush."[19] Platoons of Fox and Easy companies took an average of five prisoners from each house as they moved eastward through Vossenack. In the priest's house near the church they flushed out four German medics and two wounded soldiers. One PW could not understand why the "Amis" were attacking out of Germeter. "Why take Vossenack?" he asked. "The road leads nowhere."[20]

Fox and Easy companies secured the town by midafternoon and moved east to the nose of the ridge, where they dug two-man foxholes. It would be necessary for one man to stay awake while the other slept. Holes were quickly dug, for laboring GIs were in plain view of the enemy. All the while they waited tensely for the counterattack of which *Oberleutnant* Vennemer had spoken. They were not disappointed when it did not materialize.[21]

The heavy-weapons unit, H Company, which moved forward to support 2nd Battalion rifle outfits, suffered fiercely as it relocated. The last man in George Company, just ahead of Howe, stepped on a booby trap just beyond the line of departure. Then a sergeant from Howe's machine-gun section stepped on another one and went down injured. Sergeant Earl Janson went to help the injured men and he stepped on still another trip wire and was killed by the resultant explosions. At that moment five other mines went off simultaneously. Of 27 men in the group, 12 were killed or wounded, leaving the machine-gun section badly crippled.

The only NCOs left in the platoon were corporals Walham Strop and Robert Caldwell, both wounded. They reorganized the remaining men and moved their weapons forward to the nose of Vossenack ridge.[22]

Injured men in Vossenack were grateful to see PFC John Smedberg, a Fox Company aid man, moving among them. Casualties were heavy, both companies suffering losses of nearly 20 percent.[23] Smedberg went about his duties, ignoring mortar rounds and artillery shells landing nearby, treating casualties in both companies. He soon exhausted his supplies and made a hazardous trip from the nose of the Vossenack ridge back to Germeter to replenish his medical kit. He returned and again used up his stock of medicines and bandages. A second, third, and fourth times he made the round trip to Germeter. He received wounds sufficient to warrant evacuation, but Smedberg believed he was needed by his friends and chose to stay and treat them under nearly impossible conditions. Two days later, physically and mentally exhausted, still suffering from his wounds, he accepted evacuation to the rear.[24]

Tankers as well as infantrymen suffered that day. Enemy shells fell so thickly on M-4s on the nose of the ridge that they withdrew into Vossenack and dispersed behind buildings there. The tank of Second Lieutenant Joseph Novak, 3rd Platoon leader, struck a mine as it clanked between two buildings. Captain George West's tank also was disabled when it exploded a mine. The tank of Second Lieutenant William Quarrie, 1st Platoon leader, threw one track. A tank retriever from Charlie Company came into town to pull damaged vehicles back for maintenance. It was hit by an enemy shell and knocked out. Captain West now had only 11 operational tanks in Charlie Company. About 1600 hours he received orders to pull back to bivouac positions at Germeter for the night. Lumbering west out of Vossenack, tankers pulled into a circle about 400 yards behind the morning line of departure to gas up, receive ammunition resupply, eat, and try to get a little sleep.[25]

Vossenack and the ridge on which it sat were now seemingly secured. The regimental northern flank was protected against enemy counterattack by 2nd Battalion. But what of its sister units, the 1st and 3rd battalions, which struck out that day on their drive toward Schmidt?

Following orders of Lieutenant Colonel Carl Peterson, commander of the 112th Infantry Regiment, Major Robert Hazlett's 1st Battalion led off the attack on Schmidt at noon, 2 November. Company B, commanded by Captain Clifford Hackard, headed the column, followed by Charlie and Able companies.

Lieutenant Colonel Albert Flood's 3rd Battalion followed in their wake. The troops were to move east along the wooded southern slope of the Vossenack ridge. When they reached the Kall trail, they were to turn south and follow that path across the river and up to Kommerscheidt. 1st Battalion would hold that hamlet while 3rd Battalion pushed on to Schmidt. After securing that town, both units would prepare for further advance, on divisional order, toward Steckenborn to the southwest.[26]

Soldiers were wary as they stared off toward the gloomy expanse of forest to their front. PFC Raymond Carpenter, from Jamaica, New York, spoke for many of his buddies: "I never saw a wood so thick with trees as the Hurtgen. It turned out to be the worst place of any." He could blame only himself for being there. In earlier service with the 45th Infantry Division, an Oklahoma Army National Guard outfit, Carpenter received a foot injury. After his recovery he received assignment to a quartermaster service battalion, a relatively safe rear-area job. "But I still wanted to win the CIB [combat infantryman's badge] in service to my nation, so in Wales I requested transfer to Company M, Third Battalion, 112th Infantry Regiment, 28th Infantry Division—America's oldest division." In October 1943 he joined 3rd Battalion. Now it looked as if he would get more than he bargained for.[27]

Soldiers of B Company walked carefully forward, alert for any sign of trouble. Just as the battalions advanced in a column of companies, so Baker Company moved in a column of platoons—1st, 3rd, and 2nd. The weapons platoon brought up the rear. Suddenly the air around 1st Platoon was shattered by fire from German Mausers, Spandaus, and machine guns. First Lieutenant Ralph Spalin, 1st Platoon leader, walked point for his men. German machine-gun fire raked him from legs to head. He was dead as he hit the ground. His body lay in the path of enemy fire and was hit repeatedly thereafter. The advance collapsed as soldiers of 1st Platoon frantically sought cover.

In an effort to keep his men moving, Captain Hackard sent his 3rd Platoon forward to reinforce 1st, hoping their combined strength would force hidden Germans to retreat. The 3rd Platoon leader was also hit, suffering a broken leg. He dragged himself into a hole and directed fire with an SCR 536 radio. Only after dark was a medic able to bring him to safety. With the injury of its platoon leader, 3rd also bogged down in the face of stiff enemy resistance. Men in Dog Company fed round after round into their mortars but were unable to kill German defenders or force them to evacuate their positions among the trees of the *Hürtgenwald*.[28]

Movement toward Schmidt by two battalions thus came to a halt as the lead platoon of one rifle company making the main thrust of a divisional effort came under fire from German guns. The level of small-arms fire from the trees did not indicate a heavy concentration of Germans there. It was a force sufficient only to keep a column of platoons from moving ahead.

Regimental commander Colonel Peterson had options. He could have called in a heavy-artillery concentration on enemy hiding places. He was satisfied with using mortars. He could have committed the remainder of 1st Battalion to support Baker Company. A flanking movement on the left might well have flushed out that troublesome nest of Germans. He gave no such orders. Neither did he call upon 3rd Battalion to move up and join the fire fight. Nor did he call for support from tanks of the 707th Tank Battalion. He did not seek out direct fire from M-10s of the 893rd Tank Destroyer Battalion. And Baker Company—and its 1st and 3rd Platoons—were unable to advance.

About 1500 hours, Major Robert Hazlett, commander of 1st Battalion, walked back to the rear command post of the 112th Infantry Regiment to discuss with Colonel Peterson what to do. Upon his return to his unit, not wanting to leave Baker Company where it was, Hazlett told Captain Hackard to pull his men back. Night was fast approaching. 1st Battalion was only some 250 yards out from its line of departure.

That night Hazlett of 1st Battalion and Lieutenant Colonel Albert Flood of 3rd Battalion talked again with Colonel Peterson. The regimental commander decided to change his approach. Vossenack was in regimental hands. On 3 November the two battalions would change their order of advance. With 3rd leading, they would push east into Vossenack. There, at the crossroads by the church, they were to turn south, follow the road to the edge of the ridge, then forge down the trail, across the Kall River, and push on through Kommerscheidt into Schmidt.

Divisional air support that day succeeded no better than did the three infantry regiments. V Corps plans called for IX Tactical Air Command to lend support to the operation against Schmidt. The Army Air Force assigned five fighter-bomber groups of 36 planes each to the task. From their base at Verviers, Belgium, they were to fly armed reconnaissance sorties on the divisional front to the Rur River and toward Düren. If weather or other conditions prevented them from acquiring targets, they were to fly specific missions in the vicinity of Bergstein. Airplanes were also to seek targets of opportunity while "just looking for trouble."

One group of P-47s was to attack specific targets. Another group of P-38s would strike at locations on the divisional right front prior to 1200 hours, dropping canisters of napalm. A third group of P-51s would provide high fighter cover over the entire area throughout the day. A last group was to be grounded for two hours after H Hour on 30 minutes' alert, ready to lend aid wherever needed.

Unfavorable flying weather on 2 November prevented those planes from accomplishing their missions. The first ones did not take off until after 1200 hours, and even then haze and cloud cover prevented them from identifying their targets. One squadron leader did identify and bomb a target at about 1615 hours. Shortly after his planes dumped their loads, 28th Division Artillery frantically called its air liaison officer, Major Edwin M. Howison, at the divisional war room at Rott. Howison called IX TAC Air, which immediately contacted the squadron leader. He checked his position and acknowledged "he was over the wrong area, having mistaken the reservoir at Roetgen for the one at Schmidt." His planes had just knocked out an *American* artillery position—a command post and gun site—causing 17 GI casualties.

Elsewhere during the course of the battle, U.S. planes strafed and bombed

American soldiers both in Vossenack and in Schmidt. It was not an illustrious chapter in the history of the Army Air Forces.[29]

Early that morning Vossenack still remained largely untouched by war. Hit by shells from 0800 to 0900 hours, its church steeple a target for tank turret guns, its houses hit by tank rounds during infantry clearing actions as they moved from building to building, its frightened inhabitants cowering in cellars or fleeing toward neighboring towns, Vossenack that evening bore little resemblance to its appearance at dawn. As darkness enfolded the countryside and damp cold penetrated bodies of American soldiers, they could look toward town and watch Vossenack burn.

On the north, toward the town of Hürtgen, the 109th Infantry Regiment was pinned down in a minefield, its men stumbling among broken forest trees. On the south, the 110th Infantry Regiment was trapped in concertina wire, facing the fury of enemy bunkers and pillboxes. Life there was a face-down nightmare in foxholes as men prayed that fire logs would block splinters from tree bursts—if they had time to cut logs. Enemy 170mm and 210mm guns crumpled pines into shattered stumps, their "sheared-off trunks gleaming white against the forest green like bared fangs of animals long fled."[30]

To the east, one battalion of the 112th Infantry Regiment sat on its objective, but its sister battalions were hopelessly short of their target. Army Air Force planes bombed American positions. At *Schloss* Schlenderhan, under guidance from *Generalfeldmarschall* Walther Model, German commanders ordered reinforcements into the Schmidt sector in a desperate effort to halt any American advance. Everywhere, the 28th Infantry Division faced disaster.

28th Infantry Division
G-3 Periodic Report
020001-022400 November 1944

> RESULT OF OPERATION: . . . 112th Infantry, 2nd Battalion took its objective meeting light enemy resistance. 1st Battalion advanced against heavy enemy fire and defended positions. 3rd Battalion prepared to assist 1st and 2nd Battalions against counterattack. Division operation was successful and placed units in position for future action. . . .

THOMAS E. BRIGGS
Assistant Chief of Staff
G-3

3 November 1944

At 0730 hours, about dawn, 3rd Battalion once again started across the LD.

The woods at that hour were frosty and, as always, dank pine trees loomed threateningly. Germans had no intention of giving ground easily to their enemies, and one GI died from an artillery burst even before he reached the line of departure.[31] The auguries were not good. 3rd Battalion led the way in a column of companies: L, K, and I.*[32]

The two battalions, protected by armored vehicles of the 707th Tank Battalion, moved out along the road toward Vissenack. 3rd Tank Platoon supported K Company. 2nd Tank Platoon supported Love Company. 1st Platoon remained in mobile reserve, following the other two by some 400 yards, watching as they leapfrogged one another on the way to Vossenack.

When leading infantry elements reached the village they made a 90-degree wheeling movement toward the south. Tanks led them out across high country south of Vossenack to help clean out any dug in German positions. The M-4s fired at the near wood line as riflemen passed through them. The tanks then backed up closer to Vossenack and fired across the valley onto the tiny community of Kommerscheidt. They continued this fire until, at about 1100 hours, tank commanders could see American infantrymen moving in good formation as a double line of skirmishers on the other side of the valley slope. Tankers then drove their machines into hull defilade to await word from engineers that the trail through the Kall Valley was passable for their M-4s.[33]

The road from Vossenack to the south wood line on the slope, connecting there to the Kall trail, served as the main supply route for the 28th Infantry Division. Germans had long since prepared defenses along its route. As soldiers of 3rd and 1st battalions made their way along it, they passed *Minen* signs, warning of buried mines. An occasional harassing German artillery round fell on them as they marched south.[34]

The attack on the first objective of Kommerscheidt was to be an envelopment. King Company would come across high ground from the right, while Love Company was to move on the half-moon-shaped hamlet by following the road into town. During passage of the Kall trail, GIs met only minor resistance from small, ineffective German patrols. Item Company's mortar section, trailing somewhere behind, came under shelling in Vossenack and never rejoined the company.† Love Company continued down the steep hill

---

*Item Company's 1st Platoon remained on guard at divisional headquarters at Rott throughout these days of battle and does not figure in this story.

†The mortar section leader decided to wait in Vossenack until German shelling lifted. By that time he was uncertain of the location of the remainder of the company, by now somewhere on the other side of the Kall River. Planning to go on the next day, the men held in Vossenack the night of 3/4 November. The German counterattack on Schmidt early 4 November resulted in great confusion and incessant, concentrated enemy artillery fire both north and south of the Kall. Item's mortar section attached itself to 2nd Battalion's H Company and emplaced its tubes in the eastern part of Vossenack. When Germans counterattacked 2nd Battalion on the morning of 6 November, all its mortars were lost.

through thick woods and approached a bridge spanning the Kall. A scout walking point saw a lone German beside the arch, armed only with a pistol, and shot him. GIs crossed the bridge and moved up the road on the other side. Northeast of Kommerscheidt a single German soldier surrendered when he saw the size of the force opposing him.[35]

Men of Love's sister company, King, moved through woods on the forward slope of Kommerscheidt hill. Small groups of Germans fired desultorily at them from fringes of woods. King's troopers returned fire, and without further trouble eight Germans surrendered. Scouts then reconnoitered the hamlet, found no opposition, and the remainder of the company occupied Kommerscheidt. They suffered only two casualties in the advance: snipers shot a wire man in the leg and killed Staff Sergeant Leslie R. Marlow in the Kall gully.[36] Item Company's only casualty came when a stray shell landing close to the marching column wounded PFC Joseph Cooper as he neared Kommerscheidt.[37]

Heartened by its easy advance, King Company moved on through Kommerscheidt toward Schmidt. Passing pillboxes along the way, GIs saw one marked by wreckage of an American P-47, which sometime earlier had crashed almost on top of the structure. Several startled Germans broke from the "box" when they saw advancing "Amis" and ran frantically toward Schmidt. When K Company troopers fired at them, some fled back into their dubious shelter and later surrendered. Despite a little sniper activity against its leading elements and a few harassing artillery rounds, King Company's march into Schmidt was swift. By 1130 hours its men were at their objective.[38]

Love Company's advance was not as rapid. Captain Jack Walker deployed his men on the eastern side of Kommerscheidt, within eyesight of the minuscule settlement of Froitscheidt to their left. As they crossed high ground, some saw a German ambulance moving along the river road behind them, followed by a horse-drawn cart in which two soldiers rode. Clopping noises from the horse's hooves could be faintly heard as it crossed the bridge over the Kall. GIs saw German soldiers moving among the houses of Froitscheidt. King Company's machine-gun section set up two of its heavy automatic weapons and fired toward those enemy troops. They quickly fled, and a later patrol from Love searched Froitscheidt for them to no avail.

Walker and his men marched on toward Schmidt. In an open area southeast of Kommerscheidt they passed two German troop shelters. Smoke curled from the chimneys of each. Two bicycles stood parked outside one hut, and not far away a very seriously wounded German soldier lay untended in the open. Love's troops stared curiously at him as they tramped past. He looked so far gone no one stopped to render medical aid.[39]

1st Battalion trailed some hours behind. PFC Joe Perll, a messenger in C Company, thought the two PWs who surrendered to them just outside Vossenack were comical. "They looked funny, like Mutt and Jeff, one tall and one short." The sight kept up his spirits as 1st Battalion moved south to the tree line at the edge of the ridge. Instead of following 3rd Battalion down the Kall trail, these men stalked down a firebreak west of and parallel to that path. Reaching the river road, they turned left toward the bridge. German heavy-artillery rounds fell among them along the river valley, killing one man and seriously wounding a section sergeant in C Company, Staff Sergeant Edward Delmonico.

At the bridge, instead of crossing the river toward Kommerscheidt, C Company commander, Captain Setts Frear, ordered his men up the Kall trail. They stopped a few yards uphill near an abandoned dug-out log bunker to dig foxholes. Just before dark, 1st Battalion forward elements moved on Kommerscheidt up the winding road of the main supply route.[40]

1st Battalion operations sergeant, Eugene Holden, noted how everyone was "huffing and puffing especially when the machine guns and mortars had to be carried up the steep hill." The terrain was rugged and it was dark by the time they reached Kommerscheidt, making it difficult to set up their machine-gun positions. Even digging foxholes was hard to do in the blackness of night. As they worked, an enemy barrage fell on them and they dashed for what cover they could find. Tony Kudiak remembered his fear. A rugged 25-year-old man, he weighed 210 pounds and stood tall at six feet, four inches. When Tony first saw the Hürtgen Forest he liked it, for those trees made him think of the woods near his home in Sandy Lake, Pennsylvania. He already felt disenchanted, for among these trees man hunted not woodchucks but other men. Sergeant Kudiak determined to be one of the hunters.[41] He ordered his men to dig two-man slit trenches; one would sleep while the other stood guard. Amid the enemy barrage, they grabbed shovels and dug ever deeper, then fashioned covers to protect them from overhead explosions.[42]

All of 1st Battalion entered Kommerscheidt save for Company C, which remained north of town on the crest of a hill overlooking both that half-moon-shaped hamlet and the river valley below. It came to be called Kommerscheidt Hill. It was nearly daylight before everyone in town and on the hill finished working on foxholes and siting in weapons.[43] 1st Battalion was in place.

By noon that day 3rd Battalion entered Schmidt. For some strange reason, the Germans ignored all previous warnings of danger. Vossenack had fallen the preceding day. 1st Battalion made its abortive advance toward the Kall. Tanks fired on Kommerscheidt early in the morning to herald an infantry advance. Both American and German artillery barrages fell on the valley and hill slopes. GIs forged into Kommerscheidt and toward Schmidt in plain view of anyone wishing to watch. Still the Germans were caught by surprise as soldiers of the 28th Infantry Division entered Schmidt.

Men in K Company met no opposition. It was lunchtime as they pressed along town streets and burst into buildings. They captured astonished Germans, who looked up from their noon meal to see "Ami" rifles pointed at them. Some enemy troops fell into American hands as they wandered the streets or sprawled drunk on steps of houses. Germans stood talking on sidewalks or rode bicycles and motorcycles along roadways, without apparent thought of danger and oblivious of American soldiers until the moment when hostile rifle barrels were thrust under their noses. Two "Jerries" bicycling east through town were shot when they refused to stop.[44]

L Company soldiers learned how easily K Company had entered Schmidt. Men of Love Company then simply walked up the road into the town center, arriving about dusk. It was still a danger-ridden place. They received sniper fire and machine-gun fire from now alert enemy soldiers hidden within buildings in the southeastern part of town. Sergeant Frank Ripperdam ordered his men to dig in for the night along a hedgerow on the eastern end of Schmidt.[45]

K Company also established defensive positions. These faced south, protecting 3rd Battalion from counterthrusts from that direction. Men in both King and Love companies found themselves targets of enemy snipers. Each such marksman had to be searched out and killed or captured. By day's end, King Company counted 45 PWs, and Love Company controlled a similar number; nearly 100 enemy soldiers had been captured out of a total German garrison at Schmidt of approximately 250 men.

Members of the divisional Military Police unit did not arrive in Schmidt, so German PWs could not be evacuated as planned. They were held under light guard in the basement of a house. Their captors growled orders. If they attempted to make trouble or were noisy, they would be dispatched with grenades. Those captured soldiers remained very quiet.[46] Outside the basement occasional harassing rounds of artillery dropped on the town.

In his command post war room at Rott, General Norman Cota and his assistant division commander, Brigadier General George A. Davis, congratulated one another. The "Bloody Bucket" was once more on its way to another victory. One battalion of the 109th Infantry Regiment sat partially on its objective. Vossenack was held by 2nd Battalion, 112th Infantry Regiment. Its two other battalions were across the Kall, one in Kommerscheidt and the second in Schmidt. They were in possession of the divisional objective assigned to Cota by Gerow and Hodges. With the fall of Schmidt, Americans severed the Germans' main supply route to the Monschau corridor. All Cota's men now had to do was hang on; as soon as possible he would send other units to reinforce them, and they could then attack once again down the Strauch–Steckenborn axis. Cota was elated. When corps and divisional commanders in other sectors of the American front lines began to telephone him with their congratulations, Cota's earlier misgivings faded completely away and he described himself as feeling like "a little Napoleon."[47] Perhaps he thought of Napoleon's overwhelming defeat of Prussia's army at Jena in 1809. It would have been more apt had he pictured a cold Russian winter during which

Napoleon ordered his once-proud legions to begin their retreat from an empty and burning Moscow.

A supply train started from the rear area for Schmidt at about 2000 hours, led by 3rd Battalion motor officer, First Lieutenant William George. With him rode First Lieutenant Leon Simon, the battalion assistant S-3; an artillery forward observer; I, K, L, and Headquarters company supply sergeants; and several others. The vehicles they drove were those recently acquired M-29 Weasels, loaded with rations, ammunition, a 4.2-inch mortar, and 60 antitank mines.

As they maneuvered down the narrow, twisting Kall trail, they passed a log dugout just above the bridge that looked to Simon "like an old German aid-station."[48] Just south of the bridge, the convoy was forced to stop for nearly an hour while its men cleared tangled barbed wire from the track of a Weasel. Finally reaching their destination, first at Kommerscheidt and later at Schmidt, they began their hour-long unloading process. Guides and carrying parties hauled supplies to various companies. In Schmidt tired soldiers of K and L companies took their share of antitank mines. Too tired from the long day to emplace them properly, they simply laid them on road surfaces leading into town, completing their task by 0200 hours.[49]

As they worked, Lieutenant Colonel Albert C. Flood, commander of 3rd Battalion, and his S-3 operations officer, Captain Joseph Meadows, wandered through Schmidt talking with officers and noncoms of their rifle companies. They warned Captain Jack Walker of Love Company that regimental headquarters in Germeter predicted the possibility of a German counterattack in force. Perhaps as many as 4,000 or 5,000 enemy troops might assault their positions within a few hours. Riflemen, bazooka teams, and light- and heavy-machine-gun crews tried to be alert as they manned approaches into Schmidt, scanning the black-shrouded surrounding countryside. All too many men were unable to remain awake and slipped into a troubled sleep.[50]

Prior to his return trip, Lieutenant George asked Colonel Flood if there was anything he could do for him at rear headquarters. "Yes," responded the colonel, "tell Colonel Peterson that 3rd Battalion absolutely must have tank support available by daylight." Lieutenant Simon informed Flood that two companies of engineers were working on the divisional MSR, the road and trail from Vossenack, trying to put it into shape sufficient to withstand the pounding from tanks that were waiting to traverse it. At 0400 hours the convoy left Schmidt on its trip back to Germeter.[51]

Those engineers of whom Simon spoke were part of the 1171st Engineer Combat Group, commanded by Colonel Edmund K. Daley, and consisted of the 20th Engineer Combat Battalion and the 1340th Engineer Combat Battalion. For this operation they were strengthened by addition of another unit attached from 30 October through 19 November, the 146th Engineer Combat Battalion.[52]

Those engineer outfits were responsible for repair and construction of all roads in the Vossenack–Germeter–Schmidt sector, for clearing enemy minefields and cleaning up rubble from Vossenack's streets, and for demolition of any captured pillboxes. To add to their labors, they had only light vehicles available and were required to provide their own security while working.[53]

Colonel Daley knew his most important task was to ensure the flow of traffic over the divisional main supply route along the Kall trail. He placed the 20th Engineer Combat Battalion, commanded by Lieutenant Colonel Jonathan E. Sonnefield, in charge of that work.[54] None of the engineer commanders expected the Germans to commit any considerable number of their tanks in the area. Even so, it was essential for American armor to find a way across the Kall to support infantrymen of the 1st and 3rd battalions, 112th Infantry Regiment. Engineers hoped to find some route through the Kall Valley capable of development, for available air reconnaissance data failed to confirm continuation of the Kall trail across that defile.[55]

Early reports filtered to the rear corroborating the existence of a bridge across the river, but rumors persisted that it had been blown up. Capt. Henry Doherty, commander of A Company, 20th Engineers, ordered his 2nd Platoon leader, Second Lieutenant Robert Pierce, to reconnoiter the route and establish its condition. Pierce followed the Kall trail south into the valley as far as the river and found it open and passable except for scattered debris and abatis.[56]

At 1300 hours, 3 November, Captain Edwin Lutz, commander of B Company, 20th Engineers, received an erroneous report indicating the river crossing was a ford that needed corduroy laid on its approaches. He and Captain Joseph Miller, liaison officer of the 20th Engineers to the 112th Infantry Regiment, walked down the trail to check its condition. Captain Miller examined the bridge and estimated it to be a Class 30 stone arch structure, capable of handling loads up to 30 tons.[57] Lutz and Miller believed it would bear the 33-ton weight of Sherman M-4 tanks. The trail was in sad shape, its left shoulder on the decline soft and crumbly. On the right were occasional granite outcroppings.

At 1545 hours, Lutz and Miller informed Lieutenant Colonel Richard Ripple, commander of the 707th Tank Battalion, of their findings. The road needed work, and men of B Company, 20th Engineers, were on their way to improve it. Those engineer troops began their labor in late afternoon and worked on into the night, primarily using hand tools. At 1700 hours, Lutz sent word to Captain Bruce Hostrup, A Company tank commander, that the road was now passable. If armored vehicles hugged the right bank, they could negotiate the trail.[58]

Colonel Daley, engineer group commander, arrived at the command post of the 20th Engineer Combat Battalion, where he discussed with its commander, Lieutenant Colonel Jonathan Sonnefield, the advisability of sending forward during the night a small bulldozer and air compressor to expedite work on the trail. Daley and Sonnefield believed from various reports that tanks could pass down the trail but that it needed considerable improvement to facilitate continued heavy traffic. Cota's staff at Rott informed Daley that tankers did not agree with engineer estimates and were very concerned about those rock outcroppings. Daley knew his own officers' reports indicated their confidence that such barriers would not be a serious hazard if tankers maneuvered their M-4s carefully. "Nevertheless," Daley related, "I ordered it removed."[59]

Daley further warned Sonnefield not to rely on infantry protection for his men. They were to be responsible for providing safety around their own work sites and for the bridge. Previous experience, said Daley, showed how infantry soldiers sometimes moved rapidly from one position to another without particular regard for protection of engineer units. Sonnefield passed on this information. By the time it reached his officers and NCOs in the Kall Valley, it seemed to require them only to provide guards for their own work parties and not the bridge itself. Engineer work parties paid little attention to the river road down which increasing numbers of Germans would soon move unchallenged and unmolested.[60]

Captain Hostrup's A Company started forward. A tank company's normal complement consisted of 16 M-4s. Three were already missing—one destroyed by a mine, another with a thrown track, while a third lay bellied on a ridge, unable to free itself. Hostrup knew the trail from an earlier reconnaissance trip. He was concerned it might not be as passable as engineers were claiming.

Hostrup inched his command tank down the steep incline. Even in the dying light of dusk it was difficult to keep his M-4 on the slippery roadway. The left shoulder, which sloped toward the draw, kept giving way. Nor did Hostrup have any leeway. Both the trail and his tank were nine feet wide. At one point his tank slewed dangerously, almost plunging off into the draw. Darkness set in. Hostrup was convinced. He backed his tank up to open ground and returned to where his other tanks waited.

Radioing Colonel Ripple, Hostrup told his impressions of the trail. Ripple checked with divisional headquarters and engineer command posts and learned work parties would be laboring on the trail throughout the night. Ripple told Hostrup to hold his tanks back until dawn. By then engineers should have improved the MSR sufficiently to allow M-4s to pass through the valley.

Tankers that night huddled inside their buttoned-up machines while enemy artillery batteries focused on their dark, hulking shadows. Several tanks received hits, having sirens, headlights, and other minor fixtures blown off. Shrapnel perforated and tore through men's personal gear—bedrolls, shelter halves, haversacks—stored and tied outside the tanks. Fortunately, no Sherman suffered material damage. All remained in working order throughout the black, rainy night. As dawn lightened eastern skies, Hostrup and his men cranked their engines.[61]

German commanders worked desperately to staunch hemorrhaging of their lines caused by the American advance. Losing Vossenack was concern enough. When "Amis" jumped off toward the Kall Valley and into rear areas of the *89th Infantry Division,* its commander, *Generalmajor* Walther "Papa" Bruns, ordered Hauptmann Olbricht to form the initial opposition with two Russian companies and to prevent further unopposed "Ami" advance.

Bruns also contacted the *1055th Regiment,* then in the process of moving toward Harscheidt and Nideggen. He ordered the unit to halt. It was an experienced outfit. Since the beginning of the battles for the Westwall it had repeatedly repulsed Allied attacks and—despite heavy losses—kept American reconnaissance and patrol activity to a minimum. Its men now faced a sudden change in their expectations. Intent upon moving out of front-line duty for a period of rest and relaxation, some were already thinking of furloughs to visit their hometowns and see loved ones. Now hard necessity once again forced them back into battle.

Mestrenger Mühle fell. Kommerscheidt dropped into American hands. Bruns knew that further retreat of his men must be prevented at all costs "or all battles, all hardships, all sacrifices of the last weeks and months will have been in vain." He ordered roadblocks installed and bridges prepared for demolition. Patrols returned with reports of new losses. The American advance continued under a protective umbrella of intensive artillery fire.[62]

Generalleutnant Hans Schmidt, commanding general of the *27th Infantry Division,* was also aware of the dangers this new American thrust posed to German troops who at best were borderline soldiers. Few could have been called crack warriors, made up as they were of men drawn from all parts of the Army, Navy, and Air Force. "Command of such troops," Schmidt noted, "was a matter of command personalities [for] the fighting worth of single parts of the division was then so small they, when suddenly attacked, did not know the proper things to do."

In initial phases of the American attack on Schmidt, artillery was the most valuable German weapon. "Our artillery," said Schmidt, "was well registered in, and contributed a great deal to our successful defense." He was grateful that Americans followed habitual patterns in launching attacks—an artillery preparation followed by an infantry advance. "[T]he Division command was enabled to use the time remaining [following the end of artillery barrages] until the beginning of the attack to bring up reserves to threatened points. . . . Surprise is more important than artillery preparations."[63]

German soldiers moving into threatened areas of their lines noticed with relief tanks and assault guns clanking past, also headed into battle. "Our soldiers are overjoyed," stated one report. "It's a long time since they have seen these 'big brothers.' Now they know that the necessary weapons are on hand. Artillery gets the range of new targets [and] our own fighter planes are reported . . . in the Germeter sector . . . attacking the enemy with bombs and machine guns." [64]

Then, at 1615 hours, a demoralizing message was sent through channels from the field to higher headquarters: "SCHMIDT taken by enemy." Bruns and Schmidt shared their dismay with their superiors. By early evening of 3 November the report reached *Seventh Army,* and *General der Panzertruppen* Erich Brandenberger, its commander, learned of the capture of that town. His reaction was swift. He signaled *LXXIV Corps* that it must launch two attacks. The first, employing the *1055th Regiment* of the *89th Infantry Division,* reinforced with a tank regiment from *Generalmajor* Siegfried von Waldenburg's *116th Panzer Division* and a 15-tube assault gun brigade, was to retake Schmidt and Kommerscheidt.

The second attack, employing the remainder of the *116th Panzer Division,* was to be a concentric squeeze on Vossenack. All possible support—artillery, assault guns, tanks, automatic weapons—were to be used in this counterattack. Brandenberger further ordered the *272nd Volksgrenadier Division* artillery to displace northward to add its fires to the fury of this German effort.

German assaults, said Brandenberger, would begin at dawn on 4 November. *Generalmajor* Rudolf Freiherr von Gersdorff, chief of staff for *Seventh Army,* described well what happened: "The tired and embattled American soldiers there were then faced with a major infantry and armor threat. . . . In what was probably the heaviest fighting in the war, soldiers of both sides performed, under unbelievable hardships, acts of great gallantry and perseverance."[65] An American soldier put it differently: "They sent us into the valley of death."[66]

Soldiers of 2nd Battalion, 112th Infantry Regiment, occupying Vossenack suffered constant and relentless artillery fire. Throughout 3 November the Germans built up an ever stronger fire concentration, and increasing numbers of bursting shells fell upon hapless troops in town and at forward positions on the ridge's exposed nose. German accuracy was excellent, and the effect of constant bombardment decayed American morale. Officers and noncoms could not maintain effective communication with their platoons and squads. Men of Fox and George companies huddled hopelessly in their foxholes.

Twice that day Germans sent patrols in force against 2nd Battalion positions—at 1500 and 1800 hours. Somehow GIs repulsed them and hung on. Several times shells hit the battalion command post, and communication with regiment became impossible. Colonel Peterson made his way that day from his rear command post to Vossenack, but that was the last his beleaguered men saw of him. After that his time was taken up by events south of the Kall. Thereafter 2nd Battalion had no more contact with him, instead taking all its tactical orders directly from Generals Cota or Davis. Captain Jim Nesbitt, the battalion's S-1 personnel officer, went so far as to say that the regiment forgot them in favor of its own private war elsewhere.[67]

First Lieutenant Cliff Beggs, 2nd Platoon leader in Easy Company, became increasingly concerned about German artillery barrages. "Enemy fire," he said, "continued so intensively that one day seemed like an era. They concentrated on the town and positions just east of it, but the field to the south was thoroughly pock-marked as well."[68] E Company's commander, First Lieutenant Melvin Barrilleaux, put it differently. Germans, he said, "pecked away with deadly accuracy, the fire continuing incessantly by daylight and intermittently at night."[69]

As each hour dragged hopelessly past, American soldiers fell into an ever worsening condition. Even at night they got little sleep, and a calm moment during daylight was only a dream. It got worse as Germans began concentrating mortar and artillery fire on successive individual foxholes, firing round after round at each one until they killed its inhabitants. Then they shifted fire to the next hole and began the process over again. It was a cold-blooded, nerve-shattering, and extremely effective device. Defenders knew they would continue to face imminent death every hour they remained on the Vossenack ridge.

6

"I'll do what I can, boys"

4 November 1944

The course of battle seriously disrupted planned duties for engineers. Colonel Edmund Daley, commander of the 1171st Engineer Combat Group, clearly knew what he wanted his units to do. The 20th Engineer Combat Battalion, commanded by Lieutenant Colonel Jonathan Sonnefield, was to provide support for the 112th Infantry Regiment in its advance from Germeter to Schmidt. Lieutenant Colonel Truman Setliffe's outfit, the 1340th Engineer Combat Battalion, was to assist the 110th Infantry Regiment. The 146th Engineer Combat Battalion, commanded by Lieutenant Colonel Carl Isley, was part of the 1121st Engineer Combat Group attached to the 1171st specifically to strengthen engineering capabilities during the fight for Schmidt. That was the plan.[1]

Work for the 20th Battalion failed to materialize. Because of the 112th Infantry Regiment's lackluster performance on 2 November, Colonel Daley assigned Baker Company, 20th Engineers, to work on Germeter's roads. He attached Charlie Company, 20th Engineers, to the 146th Engineer Combat Battalion as it worked clearing roads behind the advance.

Baker Company reverted to Colonel Sonnefield's control on 3 November when Daley ordered him to clear rubble from Vossenack's streets. Sonnefield sent Baker Company to perform not only that task but also to clear the road to the Kall river. He charged Able Company to prepare to bridge the river if necessary. He held Charlie Company in reserve to carry out any necessary pillbox demolition and mine clearance. Able and Baker companies moved into Vossenack and bivouacked there.

On 4 November Sonnefield ordered Charlie Company to straighten out

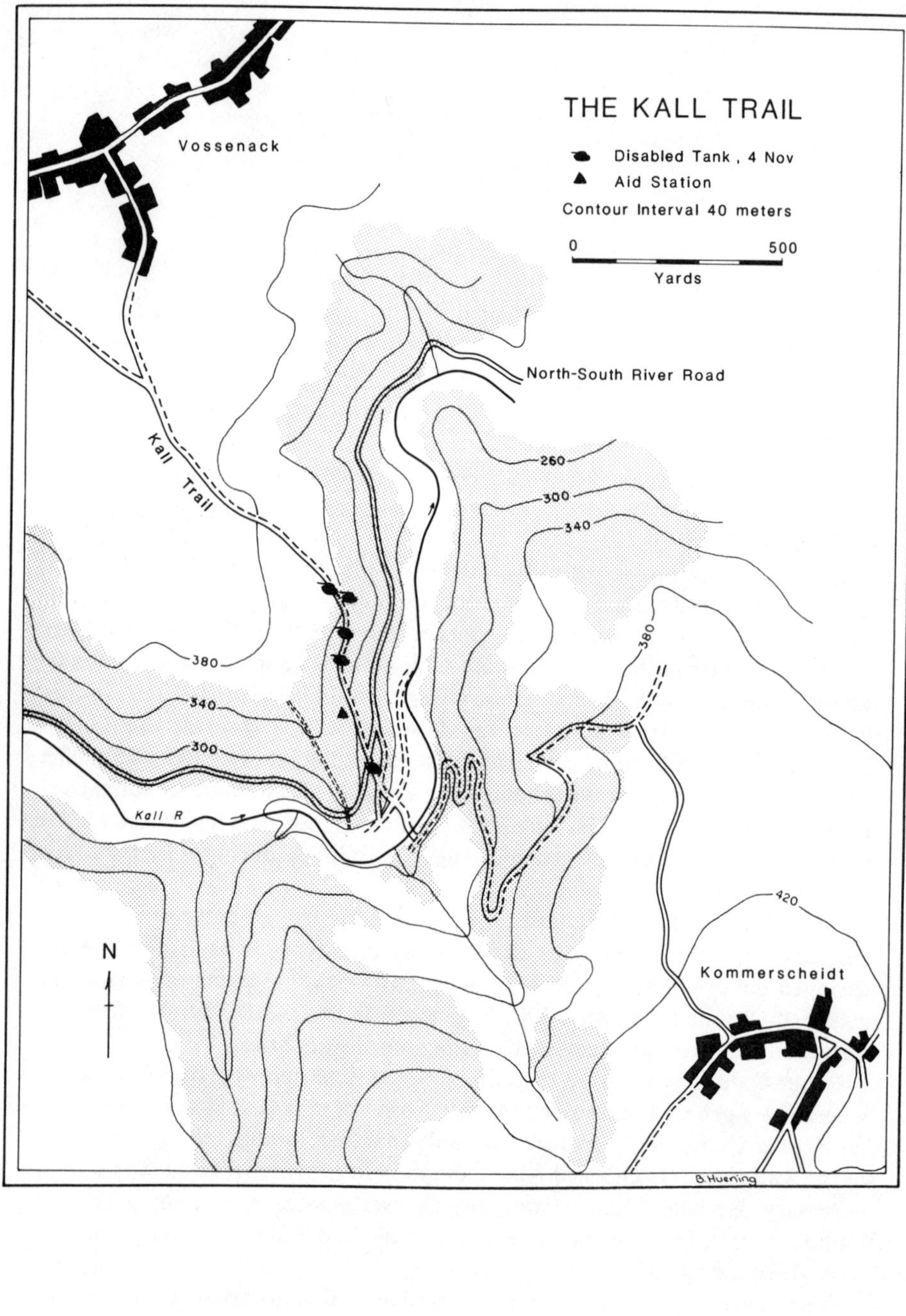
THE KALL TRAIL
Disabled Tank, 4 Nov
Aid Station
Contour Interval 40 meters
0
500
Yards
Vossenack
North-South River Road
Kall Trail
260
300
340
380
380
340
300
Kall R
420
Kommerscheidt
N
B. Huening

hairpin curves south of the Kall and to demolish German pillboxes in Kommerscheidt. The company was short the 2nd Platoon, which was already assisting the 109th Infantry Regiment in clearing mines from its sector. 2nd Squad, 3rd Platoon guarded the ammunition dump throughout the action. 1st and 3rd squads of 3rd Platoon drew TNT from the dump and tried to transport it across the river. They never succeeded. The rest of Charlie Company moved out for Kommerscheidt.[2]

Captain Edwin Lutz commanded B Company, 20th Engineers, which was responsible for clearing a route from Germeter by way of Vossenack to the Kall bridge site, making it into a usable divisional MSR. Initially he thought it could be done despite German shelling that peppered his work area.[3]

During long night hours of 3/4 November, elements of both A Company and B Company engineers labored on the MSR, working with picks and shovels to widen the trail. Such work was slow, and Lutz was impatient. Sometime after midnight he climbed onto the seat of an R-4 bulldozer. Strapped behind him on the heavy machine was an air compressor. Cranking the gasoline engine, he punched the starter on the diesel. The 'dozer roared to life. Gripping his brake handle levers, Lutz edged the 'dozer down the inclined Kall trail to a rock outcropping about halfway to the river. One of his work parties stood there picking ineffectually at the granite face thrusting out into the narrow roadway from the cliff. Lutz hoped the compressor and 'dozer blade might do what his men thus far had not accomplished. The 'dozer broke a cable at 0330 hours after working on the outcropping only a short while. Weary men once again reached for picks and shovels. Technological efficiency reverted to that of the Bronze Age.[4]

Above on the Vossenack ridge, tankers waited anxiously for word that the trail was maneuverable. The night was inky, and rain sluiced through black skies onto metal tank hulls. Harassing German artillery rounds kept tank crews awake and nervous as they heard shrapnel clang and shriek across the steel skin of their M-4s, ripping and tearing through personal baggage roped outside, snatching away antennas and searchlights.

First Lieutenant John Webster, A Company engineers, finally sent up word to the tankers. The route was free of mines as far as the river. Tank engines roared and drivers engaged their clutches. At 0500 hours the tank platoon of First Lieutenant Raymond Fleig rolled forward. At the very entrance to the draw trail Fleig's lead tank struck a mine and threw a track. His A Company commander, Captain Bruce Hostrup, fumed in angry frustration. Hostrup ordered Fleig to get his tank out of the way. "We *HAD* to go through."[5]

Fleig was able to get his tank only partially out of the way. He then crawled from his disabled machine and moved back to the second Sherman. He tried to drive it around his own tank, but there was insufficient room. The second tank slipped off the left shoulder and got stuck on the steep, slippery slope. Staff Sergeant Anthony Spooner came up and spoke with Fleig. He could, Spooner said, get their tanks past the obstacles. He took a tow cable from

Fleig's dead tank and hitched it to the Second Sherman. Using the first M-4 as a pivot, Spooner winched the second tank around it and back onto the road. Fleig was delighted.

"I told him," the lieutenant said, "to take charge of the others and get them around." Spooner did so, successfully winching the two remaining tanks onto the trail. Fleig once again started down the treacherous pathway. Its sharp bends had not shown up on either 1:25,000 or 1:10,000 maps he had consulted. Confronted by unsuspected folds in the trail, Fleig and his other two tank commanders were forced to do a great deal of hard braking, stopping, and backing. Fleig noticed his tank was tearing away part of the left shoulder as it skidded down the draw road. He hoped it was not damaging the trail enough to delay any of the remaining tanks still bivouacked above him.

Finally reaching the river, Fleig nervously edged his tank across the stone bridge, grateful when it did not collapse under him. His two following tanks also crossed the arched span. Their difficulties, however, were not yet at an end. The road now went into a series of three steep switchbacks, so curved back upon themselves, Fleig dismounted to lead his tank around them. He walked in front of his M-4 nearly to the top of Kommerscheidt hill. After a hasty check of the terrain in front of him, he mounted his tank, and all three Shermans roared down the road into Kommerscheidt, arriving in the half light of dawn a little after 0730 hours. Several infantrymen were so glad to see Fleig they almost cried.

Some riflemen pointed south. "There are Heinies with lots of tanks over that hill," they shouted. "I'll do what I can, boys," Fleig replied.[6] He halted his tanks beside 1st Battalion command post. Inside, Fleig reported to Major Robert Hazlett, the battalion commander, that more A Company tanks would arrive by 1200 hours. Little did he know.[7]

Fleig's commander, Captain Bruce Hostrup, surveyed efforts of his men as they maneuvered those remaining tanks down the trail. Walking down the miry road, wet through to the skin, thick, gooey mud clinging to his boots, Hostrup came upon Staff Sergeant James Markey's tank. It had slewed off the left shoulder of the road and was slipping its treads in a frantic effort to back onto a harder surface. Hostrup shook his head in dismay as he passed by. A hundred yards farther on he caught up with Sergeant Spooner. Spooner's M-4 idled motionless, blocked by Staff Sergeant Jack Barton's tank, which lay partially off the road, having slipped dangerously while negotiating a tricky turn past the troublesome granite rock outcropping. Nodding to Spooner, Hostrup trudged on to Barton's lead tank. One track was partially thrown. Hostrup ordered Spooner to pull the thrown track back in place with his tank. Then, using Spooner's Sherman as an anchor, Barton ground his machine around the difficult turn. Spooner then winched his own tank around the bend. Both tanks inched on down the trail.

Captain Hostrup walked another 100 yards south and saw an engineer platoon at work. He spoke to Second Lieutenant Robert Huston, asking if the men could blow off the rock face that was causing tank crews so much difficulty. Lieutenant Huston shrugged. They had no demolitions with them, but they would try. Hunting around, engineers located three German teller mines dug up from the surface of the trail by some earlier work crew. They exploded them without much effect against the granite outcropping. There was nothing more they could do.

At the top of the draw, tanks of 2nd Platoon, A Company, started forward, inclining sharply as they pitched onto the downward slope. Staff Sergeant Anthony Zaroslinski, commanding the lead tank, suddenly saw Fleig's dead tank. Unaware of Spooner's winching technique, he forged ahead, trying to maneuver through the barrier. His tank lost its grip on the slippery incline, slid off the trail, and was unable to back to safety. Zaroslinski and a lieutenant riding with him dismounted to survey their situation. A German artillery round landed nearby without warning, killing Zaroslinski and wounding the lieutenant.

In the M-4 immediately behind Zaroslinski's machine, Staff Sergeant Walton Allen climbed from his machine and walked down the trail to locate Captain Hostrup. He told his commander he believed he could squeeze between Fleig's and Zaroslinski's tanks. Hostrup told him to try.

Allen managed to move his own Sherman past the two dead tanks. Then he went back and drove the third tank in line past the disabled hulks before returning it to Staff Sergeant Kenneth Yarmon. Allen and Yarmon ground forward for some distance. Then Yarmon's tank slipped off the road, throwing its left track as it attempted to negotiate a tight corner. At almost the same moment, Allen lost control of his M-4 and it slipped off the left shoulder, throwing *both* tracks. Allen walked disconsolately down to Captain Hostrup once again. As they spoke, Sergeant James Markey walked up from below; his tank was stuck at the bottom of the draw and had thrown one track. The three men could hardly contain their frustration.

An exasperated Captain Hostrup send word up above to Second Lieutenant Richard Payne to take command of A Company tanks remaining on high ground south of Vossenack and wait until further notice. He was unwilling for any more of his M-4s to try the Kall trail. It was now 1100 hours. Sunrise had occurred at 0732. *All* of Hostrup's A Company tanks were needed in Kommerscheidt and Schmidt by daybreak. That had been their orders.

Captain Ed Lutz decided to check on his engineers along the trail and determine what condition it was in. Arriving from Vossenack, he saw how badly the path was now blocked. He complained about tankers who failed to exercise sufficient caution in their transit of the trail. They allowed the left tracks on their M-4s to creep up on the road's soft shoulder, bending them, causing bogies to slide out of treads, and losing all traction. There was, unfortunately, no alternative road to use. Terrain along the only other possible route was mostly swamp, lined with enemy soldiers and blocked by trees. Lutz told Colonel Sonnefield about conditions on the Kall trail. Sonnefield went to see for himself, looked at the first disabled tank, and told its crew to get "that goddam thing" out of there. They complained bitterly.[8]

Lutz and Sonnefield were not the only ones to inspect laboring tanker crews on the trail. Major Jack Fish, S-3 operations officer of the 707th Tank Battalion, arrived and conferred with Captain Hostrup. As they spoke they noticed an abnormal number of infantrymen coming up the trail. "They said they belonged to Third Battalion [112th Infantry Regiment] and were retreating from Schmidt. All they could talk about," Hostrup said, "was enemy tanks and having been hit by our own air strike."

In despair, Hostrup and Fish went back up the draw road to a tank equipped with a radio transmitter. They reported their situation to Colonel Ripple, telling him "the draw road looked as he might imagine the Burma road looked in flood season, that if more tanks were to get through to Kommerscheidt more Engineers were needed and soon." Fish added that tanker crews were doing everything possible to get their machines across the Kall. Ripple told them to go back and try to get the engineers to work faster. More engineer troops would be sent up during the coming night.

That afternoon Colonel Daley, commander of the engineer group, inspected work progress on the trail. He came forward after receiving a call from General Cota, who wanted up-to-date information on it. When Daley returned to his command post he called the general and relayed his findings; the trail was blocked by disabled tanks. Cota replied that it was imperative the road be cleared by the following morning at daylight. If necessary, Daley could order the tanks thrown off into the gully.[9]

Night approached rapidly. It was nearly 1700 hours, and sunset on that cloudy day occurred at 1705. Hostrup had no time to lose. He located Lieutenant Huston, the engineer officer who earlier tried to help him, and told him "the road had to BE FIXED!" Tankers blamed engineers for working too slowly as they improved the trail. Engineers thought tankers were too careless. Colonel Daley summed up their attitude when he said, "I have no evidence to show that the tanks thoroughly reconnoitered an acknowledged difficult passage nor that the drivers were briefed on the need for extreme caution."[10] Whoever was at fault, combat infantrymen in Kommerscheidt and Schmidt were the ones who suffered.

It was not until 1900 hours that First Lieutenant Stanley Lisy, A Company maintenance officer; Captain George Harris, 707th Battalion maintenance officer; and a work crew arrived on the trail to help their fellow tankers. After three hours' work they succeeded in replacing the track on Yarmon's tank. He moved it ahead 25 yards and off it came. This time they broke the twisted track while laboring to replace it. Lieutenant Lisy sent two men up the trail to Fleig's useless tank. They removed a good idler from the hulk, brought it down the trail, installed it, and put a new track on Yarmon's M-4.

At about midnight a Weasel supply train led by Captain William Pinchon, tank battalion S-4 supply officer, came down the trail, maneuvering carefully around tank hulks. Pinchon brought urgent orders from "Holiday 6," the radio call sign for General Cota. The general, Pinchon informed Hostrup, "wants to give you all the time possible to retrieve your vehicles, BUT, this route must be open by daybreak. If necessary, you will roll your immobilized tanks down the slope and into the draw."[11]

"We renewed our efforts," Hostrup later recalled. "By 0200, we had gotten the track back on the tank. It started forward, moved about ten yards and the left shoulder of the road gave away and off came the track. By this time everyone of us was ready to pull out his hair, root by root."

Hostrup ordered Sergeant Allen to fasten his tow cable to some nearby trees and pull his tank as far off the road to the left as possible. They then pulled Yarmon's stubborn machine over to the same side of the trail. Markey's stuck tank was left where it was in the bottom of the draw after Pinchon and Hostrup surveyed the area there. They checked up and down the river road, walking it some 300 yards each way. Seeing no American troops, Hostrup assumed it was held at both ends by Germans. Pinchon marveled at their luck. "Had we gone much further," he said, "we would have walked right into German positions." Just above the bridge, they located a difficult series of switchbacks that would allow tankers to avoid Markey's M-4, bypassing it by turning right, backing for 150 feet, and then starting forward again.

Hostrup and his men finally cleared the divisional MSR for other traffic in the early morning hours of 5 November. In 24 hours of agonizing, brutal labor, tankers managed to get just eight tanks down the trail and across the Kall. Under better conditions, the task would have taken perhaps a little over an hour.[12]

In Schmidt, the hours before dawn on 4 November were reasonably quiet for tired men in 3rd Battalion, 112th Infantry Regiment. Just before daybreak a very heavy German artillery and mortar barrage hit the south end of Schmidt. Enemy cannon cockers elevated their tubes, and the bombardment slowly traveled through the community until shells exploded in the northern limits of the village, some raining upon a building where German PWs were held under guard. The explosions searched out every nook where Americans hid, so intense it seemed to come from every corner of the compass.[13]

At 0730 hours, a soldier burst into Item Company command post, shouting to Captain Raymond Rokey. Some 60 German infantrymen were milling around and appeared to be forming for an attack in a light patch of thin woods almost due east of town about 1,000 yards away in front of and on the left flank of 2nd Platoon.

A few minutes later, those Germans advanced. They moved forward in a wavering, uncoordinated effort, swinging against the left flank of Item Company. A brief mortar barrage fell on American defenders. Then German soldiers swung against Item's right flank.[14]

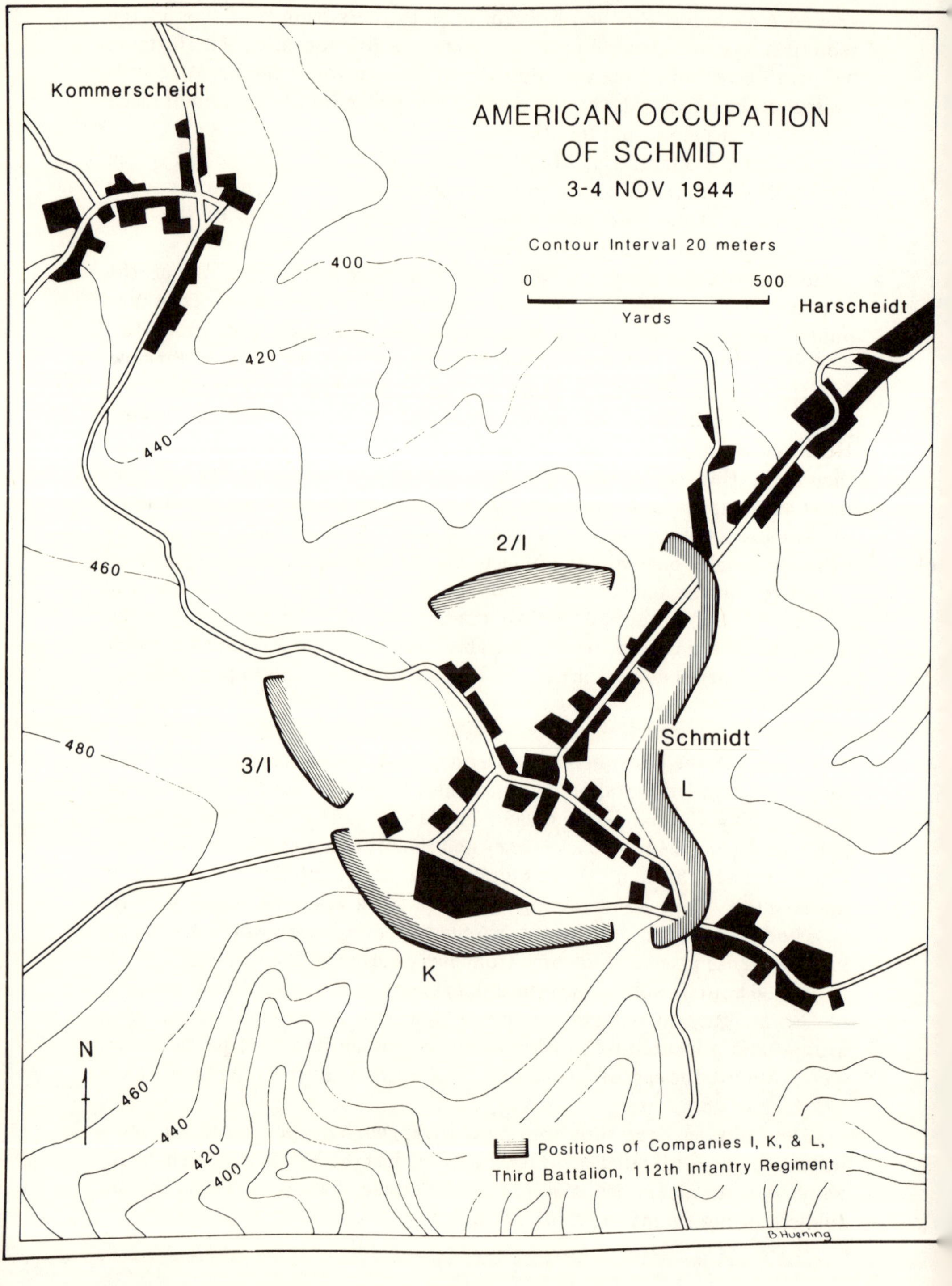
AMERICAN OCCUPATION
OF SCHMIDT
3-4 NOV 1944
Contour Interval 20 meters
0
500
Yards
Kommerscheidt
Harscheidt
400
420
440
460
480
2/I
3/I
Schmidt
L
K
N
460
440
420
400
Positions of Companies I, K, & L,
Third Battalion, 112th Infantry Regiment
B Huening

In King Company, 1st Platoon leader, Lieutenant Richard Tyo, lay in a corner house near the edge of town with one of his squad leaders. They had good observation of fields outside Schmidt and saw some 90 Germans crossing the road in front of their position. Then three enemy soldiers appeared in an orchard immediately beside the house. Tyo killed one, and the other two fled.[15]

First Sergeant Frank Ripperdam of Love Company spied six Germans approaching over a hill from the southeast. He and his men fired at them with BARs. At the sound of their shots, a German machine-gun nest no more than 50 yards away fired back. The six Germans were perhaps 900 yards out, so Ripperdam's immediate concern was to silence the automatic weapon. With two men he crawled toward the machine gun. As they came closer, German gunners saw them, and five *Wehrmacht* soldiers leaped to their feet with cries of "Don't shoot! Don't shoot!" Ripperdam and the others stood up, weapons pointed at their enemies. The Germans dropped back into firing position and triggered the machine gun, wounding one of Ripperdam's men. Angered by this trick, the sergeant ordered his other trooper to fire a rifle grenade. The machine gun kept firing for a few moments and then fell silent. When Ripperdam worked his way up to it, he found the Germans gone.[16]

Mortar shells exploded among American defenders with increasing ferocity. Gray-clad infantry worked their way through King Company's sector as GIs fired at them, trying to break up their advance. German infiltrators entered Schmidt from all directions.[17]

Ripperdam noticed a platoon-sized group of men from King moving back. One attempted to dash across a street but was cut down by machine-gun fire. Ripperdam was worried. If K Company withdrew, it left Love's right flank unprotected. He moved to his command post near the center of Schmidt as frantic GIs shouted at him that all their buddies on the right had withdrawn.[18]

It was no wonder American defenses were hemorrhaging. Germans brought up the best possible reinforcements. Mark IVs and Vs rumbled and clanked toward Schmidt. Captain Jack Walker, Love Company commander, remembered that five enemy tanks moved out of a draw northeast of town.* One tank moved directly down the center of the road; the others rode parallel on both sides of it.

The tank on the right barreled ahead, its gun knocking out two 60mm mortars with direct hits. Love Company men fired ineffective bazooka rounds at the behemoths, but they bounced off their armor. One received a direct hit but simply stopped, swung off to the side, and clanked on its methodical, destructive way. Tanks fired into foxholes and buildings as they came, demoralizing and frightening their "Ami" enemies. It took only a few

*Those later interviewed never agreed on the total number of German tanks in that initial armored assault; their estimates ranged from five to 10 vehicles.

minutes. Then panicked men streamed back from the German strike force, headed north toward Kommerscheidt and possible safety.[19]

Lieutenant Tyo ruefully watched his men flee. "Everyone had a strong desire to be elsewhere than in the path of the German tanks' deadly fire," he said.[20] Men pulled back, filtering through yards and gardens, over fences, across alleys and streets. Taking all cover possible, fearful of seeing the deadly snout of a German Mark V pointing their way, soldiers watched buildings burn and heard the crump of mortar shells landing nearby. As they ran, many fell from German automatic-weapons fire from guns they could hear but not see. GIs were so frightened they forsook their wounded, abandoning helpless men where they fell. Some later claimed they were "unable" to evacuate wounded comrades; in reality, those who ran thought of no one other than themselves. Wounded men had to fend for themselves.[21]

Some men were so frantic and confused they ran into woods southwest of Schmidt right into the arms of waiting Germans. "That," said Captain Walker, "was the last we saw of them." Carried on unit rosters for some days as missing in action, it was common knowledge that at least some of them were quickly captured, perhaps as many as 100. Others who disappeared into those woods held out for some days prior to surrendering.[22]

Lieutenant Tyo querulously asked men in his 1st Platoon and machine-gun section why they were pulling back. "They said they had orders to withdraw." Their panicky response was good enough for Tyo, who joined them and led them toward the rear. On the way they passed one man with a broken leg and another lying wounded in a foxhole who told Tyo of others who had fled into those woods to the southeast. Tyo and his men turned north toward safety.[23]

Along the Weisser Weh creek west of Germeter, at the 112th Infantry Regiment's rear command post, Colonel Peterson was understandably worried. His radio operator received a stream of calls all indicating that 3rd Battalion was under counterattack by infantry and tanks entering Schmidt from both the northeast and southeast. By 0900 hours, Peterson heard how L Company was falling back from Schmidt. He did not know the status of Item or King. Communication was of poor quality, and messages gave few details. They were not much help in clearing up for Peterson what was happening south of the Kall. He passed on to General Cota what little he knew.

Cota was bewildered. How many attackers were there? How many tanks supported German infantrymen? How effectively was enemy artillery supporting their counterattack? Were only a scattered few of his troops pulling back? Or were all three companies of 3rd Battalion crumbling from the German onslaught? He needed to know.

General Cota ordered his assistant G-3 operations officer, Lieutenant Colonel Benjamin Trapani, to investigate as soon as possible and report back with what he learned. Trapani left Rott to visit the regiment but could not get through because of enemy artillery. Brigadier General George Davis, assistant divisional commander, then called the regimental command post and ordered its executive officer, Lieutenant Colonel Landon James Lockett, to make his way across the Kall and learn firsthand what was happening.

Captain Hunter Montgomery, regimental S-2 intelligence officer, and two Army Signal Corps photographers asked to accompany Colonel Lockett. They rounded up a jeep and driver and set out for the two forward battalions in Kommerscheidt and Schmidt. They never reached their destination. Near Mestrenger Mühle, in the valley south of Vossenack, they were ambushed and captured.*

Despite these efforts, no one at regiment or division yet knew the extent of the enemy counterattack at Schmidt or the condition of American defenders there. Then Colonel Peterson learned that scattered and disorganized stragglers from Schmidt were retreating as far as Vossenack and even Germeter. He ordered officers to corral as many of them as possible and return them to their units. He also knew he could wait no longer, and he set out for the front to see for himself the situation of his units.[24]

Then Cota called upon General Davis for help. Cota ordered Davis forward to make a firsthand survey of conditions in 1st and 3rd Battalion areas. Accompanied by his aide, Lieutenant William Hambrick, Davis sought out Colonel Trapani and the colonel's driver. The four men piled into a jeep and set out. Some 600 yards south of Vossenack they dismounted and walked down the Kall trail toward Kommerscheidt.[25]

Enemy soldiers pressed forward, inflicting heavy casualties on remaining American troops in Schmidt. German infantrymen were willing to absorb punishment, for they did not stop their advance despite U.S. artillery raining down on them.[26] Soon the last GIs pulled back to the center of Schmidt, freeing themselves from the methodical advance of their enemies. Increasing numbers of Americans streamed back in disorder, fleeing north over open ground to Kommerscheidt and even beyond. One man from M Company's heavy-weapons section was so stricken with fear he sped through 1st Battalion positions, down to the river road, across the bridge, and up the Kall trail to the hill south of Vossenack, all the while carrying his machine gun. "We could not find him," said Captain Piercey, his commander, "to get it back in action. As a result it was the only gun to survive the battle."[27]

Guy Piercey watched Germans come out of the woods into Schmidt. He did his best. He ordered his mortars to fire on them and called in an artillery barrage from supporting batteries in the rear area. Their shells dropped on German troops for nearly an hour. Nothing slowed those *Wehrmacht* troops.

---

*During the ambush, Captain Montgomery was wounded. German soldiers marched Colonel Lockett, the two photographers, and the hapless jeep driver away as PWs, leaving Montgomery behind. Enemy medics found Montgomery and took him to one of their aid stations, where he spent the night. The next morning, 5 November, he convinced two of them that their situation was hopeless and that they should surrender. They did, helping him back to American lines.

Then, said Piercey, "we received word from Battalion to withdraw. They said they were going to pull the switchboard which would knock us out of telephone contact with them." He ordered his platoons to grab their weapons and start for Kommerscheidt at 1100 hours. A master of understatement, Piercey added that the retreat "was not orderly."[28]

Adding American insult to German injury, frightened infantrymen of 3rd Battalion found themselves subjected to a sudden strike by Army Air Corps planes. In addition to knocking out two German tanks,[29] P-47s attacked everything else in sight. Lieutenant Simon watched them. "We could see our planes making strikes around Kommerscheidt and Schmidt. We saw a couple of P-47s make a close in strike. The next thing we knew, about four columns of ragged, scattered, disorganized infantrymen streamed back . . . in low morale. They had been taking a heavy beating from the enemy and some of them were so excited they thought our own air corps was bombing them. We managed to stop some but most streamed past us to the rear."[30]

German soldiers followed withdrawing American troops and reoccupied Schmidt. Troops of 3rd Battalion were so completely mixed together it was difficult for angry NCOs or officers to find any large group from one single unit.[31] Commissioned officers and noncoms tried to reorganize their units in the meadows and woods north of Schmidt despite their men's jittery nerves. First Sergeant Robert Toner of Item Company lost track of most of his troops. By 1030 hours he knew where only 25 of his men were. Not all the missing were PWs or wounded. Some became so unnerved they ran all the way back to Vossenack—even to Germeter—while others simply mixed in with other groups. In any case, the outlook was not bright.[32] Schmidt was now once again entirely in German hands, and only open fields and thin, spotty woods stood between them and Kommerscheidt. The Germans moved forward.[33]

First Lieutenant Leon Simon, assistant S-3 operations officer of 3rd Battalion, arrived from rear headquarters at 1020 hours that morning with a copy of a field order instructing his unit to continue its attack southwest to acquire additional divisional objectives on the Strauch–Steckenborn line. Alarmed by the noise of battle ahead of him, Simon stopped in Kommerscheidt. As he came into the hamlet, "the Germans fired two rounds of direct fire at us which landed about twenty-five yards away. We dug our noses into the ground and remained there." After a few minutes, Simon lifted his head, looked around, and gingerly stood up, instantly ready to seek shelter if need be.

Simon needed to find out what was happening. He found his boss, Captain Joseph Meadows, the battalion S-3 operations officer. Meadows lay crouched behind a nearby house. He was retching, his clothes torn, and Simon thought he seemed completely shaken and "out of touch with things." He didn't know where anyone was and could only gasp that "they had been driven unceremoniously out of Schmidt."

Simon finally found his commander, Colonel Albert Flood, in 1st Battalion's command post on the east side of Kommerscheidt talking with Major Hazlett. Flood gave him substantially the same story as Simon had heard from Meadows. He absolutely had to have more tanks "and told me to get them." Simon didn't like the situation. "It looked bad, almost hopeless."

At 1115 hours, Simon and his jeep driver, PFC Florian Champeux, headed for regimental rear headquarters to tell Colonel Peterson of Flood's demand for additional armor support. They drove around the horseshoe bends north of Kommerscheidt, over the river, and up the MSR, grinding slowly around tanks partially blocking the trail. Arriving in Germeter, Simon caught Colonel Peterson preparing to leave for the front. He made his report. The colonel and Major Richard Dana, regimental S-3 operations officer, jumped into a jeep and drove away. Ironically, Simon, who carried to Kommerscheidt an order for 3rd Battalion to attack again, brought back news that it was retreating.

Simon decided to go back to Kommerscheidt with Peterson and Dana. He caught up with them near the Vossenack crossroads and they drove as far as the woods line at the entrance to the Kall trail. There they dismounted and worked their way along the MSR until they reached C Company positions on Kommerscheidt hill at 1500 hours. After seeing the situation in Kommerscheidt, Colonel Peterson called off any resumption of attack. He had little option.[34]

In Kommerscheidt, troops of 1st Battalion felt waves of unease flow through them as ashen-faced buddies from 3rd Battalion staggered through their lines toward the rear. Debilitated from the strain and havoc of three days of combat, 1st Battalion lines now also broke as German artillery and mortar shells landed and ugly snouts of Mark V tanks fired point-blank into its positions.

Sergeant Ripperdam was surprised by what he saw. He and a few others from 3rd Battalion went into defensive positions at Kommerscheidt in the early afternoon. "Shortly after we moved into position, about 1400, the men of First Battalion units who had been placed in defense nearby took off for the rear," the sergeant remembered. "Contrary to the artillery fire in Schmidt, it seemed fairly quiet. I could see no particular reason for this sudden breaking of position by these men although apparently their nerves and spirits were pretty well shot. When my men saw the others withdrawing in haste, they took off too. There was no holding them. They were pretty frantic and panicky." Ripperdam went along with the rest, stopping only when they reached woods north of Kommerscheidt. "Their main fear," he said, "seemed to be from the fire of enemy tanks. I tried to assure them they were safe in that spot."[35]

Major Robert Christenson, 1st Battalion's executive officer, saw Ripperdam and beckoned to him. The officer asked him to find out what was happening back in town. "I told him I would try," said Ripperdam, "and went forward to the tank commander in the tank nearest the town and asked him how, from his standpoint, things stood. He told me they had knocked out three German tanks and had another under observation." Ripperdam took that news to the major, who then went back into Kommerscheidt.[36]

At about 1400 hours, five German tanks "in a column of aces" wheeled directly down the road from Schmidt toward Kommerscheidt. Some worked their way into the village despite the loss of one tank to a P-47 air strike, again disrupting defending Americans who ran into woods northeast of town. Other German tanks on high ground to the south fired point-blank at American infantrymen.[37]

Among those panicky men of 1st Battalion who retreated from Kommerscheidt were Private Dorn* and eight others who ran into the forest north of town. They kept going across the Kall River and through trees on the north slope of the valley until they could see the town of Vossenack. "Quite by accident," said Dorn, "we ran into a group of Germans, two in each of two holes about one hundred yards apart, in what looked like a communications set up." A sergeant yelled for them "to get the hell out of there." Dorn yelled "Let's go" to one man who replied, "It's too late now" and put up his hands to surrender.

Dorn and four others ran back the way they came. They recrossed the river under cover of darkness and found some American land-line telephone wire. Following it, they came to a group of men from the 20th Engineers, who gave them something to eat and invited them to spend the night.[38]

Twenty-four-year-old PFC Joseph Perll, of Erie, Pennsylvania, saw panicky soldiers running past him toward the Kall Valley and Vossenack. This was his first action since being wounded at Hill 210 in France. As messenger-radioman in C Company's reserve position on Kommerscheidt Hill, Perll knew there was no immediate danger that far north. He saw his regimental commander, Colonel Peterson, and his battalion executive officer, Major Christenson, roughly grabbing frightened troopers and insisting they remain in place. So Perll also ran after some fleeing men, shouting for them to stop. "I turned one man, Private Lawrence, a BAR man from Company K around only because I knew him."

Perll continued to shove men into line, trying to organize wandering soldiers into a fighting force. He formed a platoon of 25 men and scrounged weapons for those who had discarded their own. Ordering them to dig in, he maintained radio communications with other units and acted as observer. Perll alerted them for night attacks, assigned them sectors, and kept their morale high even though for the next three days they received no resupply of food or water. When one of his mortar crews was wiped out by artillery, he operated the tube himself. When he noticed attempts by German soldiers to infiltrate C Company's right flank by way of a wooded ravine, he radioed for artillery fire support.

---

*Captain William J. Fox interviewed this man on 3 December 1944, at Company K command post near Sevenig, Germany, but neglected to list Dorn's given name.

Perll saw three guards stampeded when 44 prisoners of war began running, frightened by bursts from their own mortars falling nearby. PFC Perll, who was Jewish and who spoke some German, calmed the PWs and found other guards for them. For Joe Perll, who would end the action as an acting platoon leader, it was a big day.[39]

Infantrymen feared most the dreaded German tanks and the damage they could cause with their high-velocity turret guns. Defense against them was difficult at best. 3rd Battalion had no antitank guns with it, since the first divisional MSR road priority was for Colonel Ripple's 707th Tank Battalion. GIs had little to use to stop German armor thrusts except for land mines, which enemy tanks simply bypassed, and ineffective bazooka rounds, which often bounced off steel hides of Mark IVs and Vs. Rifle grenades were less than useless.[40]

First Lieutenant Ray Fleig, Sergeant Jack L. Barton, and Staff Sergeant Anthony R. Spooner were the heroes in the American defense of Kommerscheidt. Their tank crews that day engaged and knocked out between three and four Mark IVs and one Mark V. The German armored thrust at Kommerscheidt began at 1100 hours.[41]

When 12 German tanks rolled forward, Fleig radioed his commander: "We can hold them." He did so until Lieutenant Dick Payne came with five more tanks many hours later. Fleig edged his Sherman into an orchard on the eastern outskirts of town. He spotted a Mark V Panther moving closer. Fleig's tank fired twice, hitting the Panther with two rounds of high explosives. The crew of the German tank bailed out and took cover. It was only then that Fleig discovered there were no available rounds of armor-piercing ammunition for his turret gun. It was all in the sponson rack on the outside of the tank. They ceased firing and turned the turret to get at the rack. This took a few moments, and during the lull the Germans reentered their tank and opened fire at Fleig's M-4. "By that time," Fleig said, "we had our AP. We opened fire and scored four hits. The first hit cut the barrel of their gun. The other three tore open the entire left side of the hull on the tank and set it afire. None of its crew escaped."[42]

The other two tanks of Fleig's platoon were also engaged in a sharp fight, so he maneuvered his Sherman over to support them. They beat back the German armored thrust at about 1500 hours, when surviving enemy tanks withdrew. It was no wonder admiring infantrymen called him "General" Fleig! His tank platoon spent the afternoon firing on two pillboxes west of Schmidt that enemy soldiers were attempting to reoccupy.

At 1700 hours, Colonel Peterson ordered Fleig not to withdraw his machines for servicing, but to go into defiladed firing positions. The regimental commander was concerned his troops would once again pull out with or without orders if they saw Fleig's tanks moving back. No infantrymen were available to secure the tank position perimeter, Peterson said. Tankers would have to do so themselves. He also warned of a possible enemy night attack, spearheaded once again by an armored thrust. German tanks, Peterson believed, might use their headlights "to dazzle, blind and rattle" defending soldiers.*[43]

After a final conference with Major Hazlett and Colonel Flood, his battalion commanders, Colonel Peterson started back for his regimental rear command post at Germeter, accompanied by his S-3 operations officer and his S-2 intelligence officer. On the way out of Kommerscheidt they encountered some walking wounded and helped them to the aid station, set up in a log bunker north of the Kall River bridge.

Shortly after leaving the dugout, Peterson saw General Davis and his party walking toward him down the Kall trail. Davis ordered Peterson to escort him back to Kommerscheidt. The colonel and his companions retraced their steps.

Davis saw a number of soldiers still dazed by the disastrous German attack. He inspected 1st Battalion positions and found its men dug in forward of Kommerscheidt and in locations near some scrub oak. The general spoke with Major Hazlett at his command post and seemed convinced the battalion could cover the withdrawal of troops from Schmidt and hold its ground. The assistant division commander saw Fleig's three tanks and acknowledged their hazardous journey down the MSR from Vossenack. "This information," Davis said, "was sent back to General Cota, giving him the first clear picture of what had happened."[44] His comment was telling. By the time he sent his message, it was well after dark. Cota had been out of touch with developments in his own units *all* day. He never thereafter regained control.

At about the time Colonel Peterson met General Davis on the Kall trail, First Lieutenant William George, 3rd Battalion motor officer, was readying a four-Weasel convoy with food, mortar ammunition, and other vitally needed items for a run to Kommerscheidt. Enroute from Germeter to the Vossenack turnoff to the south, the convoy received rounds from a German artillery barrage. Men in the vehicles bailed out and "hit the dirt," throwing themselves into nearby foxholes or sprawling in ditches to avoid explosions. George believed Germans had the group under direct observation, so well aimed were shells falling around him.†

---

*No night attack occurred, but tankers and infantrymen endured a continuous artillery and mortar barrage fired from several directions.

†Interviewer Captain William J. Fox later wrote: "I was standing only one hundred yards from George's weasels when they stopped because of this artillery fire. As far as I was concerned, it was not very 'intense.' In fact, on a couple of occasions when I went into Vossenack and met some of these people in their cellars, they all told me of the 'intensity' of the fire although none of it seemed to strike me as being too terrible. I walked and drove up and down in the open here without feeling that the enemy was looking right down my throat. Of course, much of the effect of this fire came as a result of being exposed to it in blasted buildings and holes for days and hours on end. The cumulative effect was terrible."

After the barrage lifted, George's convoy moved down into the woods toward the river, encountering on the way a group of about 20 men from 3rd Battalion headquarters and an officer from Item Company and one from King. George asked what they were doing on the trail. "We tried," he said, "to get some sense out of the officer from Company I but had no luck. The one from Company K said he planned to stay where he was." Further questioning revealed only that they "appeared very confused and said the whole situation was completely mixed up. . . . That was obvious." They told George that Lieutenant Joseph L. Dooley, 3rd Battalion S-2 intelligence officer, and Captain Joseph Meadows, battalion S-3 operations officer, had disappeared to the rear. Later, George said, he found Dooley and Meadows, who said "they had been forced to pull back in confusion." It would seem that Meadows' earlier terror when Lieutenant Simon saw him crouched and retching behind a house in Kommerscheidt had only gotten worse. The convoy remained on the trail, not trying to move to Kommerscheidt until 0300 hours on 5 November.[45]

Those in besieged Kommerscheidt were scared and wanted to get out. Some men continued to drift back. Only close supervision by officers and noncoms kept men in position. They continued to receive heavy fire for at least twenty minutes out of every hour.[46] Beset by enemy infantry, tanks, and barrages from heavy guns, floundering in the midst of chaos, 1st Battalion and 3rd Battalion soldiers continued to hold on to Kommerscheidt and the hill to its north. They had to. As one laconic private first class put it: "Our mission was to hold till further orders."[47] Germans failed to overrun Kommerscheidt as riflemen, cooks, messengers, runners, clerks, tankers, and mortarmen combined to defend it.[48]

By the summer of 1944, each infantry division was authorized a medical unit consisting of 32 medical, dental, and administrative officers and 383 enlisted men. Each regiment and battalion had its own medical section, supervised by a medical officer with enlisted technicians attached as aid men at company levels. Two medics were normally assigned to each company.

The first treatment received by a wounded man was given on the battlefield by a medic who applied dressings, administered drugs to relieve pain, and in general tried to make casualties as comfortable as possible until litter bearers could take them to a battalion aid station, usually located a few hundred yards behind the front lines. Physicians at such aid stations performed all urgent functions, such as assessing a wounded man's condition, redressing wounds, administering plasma to combat shock, sulfanilamide to prevent infections, and morphine to relieve pain. They applied splints and arrested hemorrhages. As soon as possible, seriously wounded men needing more treatment were evacuated by litter carrier, jeep, or ambulance to a collecting station. Located a few miles to the rear, such stations functioned much as does a hospital emergency room, providing still additional temporary treatment. Casualties were then taken rearward to a clearing station four to eight miles behind the lines. More elaborate care could be given there; patients could be held for some time as they recuperated, or evacuated to a hospital if their wounds required such consideration.[49]

On 3 November, the divisional medical company prepared to receive casualties from the Schmidt action. 2nd Battalion established its aid station in Vossenack; 3rd Battalion occupied the log dugout near the base of the Kall trail; 1st Battalion set up in a house cellar near the edge of Kommerscheidt. Casualties were ferried by Weasel or hand-carried by litter teams up the Kall trail to an ambulance loading point for transportation to a collecting station at Germeter.[50]

Technician Third Class John Shedio and Second Lieutenant Alfred Muglia, medical assistance corps officer for 3rd Battalion, first saw possibilities in the dugout along the Kall trail. Engineers already utilized it as a shelter in which to rest from their labors when Shedio and Muglia happened upon it. The bunker was entirely dug into the hillside except for the front, which was reinforced and barricaded by rocks. The roof consisted of two layers of logs about 12 inches in diameter, which provided good protection from everything except a direct artillery hit. Inside dimensions were 12 feet by 18 feet by 8 feet. They told 3rd Battalion surgeon, Captain Michael DeMarco, of their find. He ordered engineers to find another shelter; he was designating this one as an aid station. DeMarco hung a Red Cross panel outside in the most conspicuous place he could find.

DeMarco brought personnel and equipment down the trail, and they began to receive patients. From the beginning, the physician was frustrated that the only evacuation route, the Kall trail, was blocked by disabled tanks.[51] At the very top sat Fleig's tank, partially blocking the trail and around which all other vehicles must maneuver. It encroached so far onto the narrow trail that even medical jeeps climbing the hill, grinding up in "grandma" or super-low gear as they came north, were often unable to make it past on the first try. Trucks found the squeeze impassable. Three hundred yards farther south was the second A Company tank. Engineers pushed it off the road and threw fill dirt around it to build up the trail. Vehicles could pass at that point. Three hundred yards south sat a third tank, still in operating condition but with a thrown track. It sat astride the road, blocking traffic.[52]

Frustrated as they might be, those who worked at the dugout were at least spared dangers faced by those in Kommersheidt at 1st Battalion aid station where confusion, ignorance, and contempt violated provisions of the Geneva Convention. Captain Paschal Linguiti, 1st Battalion surgeon, caustically noted that just 10 yards from his aid station sat an 81mm mortar. To the right and forward 10 yards was a machine-gun site. Two of Fleig's tanks parked for some time not more than 25 yards to the rear of Linguiti's aid station, and an artillery observer took up a post in a concrete shelter only 5 feet away on the left. Such actions, Linguiti warned, invited German retaliation.[53]

The measure of suffering that day was not meted out solely to men of 1st and 3rd battalions at Kommerscheidt and Schmidt. 2nd Battalion at Vossenack also endured the worst day since the attack began on 2 November. Starting at daybreak, the Germans covered every inch of town with 150mm and even 210mm shells. Rounds fell in a continuous rain lasting all day across the entire area from the east end of the ridge to 300 yards west of the crossroads church. German artillerymen methodically fired concentrations on every house in succession, moving down both sides of the main street. It was a day of drenching artillery fire, the effect of which became ever more apparent on morale of soldiers there.[54]

No one was safe. American foxholes were spread out like a fan on the exposed forward nose of the Vossenack ridge. The enemy barrage was "fiendish and unnerving." German fire direction centers singled out an individual foxhole, and their batteries fired at it until they scored a direct hit. They then shifted fire to the next hole. Sergeant Baker, a machine-gun squad leader in Easy Company, reported that Germans fired *two hundred* rounds at his hole, covering him with dirt *six* times. He was lucky. He survived with only a broken leg.[55]

Easy Company command post, located in a cellar, was hit six times by heavy-caliber shells and finally set afire. Earlier that day, Private First Class Ogburn sat in the house's kitchen, now converted into a radio room, operating the set and monitoring it for messages. He left the room for a few minutes to sit outside on the steps. While outside, a shell burst through the wall of the house, exploding in the kitchen and obliterating his radio set.[56]

Private John Allard holed up in the basement of a house. He wondered if his parents were hearing about the battle. He thought of his brother, Howard, assigned to B Company, 1st Battalion, 110th Infantry Regiment, and worried about his safety. He prayed for another brother aboard a ship bound for the China-Burma-India war theater. 4 November was his parents' 25th wedding anniversary. "What a way to celebrate," Allard thought, "with three sons off to war."* Private Allard's musings were constantly interrupted by explosions from German barrages overhead. "We saw buildings destroyed above us . . . we were splattered with mud by unexploding shells; we cried and prayed some more, were hungry and low on ammunition, but kept doing all those things that seemed so senseless in basic training, but appeared to be so important

---

*Howard Allard was listed as MIA on 14 November. John didn't learn of his loss until 13 December when he received a letter from his father informing him of his brother's classification. Howard was captured just as the 110th Infantry Regiment was leaving the front lines and was not liberated until months later by advancing American armies.

now. . . . our sanity and numbers grew weaker. . . . we held Vossenack, only to wonder what could be so important about it."[57]

Two MPs in Vossenack also wondered why they were there. "We were sent," said Sergeant Bernard Margasak of Philadelphia, "to direct traffic—that was a joke. There wasn't any traffic to direct and no place to go if there had been. Every time a jeep or a head showed on the road, the Germans threw everything but mess kits. We didn't get out of cellars for 24 hours."

Margasak's friend, another combat MP also from Philadelphia, shook his head like a punch-drunk fighter in a dressing room after the 15th round. Corporal Michael McDonald added his opinion of German barrages. As mortars opened up on them, they ran toward a blasted building. "Some G.I.'s poked their heads out of holes and basement windows and yelled at us, 'Holy Cripes, here come the M.P.'s. The town must be off limits already.'" He shook his head again. "Did I do any shooting? Not me. I was too damn busy digging. . . . And look here. If I ever reach Philadelphia again, I'll never leave, so help me God. I won't even go down to Wildwood."[58]

Officers and sergeants gave orders to stay out of sight during the day, remaining under cover in basements and cellars. Only one man in each squad was to stay on duty in the line. At nightfall, when barrages eased off, others resumed their squad positions outside, staying until dawn. So severe and deadly accurate was German shelling that any man left outside all day was by nightfall unfailingly dead or a combat exhaustion case.[59]

GIs learned to set their watches by the last round, which fell each day at 1750 hours. Save for occasional harassing shells, it would remain quiet until the next day.[60] Only at night were supply vehicles able to move as far forward as the church. From there, carrying parties from each company picked up supplies and moved them to their units.[61]

At intervals throughout the day, Germans sent patrols out in strength to probe American positions. Each time infantrymen of the 2nd Battalion threw them back.[62] It was too much. Riflemen were pounded to bits and blown to pieces. Casualties mounted steadily from enemy pressure. Mortar crews could not even keep extra ammunition close to their tubes, so heavily did German guns bombard them. Consequently, ammunition carriers moved back and forth on a constant run carrying shells, wearing down their physical stamina.[63] Some men broke completely. Medics evacuated them to the rear, advising against sending them back into combat. Nerves were so shot, morale so alarmingly gone that men could not even move to protect themselves and sat stiffly, crying uncontrollably.[64]

At 2100 hours, 4 November, five Germans came into American lines and gave themselves up. They said they were part of a regiment ordered to retake Vossenack the next morning. Their units were disposed to the north and east, with one battalion in the bottom of the draw below Brandenberg, one in the woods to the north of Vossenack, and the third in reserve. American artillerymen laid down a barrage on those areas. There was no German attack the next day.*[65]

German records summed up their progress for the day. They designated battalions by the names of their commanders. Documents of the *89th Infantry Division* spoke of *battalions Wolf, Wilschewsky,* and *Schindler* that morning attacking westerly from Harscheidt. *Battalion Onnen* thrust from the west of Kommerscheidt. *Wolf* broke into Schmidt with assault guns, forcing "Amis" out of town toward the north.

The Germans then learned that the 110th Infantry Regiment had captured Simonskall. "The whole sector," the report read, "is seeing activity. Foot by foot the battalions fight their way forward. The *1056th Regiment* receives the order to participate. A pitch-dark night envelops the mountains of the EIFEL. Rain drenches the men as they move up into the new battle area. Many a curse relieves the mind. If one cannot go into a rest area, one could at least have stayed in old positions where, under dangerous labor, positions had been erected and everyone is familiar with every inch of ground. But if the enemy succeeds in pushing further to the south, he will be able to roll up our positions from the rear."[66]

There was little danger of that happening. The 112th Infantry Regiment would never penetrate the Strauch–Steckenborn line. Its 2nd Battalion reeled under German bombardment at Vossenack. 1st and 3rd battalions maintained a precarious hold on Kommerscheidt and its hill to the north. Even there they were in trouble.

---

*The five PWs were from the *156th Panzer Grenadier Regiment, 116th Panzer Division.* They were to have attacked 4 November at 0700 hours, but the assault was postponed until 1200, then 1500, and finally canceled for the day due to casualties inflicted by both American and German artillery. It was rescheduled for the next morning. The 28th Infantry Division interrogation report indicated some of the difficulties that beset the German army at that stage of the war. On the way into the area, the PWs' vehicles ran out of gas at Langenbroich and were abandoned. "They may still be there," one of them said. The regimental *3d Company* suffered, in addition to the five desertions, 20 casualties on 4 November from American artillery fire. Most replacements were between eighteen and forty and without battle experience. Fifteen other men waited for an opportunity to surrender. Like many soldiers, they did not know the name of their divisional commander, referring to Siegfried von Waldenburg as "Waldenstein." The same was true for Americans. One of these combat interviews refers to Major Robert Hazlett, commander of 1st Battalion, 112th Infantry Regiment, as "Wade Haislep."

7

"We were in very bad straits"

5 November 1944

Major General Norman Cota did not feel at all worshipful that Sunday morning. It was not going to be a good day. Frustrated by the loss of Schmidt, embarrassed by his division's failures, uncertain what was happening to units of his regiments, Cota's mood did not improve when he learned his superiors planned to stop in for a visit.

Early that morning General Leonard Gerow came to 28th Division headquarters at Rott, insisting on receiving from Cota an explanation of events south of the Kall. Some hours later, Gerow returned in the company of others. Filled with trepidation, Cota welcomed Lieutenant General Courtney H. Hodges, commander of First Army, and his crusty chief of staff, Major General William B. Kean. Hodges brought along another man, his favorite corps commander, "Lightning Joe" Collins, of VII Corps.

It is reasonable to suppose that Hodges informed Cota he had postponed Collins' drive for the Rhine because of continuing bad weather. Collins was to have begun his attack that day. Cota could not have been pleased to learn that his unit would continue to be the only American unit engaged in combat along the Western Front. It is further reasonable to suppose that Hodges and Gerow questioned Cota closely on the reasons for the loss of Schmidt and strongly urged him to rectify matters. What is clear is that only a few hours after their departure, "Dutch" Cota brought forth a new plan for the reconquest of Schmidt. "Task Force Ripple" would save the day and free Cota from further criticism by his superiors.[1]

German artillery batteries continued their unremitting pressure on Vossenack. So severe was their shelling that they forced Easy Company, 2nd

Battalion, to change location of its command post three times. Lieutenant Colonel Jim White, executive officer of the 1171st Engineer Group, was in town from early in the morning until 0930 hours. "While I was there," he said, "we experienced the heaviest type of barrage . . . so continuous that I couldn't count the shells."[2]

George Company weapons platoon leader, First Lieutenant Clyde R. Johnson, also described German shelling that morning: "It was," claimed Johnson, "the heaviest artillery barrage I have ever seen, a continual and devastating rain of shells on the whole area from a heavy concentration of guns on the semi-circular ridge to the northeast, east, and southeast. They fired time-fire and armor-piercing shells . . . directly at each individual foxhole—as many as twenty to thirty rounds at one hole—and their aim was deadly. So good was their observation that as soon as one man moved, a concentration almost immediately followed him. . . . We were in very bad straits."[3]

Soldiers everywhere on the ridge faced disaster and death. Four men sought cover in a nearby barn. Rounds from enemy guns ranged after them as they ran toward it. The entire upper floor of the barn collapsed from a direct hit, dropping a ton of hay bales onto those hapless, cowering soldiers. Then flames began to lick at the dry hay. Other troops tried to dig their buddies out but were driven back by heat from the fire. They were unable to save their friends.[4]

First Lieutenant Melvin J. Barrilleaux returned from a leave in Paris to resume command of Easy Company, 2nd Battalion. Early that morning, his executive officer briefed him on conditions in the company. Concerned by what First Lieutenant James Condon told him, Barrilleaux crawled under fire throughout his area, visiting men in his platoons as they crouched in their foxholes. They were so battered Barrilleaux believed all of them should be evacuated. Platoon leaders told him their troopers were so affected by constant artillery fire they practically had to be ordered even to eat.

Barrilleaux spoke with First Lieutenant Eldeen Kauffman, commander of Fox Company. They discussed their men's deteriorating morale, their shell shock, and mounting casualties caused by combat exhaustion. Kauffman told Barrilleaux how his men pulled back from exposed foxholes during methodical German barrages; once they left a dangerous gap for several hours between F and G Company positions. His men, reported Kauffman, could no longer endure such poundings. "They were," he said, "just too nerve-shattered, tired, and many were crying."[5]

Kauffman and Barrilleaux decided to inform their battalion commander of the sorry state on the nose of Vossenack ridge. They reported to 2nd Battalion command post and were shocked to see that their commander, Lieutenant Colonel Theodore Hatzfeld, appeared to be in a state of stupor. Lethargic and nonresponsive, he ignored their presence and sat, head down, staring into space. His executive officer, Captain John Pruden, spoke with Kauffman and

Barrilleaux, explaining that the colonel was distraught because of his battalion's terrible casualty losses.

Their soldiers, the two lieutenants agreed, could not take any more. "They had gone through hell."[6] Pruden was sympathetic; those at the command post were also exposed to unremitting enemy artillery. But what could he do? No troops were available to relieve men of 2nd Battalion, allowing them even a brief respite from tension and combat terrors. They were under orders to hold their ground at all costs, even if it did seem that division and regiment had abandoned them. All of them, from battalion staff officers to riflemen in exposed foxholes, had to endure and hope for the best. It was not a very good solution.[7]

South of Zweifall, in positions to lay indirect fire where needed on call, the 893rd Tank Destroyer Battalion was on 15-minute alert to move forward to support infantry combat units with direct fire if the need should arise.[8] Its commander, Lieutenant Colonel Sam Mays, remained concerned about the divisional role expected of him and his tank destroyer crews. During the night of 4/5 November, Mays received notice. Help was needed by two of the divisional infantry regiments. Colonel Mays ordered B and C companies to move out. B Company was to support the 2nd Battalion in Vossenack, C Company was to move down the Kall trail and aid 1st and 3rd battalions in the Kommerscheidt area.[9]

As First Lieutenant Howard Davis, a B Company platoon leader, started moving his M-10s into Vossenack, they were the targets of "many gun flashes" and were also in danger from 170mm artillery and 120mm mortar rounds. They continued toward the little town amid exploding shells. Shrapnel fragments whistled around Davis' M-10s, endangering his foot guide, a soldier from the infantry 2nd Battalion's George Company. Davis ordered the man to clamber up on his M-10 and crouch down inside the thin-skinned, open, boxlike turret of the armored destroyer. Davis' kindness doomed the man.

"When we reached a point just due north of the church," said Davis, "an enemy artillery shell hit the counterbalance of my M-10 and blew half the doughboy guide's head away. We continued, keeping his body with us."

Davis and his destroyers located George Company, dug in at the extreme east end of Vossenack and stretched along the nose of the ridge. He placed his four M-10s to fire east, north, and southeast. The lieutenant was appalled by the saturation shelling from German mortars and artillery. "We had three or four men hit by shell fragments while [they were] inside the TDs. No medics were around to treat the wounded. All four TDs received at least four direct hits. Our individual equipment stored on the outside of our vehicles was torn and ripped. By noon, six men in my platoon were injured."*[10]

---

*Interviewer Captain John S. Howe noted that "Tank destroyer men saw their open turret, in an enemy artillery barrage, expand to dimensions of about 100′ x 100′."

Only once did destroyer crewmen spot any enemy armor during their first three days in Vossenack. One sergeant that first afternoon saw two German tanks at a range of more than 3,000 yards—too far away to fire at them. They wondered why they were there.*[11]

Engineers informed Major John Lavin, TD battalion S-3 operations officer, that the Kall trail was to be clear of mines by 0100 hours, 5 November. Lavin ordered First Lieutenant Jack Fuller, a reconnaissance company platoon leader, and Captain Sidney Cole, commander of the reconnaissance company, to reconnoiter the trail and find out if it was passable.[12]

Fuller took an M-20 armored car and drove down the MSR until he could go no farther. He dismounted and continued past groups of tankers repairing a thrown track on one of their M-4s, crossed the river over the stone bridge, and then returned to his own vehicle and drove back to Vossenack. He reported by radio to his company commander, Captain Marion Pugh, that the trail was blocked by tanks, it was impassable, and the surface itself was badly in need of repair. Engineers would try to have it in shape by 0800 hours, "but if so, the Engineers will need more help or will have to work a great deal harder," Fuller said.[13]

Captain Pugh learned at 0530 hours that the Kall trail was finally open. He ordered his platoons of armored destroyers to move out immediately and get as far as possible before dawn broke. Fuller and his reconnaissance platoon moved through the draw and into Kommerscheidt by 1000 hours, losing only one M-10 tank destroyer along the way from a thrown track.[14]

Destroyer crews of Pugh's C Company managed to get nine destroyers into the Kommerscheidt sector during the day.[15] When Pugh arrived at 1530 hours, he sought out Colonel Peterson to learn how he could best place his units to help the 112 Infantry Regiment. Peterson directed him to protect the right and left flanks of the few available tanks.[16] Eight tanks and nine TDs now sat in Kommerscheidt to support frightened and endangered infantrymen there.[17]

They provide what today is called "beans and bullets." Their work is often unsung yet is as vitally important to success in combat as is that of the bravest infantryman, the most daring tank commander, the most reliable artilleryman. Without infantry, armor, or artillery, battles could not be won. Those units prepare the battlefield, engage the enemy, capture the ground. Yet combat soldiers could not fight for even one day without help provided by other, less glamorous military units, categorized as "combat support" and

*Staff Sergeant Gardner reported that the German tanks were in Kleinhau. It is unlikely he saw tanks there unless he was standing in the steeple of the Vossenack church. The range to Kleinhau was approximately 4,600 yards, and its elevation was 375 feet. The range to Hürtgen was more nearly 3,000 yards and its elevation was 390 feet, a more visible location from Vossenack's 365 feet. Sergeant Gardner may have meant Hürtgen instead of Kleinhau.

"combat service support" organizations, such as engineers,* medics, ordnance, signal corps, quartermaster, transportation, and others. Some nations have emphasized these missions less than has the United States, but no country in history has ever been able to do away entirely with functions performed by such organizations.

All these units work at absolutely vital endeavors; they must perform effectively and efficiently if battles are to be won. Some of them—such as engineer crews—have a limited combat capability, but when they face situations requiring them to lay down their tools and fight, they are no longer able to perform their designated tasks. So they work behind the scenes and do their best to ignore the din of battle.

Many work just behind the lines or in even more remote rear areas. They can sometimes hear the sounds of combat but rarely are called upon to participate. They carry out their duties on the periphery of battle, or during lulls, or at night. If the hours of daylight belong to fighting men, the moments of night are seized by those who must attend to the needs of warriors.

At 0015 hours, 5 November, Lieutenant Howard Rogers, a platoon leader in 707th Tank Battalion, started a resupply convoy into the Kall Valley. A guide holding a white handkerchief, as a visual aid in the darkness, preceded each Weasel on the hopelessly inadequate and dark trail. Partway down the path the lead Weasel cargo carrier threw a track, its small bogey unable to accommodate the surface slant on that portion of the trail. Motors idled for 15 minutes as men replaced the track before the convoy could proceed.

Harassing fire from German guns increased during the first 45 minutes of the trip. Some 60 rounds exploded on high ground just above the draw road entrance and in the Kall gully itself. At 0100 hours, the convoy reached the third tank hulk setting astride the road, minus one track, completely blocking traffic. Lieutenant Rogers noticed how someone had tried to repair it, for the M-4 sat some 100 yards farther down the trail than the last time he had come upon it.

Rogers ordered his men to repair the tank. They worked for nearly two hours on the task, trying to cope with a damaged idler wheel before giving up in frustration and pushing it over the left bank of the trail. The hulk refused to roll completely free of the road and still partially blocked it. The convoy crew attacked the right bank with shovels, trying to widen the trail so they could get their vehicles past the blockage. Nearby engineer troops, working on the road, were also pressed into service. Lieutenant Rogers later complained that the engineers labored so slowly "we grabbed shovels and picks and worked on the cutaway ourselves."

It was 0300 hours before the supply train could move forward. Its crew were a long way from their destination, and sunrise would occur at 0734. They

*At times classified as "combat," at others as "combat support."

must still cross the river, deliver their supplies, and return to safety before daylight allowed enemy artillerymen to fire upon them. Even now they were in danger. "By this time," Rogers observed, "the moon was up and visibility was good in the draw. It worried us."

At the bottom of the draw another headache confronted them. An A Company tank sat there, blocking the road. They were forced to use the switchback bypasses to get around it. M-29 cargo carriers, or Weasels, pulling quarter-ton trailers, could not maneuver around those turns. Men were forced to unhitch heavily loaded trailers and watch as drivers backed and filled each tracked Weasel 150 feet up the switchback and then forward again back onto the trail. They then manhandled those trailers the entire distance over chopped up, slippery, and uneven surfaces of the pathway before rehitching them to the Weasel cargo carriers. It was brutal labor made more awful by the confusing network of alternate trails. Rogers complained correctly that there should have been signs or guides available or at least engineer tape stretching along the correct route to ease passage through the switchbacks. Engineer crews working along the trail might easily have marked the route, but they failed to do so.

"During the two days we used this route as an MSR," Rogers noted, "various people attempted two-way traffic. It was impossible. Both nights we sent supply trains, I set up control points using NCOs of the Recon Platoon on each difficult turn or bend in the road to halt traffic until we got through." Rogers concluded, "It didn't help us much and simply interrupted other unit trains and even medical evacuation."

Finally they were across the river, faced now on the south side with two more switchbacks of 180 degrees. Once again they repeated the process of disconnecting and pulling the trailers by hand while tracked Weasel cargo carriers negotiated the turns.

It was 0330 hours before they reached their objective—three A Company tanks parked in a shallow draw just north of Kommerscheidt. They unloaded gasoline, ammunition, rations, and water. By 0430 their trailers were empty and they started back. Engineers had slightly improved the trail, so it didn't take quite as long to return to the Germeter assembly area as they feared. They reached safety at about 0700 hours, just as it was getting light.[18]

A second tank supply train started toward Kommerscheidt that evening at 2030 hours, led by Captain William Pinchon, battalion S-4 supply officer. He tied a white handkerchief around his helmet and led the column on foot. It was so dark it was impossible to see more than a few feet. At the dugout aid station Pinchon saw two infantrymen walking along the trail burdened down with several rounds of bazooka ammunition and 12 bandoliers of .30-caliber bullets for M-1 rifles. He invited them to climb into the rear jeep, and they did so gladly. All the way down to the river, the convoy repeatedly found it necessary to squeeze against the right bank to allow medical jeeps carrying wounded to get past them on their way to the rear.

They reached their destination just north of Kommerscheidt by 2230 hours and distributed rations and water. Captain Donald Kelly spoke to "General" Fleig, who told how his tanks were under almost constant fire during daylight hours from artillery, assault guns, and tanks. Kelly was to tell Captain Hostrup that Fleig planned to use his radio transmitter only when absolutely essential. Every time he turned it on, said Fleig, he drew enemy fire. Worse, his tank batteries were so low, the engine would not start. Another M-4 had to tow it before it would catch.

Kelly and Pinchon started back at midnight. On the return trip another Weasel threw a track. Kelly remarked that "drivers were infantry with only about three days experience on them. Lacking training and experience, they were unable to handle them so as to prevent them from throwing tracks."[19]

First Lieutenant William George, 3rd Battalion motor officer, also took a supply train to the front. It arrived before daylight that Sunday, carrying enough rations to feed everyone in 3rd Battalion, with enough left for three companies in 1st Battalion. George returned to his motor pool in Germeter shortly after daylight. Turning in for some much-needed sleep, he was shortly awakened by Major Gilder, regimental S-4 supply officer, who informed George he was now in charge of getting *all* supplies to infantry troops in the forward area. Once again George organized a convoy loaded with needed materiel.

As his vehicles were about to enter the Kall trail, George "heard lots of hollering" and saw "two figures dressed in German uniforms and one dressed in an American uniform." The latter man "waved and hollered to us and we cautiously went over." George recognized Captain Hunter Montgomery, his regimental S-2 intelligence officer, who was wounded. The previous day Montgomery had joined with Lieutenant Colonel James Landon Lockett on a reconnaissance trip to Kommerscheidt to learn what was happening there. Lockett was captured and Montgomery wounded. The glib captain then talked two German medics into taking him back to his own lines and surrendering.

German artillery fire was so fierce that George decided to delay the convoy until darkness could cloak its presence. After nightfall, he saw "a fire works display from a German ammunition dump which had been hit that altogether sounded like a hell of a fight." The convoy rolled forward into the entrance to the trail, which was "so badly churned up that we had to move slowly and carefully, leading vehicles on foot around shellholes." Although one Weasel cargo carrier threw a track, the others soon made it to the bottom of the draw.

Suddenly they saw a bright glow along the river valley to the east and were mystified as to its cause until a man staggered toward the convoy through the darkness. As he came closer, George could see the man was burned almost black. Someone recognized the injured man as a squad member of 3rd Battalion's antitank platoon. The burned soldier told how Germans ambushed his squad, blasting them with three white phosphorus shells in quick succession. Fearing the German patrol might still be nearby, George ordered his convoy to move on. They found three more victims of the ambush, two of them "burned black and in bad shape."

George put two men ahead of the convoy to walk point, able to give advance warning to the rest should they encounter any enemy soldiers. At the switchbacks south of the river, Germans were close enough to hear the convoy's M-29 Weasel engines and fired rounds of antipersonnel shells. No one was hurt, and the convoy made it on into Kommerscheidt with needed supplies at 2200 hours.[20]

A resupply convoy for 1st Battalion arrived in Kommerscheidt at 0500 hours, 5 November, and dumped its load directly in front of the house used by medical personnel as its battalion aid station. For the next two hours Captain Paschal Linguiti, the unit surgeon, fumed as he watched company carrying parties arrive to receive their distribution of ammunition and rations. He was terribly concerned that such activities would compromise his work; that enemy artillery batteries would fire on the site, unaware that an aid station lay in the midst of such bellicose activities.[21]

Linguiti was only partially mollified when at 0830 hours a Weasel cargo carrier supply train made its way to his aid station carrying medical supplies. It was the first replenishment of his supplies Linguiti had received in two days. Arrival of the convoy did not herald a change in Linguiti's luck. In the afternoon, the aid station received three direct hits, destroying his new supplies and killing one private.

Captain Linguiti realized the aid station had to be moved if he were to ensure safety for his people and the casualties who crowded their facilities. After dark he evacuated his staff and patients along the road leading north out of Kommerscheidt toward the river. They followed the winding and narrow route through the series of switchbacks, across the stone bridge, and up the train until they reached 3rd Battalion aid station in the log dugout. Both battalions operated their medical facilities at the bunker on the Kall until the evening of 9 November.[22]

Linguiti left eight litter bearers in Kommerscheidt. These men would collect casualties and hand-carry them to the dugout. Evacuation from the Kall aid station could be made up the trail by jeep or litter bearers to the ambulance loading point on the meadow above. From there injured men would be taken to collecting stations in the Germeter area.[23]

That Sunday chaplains of both battalions decided to stay at the medical dugout, where many of the wounded cried out for religious succor. Chaplain (Captain) Alan P. Madden, of 1st Battalion, and Chaplain (Captain) Ralph E. Maness, of 3rd Batalion, remained there until 9 November, ministering as best they could to those who were brought to the bunker. They represented both major Christian faiths; Father Madden succoring Roman Catholics while the Reverend Ralph Maness cared for Protestants.

Second Lieutenant Alfred Muglia, a surgeon's assistant and Medical Assistance Corps officer, arrived at the aid station. He saw to his astonishment two American tanks and two mortars sited on each side of the dugout, using it as a firing point from which to lob shells at the Germans. He and the two chaplains convinced the weapons crews to move elsewhere. Chaplain Maness offered his jeep and driver, Technician Fifth Class Owensby, to Muglia to help ferry patients from Kommerscheidt to the dugout.[24] It is doubtful if either Madden or Maness found that Lord's Day to be particularly inspirational.

Sometime during the evening, PFC Delmar Putney ran into the aid station shouting that German medics, armed with Lugers or P-38s,* had forced him at gunpoint to help them carry wounded comrades to safety. Then they released him and he came straight back to the dugout.[25] Later that night, medics were attacked by a German patrol, which wounded two of them. When the enemy soldiers walked up to inspect the "infantrymen," they were surprised when they realized they had attacked men protected by the Geneva Convention. They apologized for their mistake, telling the frightened medics they had not noticed the Red Cross armbands on their sleeves in the darkness.

As night wore on, other Germans stopped at the dugout, not knowing whether occupants were fighters or noncombatants, and entered with weapons at the ready. Seeing medics inside caring for their patients, German soldiers made no effort to molest anyone and backed out of the rude structure, indicating they intended no harm to anyone inside. One German even informed Linguiti and DeMarco that they would be mining the trail and to be careful during evacuations. Still later, at the top of the hill, a German soldier stopped a medical jeep about to start down the trail to inform its driver the road in front of him was now mined. They let him proceed on foot.[26]

The aid station on the Kall remained filled to capacity as litter bearers evacuated men from Kommerscheidt who were wounded by enemy fire or who broke down under the stress of prolonged combat. Once again, beset by this exhausting and terrible conflict, some American soldiers voted with their feet. Captain Henry Doherty, an engineer officer, watched them leave. Throughout the morning of 5 November, he saw groups of men from near Kommerscheidt "filtering up through the woods from the south. . . . I tried to stop them but couldn't do it."[27]

Consumed with fear, those who remained in place remembered such contradictory things. Lieutenant Tyo recalled the night of 4/5 November as a momentary reprieve. "During the night it was absolutely quiet and a beautiful moonlit night. Not a shell landed in our positions. We had no blankets or coats so had to do something to keep warm so we kept digging."[28] In a nearby

---

*Unlike their American counterparts, who carried neither pistol nor rifle, German medics customarily armed themselves with a side arm, usually a Luger or a P-38.

company area, Captain Walker had a different recollection. "We received heavy artillery all night and could hear tanks maneuvering to our front and side throughout the darkness."[29]

Whether or not shells landed during the night, they did so with a vengeance that Sunday morning. Germans poured murderous concentrations of artillery, continuing for hours on end without respite. "We could do nothing," said Sergeant Bob Toner, "but sit tight, all the while losing men as casualties mounted. Everyone stayed in his hole, even to the point of disposing of excreta in K ration boxes, pieces of paper, or handkerchiefs, throwing it out of a foxhole when the chance came, since it was worth a man's life to be seen. For at least two days men had no rations or water and each one lived out his personal hell within himself. Seldom did the Boche artillery and mortar fire let up."*[30]

The bravery of some continued unabated. During a barrage in which *600* rounds fell within a 30-minute period, Staff Sergeant Paul Kerekes of Mike Company dashed out from his hiding place to repair breaks in communication wire.†[31] As Army Air Forces planes soared in to bomb and strafe enemy attackers, Staff Sergeant Arthur Johnson of King Company dragged identification panels marking American positions into view so pilots would be able to differentiate between foes and friendly troops.[32]

At about 1200 hours that Sunday, Eugene Holden, operations sergeant of 1st Battalion, counted 11 German tanks poking their snouts down the ridge from Schmidt toward Kommerscheidt. As they moved forward, a P-47 zoomed down and blasted one with a bomb. Other P-47s could be seen strafing and bombing Schmidt.[33] Those German tanks, many of them camouflaged to look like haystacks, slowly rolled forward. No American armor was at hand to repel them. They were behind the crest of a large hill to the north.

---

*Although interviewer Captain William J. Fox recorded the words of his conversation with Sergeant Toner as they are reproduced above, it seems doubtful that the speaker actually phrased his words so delicately as to refer to his men's bowel movements as "excreta." In this, as in so many other cases in these records, what we read was as much formed by the interviewers' own attitudes as by the words of those interviewed. It is interesting to realize that in Fox's interviews, all those with whom he spoke talked in the same way; those who conversed with Captain John S. Howe sounded very much like *he* did, and everyone in the 109th Infantry Regiment addressed Lieutenant Harry Jackson using the same phrases. What was actually said will, of course, forever remain unknown.

†During the entire course of this battle communications were one of the most severe problems faced by fighting men. Radios gave out without warning and even when they worked reception was often poor. Nor were telephones much more reliable. Signal Corps troops strung telephone wires along road shoulders or tacked them to tree branches. Wire crews did not often venture far from roadways because of the possible danger of mines. Wires consequently hung with a great amount of slack or lay unprotected beside roadways. Passing trucks and armored vehicles snagged and broke them. Artillery barrages regularly also broke wires, severing all communication.

Tankers told Holden they no longer had enough gasoline to maneuver. Help for infantrymen came from tank destroyers. Back behind the same hill with the tanks, M-10s cranked up, moved up to the hill's crest, fired, then ducked behind the slope once again. But German tanks were not easily repulsed this time and continued to close on Kommerscheidt. The world became a chaos of blood and steel in which men fired and cursed like automatons. Sergeant Tony Kudiak and Second Lieutenant Horace Smith worked as a bazooka team, trying to hit the steel monsters with rounds from their launcher, risking their lives as they did so. Each time they missed. Mark IVs and Vs churned through rain-soaked meadow glades toward them.

Waiting Americans felt their threat as they faced a danger greater than decimation. Sergeant Holden decided to wait no longer. He ran for cover in a storehouse, a small cement structure "about the size of an 'out-house.'" It was not the best possible protection. When it received a direct hit, two other men hiding with Holden were killed. The blast knocked him down and piled chunks of concrete on top of him. It was some time before he could get free.[34]

More infantrymen were desperately needed in the lines at Kommerscheidt. Technical Sergeant Carl Beckes took Charlie Company's 2nd Platoon forward from its position on Kommerscheidt hill north of town. "None of them came back," Joe Perll remembered.[35] During one assault Second Lieutenant Ray Borders, a member of Mike Company, used a BAR to knock out almost two full squads of German machine gunners.[36]

As battle flared in Kommerscheidt, First Lieutenant Leon Simon at regimental headquarters near Germeter was told to lead 3rd Battalion's Baker Company to Kommerscheidt to reinforce troops there. Simon and the company arrived on Kommerscheidt Hill at 1530 hours. Baker Company went on forward into the line of defenders inside the town, the rictus of death already on the faces of men of the company. No one knows what happened to it. None of its troops returned to describe their experiences.[37]

1st Battalion's Baker Company also suffered. Its 2nd Platoon, fighting near Able Company, had no remaining officers. Technical Sergeant Bruce Pitman took over the platoon and noticed one of his men missing. He went to look for him and did not return. The platoon guide, Technical Sergeant Roy Littlehales, set out to find Pitman and located him about 25 yards away with his left leg torn off from the knee down, the victim of an artillery explosion. Littlehales screamed for a medic, who said there was nothing he could do "but finally gave him a shot of morphine. . . . We went back to the aid station and wrangled there but it got us nowhere. . . . I went back later that night and found he had died. He was a grand fellow and up for a commission."[38]

Staff Sergeant Nathaniel Quentin saw a German tank move within 75 yards of A Company's command post. The Mark IV fired directly at it and missed. Disaster was avoided only when a lone P-47 flying overhead saw the tank, peeled off, and dove toward it, dropping a bomb that knocked it out. "That night," said Quentin, "their infantry got within talking distance of our positions and asked for our surrender. They received a lot of small arms fire in return."[39]

At about 1200 hours on that horrible Sunday, Colonel Albert Flood, commander of 3rd Battalion, confessed to Captain Jack Walker that he had been relieved of command. He was later evacuated because of minor wounds and combat exhaustion. Major Bob Christenson informed Walker he would now take orders from Major Robert Hazlett, commander of 1st Battalion. Since both units were so battered, they now united, and Hazlett commanded both. He directed Captain Walker to take charge of the combined battalion's right flank. Walker's force was a thin one, comprised of a platoon of A Company and the remnants of his own L Company. "After dark," Walker said, Hazlett "moved a platoon of Company B up to me."[40]

Lieutenant Simon, who brought 3rd Battalion's doomed Baker Company to Kommerscheidt from Germeter, sought out his regimental commander, Colonel Peterson. He found him in his forward regimental command post on Kommerscheidt Hill. The colonel wanted Simon to go into Kommerscheidt and bring back either his two battalion commanders or their executive officers for a meeting at 1600 hours to decide on a course of action.

Simon found Major Hazlett and Major Christenson talking to one another. Before he could deliver his message, Christenson "took off on the double" for the east end of the hamlet. "Burp gun fire was sounding in the streets from the east and west and the enemy apparently were closer," Simon noted. He assumed Christenson was "apparently concerned with the defense." He told Hazlett about the meeting at 1600 hours and went to look for Colonel Flood. He finally found him in a shattered building. "He seemed exhausted," the lieutenant remembered. "I passed on Peterson's information," and the colonel accompanied him back to Kommerscheidt Hill. At the end of his tether, Flood asked Simon to "get him out of town." Colonel Peterson insisted that Flood remain there that night.

The regimental commander then sent Lieutenant Simon back to the rear "with a message for General Cota." The contents were stark. Both 1st and 3rd battalions were as cicatriced by scars as the ridge they fought on. Their men were shell-shocked and in poor condition. There were only six to seven tanks in Kommerscheidt, and tank destroyer crews were not sufficiently aggressive. He was, however, going to try to reorganize his men and hold Kommerscheidt and, if possible, retake Schmidt. "I went to divisional headquarters and relayed the message to General Cota."[41]

Carl Peterson lived in a dream world. The idea of recapturing Schmidt was folly. Americans would be lucky to cling by their fingernails to the narrow salient south of the Kall they still possessed, which included Kommerscheidt and Simonskall. Facing that bleak reality, the colonel fantasized about renewing an attack upon Schmidt.

If the regimental commander was a myopic visionary, General Cota was even more blinded by his unrealistic hopes. Loss of Schmidt the previous day stung him to the quick. Critical comments by General Hodges and General

Gerow in the early-morning hours gave Cota warning his head might soon roll unless he redeemed himself. He was popular with troopers of the "Bloody Bucket." They would do whatever he called on them to accomplish. After his superiors left the war room at divisional headquarters, Cota tried to determine a way out of his predicament. His solution, after all these years, is worth reproducing:

SECRET

Headquarters
28th Infantry Division
5 November 1944
In the Field

MESSAGE TO: Commanding Officer, 112th Infantry Regiment

1. It is imperative that the town of SCHMIDT be secured at once. Task Force "R", under the command of Lt. Col. RIPPLE, is attached to your command effective upon arrival at KOMMERSCHEIDT.

2. You will use this Task Force as the spearhead of your attack to capture SCHMIDT. The remaining elements of your command now at KOMMERSCHEIDT will follow close behind this Task Force and occupy and defend route of approach to SCHMIDT from all directions with special attention to the high ground SW of the town. SCHMIDT, when captured, will be held at all costs.

3. Details will be arranged between yourself and Lt. Col. RIPPLE.

4. . . . It is imperative that no time be wasted in getting this attack under way and it will be launched prior to 061200A November 1944.

5. . . . Reports will be made to DHQ every half hour.

6. I again caution you that men defending road blocks or a terrain feature must dig in and must be able to fight from the foxhole they dig. Great care will be exercised to prevent any recurrence of the episode of the 3rd Battalion.

7. All previous instructions relative to Task Force "R" in conflict with this message are rescinded.

8. "ROLL ON."

COTA
Comdg

OFFICIAL

BRIGGS
G-3

This was General Cota's plan by which he would redeem himself in the eyes of Gerow and Hodges. Task Force Ripple was to consist of (1) the already weakened 3rd Battalion, 110th Infantry Regiment, now numbering only 316 men; (2) "General" Fleig's A Company tanks, even now facing the wrath of German armor in Kommerscheidt; (3) D Company, 707th tanks, which never actually participated in the task force but remained in blocking positions southwest of Germeter until 8 November; (4) one platoon of B Company tank destroyers, which were to move forward along with 3rd Battalion infantrymen; and (5) C Company, 893rd TDs, which already had nine M-10s in Kommerscheidt.

Even keeping his desperation in mind, one wonders how General Cota imagined such a group could achieve a divisional objective. One *regiment* of infantry, supported by parts of a tank *battalion* and a tank destroyer *battalion,* had been unable to retain Schmidt. Yet Cota now ordered an infantry *battalion* already so decimated in battle that it now had less than half its strength, supported by eight tanks and nine tank destroyers, all of which were currently tied down by enemy armor, plus four more TDs, to achieve what the much stronger force had earlier been unable to retain.

It was late in the afternoon of 5 November when Colonel Richard Ripple, commander of the 707th Tank Battalion, received these astonishing orders. With the minuscule force assigned to him, he was to move through Vossenack at about 0200 hours on 6 November, pass through the Kall Valley, and join forces in Kommerscheidt with the depleted and exhausted 112th Infantry Regiment. Together they would forge on to retake Schmidt, after which the 112th was to pass through Task Force Ripple and continue the attack of the 28th Infantry Division toward the southwest. A good soldier and a man who followed orders, Lieutenant Colonel Richard Ripple set about trying to organize his force for this hopeless endeavor.[42]

For the second day in a row, General George Davis traveled to Kommerscheidt to observe the fighting there. He spent the night of 5/6 November with Colonel Peterson, regimental commander of the 112th, in A Company's 3rd Platoon command post. Even those outside could hear the two men arguing. The general accused Peterson of having a "poor plan."[43] Peterson's primary concern was to reorganize his command to ensure its ability to hold Kommerscheidt without further loss of ground. It was an eminently sound approach. If he were successful, Peterson hoped to make a second attack on Schmidt, a much less likely possibility. General Davis knew all about Cota's plans for Task Force Ripple. If Peterson's plans were "poor," then Cota's creation of Task Force Ripple was ill conceived indeed.

Engineers spent most of Sunday, 5 November, repairing roads, clearing minefields, removing rubble from Vossenack's streets, and sweeping the Kall trail and other sections of the divisional MSR for mines. Their difficulties did not begin until after sundown, when minesweeper crews were pinned down by artillery for two hours.

As they had done on the previous night, two squads of Charlie Company,

20th Engineers, tried to move 5,000 pounds of TNT down the Kall trail under cover of darkness. Second Lieutenant Benjamin Johns supervised their efforts. They were unsuccessful for the second night in a row. Conditions on the trail persuaded Lieutenant Johns that he would be unable to use his vehicles to transport the explosives. So he and his men made their way on foot along the trail, which was illuminated by brilliant moonlight. After crossing the bridge, they took an almost direct burst from German artillery fire. Transporting their wounded back over the bridge to the aid station along the Kall, Johns and his men walked some 25 yards above the dugout to wait out the night hours.

Below Johns' two squads, down near the bridge, were other engineers of A Company, stationed there to provide the bridge site with local security. One of them, Technician Fourth Class James Krieder, "heard two blasts of a whistle and the sound of firing up the hill" at about 0230 hours. "Later I saw Germans on the far side of the stream about seventy-five yards from the bridge," Krieder said. "I saw five Germans jump up on the bridge [and] about twenty-five to thirty came across it. We did not open fire because we felt we could not overcome the superior force."[44]

In addition to Lieutenant Johns' two squads, other members of B Company were also on the trail. Its 3rd Platoon moved toward the bridge, behind and separate from Johns' troops. Men in 3rd Platoon heard the artillery explosions landing south of the bridge that wounded some in Johns' party. Fearing they would be next, members of 3rd Platoon sought refuge and hid in a culvert about 20 yards off the trail. At 0230 hours they saw Germans on the trail fire three pistol flares into the air and they heard the sound of shots. One man, Corporal Marion Martone, reported why they continued to hide. "There were," he said, "enemy machine gun nests set up a few feet from the culvert and small arms fire. The men were instructed to remain silent and at daylight we made for the hills."[45]

What both Krieder and Martone heard was the destruction of Lieutenant Johns' two squads. After leaving their wounded at the Kall aid station, Johns and his men walked up the trail a little distance to dig in for the night. Some men worked quickly, scooping out foxholes for themselves, while others took their time. Two men, Sergeant William O'Neal and Private Joseph Sabol, started a hole, hit a rock, and moved a little away from the end of the squad line to try again. O'Neal lugged his gas mask and rifle in one hand, holding it by the sling. In the other he carried his mackinaw. He started to lay them down to resume digging. They had been in that area of the Kall trail for 10 minutes.

Suddenly a German soldier slipped out onto the road from the brushy slope. He blew a whistle twice in rapid succession and shouted at the American engineers. "When the German blew his whistle," Sergeant O'Neal said, "I looked around to see what it was. A lot of the other men did the same thing." Simultaneously with the sound of the whistle, other Germans appeared on the roadway. "That's when they blasted us," O'Neal remembered, "firing at us from all sides." Stunned engineers had little chance from "about ten burp guns and some rifle fire."

O'Neal recalled his own circumstances. "A German with a burp gun fired at me from about seven yards away. I was standing right out in the open. He was behind a six foot bank of earth. Most of them seemed to be firing from that position. I couldn't fire because I had my rifle by the sling in the same hand with my gas mask. I jumped and rolled into a small patch of scrub pine to get out of the way. It was only a few feet from me but I reached it swiftly. When I got in the pines, someone else was shooting at me with rifles from farther up the road."

Then German soldiers began throwing hand grenades and fired the three flares seen by Corporal Martone from his culvert hiding place down the road. From the glare of their light, O'Neal "could see some of the boys lying on the ground and couldn't tell if they were wounded." O'Neal knew how outgunned his men were. "Our only defense was rifle fire. They probably got most of our boys with the first blast. What little fire power we had was on the right. We could see we were outnumbered and had less firepower." O'Neal worked his way up the slope above him and behind the reverse side of the hill. "There was no rifle fire coming up from the stream and woods there. I got lost in the trees," O'Neal said.

The sergeant and three others eventually made it back to Vossenack, reporting to the engineer command post there. Major Bernard McDonnell, S-3 operations officer for the 20th Engineers, received their report about "some trouble" down on the Kall trail. One survivor, Private Patzner, told the major how two Germans jumped on him as he hid in his foxhole. One came down on his feet, the other on his head, knocking him out. They then pulled him from his hole, laid him alongside a tree, and departed without further harming him. Patzner laid there watching enemy soldiers go through the pockets of the dead and wounded, taking watches and other valuables. They then put their guns in the backs of Lieutenant Johns and other captured men and marched them away.[46]

It was little wonder the Germans were able to move through the woods and along the Kall trail and river road with impunity. No one was in charge of security for those key points! Without the lifeline of the Kall trail, all military efforts in Kommerscheidt were doomed, whether of those already there or of members of Task Force Ripple, who would within hours move across the river hoping to "retake Schmidt." No TD crews, no tankers, no engineers, no infantrymen had responsibility for guarding the trail. All previous planning by division, regiment, and battalion officers ignored this one crucial necessity.

The area of the trail, bridge, and river road was under the supposed jurisdiction and control of the 20th Engineer Combat Battalion, which was disorganized and hopelessly overcommitted given its capabilities (it went into battle at less than full unit strength) and its inordinate responsibilities, which included improving roads, clearing mines, blowing up pillboxes, guarding an explosives dump, clearing rubble from streets, removing mines from the Kall trail, and providing *local* security for the Kall bridge. It was to perform additionally any other normal engineer task that might be required of it. The 20th Engineer Combat Battalion was further required to complete its duties using only light vehicles and to provide for its own security.

Its mission was thus grossly overextended. To make matters worse, its commander, Lieutenant Colonel Jonathan Sonnefield, assigned tasks piecemeal to his platoons, which resulted in his company commanders losing control of their own platoons, just as he lost control of his companies when General Davis and Colonel Daley, commander of the 1171st, later began to assign them to combat as infantry. When superior officers bypass the chain of command to give orders to lower organizations, commanders at every level suffer.

Even when his men suddenly became infantrymen, Sonnefield continually tried to provide engineer support for the 112th Infantry Regiment. This effort to execute both missions was unrealistic and ignored basic military doctrine, which requires that when engineers are called upon to fight as infantry, their engineer support thereafter must be limited to requirements necessary for the infantry mission of their *own* unit.[47]

Other engineers heard noises from the fire fight as enemy soldiers destroyed the two squads of Lieutenant Johns. Captain Walter Mahaley, commander of C Company; First Lieutenant Clarence White, one of his platoon leaders; and their men waited along the trail until sounds of combat died away. Carefully they pressed on down the roadway, searching for friendly troops. They reached the former site of the 112th Infantry Regiment's command post, not knowing it had been relocated still farther forward before darkness fell. Several vehicles remained parked there, persuading Captain Mahaley that the half-underground shelter, which Germans had used as an officers' billet, was still functioning. Entering, he found it abandoned. The captain was upset to learn they had moved out without notifying engineers. It was part of a pattern south of the Kall—indeed, everywhere within the combat area of the 28th Infantry Division. No coordination existed among units, and no efforts were made to do so, a result of poor standing operating procedures and constant communications breakdowns.

Mahaley and his men went on into Kommerscheidt and came upon a lieutenant and crews of a 57mm antitank gun site. Mahaley asked them for protection of their guns for his engineers. Since it was no longer possible to do roadwork, Mahaley reasoned that his men could at least do something worthwhile if they aided the very much understrength crews of the antitank guns.

Mahaley's men began digging in. As the night waned, stragglers from the decimated 1st and 3rd battalions filtered back. Seeing other friendly troops, stragglers decided to stay with them and dug foxholes for themselves. Mahaley may have been among the first to realize a new predicament faced by all those south of the Kall. "We were cut off," he said. "We realized this in daylight when I tried to get patrols out and they were unable to cross the valley."[48]

German records reflected their growing optimism. Victory in the Hürtgen Forest was within their grasp. Battalion *Onnen* pressed its attack. *89th Division* command post received glowing reports from *1056th Regiment* as its reconnaissance and combat patrols turned in news of battle gains. Elements of Battalions *Wolf* and *Wilschewsky* "with their commanders at the head of their troops" overpowered bitter and stubborn American resistance and broke into the eastern part of Kommerscheidt.

"Battle proceeds with almost unbelievable intensity," German records claimed. "House after house must be stormed again and again as enemy soldiers shoot from a cellar or attic window." German pincers gradually shut down the vital Kall MSR. "Behind the enemy the gap is being slowly closed. He tries with all his force to break out in several places but is repulsed everywhere."

Information released to its troops by the *89th Infantry Division* became almost euphoric. "Enemy tanks are again pushing forward but cannot break the spirit of our men. The first prisoners of war are brought in; isolated in SCHMIDT they withdrew to the woods southeast of town. Others come in from KOMMERSCHEIDT. The number is slowly growing: first 7, then 9, then 15. A few comrades, who had fallen into enemy hands, are freed. Then the results of a hard day's battle are learned: 41 PWs, two Sherman tanks knocked out, one damaged, one plane shot down. That night patrols are sent against the enemy from all directions. He cannot be permitted to rest. Our artillery provides continuous and successful harassing fire."[49] As is often the case for Army information releases past and present, those claims were extravagant. Only their tone was correct. The Germans made days disastrous and nights merciless for American soldiers who came to believe that if hell existed, they were in its midst. And at the command post of the 28th Infantry Division in Rott, General Cota remained totally unaware of impending disaster.

(above) Stateside training for troops of the 28th Infantry Division prior to being sent overseas during World War II. These men still wear the American helmet utilized during the previous war.

(below) A view looking south along a portion of the Siegfried Line fortifications of western Germany. The 28th Infantry Division penetrated these "dragon's teeth" anti-tank barriers on the morning of 13 September 1944.

As American troops entered the borders of Germany, they were frequently met by signs such as the one in this photo, which proclaims "Death to the Destroyers of Europe."

The following series of four photos shows the muddy terrain of the Hurtgen with which members of the 28th Infantry Division had to contend during the fighting in the Schmidt sector.

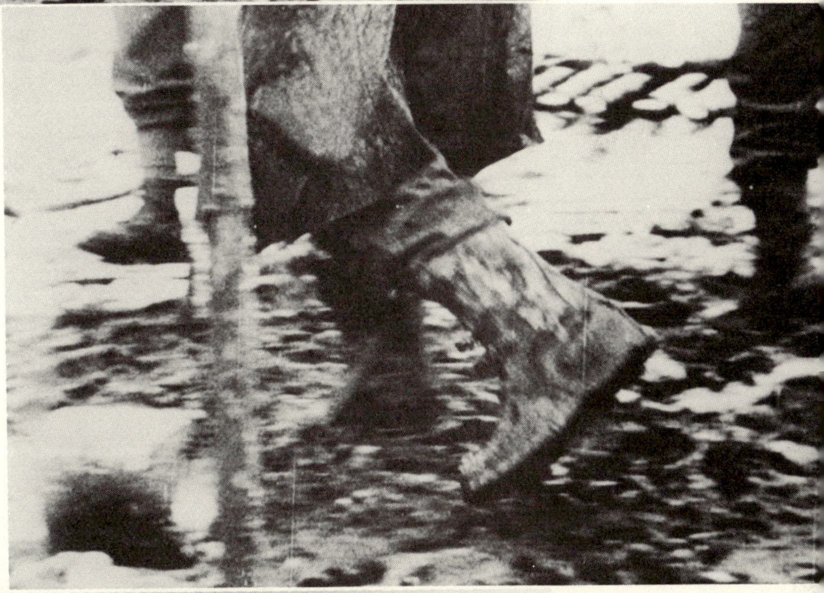

Roads and trails were so muddy that vehicles frequently bogged down. In these four photos an engineer unit lays down a corduroy road in an effort to defeat "General Mud."

Two views of a camouflaged American artillery battery in operation.

Two views of American soldiers warily dashing through the pine forests of the Hürtgen during an attack.

Although the photos are of poor quality, these are three views of American filler replacements marching down the Kall trail on their way into combat.

(right) The church steeple at Vossenack in flames during the course of the battle.

(below) A unit moves forward through Vossenack, its men well-spread out on both sides of the road.

American M-10 self-propelled tank destroyers of the 893rd Tank Destroyer Battalion move up through the Hürtgen Forest on their way toward Schmidt, Germany, where they will go into combat against German tank units there, 4 November 1944.

Backed by the armored support of a Sherman M-4 tank, infantrymen of the 28th Division advance with flame throwers toward a pillbox in the Siegfried Line to mop up any last signs of enemy resistance.

An explosion of white phosphorus directly in front of a kneeling American infantryman.

A rifleman drawing a bead on a target during the fierce forest fighting.

(left) Major General Norman D. "Dutch" Cota, commander of the 28th Infantry Division, strikes a formal pose for the photographer.

(below) General Dwight D. Eisenhower visits Major General "Dutch" Cota at his command post at Rott. "Ike's" famous smile is nowhere in evidence as he learns of the disasters besetting the 28th Infantry Division.

Brigadier General George A. Davis, Assistant Division Commander of the 28th Infantry Division.

Lieutenant Colonel Carl L. Peterson became commanding officer of the 112th Infantry Regiment on 10 September 1944. Relieved by General Cota and wounded during his trip back from the front, he was replaced by Colonel Nelson.

Colonel Gustin Nelson, commanding officer of the 112 Infantry Regiment during the closing phases of the attack in the Hürtgen.

Lieutenant Colonel Daniel B. Strickler commanded the 109th Infantry Regiment during the Schmidt battle.

8

"The saddest sight I have ever seen"

6 November 1944 (Part One)

American forces faced disaster across the entire Vossenack–Kommerscheidt front as night gave way to the first light of dawn. Vehicles moved forward with supplies from rear areas along mud-sluiced roads, the cold penetrating their drivers' clothing. Four-wheel-drive gearboxes chattered as wheels sank hub deep in mud, slewing carryall trucks and jeeps erratically along roadways. To the south the brittle beauty of the wintry morning echoed to deadly artillery explosions.

On the Vossenack ridge, men of 2nd Battalion, 112th Infantry, shivered in their exposed foxholes and huddled deeper to escape the frosty morning wind. They had grown to dread mornings, which were inevitably heralded by a hail of German artillery rounds fired at them with card-index certitude. Minds benumbed by pervading cold, they finally sensed that this day was different. Then they realized what it was. Around them was only silence.

"Because it was so unusual," said Lieutenant Clyde Johnson, a weapons platoon leader in G Company, "we became suspicious and I mentioned the oddness of this fact to one of my sergeants. No sooner had I said this than one of our men was hit by small arms fire and let go with a piercing scream. This further frayed our already frazzled nerves."[1]

Corporal Joe Philpot, a front-line company clerk in G Company, remembered nothing unusual about the preceding night, interspersed as it had been by periodic explosions from German harassing artillery fire, but he also noted the strange lack of heavy shelling that morning. Then, about dawn, a sudden burst of enemy small-arms fire hit men of George Company "from all sides, even from behind."[2]

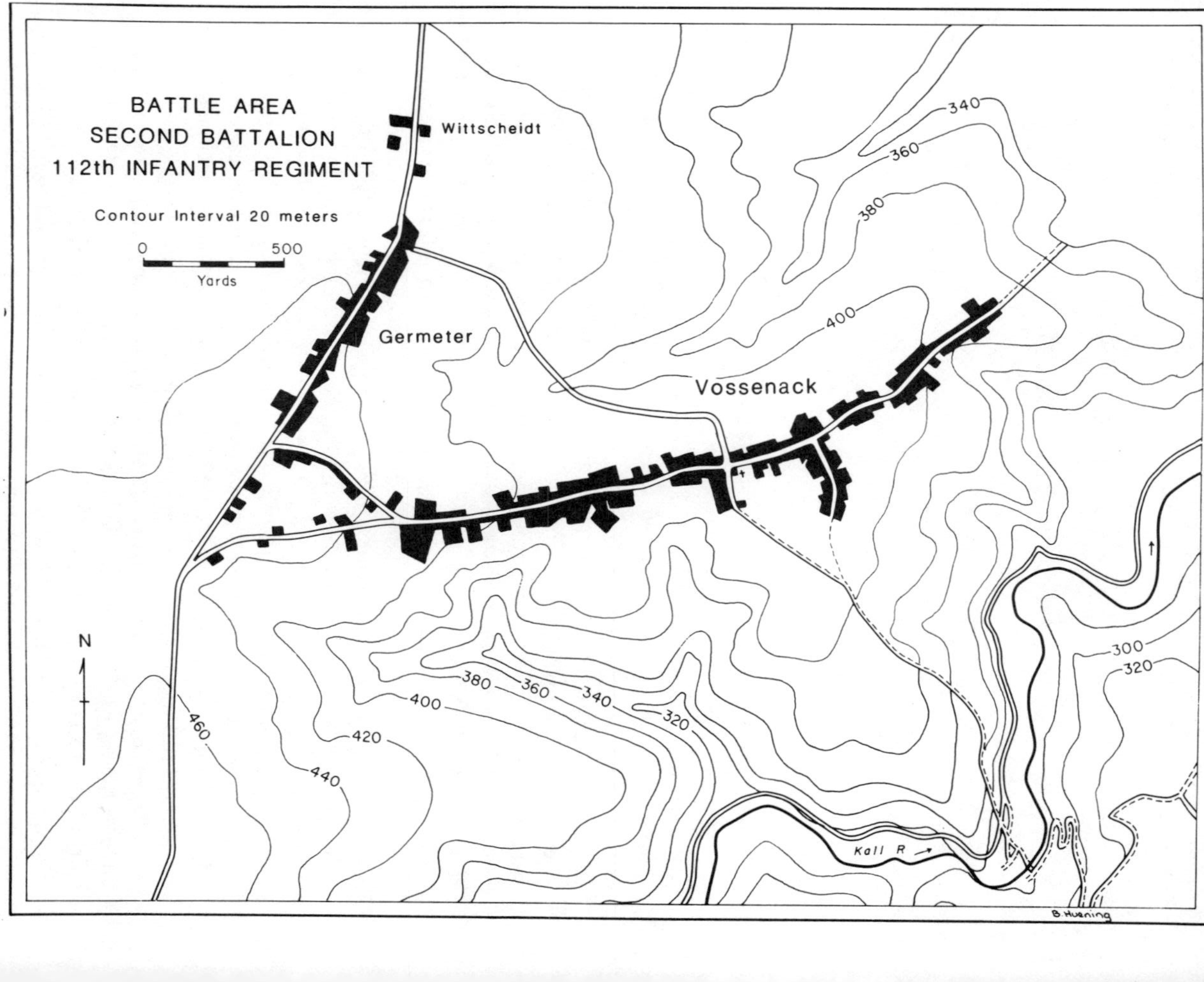
BATTLE AREA
SECOND BATTALION
112th INFANTRY REGIMENT
Contour Interval 20 meters
0
500
Yards
Wittscheidt
Germeter
Vossenack
340
360
380
400
300
320
380
360
340
320
400
420
440
460
Kall R
N
B. Huening

Then the morning barrage finally began. It was more than those tormented soldiers could take. They had already given far more than anyone had a right to expect through the preceding five days as they occupied positions on the Vossenack ridge. Now it was at an end. Primal drives surged to the forefront of their minds. They could only accept their screaming need to protect themselves.

Philpot and First Lieutenant Julian Ferrier, executive officer of George Company, were alone in their cellar command post. Hearing unusual sounds, they went upstairs into the lower floor of the ruined house above them. Looking outside, they saw their buddies darting around in the half light. Those on the company's flanks were pulling back, trying to make an orderly withdrawal. In the middle were other men, all headed west, making a general exodus in the midst of great confusion. Most seemed not to know what was happening, but as their friends pulled out they moved back also, "some even trotting." Philpot and Ferrier broke out a window of the house, quickly jumped to the ground outside, and ran over to see what they could do. They found out only that everyone was leaving, so they went along with the others. Some few tried to take up occasional defensive positions, but most kept moving steadily back, retreating toward the Vossenack church.[3]

Defensive lines began to disintegrate elsewhere as well. Lieutenant Howard Davis, commander of an M-10 tank destroyer parked on the forward slope of the ridge, saw infantrymen passing his vehicle as they moved back from their foxholes. "I stopped three or four and asked if they had orders to withdraw," he said. "No," they replied, "but the Germans are sending direct high explosive fire at their holes, blowing them out of their holes."

At about 0700 hours,* two soldiers ran toward Davis' M-10. "All out of breath," they stopped momentarily "to tell me no more men were left in the line. I could see no sign of friendly life or activity. We remained in position for an hour or so. No enemy attack materialized." Finally, unwilling to remain where he was without infantry support, Davis gave orders for his tank destroyers to pull back.[4]

Davis was wrong about German infantrymen. Although they may not have launched an attack, they did move forward at just about first light that fatal morning, following American troopers and moving into their deserted positions. Captain John Pruden, executive officer and acting commander of 2nd Battalion, reported sightings of enemy soldiers moving past foxholes occupied by men of G Company before daylight. Those GIs pulled back in panic. Others, seeing them flee, started to follow. That, Pruden believed, was the start of the rout.[5]

Captain Ed Lutz of the engineers saw "a general exodus" of infantry passing his position at the west end of Vossenack at about 0730 hours. "We tried to get the situation from them but they were in a hurry. . . . They said they

*Sunrise on 6 November came at 0735, so at 0700 it was just getting light.

were pulling out and claimed Germans were all over their area." Further questioning was futile, Lutz said. "They did not pause long. . . . They appeared to be sadly disorganized. There were officers among them. We could get no coherent story."

Lutz sent his administrative officer, Second Lieutenant Henry Gray, forward to learn as much as he could. He came back promptly and told Lutz the infantry positions to the east were being rapidly vacated. "He had met a captain there who told him that he and the small group of men with him were the last ones around and that they were leaving." Gray told Lutz, "the captain almost knocked him down in getting out." Lutz looked around. "The tanks in and around Vossenack were also pulling out. Then we decided we had better withdraw too." As they evacuated, a German artillery shell killed Lieutenant Gray and knocked Lutz unconscious, deafening him for nearly five hours.[6]

Company G occupied the left portion of the Vossenack ridge's nose; F Company held onto the right section. Fox Company commander, Lieutenant Eldeen Kauffman, saw G Company men running toward the rear as early as 0630. "I had a suspicion of what had happened and realized the situation was critical," Kauffman said. He knew there was no way his men could retain their tenuous hold on the ridge with their left flank exposed. "I told my people to move out for we were receiving small arms fire . . . and I was afraid we might be wiped out or captured." One group of his men was unable to withdraw. Pinned down by advancing Germans, they were killed or captured.*

Kauffman ordered his men to retreat in orderly fashion, but complained "I had no control" over them. When they reached the "safety" of Vossenack, most continued on through town toward Germeter, despite Kauffman's efforts.[7]

Fox Company's Staff Sergeant Charles Cascarano knew how upset his men were. The company had received several replacements, all of whom were now scared. As the company moved back, many of them disappeared. "I don't know what happened to them," Cascarano said. He could see other men running west down the ridge road. "Everyone was excited and nervous." Cascarano followed them back to Germeter, where they finally all stopped, safe at last.[8]

At about 0730 that morning, Captain Charles Crain, commander of H Company, saw men from Dog Company "racing past our positions. From their shattered and scared attitudes, it was evident that the unmerciful shelling had finally broken their nerves. All hell had broken loose and the situation was very confused. I called battalion and was told to hold. We did. E and F

*Two of the captured men, Staff Sergeant George A. Christian and Corporal James Klinginsmith, were held under loose guard in a nearby house. At nightfall, they managed to escape and worked their way down the draw to the east, ultimately reaching the safety of their own positions under artillery fire from both the Germans and their own guns. The return trip took them nearly a day.

pulled out. We managed to get our machine gun section out too. Then I told the mortar sections to pull back and we did so also."[9]

Everywhere men were running for some ephemeral place of safety. "I don't know why they withdrew," mused Captain James Nesbitt, battalion S-1 personnel officer, "for battalion had orders to stay in position regardless."[10]

Easy Company's Lieutenant James Condon had a ringside seat for what happened. At about 0700 hours his radio operator received a message informing them that Germans were attacking and George Company was retreating. Two minutes later another message confirmed the first. Outside the command post fell repeated rounds from a barrage.

"I came up out of my cellar command post," Condon related, "in an effort to find out the situation and saw the saddest sight I have ever seen. Down the road from the east came men from F, G and E companies; pushing, shoving, throwing away equipment, trying to outrace the artillery and each other down the main road, all in a frantic effort to escape. They were all scared and excited, some were terror-stricken. Most of them were running. Some were helping the slightly wounded to run and many of the badly wounded men, probably hit by artillery, were lying in the road where they fell, screaming for help. It was a heart breaking, demoralizing scene."[11] Retreating men tossed officers and noncoms about like chaff before the wind.

Captain Nesbitt concurred. "There was no sense fooling ourselves about it," he said. "It was a disorderly retreat. The men were going back pell-mell. . . . No matter what we did to build up a line, they kept drifting back to the rear."[12]

Jim Condon and Lieutenant Melvin Barrilleaux, commander of Easy Company, decided there was probably little they could do. Whatever had caused the rout, their chances of stopping or slowing it were slight. "From the passing stream of men," said Condon, "we were able to gather garbled bits of information that the enemy was attacking." He was not convinced. "It is my opinion that either there was no attack or one too small to cause such a rout. I feel the men simply had had too much. They could not stand any more of the hell of lying in a foxhole waiting to be killed." Condon and Barrilleaux decided it was time to move Easy Company west as well.[13]

As they moved through town, Captain Nesbitt ran out to them from the battalion command post. He ordered Condon and Barrilleaux to stop as many men as they could and establish a temporary line of defense along both sides of the road. The area of the command post now became the American front line.

German soldiers infiltrated into Vossenack in the footsteps of retreating Americans. "I don't think there was any real attack," Condon said. "The Germans just seized this opportunity when our troops broke and reoccupied the town."[14] All the while, artillery fire fell on the frightened and miserable defenders of 2nd Battalion.

Clifton Beggs, a first lieutenant and platoon leader in Easy Company, was shocked by the sudden withdrawal. Warned by a lookout in the hayloft of a commandeered barn that men were running west along the street, Beggs ran out into their midst. "I managed to stop a few, tried to question them, but the only thing I could get out of them was that G Company was withdrawing. The men were wild-eyed and scared, the first few were running helter-skelter, and no one seemed to know what to do." He saw Barrilleaux and Kauffman, and the three officers went into a huddle. With none of them able to halt the flight, they decided to follow it.[15]

When "all hell broke loose," Lieutenant Johnson and two other men were in the George Company command post. It was a hole burrowed into the earth, its top concealed by a well-camouflaged cover. "Suddenly we heard a great deal of commotion and a lot of our men hollering and sounds of running. We didn't know what had happened." Johnson told the two men with him, Technical Sergeant Kenneth Jones and PFC I. Ortiz, to go outside with him. As they started to clamber out, a German soldier stepped on the hole's cover and stopped.

"He hollered something, probably a command, so we decided to lay low," Johnson said. "From the confusion and commotion we decided the Germans had come up through the woods on the left and overrun us. We were cut off." They remained hidden in their hole from 0800 to 2000 hours that night. "All the while we could hear German voices around us and our tanks far off in the west. We did not know what our chances were, but kept hoping someone would come back to help us."

No one did, and the hours slowly passed. Using their limited observation, the three men saw about 35 Germans not far away as they established for themselves a battalion command post. Without moving, Johnson and the others had passed from a position in their own front lines to one in the rear area of an enemy battalion! It was a nerve-racking ordeal to wait quietly, peeping out from time to time, watching a sentry pacing up and down. "The thing which tried our nerves," Johnson recalled, "was a God-damned chicken which wandered around our hole all day long, scratching intermittently. It always sounded like a man crawling and nearly drove us crazy."

The trapped men noticed that enemy sentries were changed every two hours, making a lot of noise in the process. They decided to make a break for their own lines during a changing of the guard. After dark, they removed part of the roof from their shelter and, at 2000 hours, they crept out. Even the heavens seemed against them. For a change, no rain was falling, and stars shone brightly in the night sky. They crawled through the oozy mud of a pigpen, noting that two houses and an orchard that had stood nearby that morning simply no longer existed, shelled into atoms.

Moving on their hands and knees, they edged rearward past Germans scattered throughout the woods. The three soldiers were grateful that their enemies were careless, striking lights and shouting to one another. Occasionally they tried to move standing up, but each time some German among the tree boles spotted them and fired. They finally made their way along the draw north of Vossenack until they at last staggered into Germeter, where they spent the few remaining hours of darkness with a chemical mortar unit.[16]

Others that day did not fare so well. At the battalion command post west of the church, Captain Pruden and Captain Nesbitt vainly tried to staunch the flow of men toward Germeter. "We rushed into the street to hold retreating men up," Pruden recalled. "We were able to corral men for a time but, when no one was looking, our hoped-for defensive line dissipated as men took off again singly and in pairs."

By 0930 hours their efforts began to pay off as they managed to hold a few frantic men in place. "A few of the men were rational," Pruden observed, "all were shocked, but the majority instinctively carried their weapons with them. As we built up a fire base, we sent word to the rear and hoped for help."[17] Barrilleaux had 30 men from Easy Company.[18] Kauffman had 20 men of F Company.[19] Lieutenant Beggs came with 10 stragglers from E Company.[20]

Again disaster struck. Barrilleaux stood talking with Beggs and others near the entrance to the battalion command post. An American artillery barrage landed among them, shrapnel striking Barrilleaux. "I had about a dozen men with me in good spirits," he said, "who were kidding each other. . . . Then our own artillery started falling on us. I was hit in the face and leg." He was evacuated to a Germeter aid station, his time in Hürtgen's hell at an end.[21]

Sergeant Donald Nelson, an Easy Company platoon sergeant, lay with others behind a crumbled stone wall opposite the command post. When artillery rounds fell, he and those with him withdrew into an old house with a connecting barn. A shell hit the barn, injuring PFC Edward Shoronsky, PFC William Powers, PFC Garland Dockeny, and PFC Lawrence Whiteman. Powers was hit in the eye, shin, leg, and head; Dockeny in the legs; Whiteman received shrapnel splinters across his entire body. "I had no platoon left," lamented Nelson, "so withdrew to the aid station in Germeter," taking the wounded with him. Shoronsky died there following his evacuation.[22]

First Lieutenant Norman Woodal, Easy Company platoon leader, was evacuated with combat exhaustion. Lieutenant Beggs was wounded, treated at Germeter, and returned to action that afternoon.[23] At the aid station, officers stopped all the men they could find and formed them into groups to lead back into Vossenack.[24]

"We would gather up fifty or sixty or seventy men from the Germeter area and start forward with them," Condon testified. "By the time we arrived back in Vossenack so many had disappeared that we might arrive with perhaps four to six. The men scuttled for cellars and other places of hiding. They were tired and scared and cold and wanted no more of war for that time."[25] Lieutenant Kauffman agreed. "At every opportunity they slipped away for their nerves were in a sad state, but we kept bringing them back, forcing them and ourselves to remain."[26]

For a time that morning both American and German artillery fell silent.

Captain Pruden realized German soldiers had infiltrated as far forward as the church. He knew his thin line of GIs could not long contain them, but he decided they must try to fight it out as long as possible. "At least," he said, "it was better to see some German infantrymen than experiencing that goddam consistent artillery fire."[27] But not much. No one knew what was going on. Radio calls to the rear for help brought no succor. Casualties mounted and the tiny American force dwindled as men drifted away one or two at a time.[28]

Combat is inevitably perilous and frightening. Men have always deserted in the face of the enemy. Those who remained have been frightened, cowering and trembling under threat of death or injury. This has been a truism of history since the dawn of time. In all the annals of American history, however, widespread routs such as those that occurred at Schmidt on 4 November and in Vossenack on 6 November have been extremely rare. Soldiers normally continue to fight, even to death, no matter how awesome are the forces confronting them. Those two routs are what make this battle so rare.

General Davis appeared to be both furious and frantic. Hard information was difficult to come by. He knew American forces were in a rout from Vossenack, yet that ridge and hamlet *had* to be held to protect the left flank of the penetration south of the Kall, which itself was in grave trouble.

The previous day Davis had met with Colonel Sam Mays, battalion commander of the TDs. The general inquired of Mays where his M-10s were located in Vossenack. Mays replied that none were there. No position in town was suitable for them. There were no visible targets for them to fire at and they drew German fire whenever they moved or exposed themselves. They must, argued the colonel, be conserved and not unnecessarily expended, since they might later be needed to reinforce Kommerscheidt or to defend Vossenack from enemy tank attack.

General Davis was displeased by Mays' response and ordered Mays to send one platoon of destroyers to the eastern nose of the Vossenack ridge. It was that group of M-10s, led by Lieutenant Davis, that spotted GIs withdrawing from their foxholes under cover of darkness early that morning of the rout.

When the retreat began, General Davis once again sought out Colonel Mays. Why, he asked, were destroyers not in firing position on the ridge? Mays patiently explained. M-10s were targets of frequent German fire, both direct and indirect, from commanding heights to the northeast, southeast, and east. Crews out there with Lieutenant Davis saw no targets. Subjected to intense artillery fire in the early daylight, they withdrew to cover.

His reply irritated General Davis. Mays' attitude seemed to be that it was acceptable for infantrymen to die, but no one should hurt his armored toys. There were, Davis said, entirely too many people in rear areas. Mays withdrew his destroyers contrary to Davis' own express orders. He wanted those guns out front and wanted them there "now!" Mays countered that open-turret weapons should not be exposed to unnecessary hazards. General Davis was beyond allowing such concerns to interest him. The whole mission of the 28th faced disaster, and this lieutenant colonel was upset about dangers of open turrets. Davis ordered all of B Company TDs into Vossenack. M-10s were, he said, necessary for the morale of suffering infantrymen as they struggled to maintain a precarious hold on western Vossenack. Both tanks and TDs "*would be there.*"[29]

They went. Captain Cole, commander of the TD reconnaissance company, told Lieutenant Davis to go back into Vossenack and "cruise around," firing at any enemy positions he could locate.[30] Eight remaining tanks of C Company also arrived. They entered Vossenack in time to see infantrymen running toward the rear. C Company tanks were reinforced by others from B Company. Those crews, not knowing the situation, came into town firing their tank turret cannons, hit some houses used as shelters by their own troops, and caused several casualties.[31]

First Lieutenant Carl Anderson, a B Company tank platoon leader, led his M-4s forward. He saw about 20 infantrymen running to the rear along the Vossenack road. Continuing into town, Anderson put his platoon in position on the crest of a rise just east of the church. They received mortar fire from Brandenberg and the draw northeast of Vossenack. "We started shooting, continued forward, began receiving mortar fire. . . . I started withdrawing slowly, firing as I went at some gun flashes at a range of about 3,000 yards."

Captain George West, commander of C Company, drove his tank up beside Anderson's and shouted, "You shot your own infantry in the back and now you are running off and leaving them." Anderson asked what he should do, and West ordered him back into the positions from which he had just withdrawn. Then came sudden artillery and mortar fire on them. West turned his tank around and yelled at Anderson, "Let's get the hell out of here." They withdrew to the area of the church.

A little later, Captain George Granger, B Company tank commander, saw Captain West standing in the turret of his tank. Granger pulled alongside and asked West for a situation report. "Counterattack," replied West. Granger inquired where their infantry were located. West didn't know. What sort of fire were the tanks drawing? "Big mortars," said West, which came from the north. As Granger looked around for possible locations of those mortars, a very heavy round came in and exploded with shocking force, causing him to flinch and duck. As the dust settled, he turned back to continue talking with West. There was little use. "When I turned around . . . the hatches on his turret were gone and so was he, the explosion blowing his head off."

Only moments later, Granger heard the voice of General Davis sounding through the speaker of his tank radio asking for a situation report. Granger replied that he didn't know what to say. Another tanker broke in on the radio link crying out, "We're all alone out here." Then a nearby tank, struck by direct fire, exploded and burned furiously. Granger headed his tank toward the command post of 2nd Battalion.[32]

Arriving at the command post, Granger found Lieutenant Colonel Theodore Hatzfeld, the battalion commander, sitting in dazed silence, his face resting in his hands. "I asked him for the situation but received no reply," Granger recalled. Captain Pruden asked Granger to identify himself and the tanker replied he had tanks outside to use in reinforcing the infantry effort. After Pruden filled him in on their hopeless condition, Granger went back to his tank.

One of his crews, in a tank on the north flank of town, radioed Granger. "Captain, it's getting too hot to handle out here. We're just taking fire and doing no good." Granger told them to get out quickly.

At 1130 hours, in Anderson's tank, Sergeant Arthur Claugh suddenly opened fire with his machine guns on buildings to his immediate front. Anderson shouted at him, asking what his target was. "Krauts!" the sergeant yelled back. "Are you sure?" "Hell, yes, I'm sure . . . Sir," responded an irritated Claugh.[33]

By 1100 hours tankers built up a secondary line of defense astride the Vossenack road some 200 yards west of the thin force of infantrymen around 2nd Battalion's command post.[34] German artillery concentrated with devastating accuracy on the area in American hands west of the church. Casualty lists mounted but the aid station was in Germeter and litter bearers could move wounded soldiers there only after nightfall to provide themselves with a minimum of concealment.[35]

Between 1100 and 1200 hours, American artillerymen once again miscalculated, shelling their own men. Compounding the GIs' agony, 4.2-inch mortars dropped white phosphorus shells near the command post, setting afire the clothing of two men. It was not enough to be asked to face the enemy. GIs in Vossenack had to fear their own forces as well.[36]

Early in the afternoon, Colonel Hatzfeld, while sitting hopelessly in the battalion command post, finally collapsed into tears. So many hours had gone by without the arrival of reinforcements he had earlier asked for. In a state of shock, Hatzfeld left for Germeter with the avowed intention of obtaining help. It was, said his S-1 personnel officer, Captain Nesbitt, "the last we ever saw of him."[37]

When he arrived at the Germeter aid station in hasty dismay, medics tagged Hatzfeld as a casualty with a sprained ankle.[38] According to Captain Pruden, Hatzfeld was of little assistance after the first two days of incessant artillery fire. Overwhelmed with grief at the terrible ordeal visited upon his battalion, he suffered almost complete nervous collapse.[39]

German attackers poured small-arms and artillery fire upon weary American troops. Buildings shattered with explosive force as shells impacted upon them. *Wehrmacht* soldiers moved warily westward from one pile of rubble to the next, the angry hammer of Spandaus interspersed with the crack of Mauser rifles. Wounded troops cried out in agony, their tones of dismay muted by the snarl of shells from tank turret guns. Townspeople unfortunate enough to have been caught in this maelstrom before they could flee to neighboring towns, hid where they could, or died. Many of them crouched in cellars of houses and watched or listened to the destruction of their homes. One group of 14 hid for several days inside a community privy made of brick, one of the few buildings in Vossenack that emerged unscathed from this spate of carnage.[40] They would have appreciated the truth of an old Spanish proverb: *No son soldados todos los que van a la guerra* (All who go to war are not soldiers).

While maneuvering through Vossenack's narrow east–west street, an M-10 from Lieutenant Davis' platoon backed into a building, shattered its wall, and crashed through into the cellar, its gun pointing straight up into the air like an anti-aircraft mounting.*[41]

At 1430 hours, General Davis was back at Colonel Mays' command post. The general believed in staying in touch with new developments. Why, he asked Mays, had his outfit dropped an M-10 into a cellar? Why were other destroyers not in firing positions? Mays protested that they were sitting targets in Vossenack and unable to function there as they should. If so, the general responded, then Mays and his men evidently didn't know how to make effective use of camouflage! With that, the furious general departed. He had other pressures as well. He *had* to find additional infantrymen to throw into the Vossenack breach to bolster crumbling defenses there. Where could he find them?

Colonel Mays was in a quandary. Vossenack and its ridge were far from ideal terrain for his tank destroyers, yet the general had again ordered him to keep them there. Infantry morale, said Davis, was the vital principle they must keep in mind. Mays was more concerned about his own crews than riflemen. He sought out Major Bodine, the divisional antitank officer, and the two men went to see Brigadier General Basil Perry, commander of 28th Division artillery. They talked with him about Mays' difficulty with General Davis. "We could see no gain in having tank destroyers in town except for possible use against sneak attacks during daylight hours of limited visibility." Although General Perry tended to agree and seemed "perturbed" about Davis' requirements, he told Bodine and Mays that if they felt TDs were

---

*That night, Lieutenant Davis reported, they tried to retrieve the destroyer from the cellar. A T-2 tracked tow vehicle came forward from the battalion rear area to evacuate it and fastened its tow cables onto the disabled M-10. The TD gunned its motor to aid the T-2 in pulling it out of the cellar. Moments later, an enemy mortar round landed on the nose of the TD, killing the driver of the T-2 and wounding his assistant. The explosion also blew an arm off a motor sergeant who was hanging onto the TD turret to assist in the operation. Further efforts were abandoned for the night. Davis noted that as long as his vehicles remained quiet, there was very little enemy artillery fire. The minute they started their engines, artillery shells began to land around them.

improperly employed they should report it through channels rather than to him. Coming to him was a breach of the chain of command and was not the way to proceed.

General Perry inquired as to the number of casualties inflicted on destroyer crews thus far. Colonel Mays told him of the TD mishap and the added calamity when the T-2 tried to rescue it from the cellar. Yes, General Perry responded, but what had Mays lost by having his destroyers in Vossenack? The colonel admitted that no other personnel had been lost "so far," but "we could surely expect to suffer casualties with open turrets and the constant shelling in Vossenack." Mays pointed out how in earlier campaigns his crews suffered injuries in open M-10 turrets during mortar barrages.

General Perry suggested his men cover their turrets with logs and sandbags to reduce such possibilities. Mays returned to his basic argument. "We did not feel that morale for the infantry was sufficient reason to justify the presence of tank destroyers in town." General Perry offered no further assistance and so Mays and Bodine returned to the 893rd command post.

Upon arrival there, Mays found a message from General Davis requiring the colonel to report to him at once. An alarmed Mays sought out the general, perhaps wondering how he had learned so quickly of his conversation with Perry. That was not the issue on General Davis' mind. How many TDs, the assistant division commander inquired, did Mays have in Kommerscheidt? Mays was nonplussed. He was expecting the general to ask him once again about Vossenack. Sam Mays, in his response, employed what can only be described as evasive tactics. "We reminded the general we had been unable to get a platoon of B Company TDs down the trail for it was covered by hostile infantry, mines, wrecked weasels, and a caterpillar bulldozer." The road itself was getting worse due to rain. If he tried to send tracked vehicles down the trail, they might cause a section of it to slough off, thus denying it to other traffic.

By now General Davis had grounds to court-martial Colonel Mays. The whole operation of the 28th Infantry Division was coming apart, and the commander of the tank destroyer battalion was expressing his "worry" over some dirt caving away to avoid carrying out command orders. But Davis did not act, and after some further talk, Colonel Mays departed.[42]

While Colonel Mays talked with General Perry trying to find a way to circumvent General Davis' requirements, the assistant division commander found the additional "infantrymen" he needed to pour into the battle for Vossenack. It did not take long for word of his actions to spread to the command post of 2nd Battalion on the mutilated street west of the church: The engineers were coming!

It was the first good news of the day for weary infantry defenders. They whispered excitedly that within perhaps 45 minutes a battalion of engineers would reinforce them. "So confused and excited was everyone that some men misinterpreted this as meaning a relief and took off for the rear."[43]

Such news came none too soon. Prior to hearing about the engineers, Captain Pruden said, it looked as though all American defenders in town would be captured. As a consequence, Pruden radioed the aid station in Germeter to send medics forward to evacuate the wounded, scores of whom lay in and about the command post "screaming and moaning, most in horrible condition." In heroic efforts, medics did a yeoman job, evacuating about 40 men. Meanwhile, German soldiers were so close to the command post that "we could hear their guttural screaming and yelling in the vicinity of the church."[44]

As early as 0900 hours, 6 November, Lieutenant Colonel Carl Isley, commander of the 146th Engineer Combat Battalion, received a message from his headquarters, the 1171st Engineer Combat Group, that General George Davis wanted men of the 146th on two-hour alert for possible use as infantrymen. Most of Isley's men were scattered through the combat area, laboring on maintenance roadwork. He knew it would take perhaps three hours to gather them all in. As they reported back, they still wore their yellow boots and overshoes. Their company commanders arranged for supply sergeants to issue them weapons and basic ammunition loads.[45]

"I had," Isley remembered, "no notion of where we were going or how we would be used until we got into Vossenack except for the general term 'to be used as Infantry.'" He went to see his group commander, Colonel Ed Daley, who wanted to know where Isley's men were located. When Isley told him, Daley rejoined, "Let's get going," and they left to check on them.[46]

The two men headed for a draw outside Germeter where Isley's A and C companies were forming up. The two officers talked with Captain Vincent Wall, commander of C Company, and Captain Sam Ball, Jr., commander of A Company. The two captains indicated they needed at least half an hour to get their men ready to march into combat. Isley and Daley left for Vossenack. As they entered the western fringe of town they encountered a barrage from enemy guns and took shelter among the rubble of the same house into which the M-10 had earlier fallen. One man hid on each side of the destroyer. Isley heard a "plunk," and looking around, he saw Colonel Daley fussing with his pant leg where he had been nicked by a piece of shrapnel.[47]

As the barrage lifted, Isley and Daley worked their way to the infantry battalion command post and spoke there with Captain Pruden. He told them he had only about 40 men left. His force was falling back, no longer able to hold in the face of a determined German advance. He and all his men, he said, were suffering from combat exhaustion. He would have to withdraw unless reinforced within 30 minutes. Colonel Isley asked for an hour. He told Pruden he must get back to his troops, tell them their mission, and get them moving forward. A distraught Pruden pled with him to hurry.[48]

As Isley made his way back toward A and C company engineers near Germeter, he met his S-3 operations officer, Major Willard Baker, and Captain Sam Ball moving forward with A Company. Baker and Ball quickly filled Isley in. General Davis had been unwilling simply to issue orders to Daley's 1171st Headquarters and wait for the chain of command to take effect. The general had driven into their area, they said. Davis asked Major Baker for the unit designation of the men around him.

"I remember distinctly what he said," Captain Ball related. The general's words were terse: "Go in. Drive the enemy out of the town. Move. Get going."[49]

Colonel Isley quickly briefed Baker and Ball on what he knew, but he could tell them little. The situation in Vossenack was desperate and "we were just to go in and assist the Infantry."[50] Isley later confided his dismay: "No time was given to learn the enemy situation, issue orders, or organize in any way. But General Davis insisted violently that Major Baker get the men moving at once. Baker ordered Captain Ball forward and told Captain Wall to bring Company C as soon as possible."[51]

The engineers, marching in a column of platoons, one file on each side of the road, moved toward Vossenack, which lay about a mile away. Captain Ball commented, "I gave orders hastily as we moved along. It was pretty tough to give them notice on the fly and when there was a fair amount of artillery coming in. . . . We moved as best we could under the artillery. When it came close, we'd hit the dirt til it let up, move on, repeating this several times. . . . Tanks were also moving into town, going pretty fast. One of them forced me to jump into a ditch."[52]

General Davis was not finished. Some distance from the spot where he had talked with Major Baker, he found C Company engineers and a platoon of B Company, 1340th Engineer Combat Battalion. He issued orders to them also to deploy as infantry.

Colonel Daley, his S-3 operations officer; Major Robert Argus; and Lieutenant Colonel Jonathan Sonnefield, commander of 20th Engineers, set out to find the general to confirm the orders he had issued. The general was quick to do so.

"I am sending in a company of yours," he said to Daley, "to report to Colonel Hatchfield [sic] of the 112th in Vossenack. They are to work for Hatchfield [sic] and the tanks and retake the town."

"That is 'C' Company of the 1340th Engineers you're speaking of," Daley responded.

The general went on as if he had not heard Daley's comment. "Now you are to send these other people here back to the bridge area and retake and hold the bridge. So you have two missions to accomplish—first retake Vossenack and second retake the bridge and road between Vossenack and the bridge. After retaking it you will hold it."

Daley asked Davis to repeat his orders. The general did so. At that point, Lieutenant Colonel Truman Setliffe, commander of the 1340th Engineer Combat Battalion, joined them, listened for a time, and then set out with C Company toward the draw leading to the trail and the bridge. Before they went very far, Setliffe returned to Daley and asked to be given either one or the other of the two missions assigned by the general. Colonel Daley told him to concentrate his efforts on the bridge. He would use engineers from the 146th in Vossenack.[53]

Under German artillery fire, Colonel Isley led Captain Ball and his company of engineers into Vossenack to the infantry battalion command post. They arrived at 1500 hours. Pruden was grateful to see them. He and Isley decided that A Company engineers would defend the right of Vossenack, pushing east as far as possible and then fanning out to the south to protect the main supply route to their comrades south of the Kall. When C Company engineers arrived, they would take care of the left side of town. Pruden would use his few remaining infantrymen to evacuate German prisoners of war and as close-in security for the command post.[54]

Captain Ball and his A Company engineers began their task. They found themselves facing a continuous artillery barrage interspersed with mortar rounds. As they moved forward along Vossenack's east–west street, they were harassed by sniper fire. They advanced to the crossroads by the church, where they were pinned down by small-arms fire. Private Doyle McDaniel climbed onto a shed roof to locate enemy positions. As he jumped down, he landed beside a German soldier. Before the other man could react, McDaniel shot and killed him. He then climbed another building across from the church, still trying to locate the source of the frontal small-arms fire. Rifle slugs tore through him, killing him.

Engineers rushed the church, using "run and duck" tactics, shooting and running from one pile of rubble to the next, ducking and taking cover as they went forward in short rushes, singly and in pairs. They dashed through the front door of the church. Inside were a number of enemy soldiers. In the short battle that followed, both sides lost several men, but the engineers succeeded in clearing the church, capturing ten PWs. Captain Ball shook his head at the condition of the building. The inside was thoroughly savaged and wrecked. Then they moved on to the first building east of the church, used by Germans as a command post. Despite heavy resistance, the engineers took it also.[55]

At 1600 hours, Colonel Sonnefield brought a platoon from B Company, 20th Engineers, into Vossenack. These men received the mission of protecting the American south flank, covering the road leading out of town toward the Kall River.[56]

As it grew fully dark, Captain Ball sent a message back to Pruden in the infantry command post that the engineers now held everything west of the church on both sides of the street.[57] Colonel Daley returned to town and informed Isley that he was to assume command of all troops in town.[58]

Major Baker and Captain Wall of C Company decided to strike out through the ruined town to determine the location of Captain Sam Ball's A Company. Baker had already tried to do so earlier but without success. He scouted alone forward into the church graveyard, north and east of the church, and "wandered around there for a little while, plenty scared." He saw an officer in an American second lieutenant's uniform standing on the church steps and asked him if there was a command post nearby. Yes, responded the man, he thought there was one in the basement of a house across the street. "He said I'd better hurry because the street was pretty hot." At that point, Baker thought no more about the incident, for he also saw Captain Wall talking with the lieutenant. From the man's position, Baker assumed he was an artillery observer, and he spoke perfect English when he told the major that the situation was fluid and dangerous.

Only later did Baker begin to wonder about him. As he pondered the matter he realized the lieutenant "was facing in the wrong direction to get any observation for the artillery." Baker came to believe "this fellow probably was a German dressed in an American uniform, watching our movements and directing enemy fire on us."

Asking Captain Wall to accompany him, Baker again set out to find the location of A Company. The two men climbed over a barricade between the church and the next house east. Baker went first, squatted, and waited. Nothing happened. Then Captain Wall followed him. As Wall crouched beside the major, an unseen German threw a grenade at them, which exploded loudly. Both men pitched to the ground and lay there limply. Some German shouted "Hans!" and other enemy voices rose in a clamor. The man who had thrown the grenade decided to find out whether the two men were dead. As he came closer and silhouetted himself against the darkened sky, Wall got to one knee and picked him off with his carbine. "I shot a .45 slug at him also," Major Baker said, "for I wanted to fire the thing at least once during the war."

Angry and shouting Germans ran toward them, so Wall and Baker fled. "We dove over the barricade and around the corner of the church with Germans shooting tracers after us." Major Baker recalled how they again encountered the strange lieutenant on the steps of the church and sat down with him to catch their breath. Both of them were wounded. Baker had a piece of grenade in his neck and another in his finger. Wall was more seriously wounded, growing weak from shock and loss of blood from steel fragments in his back.

Wall's executive officer was nearby in a shell hole in the middle of the road, and Wall turned over his command to him. Baker got the captain to a medic, who advised that he be evacuated. Only after Wall was gone did Baker finally find A Company's command post in a house across the street from the church.[59]

General Davis continued to monitor the course of battle in Vossenack. At 1930 hours he came into town, accompanied by his aide and a jeep driver. Lieutenant Bill Quarrie, a tanker, complained that "he walked right through my guard who recognized him, but [still] shouted halt. General Davis came right on up to my command tank where he bawled me out for not having guards posted. Apparently he had not heard the guard challenge him. He got me out of my tank and asked me to check the TD positions. We did so. He didn't approve too heartily of them as they were dispersed among some buildings."[60]

General Davis then headed for Pruden's command post. Inside, among others, were Pruden, Isley, and Captain George Granger, commander of B Company, 707th Tanks. Davis ordered Colonel Isley to retake Vossenack during the night. Granger volunteered the opinion that as bad as circumstances were, a night attack was not feasible. The feisty general promptly told him to keep still; it was none of his business.[61]

Davis then asked Isley how he had placed his troops. When the colonel showed him, General Davis exclaimed that one could not defend an MSR by sitting right on top of it. He said to put a company of troops "out here," generally sweeping his finger toward ground southeast of town and forward of American positions. Pruden broke in. The location indicated by the general was, he said, precisely the area from which George Company troops of 2nd Battalion had run early that morning because it was so exposed to enemy fire. It was not, Pruden insisted, a very tenable location.

General Davis finally agreed to allow Isley and Pruden to choose their own troop positions, but he insisted he wanted someone out in the area he had indicated. Fulfilling his wishes required considerable shuffling of A Company engineers. That necessitated ordering C Company troops to pull out their rear platoon and move it up to take over vacated A Company positions at the church and on the Kall River road, all of which had to be done in darkness.[62]

As night hours wore on, men in Vossenack heard their first stories of what was happening in the Kall draw and south of the river around Kommerscheidt. They feared they would have no regiment left, that all their units were on the verge of destruction. It made their own situation, close as they were to the Germans, seem even more serious. In the church, enemy soldiers occupied the basement, while American engineers claimed the main floor. Above them in the bell tower were still more Germans.[63]

As 2nd Battalion tallied its survivors that night, the check showed G Company with only two officers, F Company with but one, and E Company with two. G and F companies had a combined total of *seven* enlisted men left in position; E Company had 20. At the battalion command post were another 20 officers and men.[64]

German artillery fell all night with only occasional breaks. Sporadic rifle fire resounded through dark streets. Men's voices shouted and cursed but could not entirely drown out the sounds of wounded soldiers moaning in pain. Those few Americans faced a gargantuan task, for enemy forces would not give up easily the ground they had recaptured that day.[65]

Even the tone of German records was more subdued by the intensity of the fighting in Vossenack than had been true of other days. The attack on Vossenack, *Generalmajor* Siegfried von Waldenburg claimed, was to have been launched during early-morning hours but was postponed when artillery batteries were not ready to cover an attack with a protective barrage. As a consequence, no actual assault was ever launched, for American soldiers suddenly left their positions in a rout. German soldiers only had to follow them as they fled.

The *156th Panzer Grenadier Regiment* moved toward Vossenack from wooded terrain south of Hürtgen. Simultaneously the *60th Panzer Grenadier Regiment* came toward the Vossenack ridge through bottom land southwest and south of Brandenberg. Von Waldenburg spoke of combat that day as very stiff and heavy, with troops on both sides fighting stubbornly and with courage.[66] No matter whether American or German records are consulted, the result is the same. By nightfall, German forces held half of Vossenack.

One of those German soldiers who infiltrated into town behind panicky "Amis" was *Feldwebel* (Sergeant) Baptiste Palme, a native of Vossenack. He moved into the hamlet out of the draw between the Vossenack ridge and the Brandenberg–Bergstein ridge, his eyes blurring as he saw the devastation of his home.[67]

Headquarters
28th Infantry Division
060001 Nov 44–062400 Nov 44
G-3 Periodic Report Number 112

6. COMBAT EFFICIENCY: Excellent.

7. RESULT OF OPERATIONS: 109th Inf exerted pressure against the enemy, improved positions with 1st and 2d Bns. 110th Inf cleaned out pockets of resistance by connecting "E" and "C" Cos. Prepared to continue operations on 7 Nov. 112th Inf held positions against intense artillery fire and constant pressure from the enemy. 2d Battalion received very heavy and concentrated artillery fire, withdrew to reorganize and then regained their original position.

THOMAS E. BRIGGS
Assistant Chief of Staff
G-3

One wonders what war official reports of the 28th Infantry Division spoke of? G-2 and G-3 journals of the division reveal how closely General Leonard Gerow at V Corps monitored progress of the battle, often telephoning and regularly visiting the war room at Rott. G-3 periodic reports indicate how very little information Cota allowed his superior to see. The entry just quoted has an Alice-in-Schmidtland quality about it. In reality, 2nd Battalion, 112th Infantry, had been thrown off the end of the Vossenack ridge in panic, many of its men fled without stopping to Germeter, engineers were thrown into the breach, and *none* of the lost ground had been recovered. One author has suggested that such reports "seemed designed to soften the effect of the various reverses."[68] Perhaps rather Cota's intention was to cover them up, to deny them entirely.[69]

9

"I'm dying right here"

6 November 1944 (Part Two)

Monday began early for medics in the dugout along the Kall trail. Major Albert Berndt, regimental surgeon for the 112th, reported that at 0100 hours a German patrol infiltrated onto the trail, wiped out all the GIs it could find in the sector, and mined the trail. It may well have been the same group that attacked engineers there, blowing whistles and firing flares.[1]

By 0300 hours, all communication between forward and rear regimental headquarters of the 112th were cut by enemy penetrations along the valley road and up the Kall trail. From that point on, the aid station existed in a state of siege, cut off from both the 1st and 3rd battalions to its front and from 2nd Battalion to its rear. It was now completely in German-held territory.[2]

A German squad stopped at the dugout at 0200 hours. Personnel inside heard a polite knock on the door and opened it. There stood a German private. PFC Joseph Cally, a medical clerk who spoke German, talked with him. The private told Cally they were all now prisoners of war. Then he called a German sergeant to join him. The sergeant asked Cally if there were weapons inside. There were none. Did they have sufficient rations? Enough for one day. The sergeant said he would bring them rations and some German medics to help them. He ordered everyone to remain inside the bunker and left after posting a guard at the door. Medics later found a .45 Army-issue automatic pistol on one wounded soldier and gave it to the guard.[3]

The German *Feldwebel*'s word had been good. At 0400 hours, an enemy squad stopped at the aid station to offer rations and supplies to medical personnel there.[4] At daybreak, those in the log bunker peered outside. The guard at the door was gone, but in woods facing the dugout they could see Germans patrolling the trail.[5]

From then until they evacuated the aid station on 11 November, German medics and infantry visited the bunker several times each day. They permitted walking wounded to cross through their lines as wounded men made their way back from the carnage at Kommerscheidt. Germans made no effort to interfere with operations of the medical station and even supplied its staff with dressings and sulfanilamide. Enemy officers and enlisted men alike made no effort to molest anyone except infantrymen who brought their weapons into the area. They *did* seize all medical vehicles, and subsequent evacuations of wounded were made by litter teams struggling up the steep hill. Germans forced walking wounded with only minor injuries to return to the aid station. At no time during those six days in which Germans held the Kall dugout did its medical people have any idea of the military situation outside their doors.[6]

General Davis wanted desperately to limit German movement along the Kall trail. That was as important to him as retaking Vossenack. At 0900 hours, First Lieutenant Lunar Makousky, executive officer of C Company, 1340th Engineers, received word from his company commander, Captain Ralph Lind, Jr., to assemble their men so they could be used as infantry. Makousky and his crews arrived at a road junction south and west of Vossenack at 1130 hours.

The young lieutenant was surprised to see his assistant division commander drive up in a jeep. He heard the general asking for the senior engineer officer present, and Makousky watched as Captain Lind reported to Davis.

"That's fine, Captain," said Davis, returning Lind's salute. "Here's what I want you to do." He took a map and ordered Lind to move his C Company plus one platoon from 20th Engineers down into the Kall gorge.

"Your mission will be to prevent any enemy patrols from coming up that draw," General Davis said. "Wait for me for further orders."

After their conversation, Captain Lind moved C Company slowly south, well dispersed, to positions Davis had indicated, at the bridge on the north side of the river. Arriving there at 1530 hours, they set up their defenses while behind them to the west the water wheel at Mestrenger Mühle slowly revolved in the flowing current of the Kall.[7]

Makousky and Lind put their men into a squad perimeter defense, based on two .30-caliber machine guns and two bazookas. As they worked, a sergeant scouted Mestrenger Mühle, found no Germans, but reported they had left equipment behind.[8] By 1900 hours, the engineers' defenses were ready. Men crouched in two-man foxholes, under orders for one to remain awake at all times throughout the night. Three men sat at each of the machine guns, aware that one of them must be ready to man the weapon at any moment.[9]

While they worked readying themselves for the night, Captain Lind—who was still very weak, having just been released from the hospital—sent a crew up the trail to check for mines. They discovered several teller mines under a foot of mud between the bridge and the dugout. Corporal Thomas Hamlett, in charge of the crew, came upon a litter patient lying on the trail near the aid station. He paused to look at the man and was fired upon by a hidden German using a burp gun. The noise attracted Makousky, who ran up the trail toward his men. As he arrived, Hamlett finished emptying an M-1 clip into the undergrowth. The Germans withdrew without further contact.[10]

The minesweeper crew returned to their positions near the bridge. That night at 2230 hours, another German patrol slipped toward them through the darkness from the direction of Mestrenger Mühle. Engineers estimated there were at least 80 enemy soldiers in the patrol. Small-arms fire interrupted by the crump of grenades shattered the stillness. "Potato masher" grenades flipped into C Company positions, burying two men. Sergeant Kaczmarski and Corporal Wanet tried to dig them out but failed. Then Wanet and three others leaped to their feet, shouting they were going to get help from Sergeant Szvetitz. All four of them disappeared into the night, hell-bent on escaping from the fire fight. Other C Company engineers were driven from their positions by the German patrol, ran up the hill, and later reached the location of B Company engineers.[11] Those who remained managed to fend off the German attack.

Then an enemy artillery barrage fell on them as they cowered by the bridge. "The concentrations were so heavy that at one point around midnight," Lieutenant Makousky claimed, "I counted 97 explosions within 3 minutes." The barrage killed or wounded 50 percent of the company, leaving only three officers and 18 enlisted men still able to function. Captain Lind was evacuated that night, suffering from combat exhaustion and trench foot.*[12]

Task Force Ripple crossed its line of departure at 0245 hours, 6 November, on its journey to Kommerscheidt, where—according to Major General Norman "Dutch" Cota—it was to turn the tide of battle by striking into and recapturing Schmidt. The task force made its way to Vossenack, where it was to turn south toward the Kall gorge. In the group were 316 infantrymen, including perhaps 100 heavy weapons men and their wheeled vehicles. In Vossenack, the unit was held up by still another of the incessant German artillery barrages. As members of the task force waited for the bombardment to lift, Lieutenant Jack Fuller and Captain Marion Pugh, of the tank de-

*The breakdown of unit integrity suffered by engineers was serious. At one point, due to contrary orders issued by Colonel Daley, General Davis, and others, Company A had two of its platoons mixed with one each from Company B, 20th Engineers, and Company B, 1340th Engineers, plus two officers and 12 enlisted men from Company C, 1340th Engineers. This confused deployment of the 20th Engineers and 1340th Engineers represented the least desirable tasking of engineer units for the conduct of infantry operations. Not only were companies cross-attached, but also in some cases platoons from three different companies had the same mission. There is little wonder that confusion often reigned and command was difficult.

stroyer C Company (which was a designated part of Task Force Ripple), set out to take an ammunition supply train on to Kommerscheidt. Four jeeps moved south through heavy rain, with Fuller in the lead.

Germans now operated up and down the length of the Kall trail with impunity. Under cover of rain, darkness, and their own barrage they came up out of the draw and worked alongside the road toward Vossenack to set up an ambush only 300 yards south of town. Some 40 of them waited, armed with Mausers, Spandaus, machine guns, and a *Panzerfaust*. They heard the supply convoy draw near.

Fuller, Pugh, and the Germans all acted simultaneously. Pugh saw the ambush and shouted "LOOK OUT!" Fuller floorboarded the footfeed on his jeep as his driver fired a 10-round burst from the rear-mountain machine gun. His driver, a boy named Myers, was on this occasion riding in the passenger seat and was hit in the stomach by automatic-weapons fire. As slugs tore through the vehicle, Fuller leaped from it, shouting to Myers to fire his weapon. "I can't, Lieutenant," Myers groaned. "I'm dying right here," and he collapsed from his abdomen wounds. The gunner manning Fuller's machine gun was also wounded.

As he saw shots wrack Fuller's party, Pugh fired perhaps three rounds from his jeep-mounted machine gun when the weapon jammed. He rolled out the left side of his vehicle, bouncing on the ground, hugging it for cover. At the same time, a *Panzerfaust* round grazed his careening jeep, wrecking the windshield.

"One big 'Heinie' came at me with his bayonet," Pugh said. "I batted it away, gashing the index, 3d and 4th fingers of my hand, and ran like the devil." Still carrying his rifle, Pugh turned and fired without noticeable effect at the ambush party. Skirting the danger zone, Pugh and his passenger, Second Lieutenant Louis Izzo, trudged back into Vossenack. Only a few moment later, Fuller joined them. They went up to the platoon of tank destroyers waiting to accompany Task Force Ripple on its move southward, and commandeered two M-10s.

Fuller and Pugh headed south through the dark, foggy air to flush the German ambushers and recover their wounded. Fuller drove the lead destroyer. He began firing as he neared the ambush zone, killing six Germans. The rest fled into the night. They found Fuller's wounded gunner and Myers' body.[14] Having avenged Myers' death, Fuller and Pugh waited for the infantrymen of Task Force Ripple, now freed from the barrage that had held them up, to join them near the entrance to the draw.

It was clear to Colonel Ripple and Lieutenant Colonel William Tait, commander of those riflemen from 3rd Battalion, 110th Infantry, that the Kall trail was controlled by Germans. Rifle fire sounded up and down the path and more distant staccato sounds of small-arms fire from the bridge in the gorge below meant that those defending the stone arch were also in trouble. They would have to find an alternate route to Kommerscheidt.

Unbelievably, divisional headquarters still assumed the Kall trail to be in American hands and open to uninterrupted traffic!

The only available alternative was a nearby firebreak 200 yards west of and parallel to the Kall trail. Unfortunately, it was impassable even for jeeps. So Ripple ordered all wheeled vehicles of the infantry battalion to return to Germeter. His foot soldiers could work their way down the hill along the firebreak. Pugh and Fuller had no option. They must use the Kall trail to get their M-10s to Kommerscheidt. They asked Ripple for a platoon of infantry to protect their destroyers on the trip through the gorge. Ripple knew full well the value of infantry protection for armor, but he had to refuse. His troops were too few to risk them on the trail. M-10 crews would have to make do on their own.

Men in Ripple's task force encountered stiff German resistance as soon as they entered the woods and had to fight the full length of the firebreak to the Kall River and even beyond. They lost two officers and 15 enlisted men on the passage across the Kall. At 1130 hours, 6 November, Task Force Ripple managed to reach near elements of C Company, 112th Regiment, on Kommerscheidt Hill. They then dug in to await the hour of their "attack."[14]

While his men scratched out foxholes for themselves, Colonel Tait, his S-2 intelligence officer, Captain Ashley, and Staff Sergeant Martin Joyce, intelligence sergeant, walked toward the 112th regimental command post in Kommerscheidt. The air was thick with exploding shells from a heavy mortar and artillery barrage. They made their way through trees on the western edge of Kommerscheidt Hill and passed through a shallow draw. A sniper in a patch of nearby woods fired at them, wounding both Tait and Ashley. The captain lay in a partially cleared area. Seeing his danger, he tried to struggle into cover. The sniper fired again, putting a bullet through his head.

Sergeant Joyce crawled over to help Colonel Tait. "I could see," Joyce said, "the bone in the Colonel's arm sticking slightly out where it had been smashed.... I tried to use my trench knife to cut away the Colonel's clothing. He was wearing a combat jacket over one of the grey green jackets more recently issued. The weight of the clothing, and its resistance to the knife caused the colonel so much pain I could not complete the job of clearing away the clothing. As we lay there, with very little cover, a TD pulled into the area between us and the sniper."

The destroyer, commanded by Sergeant Marshall Pritt, fired both its 76mm and its machine guns into the area where the sniper hid, killing him. Two other Germans came out of the woods, hands held high. One pointed at the body of Captain Ashley and whimpered that he had not shot him. Sergeant Pritt put Colonel Tait on the deck of his destroyer alongside Ashley's body and carried them back to the aid station, from which Tait was later evacuated.[15]

Shortly thereafter, Major Robert Reynolds, Tait's executive officer, and the commander of 3rd Battalion's Item Company were wounded as they tried to reconnoiter a line of departure for Task Force Ripple's spearhead assault against Schmidt.[16]

At his 112th Regiment command post, Colonel Peterson exploded upon hearing of these new disasters. "This situation," he fumed, "is worse than snafued.* Communication is bad, out almost all the time. Even as far forward as this CP is, information does not funnel back properly."[17] Ripple shared his frustration as the two men talked about their assignment to retake Schmidt. Heavy artillery and mortar explosions resounded around them. "General" Fleig's tanks and Pugh's TDs drew continuous fire from as far away as the Brandenberg–Bergstein ridge line whenever they showed themselves. No additional tanks or destroyers could any longer make their way down the Kall trail, which Germans roamed at will, firing from its bordering tree line and constantly mining its muddy surface. Even had they not controlled the pathway, transition would be difficult, blocked as it was by several vehicles.

General Cota's orders called for Task Force Ripple to assault Schmidt at 1200 hours, but conditions in Kommerscheidt caused Ripple and Peterson to postpone the attack until 1300. In what must surely have been a mistaken reckoning, Major Richard Dana, regimental S-3 operations officer, calculated that Tait's 3rd Battalion, which had begun with 316 men, was now reduced to *30* effectives. As he said, that was "a pretty depleted condition."[18]

Ripple then learned that two of the M-10s assigned to his task force had been knocked out by enemy fire while waiting above on the Vossenack ridge for an opportunity to move through the Kall gorge to Kommerscheidt. He ordered the others to move back to the 893rd assembly area. He also sent word that no additional tanks should try to maneuver down the trail. To do so was suicide, yet his order also meant that those in Kommerscheidt would not receive desperately needed armor support. The TDs did not move back until dark. At about 1800 hours, Lieutenant Howard Davis' M-10 was attacked by infiltrating Germans, who threw grenades on the deck of his destroyer in hopes that one would land inside the open turret. Davis shot two enemy soldiers off the deck of his destroyer before the probe stopped. Fuller also had to contend with that same attack, "fighting off Jerrie with hand grenades."[19]

In Kommerscheidt, Ripple and Peterson postponed the attack once again, from 1300 to 1500 hours. They finally decided that without supplies or armor, outnumbered, their men already shattered by exhaustion, cold, and relentless fear, the suicide mission of Task Force Ripple to retake Schmidt was out of the question. There was no way they could mount a successful attack.[20]

Lieutenant Ray Fleig had known for hours that something was wrong. At daylight that day, he and his tanks took up positions to carry out fire-support missions for the task force. Hours passed without receiving orders to begin the move on Schmidt. Eventually Fleig learned there would be no mission.

---

*SNAFU is an Army acronym for "situation normal: all fucked up."

American forces might no longer have the strength to strike against their enemies, but the Germans did. At 0630 hours, 6 November, enemy infantry and armor launched another northward probe against remaining American forces in Kommerscheidt.[21]

Reaction to this new *Wehrmacht* onslaught was almost instantaneous. "Some of the infantry by this time," said Fleig, "were so shaken up and unnerved that the mere sound of a German tank starting its motor caused a few of them to leave their foxholes and run to the rear." The lieutenant saw one sergeant running toward his tank. "I stopped him and asked why he was running."

"A German tank," he responded. Fleig held him there, talking in an effort to steady the man.

"Didn't you learn in training that a tank cannot depress its guns to hit a man on the ground when it has come within 35 yards? Didn't you learn that a tank can run over a foxhole without injury to the occupant? Didn't you learn that the safest place during an artillery or mortar barrage is your foxhole?"*

"Yessir," the sergeant replied, "but I can't stand it anymore."

Fleig knew full well the man was not an isolated case. Infantry were dug in on the forward slope in exposed positions. They were in full view of enemy artillery spotters as far away as the Brandenberg–Bergstein ridge line. High ground at Schmidt and Harscheidt also loomed over them. Worse, Germans began to use air bursts, effective against both infantry in foxholes and tank destroyer crews, whose open turrets provided little protection.[22] To add to their woes, they now faced another German armored assault. It was no wonder some ran.

During the night of 5/6 November, an unnamed German tank company commander received orders to recapture Kommerscheidt from its "Ami" conquerors. His command consisted of nine Mark V tanks, located in a wooded area 1,500 meters northeast of Harscheidt. The commander was aware that daylight attacks by Panther antitank guns and Mark IV panzers had so far been unsuccessful in dislodging American forces. Their effective use of artillery fire directed by excellently placed observers around Vossenack made armored advances difficult during the day. The German officer also held a grudging respect for American tanks and TDs, which rolled out from concealed positions to knock out advancing German tanks or force them to retire. He also acknowledged that the U.S. Army Air Forces held complete mastery of the skies.

"When the mission was assigned me," the panzer officer said, "I suggested a night attack. This was accepted." *89th Infantry Division* provided the tank officer with riflemen to support his movements and "all Panther anti-tank guns and Mark IV tanks fit for action were to be placed under my command."

---

*Although true for ground bursts, it was not correct for air bursts.

It was still full dark when the assault began. The battlefield was slightly lit by snow, and night mist was heavy.

Tanks of the German officer's 1st and 2nd platoons rolled north along the road from Schmidt to Kommerscheidt through harassing fire from American artillery batteries. 1st Platoon advanced slowly toward houses in the western outskirts of Kommerscheidt. Simultaneously, 2nd Platoon took under fire all recognized enemy positions as well as farmsteads outside the hamlet where enemy tanks might be located.

At 0630 hours, with sunrise still an hour and five minutes away, the German officer's 1st Platoon opened fire. Its platoon leader radioed him that it was in "combat with enemy tanks, which apparently are in positions between and [even] in houses." Flames from buildings set afire by tank shelling dimly lit the battlefield; smoke from their flames obstructing vision.

Lieutenant Ray Fleig's M-4 Sherman tanks waited patiently. The German battle commander reported that American armor waited until his tanks were within 200 meters before opening fire. "Ami" tanks, he recorded, were well hidden between houses and in gardens concealed by trees. This gave them the element of initial surprise but also hampered them when they tried to maneuver. "Through excellently coordinated fire, observation, and maneuver," his 1st Platoon managed to destroy "the first enemy tanks at the loss of only one [German] tank."

Outnumbered and unable to maneuver easily, with poor visibility and a restricted line of fire, "Ami" tanks began to retire. As they pulled back "They were destroyed by German tanks in ambush positions in the gardens outside the town which had advanced to the northern outskirts [of Kommerscheidt] and took them under fire." The German officer was elated by the progress of his armored assault. It was only 0830 hours.

Saddened by the death of his 2nd Platoon leader, who died when his tank was hit, the German tank officer jubilantly noted that his crews destroyed nine enemy tanks at a cost of only four of his own.* The German commander gained a grudging respect for his outnumbered adversaries, both tankers and infantrymen. "Very careful watch had to be kept," he warned, "against [infantry] close defense anti-tank weapons." This particular assault continued until 1000 hours against Fleig's tanks and "numerous, tenaciously held infantry positions." German troops following in the wake of the panzers "suffered heavy losses while crossing open terrain."[23]

When faced with the beginning of this panzer strike, Fleig and First Lieutenant Turney Leonard, a TD platoon leader, worked out a plan. Fleig would take his tanks to the crest of a hill, where they would draw German fire.

---

*His estimate was incorrect; at the beginning of his attack Americans had only eight tanks in the sector and lost no more than half of them in this battle. More realistic was a report of the *89th Infantry Division* that listed two American tanks destroyed and three more damaged that day.

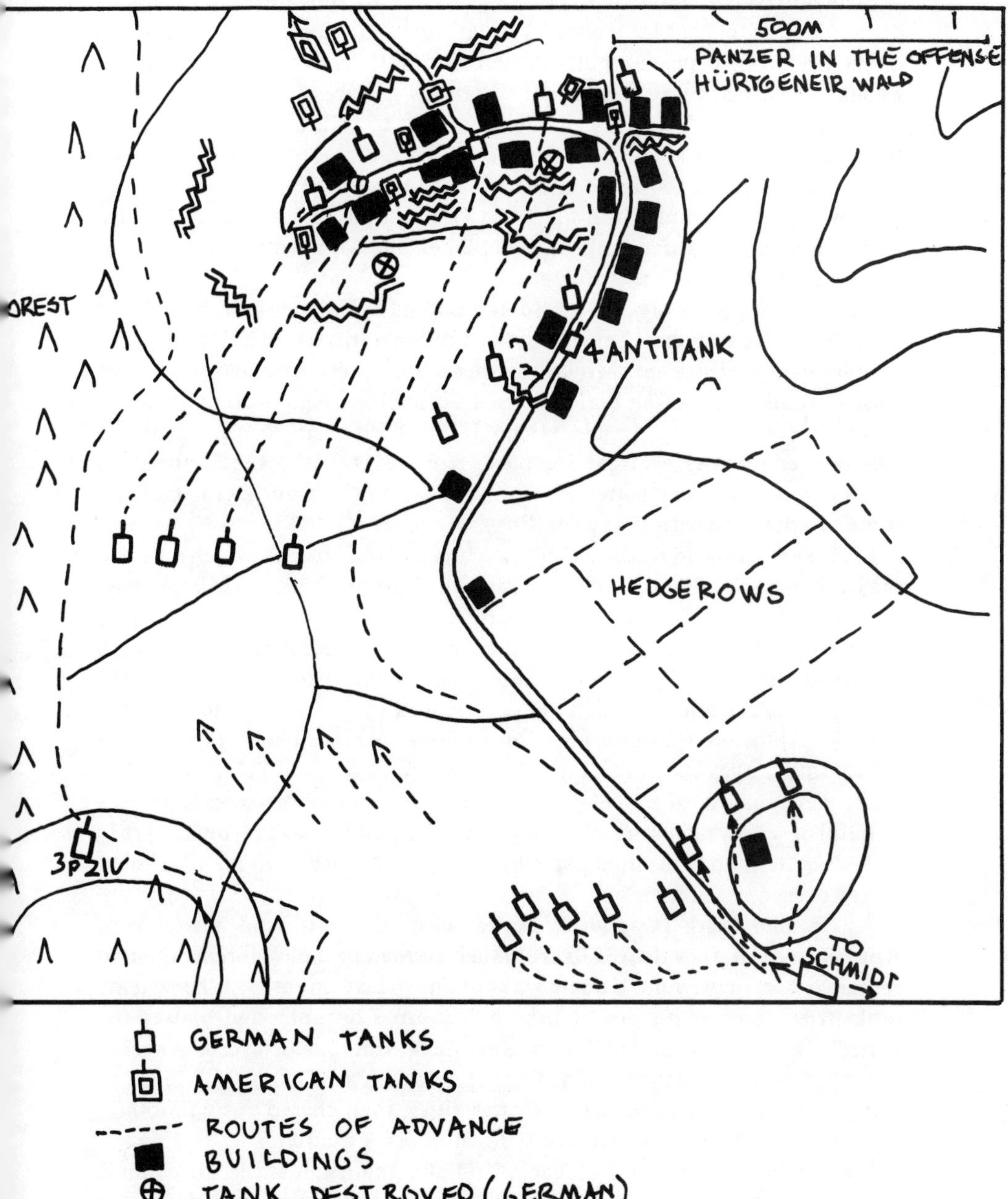

500M
PANZER IN THE OFFENSE
HÜRTGENEIR WALD
OREST
4 ANTITANK
HEDGEROWS
3 PzIV
TO SCHMIDT
GERMAN TANKS
AMERICAN TANKS
ROUTES OF ADVANCE
BUILDINGS
TANK DESTROYED (GERMAN)

Leonard and his platoon would maneuver to the right; as they saw enemy targets expose themselves, they would open fire.

Fleig moved out with two other tanks and immediately drew fire. Leonard dismounted from his M-10 to lead his platoon to the right. They came under direct fire from a nearby pillbox, and his M-10 crews refused to move. Leonard returned to his destroyer. "From his gestures," Fleig observed, "I assumed he was ordering his gun commanders to follow. Again he walked forward, still under small arms fire from the pillbox. . . . They still did not move. That was the last I saw of Lieutenant Leonard."[24]

Now receiving point-blank fire from German panzers and assault guns, Fleig withdrew his three tanks into defilade. The M-4s with him sustained damage, jamming both their turrets.[25]

At first light, Sergeant Tony Kudiak huddled in his wet foxhole in Kommerscheidt. He counted 12 enemy tanks moving north out of Schmidt for an early-morning onslaught. Moving in formation, they covered one another with mutually supporting fire, making it difficult for American tankers and destroyer crews to defend against them. If they fired on any one enemy track, they opened themselves to cannon blasts from several others.[26] Fortunately, American rear artillery batteries responded promptly, scouring the German route of approach with heavy fire.[27]

In the sky overhead Kudiak also saw a flight of U.S. planes, which dived on the German tanks. "I didn't see them drop any bombs," he said. He knew why. Rumor had it that Germans used American air identification panels on their tanks to confuse those who flew strike missions against them.[28] German artillery batteries now joined their American counterparts, laying down the heaviest concentration of shells yet experienced by U.S. troops south of the Kall. As explosions shattered the mud- and snow-wracked field of combat, an officer told Sergeant Frank Ripperdam the situation was hopeless. Their few tanks were unable to move out to engage the enemy in strength. Only a handful of scared men were left. They watched, visibly shaken from the grisly ordeal, as German tanks fired point-blank into five nearby two-man foxholes, killing everyone in them.[29]

As German Mark IVs and Vs worked in on the south and west ends of Kommerscheidt, they drove GIs from their sodden foxholes, forcing them to retreat as best they could. Kudiak was not one to give up easily. When enemy tanks tried to erase his position, he picked up a bazooka and blasted the panzer. His platoon leader, Lieutenant Mack McDonald, of Los Angeles, described what happened. "When the Heinies crawled from the wreckage, Tony and his men picked them off with rifles, then chased away [another] tank which had pinned our infantry down in other quarters."

When others around him fell back, Kudiak remained in place. He climbed into a vacant tank destroyer, manned its machine guns, and repulsed German grenadiers. When his guns jammed, he abandoned the M-10 and climbed into another one. It was also crippled but its guns worked, "so Tony fired at enemy tanks . . . and hit something, but refused to claim one because he didn't see it." He also used his M-1 to pick off enemy infantrymen like so many squirrels back on his Pennsylvania farm.[30]

At 0830 hours, Tony Kudiak peered out of a foxhole. Two other men were with him, PFC Rosslyn Schaffenberg and PFC Frank Serbea. Kudiak focused his binoculars, scanning the countryside for enemy infantry movements. A German artillery shell burst nearby, knocking the glasses out of Kudiak's hands and wounding his two companions. "Everytime we moved," he stormed, "they shot at us with artillery."[31]

Enemy tanks now maneuvered through the rubble of Kommerscheidt. Some came to regret their closeness to American lines as infantrymen moved quietly through debris, shooting at them with bazookas.[32] It was not enough. Enemy armor continued to exact a deadly toll. Sergeant Tom Hunter saw two tank destroyers start over the top of a hillock to engage German tanks. The first M-10 hadn't yet stopped rolling when it was hit by direct fire, killing the man looking out of the turret.[33] Joe Perll was also appalled at American losses. "Our tanks and destroyers were taking a beating," he said. "Three of them were burning and every few minutes another house in Kommerscheidt would flame."[34]

Perll had been awake since dawn, when the sound of machine-gun and burp-gun fire to the south jarred him back to consciousness. Knowing how thin his forces were, he gathered up five men who were sick or had broken their glasses and put them into foxholes to ward off any enemy attack. They all looked anxiously toward Kommerscheidt and Schmidt to the south, waiting for death.[35]

Capture, injury, or death seemed the only certainties. Captain Don Kelly, a tanker, heard small-arms and burp-gunfire and shouting from the Kall draw north of Kommerscheidt. Captain Bruce Hostrup told him Germans had cut the road back to Vossenack; they were surrounded.[36]

Morale kept dropping as German tanks and artillery kept up saturation fire. Casualties mounted swiftly.[37] Captain Jack Walker cowered beneath the rain of shells and watched enemy tanks fire point-blank into Kommerscheidt's buildings, blowing them apart with explosive force. He saw Sergeant Frank Ripperdam force frantic men back into their foxholes. Walker crept over to Ripperdam and urged him to do his best to stop anyone from retreating. "Sir," Ripperdam snapped at him, "there is not a hell of a lot we can do except hold."[38]

PFC Nathaniel Quentin, hiding in a house within the village, found it taken under fire by a German tank. He was knocked from his feet three times by shell explosions before he succeeded in getting out of the building. A nearby enemy tank moved back and forth, firing point-blank into infantry foxholes.[39]

The battle slackened for a time at about 0900 hours, but the respite did not last long.[40] At 1000, enemy tanks once again began to move, their fire devastating amid a simultaneous barrage of high-explosive artillery shells. The renewed attack had deadly effect; the American line broke once again.[41] Racing as best they could from cover to cover, GIs fled in twos and threes toward C Company's area behind the hamlet on Kommerscheidt Hill.[42]

Those panicked men kept Joe Perll busy. "Every so often a few men would straggle back and we held them with us, gave them holes and weapons if they needed them." One man, Perll recalled, who was shot in the leg, crawled all the way back from Kommerscheidt to C Company area on the hill. He was still struggling forward on his hands and knees when medics finally saw and rescued him.[43]

Sergeant Ripperdam knew of only 40 or 50 men left in his area, all exposed to enemy fire, meat for the butchery of German guns. As if that were not bad enough, he then learned that American remnants in Kommerscheidt were completely encircled, cut off from reinforcements from or retreat to the rear, beset on all sides by enemy forces.[44]

Then vague word began to spread among the dispirited ranks of defenders that a battalion of 110th Regiment infantry had driven through German lines and was in contact with C Company on Kommerscheidt Hill. They arrived at 1100 hours but were not to be of much help. Once again discrepancies in the records are confusing. Tait and Ripple indicated they started out that morning at 0245 hours with 316 men, losing two officers and 15 enlisted men as they fought their way through the Kall gorge to Kommerscheidt. When they reached their objective, Major Richard Dana, 112th Regiment's S-3 operations officer, described them as having been reduced to 30 effectives.[45] Joseph Perll saw them arrive and helped them into positions on Kommerscheidt Hill. According to his testimony, "they had been so badly shot up and were so tired, exhausted, and had only about sixty men that they couldn't attack. . . . they built up along the edge of the woods and on the road" north of Kommerscheidt.[46] Perhaps it does not matter whether they numbered 316 or 299 or 60 or 30. They were in no shape for an attack.

Lieutenant Bill George decided to investigate for himself when he first heard the good news about the breakthrough of a relief column. "You always hear," he commented, "lots of rumors, most of which are without foundation. I checked in C Company area and . . . the battalion was there alright, but its commander was wounded and the battalion itself so badly shot up . . . it was no longer an effective fighting force." Despite the poor condition of 3rd Battalion, George was told simply to spread the word of its arrival without other comment. This would bolster morale of hard-pressed defenders in Kommerscheidt "and insure they remained in position despite the fact most of them were in pretty bad shape from continual shelling. . . . I told my men to remain where they were."[47] It was doubtful how long that kind of manipulation would be effective. The last American fingerhold on Kommerscheidt was rapidly slipping.

At about dusk, five German tanks and two self-propelled assault guns moved north from Schmidt. American artillery laid heavy fire on them in its best performance of the entire battle. "We had excellent artillery support," affirmed Lieutenant George.[48] The German armor was also strafed by seven P-47s but kept coming, accompanied by their own infantry. Many GIs in Kommerscheidt could not face another attack.

"We pulled back out of our positions," Tony Kudiak said. "This withdrawal was not orderly. It was everyone for himself. . . . and everyone was scared and confused."[49] As Second Lieutenant Richard Tyo retreated from town he picked up 21 stragglers, including nine wounded men. They bypassed C Company positions on Kommerscheidt Hill and pulled back down into the draw of the Kall River, working their way toward the bridge. Then a German artillery concentration fell on them, wounding five more men. They abandoned the two most seriously injured soldiers and went on, "pretty well beaten and ragged." Finally they found a spot where they could ford the river. The water was cold and the suffering of the wounded men pitiful. "One went across with half his foot gone," Tyo said, "and all we had to wrap it in were dirty handkerchiefs."

As they made their way up the Kall trail they passed Sergeant James Markey's tank still blocking the road.* Trudging around it, they went on up the trail to the bunker aid station. They saw a medic talking to a German soldier outside the dugout, and they crouched among trees beside the trail, remaining hidden for half an hour until the soldier disappeared. Finally, one sergeant who had been shot in the mouth threw away his weapon and he and another casualty made their way to the aid station. Those who stayed behind covered them with their guns.

Then the sergeant shouted for them to leave their weapons and come on in. It was safe. Tyo and his men hid their rifles and carried the other wounded men to medics in the bunker. Aid station personnel warned them that enemy soldiers moved freely throughout the area and advised those able to do so to escape. Tyo and seven others ran back to their weapons cache, retrieved their rifles, and veered west. They worked slowly through the trees until they encountered a group of engineers from the 20th Battalion, who asked them to stay the night and help them hold their site against possible enemy attack. They did so.[50]

Those who had not fled from Kommerscheidt felt grim, angry at the unending spate of continuing defeats they suffered. Now they clung only to a few buildings at the north end of the hamlet. Their attitude was summed up by

---

*Only later did anyone learn that Sergeant Markey had remained with his tank ever since its breakdown, hiding quietly inside its hull. During the nights of 5/6 and 6/7 November, Germans used it as a meeting place and several times he heard them outside laughing and talking, even occasionally banging on it but making no effort to examine the inside.

Tony Kudiak. When an officer requested him to help guard German PWs, he responded with a snarl. "I told him I'd shoot them before I'd guard them."[51]

At 1700 hours on 6 November, Captain George Rumbaugh walked into the rear command post of the 110th Infantry Regiment near Germeter. He had served as commander of the regimental antitank company until 4 November, at which time he was assigned as regimental S-3 operations officer, a position he held until the night of 6/7 November. One who knew him said that Rumbaugh, from Washington, Pennsylvania, fortified himself with a "few belts of the grape" prior to entering the command post.

"Howdy" Rumbaugh marched in to see his regimental commander, Colonel Theodore Seely, and demanded to know why he had been passed over several times for promotion. The colonel, faced with disastrous losses in his regiment in the fighting south of Germeter and aware of the decimation of his 3rd Battalion in its move to Kommerscheidt as part of Task Force Ripple, was in no mood to suffer fools gladly. Hearing Rumbaugh's belligerent queries, the colonel sat silently for a long while. He then turned to the war map on the wall of his command post. Pointing to the Kommerscheidt sector, he began to speak.

Seely told Rumbaugh that Colonel Tait and Major Reynolds had both been wounded there, but the extent of their injuries was unknown. He ordered Rumbaugh to take two Weasel M-29 cargo carriers loaded with water, food, and medical supplies south of the Kall. If only one of the two men was seriously wounded, Rumbaugh was to assist the other. If both were still capable of functioning, Rumbaugh was to learn as much as he could and report back to the regimental command post with his information. If both men were incapacitated, Rumbaugh was to take command of 3rd Battalion in Kommerscheidt, "and then we will talk about your promotion."

Rumbaugh was startled. He saluted and said, "Yes sir," and left the command post. He went to the operations bunker for recent information on the enemy and current maps. Then he visited the supply bunker and made arrangements for the Weasels. Within four hours after receiving his unorthodox orders, Rumbaugh set out with his jeep and two following Weasels.

As Rumbaugh moved forward he encountered a jeep and five more Weasels from the 112th Regiment which joined his convoy. About 50 yards west of the Vossenack church, a German machine-gun crew opened fire on them. Scooting for cover, the men in the supply column abandoned their vessels. After a few minutes, fearing an artillery barrage might hit next, Rumbaugh got his supply train moving south toward the draw road.

Tracer machine-gun fire followed them, but no one was hit. The convoy gained only 400 yards when German artillery rounds began to drop where they had stopped, then shifted south to follow them. As the convoy sped toward the woods on the south edge of the Vossenack ridge, a machine pistol fired at it. Rumbaugh returned fire with his jeep-mounted machine gun, and the column continued.

As his vehicles attempted to negotiate a sharp rise, inexperienced drivers turned two Weasels over. Fifty yards farther, a third Weasel threw a track. Only four of the original seven Weasels were now left. Reaching the draw road, Rumbaugh found felled trees of various sizes blocking it, and he and his men had to force each one out of the way. Then Rumbaugh heard the sound of nearby German voices and he worked his way forward on foot, peered over the edge of the road down into the draw, and saw two men silhouetted against the night sky. He challenged them. One threw a hand grenade at him, so Rumbaugh fired back with his carbine. Others with him also sprayed the area with small-arms fire. They killed four Germans.

The column continued on down the Kall trail past Sergeant Markey's seemingly abandoned tank and around the switchbacks. They crossed the bridge and rolled up the south side of the slope. There they were stopped by a huge tree laying across the road. It took nearly an hour's labor with axes, ropes, and hand power to remove it. As they finished, a group of 15 men from the 20th Engineers drifted up and told them how they had been overrun an hour earlier by a large German patrol. They had since hidden in their foxholes until they heard the sounds of chopping on the tree. Rumbaugh wondered whether that "large" patrol might have been the small group he and his men fired at higher up the trail.

The captain ordered his convoy onward. As they drove toward Kommerscheidt they were stopped by three Sherman tanks parked along the roadway. Rumbaugh asked a tanker what they were doing, and the man replied they were moving back because their turrets had been damaged by enemy fire. In maneuvering around the tanks, another Weasel was lost when it became stuck. Somewhere—Rumbaugh was uncertain when—another jeep and trailer were lost. Two other Weasels belonging to the 112th Regiment also apparently turned off the road at some point. Rumbaugh arrived at the 112th Regiment command post at 0420, 7 November, with his jeep and one Weasel. At the CP he found that both Tait and Reynolds had long since been evacuated to the aid station on the trail down which he had come. He took command of 3rd Battalion, 110th Infantry, at 0500 hours, 7 November; he held that position until the unit was relieved from front-line duty on 16 November.*[52]

Only Germans had cause to rejoice that day. Gray-clad soldiers of *Battalion Schindler* fought their way forward to make contact with *Onnen* and *Wilschewsky* battalions. Despite heavy "Ami" artillery, German infantrymen

*A month later, Captain Rumbaugh was captured by the Germans during fierce fighting in the Battle of the Bulge.

moved closer to Kommerscheidt. Their own mortar and artillery shells hit only 100 to 200 meters in front of *Wehrmacht* soldiers as they fought their way into the northern and western sectors of Kommerscheidt. Troops of the *89th Infantry Division* searched every cellar, every barn, every house as they moved forward. "Thus," one German wrote, the American defense was "broken up under the fire of our artillery and the unbreakable fighting spirit of our grenadiers."

Generalmajor Siegfried von Waldenburg, commander of the *116th Panzer Division,* related how one of his reconnaissance battalions, reinforced by engineers and some panzers, pushed forward along the Kall River to retake Mestrenger Mühle, cutting the "Ami" line of retreat from Kommerscheidt.

As evening drew on, "Papa" Bruns, commander of the *89th Infantry Division,* called his officers together. "The trapped force must be annihilated under all circumstances," he said to them, "before the enemy has a chance to rally new strength and attempts to break into the pocket from any direction thus to free the trapped unit." He ordered that efforts the following day must be even greater and assigned the *1056th Regiment* and *Armored Task Force Bayer* to destroy American forces by evening on 7 November. He further ordered his *1056th Regiment* to link up with the reconnaissance battalion from the *116th Panzer Division* which now controlled the river road and the Kall trail. This, he said, would prevent any breakthrough from the Vossenack area to rescue encircled Americans at Kommerscheidt.

Generalmajor von Waldenburg commented that his armored losses in the Schmidt sector were not great, their principal enemy being the American Army Air Forces "which became more and more powerful from day to day."[52]

Disaster was near. All three regiments of the 28th Infantry Division were mutilated, nearly annihilated, no longer capable of serving as an effective fighting force. General Davis fitfully crossed the battlefront, arguing with regimental commanders, excoriating Sam Mays, scolding tankers for not using perimeter guards, ordering infantry battalions to send troops "out there," and sending engineer teams on missions throughout the battle area. And Major General Norman Cota sat in his command post at Rott, wondering how to salvage the remains of his division.

10

"All hell was breaking loose"

7 November 1944

Inclement weather plagued men of the "Bloody Bucket" from the first hours of their assault on Schmidt on 2 November, causing record numbers of casualties from pneumonia, influenza, colds, and trench foot. Clouds and rain also prevented IX TAC Air Command from providing adequate battlefield support. Its planes were never able to fulfill operational plans made prior to launching the divisional attack in the Hürtgen Forest. "WX infavorable" and "WX cancelled operation" continued to be regular entries in the daily log of Major Edwin Howison, air liaison officer with the 28th Infantry Division. Airplanes played a part in the battle, but unsatisfactory flying weather caused their role always to be peripheral.

Already miserable conditions worsened during the night of 6/7 November. The darkness was impenetrable, thick as mud, and a saturating mist clung to ridge lines and lay among forest trees like heavy steel wool. About 2200 hours, the sky cleared and moonrays shone brightly for an hour on the winter-cold battlefield, illuminating the ruins of Vossenack, above which rose the burning tower of the damaged but still-dominant church.

By 2315 hours, rolling black clouds once again covered western Germany, opening to sluice drenching rains upon the land. The temperature plunged as the deluge turned to driving sleet, tormenting utterly weary and bitterly cold warriors. Heavy supply vehicles churned sodden earth of roadways into a hopeless morass. An unabated sleetfall continued until 0330 hours, when once again rain began to fall, continuing throughout the remainder of the night and into the morning without letup. Exposed to the vagaries of weather, soldiers shivered helplessly as drizzling rain soaked steadily through their clothing, their arms and legs dangerously numb.

Following General George Davis' visit to Vossenack and his express desire for a night attack against German positions, Captain Sam Ball, Jr., commander of A Company, 146th Engineers, led his men against their foes. They stumbled forward in driving rain and utter blackness. At 0100 hours, Ball sent a runner to his battalion commander, Colonel Isley, informing him that A Company was pinned down on the flank of Vossenack by enemy fire. They could go no farther. Isley ordered them to withdraw to their former positions near the Vossenack church. An hour later he received word that Ball and his men had disengaged themselves and were now back near the church.

Midway during the hour in which those men moved carefully rearward, Lieutenant Colonel James White, executive officer of the 1171st Engineer Group, arrived at Isley's command post with orders from the group commander, Colonel Daley. Once again engineers would be flung into battle as mixed elements without regard for unit integrity. At dawn, Company B, 1340th Engineers, and Company A and one platoon of Company B, 20th Engineers, would press forward on the south side of Vossenack. At the same hour, men of the 146th Engineers would attack with tank support to retake the eastern half of town.[1]

During the last minutes of darkness those supporting tanks arrived. Staff Sergeant John Cook, a platoon sergeant in B Company of the 707th Tanks, did not even know they were to aid foot soldiers in an attack. Then at 0800 hours, his platoon leader gave orders for his M-4 crews to begin firing. The target was to be the first building north of the church. "Two rounds," the lieutenant called out. They fired, muzzle flashes flickering in the still, dark air. A German infantryman dashed from the building and fell kicking under a burst of machine-gun fire from one tank. Armor-clad Sherman M-4s ground their way east through falling rain as the sky slowly lightened to a dirty gray. Sergeant Cook fired two more rounds into the targeted building. Some 30 German soldiers and six nuns fled the ruins. Engineers corraled them and herded them under guard into the church basement as tanks moved on, firing into each successive building. Engineers followed closely, rushing into each house and killing or capturing its inhabitants.[2]

Captain Pruden was well pleased with the work of his combined armor-infantry force. "They did a bang-up job," he recalled.[3] It was, however, a costly procedure as Germans fought to retain their hard-won ground gains.[4] Tanks and engineers faced determined resistance as they pressed forward, blasting buildings and setting houses on fire, spraying defenders with rifle and machine-gun fire. They showed little mercy. Sergeant Cook saw German soldiers fleeing houses set ablaze by tank fire. They ran frantically along the road toward the east. "We mowed 'em down," he laconically observed.[5]

In the early afternoon, General "Dutch" Cota paid his only recorded visit to any divisional unit during the entire course of the Schmidt–Kommerscheidt–

Vossenack action. He arrived at the command post in Vossenack at 1400 hours, parked his jeep outside, and walked in to inform Pruden and Isley that 2nd Battalion, 109th Infantry Regiment, would shortly relieve battered and weary infantry and engineer troops in Vossenack. 2nd Battalion of the 109th had been evacuated from minefields and shattered forests on the divisional left flank south of the town of Hürtgen and was now available to help them. Cota remained at the Vossenack command post for half an hour. Lieutenant Jim Condon remarked in surprise that during Cota's visit "not a single artillery shell fell, the first such lull in six days." The respite did not last long. "Five minutes after he left it started all over again. One shell landed in the exact spot where his jeep had been parked."[6]

Cota's words brought hope to those in the command post. "Dutch" was popular with them, and they believed him to be a man of his word. If they could only hold out a few more hours, relief would come that night. One man's understatement spoke for them all: "We were anxious to get out."[7]

By 1515 hours, C Company, 1340th Engineers, reported to the command post that all houses in Vossenack eastward to the point where the main road started down the forward slope of the ridge were once again in American hands. There were only a few buildings beyond that location, and tank crews were no longer willing to continue onward. Further forward movement would expose them to German direct antitank fire.[8]

During the next hour, ground troops observed several P-47s droning around the perimeter of Vossenack, unable to close on targets because of intense antiaircraft fire from the Brandenberg–Bergstein ridge. "Then," said Lieutenant Condon, "suddenly something went wrong. We heard a fast rate of fire from multiple guns which sounded like German weapons. We looked up and there was one of our own planes diving with his guns blazing, surprisedly strafing our area." Stunned men leaped for any available cover.

"Only when we heard the roaring of his motor," Condon observed, "did we realize we were being strafed and hit the ground. The pilot came in from east to west and dropped one bomb somewhere east of the church, zoomed around and repeated the process, dropping a second bomb."[9] Angry men cursed the stupidity of the pilot as he flew away to clean sheets and a hot bath.

Isley and Pruden, their red-rimmed eyes glazed with fatigue, welcomed the commander of the 109th Infantry Regiment when he arrived at 1630 hours to discuss his relief of soldiers in Vossenack. His own regiment, relieved during the night just past from its stalemate north of Germeter by the 12th Infantry Regiment, 4th Infantry Division, was back in its assembly area west of Germeter. His men were eating a hot meal and receiving ammunition issues and new equipment. One battalion would replace the 146th Engineers; another would take over for the 1340th Engineers. The 146th could vacate its positions after daylight the next morning.[10] Lieutenant Jim Condon suggested that relief troops should move into town only after 1830 hours, for the regular German artillery barrage would have lifted by then.[11]

Surviving soldiers of 2nd Battalion, 112th Infantry Regiment, began their withdrawal shortly after dark.[12] Even that was not easy. Corporal Joe Philpot, of G Company, told how on the way back "a lucky barrage fell on us and First Lieutenant Julian Ferrier and First Sergeant Dale Todd were hit. Medics took care of them. The rest of us continued on back for what seemed like three miles through heavy mud up to our knees." Finally they were picked up by trucks and driven to a rear kitchen area, where they ate and pitched tents. At the time of their relief, said Philpot, George Company had only 42 men left, including its headquarters personnel and kitchen staff, who had remained in the rear. "Of those who had been in the town, only nineteen came out. Of officers, only First Lieutenant Clyde Johnson came out."[13]

Survivors of Easy Company, 2nd Battalion, were no more fortunate. Arriving in Germeter, Jim Condon turned command over to First Lieutenant Cliff Beggs. Condon went to medics who diagnosed him as suffering from influenza and evacuated him. Beggs was appalled by the casualties in his company. The 1st, 2nd, and 4th platoons were commanded by technical sergeants instead of lieutenants. Only 3rd Platoon still had an officer in charge. Technical Sergeant Edward Devers now ran Beggs' old 2nd Platoon. Beggs himself had been wounded slightly, and his former platoon was decimated. Its 1st Squad had only two men instead of 12—PFC Joseph Kuesal and PFC George Elliott. Its 2nd Squad had five men—PFC Frank Stocklas, PFC Willard Wakefield, Technician Fifth Class Warren Sorentino, Sergeant Arthur Davis, and PFC Paul Whiteside.* The 3rd Squad of 2nd Platoon also had only five men—Staff Sergeant Richard Sam, Sergeant Walter Kiballo, Corporal Walter Swiger, PFC James Jett, and PFC Merle Kepple. In platoon headquarters, only three survived—the medic, Private Bernard Piessecki; the runner, PFC Henry Lambest; and Sergeant Devish.[14]

Easy Company remained in Germeter from the early-morning hours of 8 November until 15 November, its members enduring continual cold temperatures, rain and snow, and ever-present mud. On 15 November it was relieved by 2nd Ranger Battalion.[15]

Eldeen Kauffman's Fox Company was in even worse shape. After leaving Vossenack, his men went to the rear for a rest, which lasted precisely *one* day, during which 132 replacements arrived. On 9 November the company was sent back into Vossenack to help hold the village, remaining there until 14 November. Kauffman sorrowed that "Of the original men in the company who went into Vossenack, we came out with six enlisted men and three lieutenants."†[16]

---

*Of those five men, three more were wounded before Easy Company was evacuated from Germeter!

†Authorized unit strengths were as follows: squads had 12 men; a company had six officers and 187 men; a battalion had 871 men; a regiment consisted of 153 officers and 3,049 men.

Engineers watched enviously as men of 2nd Battalion, 112th Infantry, evacuated Vossenack. Why had they not also received word to leave? There was a reason. Although General Cota authorized their relief from infantry duties, General Davis wanted those engineers to stay and help hold Vossenack. Major Robert Argus, S-3 operations officer of the 1171st Engineer Group, went to the command post of the 28th Infantry Division where he received word that although engineers were to be relieved, they should not leave Vossenack until after daylight on 8 November. This information was given him despite General Davis' actual orders for them to remain in position. Argus passed this permission to Colonel Daley, who gave it to a liaison officer, who told a sergeant in the 146th Engineers. In transmittal, even that message became garbled. Perhaps through wishful thinking, men of the 146th Engineers understood it to mean that they should be gone *by* daylight on 8 November.

Engineers of the 146th assembled in the ruins of the church and in the street outside. They began their withdrawal at 0145 hours, and by 0215 all of them were out of town. When General Davis learned they were gone he "raised hell" but contented himself with insisting that all other engineers should remain in Vossenack.[17] It is no wonder that men of the 146th pulled out of town at their first opportunity. In a note on one of the documents from this battle, interviewer Captain John S. Howe wrote how several commanders told him that many of the few officers and NCOs who survived these days of combat were never again up to par. They lost some inner stamina. Like a broken violin string, they had been stretched too far for too long.

The 109th Infantry Regiment had troubles of its own. Hurt badly by days of striking through forests and German minefields north of Germeter, trying to achieve objectives south of the town of Hürtgen, it became so weakened that General Cota ordered its relief by the 12th Infantry Regiment, 4th Infantry Division. The unit pulled back to Germeter during the morning of 6 November.[18]

In a rest and assembly area west of town, men ate hot meals, picked up overcoats, received K ration and ammunition issues, and snatched a few hours of sleep. For the first time in days these soldiers were in no immediate danger from the enemy. Replacements moved in to fill up vacancies left by battle casualties. One company had but 47 men left. Sixty new men were assigned to another company.[19]

General Cota already had a new mission in mind for the three battalions of the 109th Regiment. 1st Battalion would remain at Germeter to protect that sector. 2nd Battalion was to move into Vossenack, relieve bedraggled American troops there, and complete recapturing the town and its ridge. 3rd Battalion would move onto the southern slope of the Vossenack ridge and guard the main supply route of the Kall trail, freeing it from German possession, so at least some supplies and reinforcements might reach encircled men on Kommerscheidt Hill.[20]

The companies of 2nd Battalion left for Vossenack between 1800 and 1900 hours, 7 November, the night so dark men had to hold on to one another as they walked so as not to get lost. Arriving at the church, they began relieving waiting engineers.[21]

Major Howard Topping, commander of 3rd Battalion, 109th Regiment, ordered a lieutenant to guide the unit into position while he went on a reconnaissance mission. The young officer was to guide the battalion along the road into Vossenack, turn south at the crossroads until he reached the edge of the ridge, and then follow the woodsline until he reached the battalion's designated position. During Topping's absence, the lieutenant became lost, turned at the wrong crossroads, and guided the battalion back west along the wrong tree line. Now thoroughly confused, he struggled along through driving rain and finally stopped at 2100 hours some 3,000 yards south of Germeter.[22]

Upon his return, Major Topping could find no sign of his battalion. He and his staff spent the entire night looking for it. Captain William Rogers finally located their men on the morning of 8 November in the wooded draw south of Germeter where they had bedded down. Rogers encountered the "lost battalion" at 0700 hours. Before he could get the men moving, General Davis arrived and Rogers briefed him on the mishap. Using one platoon as a personal bodyguard, Davis led the battalion 2,500 yards east to the Kall trail MSR, at which time he relinquished the unit to Major Topping.[23]

Early on that Tuesday of 7 November, Lieutenant Colonel Sam Mays once again found himself standing in front of General Davis trying to explain his actions. The general informed him that two columns of Weasels had transited the Kall trail during the preceding night. Why had no tank destroyers done so?

Mays replied that he was aware of the Weasels' passage along the besieged MSR. He had even tried to send destroyers along, but ponderous M-10s did not keep up with Weasels at night on the area's hazardous and sodden roads. If they preceded Weasels, they slowed their speed and subjected them to hostile fire. If they followed, they could not keep up. The general should further realize, added Mays, that Weasels could move safely over an average German pressure mine, which destroyers would set off.

The trail was difficult to cross at night, Mays continued, for it was so narrow and full of twisting turns even jeeps had to back and turn several times as they negotiated their way. If M-10s tried to travel the trail during daylight, they became excellent targets for German direct artillery barrages from nearby commanding ridges and for concentrations of shells laid in defiladed areas. The stubborn colonel pushed on with his arguments. Hostile infantry constantly mined sections of the road and often waited in ambush. One M-10 platoon was forced to withdraw when ambushed on an attempted run through the gorge. On this point Mays was mistaken, for he had in mind not

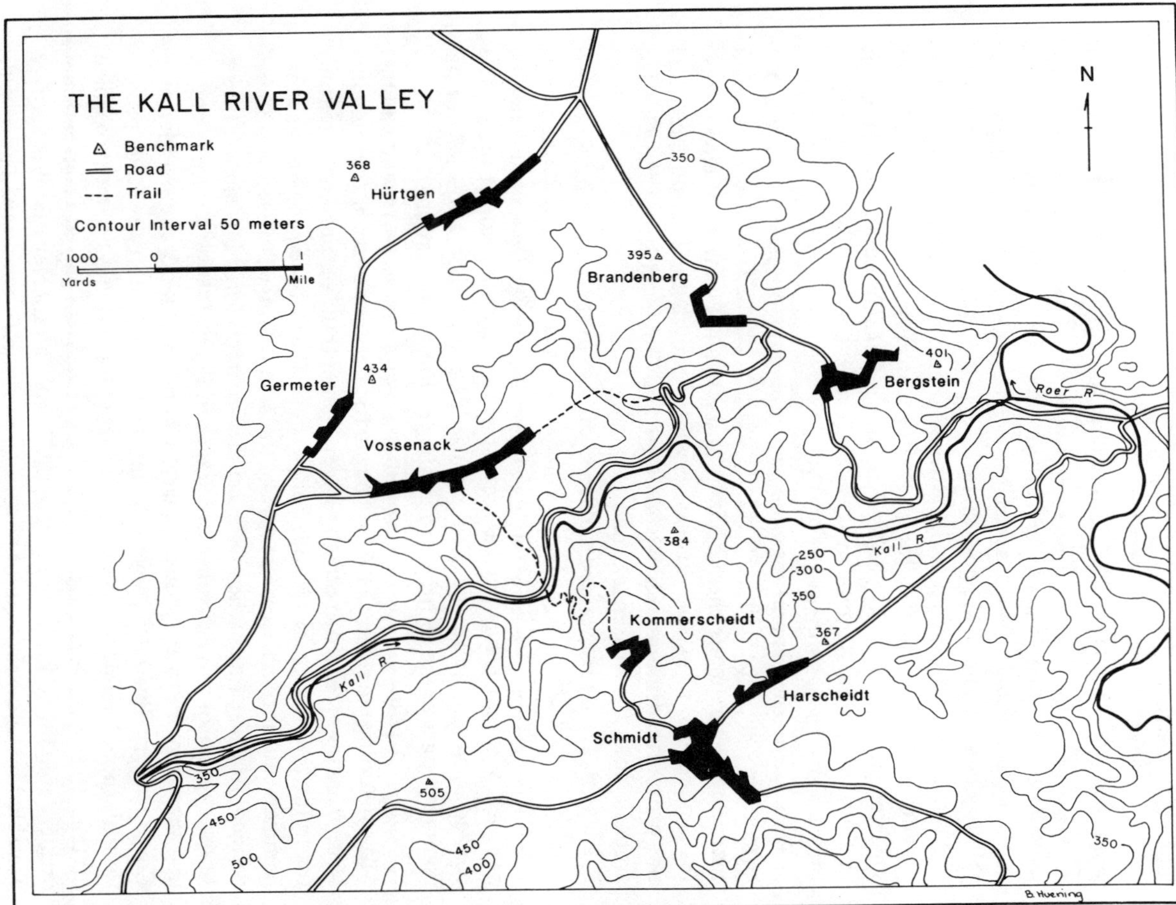
THE KALL RIVER VALLEY
Benchmark
Road
Trail
Contour Interval 50 meters
1000
0
1
Yards
Mile
N
368
Hürtgen
395
Brandenberg
401
Bergstein
Roer R
434
Germeter
Vossenack
384
Kall R
250
300
350
Kommerscheidt
367
Harscheidt
Schmidt
505
450
500
400
B. Huening

M-10s but Fuller and Pugh's jeep supply column attempt of the previous morning. Mays went on to tell General Davis how other destroyers had to shoot German soldiers off their decks as they tried to drop hand grenades into open turret areas.

The general finally cut Mays short, his patience exhausted. He asked how many TDs were available. The Colonel admitted there were still 11 M-10s in B Company around Vossenack and four more with makeshift crews in the rear echelon of C Company. Davis demanded that all 15 of them start immediately for Kommerscheidt. Mays asked for a company, or even a platoon, of infantry to go along to support them.

Mays advocated sound doctrine when he requested infantry support before moving his destroyers, yet the preceding morning Fuller and Pugh used machine guns on their M-10s to clean out a German ambush without any infantry protection. Bending to Mays' entreaties, Davis said he would "try" to find infantry to accompany the M-10s.

Were there, the general inquired, machine guns on destroyers? Yes, the colonel replied, each had a .50 caliber weapon on an awkward antiaircraft mounting, which made them difficult to use against infantry at close range, for gunners had to expose themselves while firing them. That difficulty had not proven insurmountable when Fuller and Pugh broke up the German ambush along the Vossenack road.

Davis was firm. He wanted a platoon of destroyers to leave for Kommerscheidt immediately, regardless of consequences. Mays told him it was against his wishes. In his judgment it was a mission that should not be assigned. General Davis put his request in the form of a direct order. The conversation was at an end. Still opposed, Colonel Sam Mays left for his command post at the 893rd Tank Destroyer Battalion headquarters.

From that point on, the relationship between General Davis and Colonel Mays deteriorated so far that Mays began to issue his destroyer commanders written orders of record in order to have a "paper trail" supporting his reasons for trying to circumvent his superior's orders. Part of the problem was that command authority between Mays and the 28th Infantry Division was poorly defined. At those times when his mission was to reinforce Division Artillery, Mays' supervisor was Brigadier General Basil Perry, DVARTY commander, and through him to Brigadier General Charles Helmick, commander of V Corps artillery. But when Mays' mission changed to infantry antitank protection, his supervisor became the commander of the infantry regiment to which his tank destroyers were attached. Tank destroyers had played a conventional artillery role for so many months in the European theater that it is entirely possible Mays now thought of himself as an artillery, rather than an assault gun antitank, officer and commander. It would be unfair to conclude that Sam Mays was inept in the performance of his duty as he saw it. He was a competent officer, and his concern for men in his unit was admirable. He should have remembered, however, the limits of his role and the *mission,* which should have been his primary consideration.

General Davis was pursued by other furies that caused him to want to use Mays' tank destroyers as a substitute for tanks—a role for which they were clearly unsuited. Heavy losses among the few tanks of the 707th that had reached the Kommerscheidt sector were disastrous. Even those still capable of functioning needed servicing and resupply. Reloading ammunition, topping off gasoline tanks, and preventive maintenance are difficult chores to perform under nearly continuous artillery fire. Rotating those tanks rearward to conduct such routine chores would be possible only if *something* took their place. The only available substitutes were M-10s. Davis seemed to feel that if tankers and infantrymen could die on the exposed Kommerscheidt ridge, so also could tank destroyer crews. He may not have known governing doctrine for TDs as well as did Mays, but he knew that an order from a superior officer stands on its own.

Colonel Mays reluctantly totted up his forces. During the entire period of battle, only B and C companies were available to him, for A Company was occupied elsewhere, attached to the 102nd Cavalry Group. Only 24 destroyers were his to use when the assault in the Hürtgen began on 2 November. Of those, one was evacuated to the rear for maintenance after its initial firing mission due to a leaking recoil mechanism. A second M-10 fell prey to an exploding mine near Rickelskall. Another mine knocked out a third destroyer in a draw north of Vossenack. A fourth was destroyed by enemy fire on the eastern nose of the Vossenack ridge. A fifth sat in a Vossenack cellar with its cannon pointing skyward. Nine destroyers had gotten through to Kommerscheidt, and several of them were already casualties of armored combat there. Those still operating there might as well also be written off, for they would not last much longer. Fourteen down with 10 to go. Now Mays faced the necessity of sending additional crews and machines to Kommerscheidt. He *knew* it was wrong to do so.

Colonel Mays felt General Davis was not acquainted with appropriate doctrine regarding tactical deployment of tank destroyers. Mays was probably correct. Yet Mays would have done more to help the mission of the 28th Infantry Division had he demonstrated a willingness to support fully those rifle units that were his main responsibility. Small men with insufficient courage cost more lives in wartime than they save. Mays' inability to do what had to be done was his contribution to the disaster that faced the division.

Only after General Davis sought him out for the second time that day did Colonel Mays finally order Captain John Cook of B Company to dispatch one platoon of his TDs to Kommerscheidt. Just as Mays resisted orders from Davis, so also did Captain Cook argue with his battalion commander. Mays had no option. On that second visit, General Davis complained tellingly of Mays' slowness in carrying out orders. Cook reluctantly sent forth his crews across open ground during daylight. He made no effort to call on the artillery for a smoke cover on the ridge to conceal the movement of his platoon. The cost for this lapse in tactical expertise was high. Two M-10s received direct hits from enemy guns and were knocked out. The other two went out of control while taking evasive action, were unable to maintain traction on the slippery Kall trail, and skidded over the left bank into the draw. As their crews clambered out, they found themselves under artillery and machine-gun fire from several points. Doing as much damage to their vehicles as they could, they sought cover and finally worked their way back to safety, having suffered several casualties.

Captain Cook broke down. Other orders might come requiring him to send still more crews to their deaths, and he could no longer face that possibility. If he refused orders from Colonel Mays he could be court-martialed; if he obeyed them it would mean possible death for himself or others. He chose insanity instead, relieving himself as a combat exhaustion casualty. Cook turned over command of his company to Captain Sidney Cole, who then happened to be at the B Company command post. Mays saw Cook at 1430 hours, heard what had happened, and told him to report to Captain Shibler, surgeon for the 893rd, at the battalion aid station.

No additional tank destroyers ever got through to Kommerscheidt. Colonel Mays may have felt his judgment was vindicated by the loss of Cook's four M-10s,* but doughboys in Kommerscheidt would have been hard pressed to sympathize too deeply. There was not a GI alive who could have appreciated Mays' reluctance and his civilized disputation with General

*As late as 9 November, Colonel Mays still attempted to find ways to save his remaining destroyers and crews. On that day he went into Vossenack for a talk with the new commander of 2nd Battalion, 109th Infantry Regiment. "He understood our problems of remaining in town," wrote Mays, "which were explained to him in detail. He . . . agreed our TDs should be conserved. . . . that we possibly did more harm than good by being in town . . . . and wanted us to show ourselves no more than necessary and to fire only at remunerative targets of opportunity."

From Vossenack, Colonel Mays went on to DIVARTY to speak with General Basil Perry. Afterward Mays drove to the divisional command post at Rott "to arrive at a plan for relaxing requirements of keeping guns in Vossenack." As Mays talked with staff officers there, General Davis walked up, listened for a while, and Mays "oriented" him on his new understanding with the commander of 2nd Battalion, 109th Regiment.

Exasperated beyond belief, Davis informed Mays that "there had been too much movement in and out of town by the TDs and that we would keep them there or he would take steps to see that we did."

One of my students, Colonel Richard Ehrhardt, USAR (Ret.), commented in notes to his seminar paper "The 893rd Tank Destroyer Battalion in 'The Forest Frolics'" (University of South Florida, 1979), that "After 40 [sic] years I am still able to get angry at Mays. I would have sent him to Leavenworth for a twenty-year refresher course and forfeit of all pay and allowances. It is an irony that this document he intended to be an explanation of his actions condemns him beyond any doubt."

Davis while riflemen fought and bled in the snow south of the Kall on Kommerscheidt Hill.[24]

Some few Americans were escaping from the Kommerscheidt pocket. Late the previous evening, Lieutenant Richard Tyo and seven men slipped through German lines and spent the night along the river with a group of 20th Engineers who needed help holding their positions. By the morning of 7 November, all of them—engineers and infantry alike—were suffering intensely from exposure. Their clothes were sodden from rain, and their feet were in agony from cold and dampness. A wounded engineer offered to show Tyo's men a cross-country route toward Germeter and safety. They moved out through trees and brush, avoiding clearings where they might be seen by roving German patrols. Moving in column, very close together, they passed through a former enemy position littered with equipment and stiff German corpses. Tyo and his men did not realize the area was booby-trapped.

"Through some freak chance," Tyo said, "I passed one spot safely but the man behind me stepped on a buried grenade which was booby-trapped to another. Both exploded, blowing half his foot off, blinding another man, breaking the leg of the wounded engineer in two places and throwing me to the ground." Leaving the two men with leg wounds, they led the blind man, working their way among trees until they reached elements of a cavalry reconnaissance unit. An officer pointed the way to the command post of the 110th Infantry Regiment.

Tyo picked up four aidmen, two litters, and a mine detector crew. They returned to the two wounded men and carried them to the 110th aid station. All except Tyo and one sergeant were then evacuated because of wounds or trench foot.*[25] As Tyo sought out the unit kitchen to get something to eat and try to warm himself, he could hear thunderous explosions in the gorge behind him as a savage German artillery barrage blasted its way into the encircled ring of American troops north of Kommerscheidt.

Another few men also escaped that man-made hell during the night. At 0300 hours, 7 November, a convoy of seven M-20 Weasels and nine trucks succeeded in crossing through German-held territory down the Kall trail to reach troops on Kommerscheidt hill with water, rations, blankets, ammunition, and medical supplies. Their crews quickly unloaded, impatient to begin their return trip so they could reach safety before daylight.

Lieutenant William George, motor officer of 3rd Battalion, 112th Regiment, had come forward many hours earlier with a supply train of his own. Now he decided to get out of the encirclement and go back to Germeter with

*Interviewer Captain William J. Fox noted that Tyo's K Company, 3rd Battalion, 112th Infantry, suffered heavily in actions south of the Kall, losing its company headquarters, most of the 2nd Platoon, and all of the 3rd and 4th platoons.

the Weasel convoy. He still had his own jeep, two Weasels, and two half-ton trucks, so they set forth with George driving a Weasel cargo carrier.

They moved toward the switchbacks on the road north of Kommerscheidt Hill through driving rain so heavy it was almost opaque, squinting through water-sheeted windshields at the battered road. Two German flares suddenly exploded in the sky above, illuminating the column. As the flares blew away the rain-soaked night, a barrage began to fall on them. There was, said George, "so much stuff it gave us a panicky feeling." They lumbered down the trail as rapidly as they could "so we could get the hell out of there." The shelling followed them until they crossed the bridge over the Kall.

On the north side of the river, the trail was a mess, covered with fallen trees and scattered brush on which lay bodies of fallen German and American soldiers. They snaked their way through the tangle to within 150 yards of the top, where they were stopped by a large tree, sawn off and fallen across the trail. They worked the jeep and Weasels under its bole but had to abandon the two trucks.

As they came out of the woods, they discovered Germans dug in on a slight rise to the east in firing positions. George told his men "to fire like hell" as they went past. The convoy raced up out of the draw. "The men with me were all so scared they didn't fire a single shot until we were past the German positions, then a few fired a couple of desultory shots." They finally arrived at a kitchen area near Germeter, where kerosene stoves sent out roaring waves of warmth and where cooks worked in snug tents while the aroma of boiling coffee filled the air. Lieutenant George was now out of the fight. He made no more trips to Kommerscheidt Hill. To the south he could hear the increasing ferocity of a German artillery barrage.[26]

Others continued to escape from the jaws of the German trap slowly closing around Kommerscheidt. Men of B and C companies, 1340th Engineers, saw them pass as they waited in their positions near the bridge over the river, enduring regular barrages that Captain Thomas Creegan, B Company commander, believed to be of at least 150mm caliber. Those engineers were scared and confused. Roaming enemy patrols and artillery barrages frightened them. They also received reassuring radio messages from the rear that claimed they were in no real threat. Yet passing stragglers told them how badly their outfits were chopped up and so they were getting out while they could. This confused the engineers and, Creegan said in understatement, "left us in a bad position."[27]

At 1000 hours, 7 November, Staff Sergeant Ben Cipra, an engineer in C Company, saw an infantry lieutenant and nearly 30 enlisted men come across the bridge and up the road toward Vossenack "in single file, closed up, going damn fast." There were no shots being fired nor any artillery or mortar rounds falling. "It was a strange sight and we didn't know what to think," Cipra said.

As the infantrymen disappeared up the trail, Cipra heard shouting from his own 3rd Platoon in positions across the river. "They came racing across the bridge," Cipra recalled, "the whole crowd of them, running." A German machine gun sited near Mestrenger Mühle opened fire on them. It was enough for Cipra. "I tried to make my way to the rear. Men were strung out all along the road." A little way up the hill, engineer Captain Tom Creegan of B Company stopped Cipra. The sergeant told Creegan that C Company had fallen back from its positions. "He put me in charge of some C Company men and told me to dig in." It was nearly noon.

Creegan was dismayed as he saw men retreating up the trail. "At one point," he said, "I ordered one infantry lieutenant accompanied by six to eight men to dig in. He balked at first, but since none of his men were wounded, he finally obeyed my order." After a few hours the lieutenant told Creegan they were going back to the vicinity of their artillery "where they would find no Germans." Apparently, thought Creegan, they had been through a "very grievous strain." So had Creegan. His Company B suffered 44 casualties out of 99 men who went down into the gorge.[28]

In the afternoon, Sergeant Cipra saw one of his company officers, Lieutenant Lunur Makousky. The two men, accompanied by a few other troops from C Company, 20th Engineers, walked back down the trail to the bridge, where they found Staff Sergeant Earlis Gillespie still at his machine gun trying to care for six shell-shocked men. During the afternoon small groups of Germans kept pressing in on them from the direction of the mill. Gillespie slipped away about 1700 hours that afternoon, leaving behind him only three officers and 14 men in C Company.[29]

By full dark, Sergeant Cipra recalled, he had but six men with him; 24 hours later, only two others remained. By the night of 9/10 November, he had only one companion. All the others had been evacuated, or were missing, or had helped carry wounded men back to safety and had not returned.[30]

Aid station facilities at the dugout on the trail were strained on 7 November as personnel there cared for casualties from the 109th, 110th, and 112th Infantry regiments, the 893rd Tank Destroyer Battalion, the 707th Tank Battalion, and men from Companies A and C, 1340th Engineers.[31]

First Lieutenant Loyd Johnson attempted one evacuation trip. He drove from Vossenack to the bunker in a Weasel cargo carrier pulling a jeep trailer. When he arrived at the aid station, he told four walking wounded casualties to climb in the Weasel and put two more walking wounded and a litter case in the trailer. Up the trail he went and onto the near slope south of Vossenack past some 707th tanks there, which were drawing enemy fire. Johnson threaded his way around the M-4s and past numerous shell holes. On one part of the slope, unable to shift quickly enough, Johnson stalled the Weasel's engine. He jammed his foot against the brake pedal to hold the vehicle in place while he restarted its motor. Its brakes failed to hold, the Weasel rolled backward, and the trailer jackknifed before coming to a stop.

Later, driving through the wrecked streets of Vossenack, a Sherman tank sideswiped Johnson's Weasel, dragging it and the trailer backward until the treads of the two vehicles finally disentangled. Again the trailer jackknifed, this time into the path of the tank, which pushed it to the edge of the road with its treads rather than crushing it. "Little wonder," Lieutenant Johnson marveled, "the litter patient in the trailer was hysterical when we reached our objective."[32]

Grievously concerned about the number of unevacuated patients at the Kall aid station and wounded men in the Kommerscheidt sector, Major Albert Berndt, regimental surgeon for the 112th, suggested at 1900 hours that a truce be arranged with the Germans enabling him to sweep the Kommerscheidt area for dead and evacuate the wounded. The S-2 intelligence officer and S-4 supply officer of the regiment declined to entertain his idea. Berndt then suggested an air drop of medical supplies to those at the dugout and to the men of 1st and 3rd battalions at Kommerscheidt. That too was vetoed.[33]

When it proved impossible for Task Force Ripple to carry out its assignment of attacking and retaking Schmidt, the two divisional generals, Cota and Davis, sought an alternative. By 0830 hours on Tuesday, 7 November, they came up with the idea for Task Force Davis. The peripatetic assistant division commander would finally get his own "army," which, under his leadership, would accomplish what all others had failed to do.[34]

It now became clear why 1st Battalion, 109th Infantry Regiment, was retained in the Germeter area after its relief by the 12th Infantry Regiment, 4th Infantry Division, from the forests and minefields south of the town of Hürtgen. 2nd and 3rd battalions had been thrown back into the fray—one against Vossenack and the other onto the slope of the Vossenack ridge to protect the Kall MSR. Neither received filler replacements prior to these moves. Only 1st Battalion had been reinforced. Some 200 new men replaced those who fell as casualties in the fierce forest fighting of previous days. 1st Battalion, 109th Infantry, would form the core of Task Force Davis, to be strengthened later as it churned over the Schmidt plateau by surviving members of 1st and 3rd battalions, 112th Infantry, presently encircled at Kommerscheidt, and by existing remnants of 3rd Battalion, 110th Infantry Regiment, which had already fought its way through the Kall Valley as part of Task Force Ripple.

For armored support, Task Force Davis was to use B and C companies, 893rd Tank Destroyer Battalion, and A and C companies, 707th Tank Battalion. Surely four battalions of infantry and four armored battalions would have the strength to thrust through German forces where others had failed and seize Schmidt from stubborn *Wehrmacht* defenders. It might have worked if components of Task Force Davis had not been so depleted by previous fighting.

When withdrawn from combat north of Germeter on the evening of 6

November, 1st Battalion, 109th Infantry, was a shambles. Only one officer remained out of the entire battalion staff. Able Company needed 60 replacements, while B Company was down to 74 officers and men. Its other companies were in similar straits. Two hundred new men dropped suddenly into battalion ranks could hardly transform it overnight into a top-notch fighting machine ready for renewed combat.

3rd Battalion, 110th Infantry, was even more wasted. Estimates of the number of its riflemen still capable of functioning varied from 30 to 60 to 299 at the time of its linkup with 1st and 3rd battalions, 112th Infantry, at Kommerscheidt Hill. The pathetic condition of its few remaining "effectives" was a major reason for Colonel Ripple and Colonel Peterson canceling the attack of Task Force Ripple on 6 November.

Riflemen of 1st and 3rd battalions, 112th Infantry, had been in no shape to launch or renew an attack on Schmidt since the German counterattack on 4 November. Beset by constant enemy artillery, struck repeatedly by German armor and infantry, ravaged by weather conditions, and with morale at low ebb, no responsible commander could have expected these men to have been able to renew an attack.

Armored units scheduled to form part of Task Force Davis were also inadequate. Colonel Mays told General Davis that so far as he was able to determine, only two M-10s in Kommerscheidt were still functioning, and one of them was damaged. Concern for his new task force was a major reason for Davis' insistence that Mays send additional destroyers down the Kall trail; this resulted in the destruction of four more of them. Tanks in Kommerscheidt were in as much trouble as were TDs. Although some M-4s and M-10s were available to General Davis, he could use them for his task force only by stripping all remaining armor from the Vossenack ridge. Even then there was little likelihood they would be able to transit the deadly Kall trail.[35] Despite his best efforts, General Davis was never able to launch his "paper tiger" through the Kall Valley and on to Schmidt. The concept was unrealistic from the beginning, refusing to take existing conditions into account—a desperate effort by two divisional generals under pressure from Corps and Army superiors to accomplish an impossible task.

In the encircled pocket of Americans at Kommerscheidt and on the hill just north of the hamlet, murderous concentrations of artillery fire from German guns exploded with ear-shattering ferocity directly upon surviving soldiers of the *"Blutiger Eimer,"* continuing hour after countless hour without respite. Men were soaked to the skin and hopelessly miserable as they crouched fearfully in their waterlogged holes while concussive waves burst around them. No longer, as had occasionally been done on earlier days, did a trooper climb from a hole during a barrage to walk into the open, drop his pants, and squat for a bowel movement as an obscene gesture of contempt for enemy artillery gunners.[36] Fearing for their lives, shaking from the cold, often wracked by their own sobs, with no rations or water for the past two days, each man lived within his own personal hell.[37]

Major Richard Dana commented on the fierce artillery barrage. "I counted explosions as fast as I could and, at one point, they put down fifty rounds in one-and-a-half minutes."[38] Colonel Ripple believed there must be at least four or five battalions of German artillery firing simultaneously for such a concentration of fire to fall on the area. It was coming in from Bergstein, Hürtgen, Harscheidt, and Schmidt, creating a 180-degree arc of explosive rain and causing heavy casualties.[39]

At 0540 hours, 7 November, PFC Clarence Skains saw five German tanks moving through an orchard toward Kommerscheidt.[40] Captain Bruce Hostrup saw nearly ten.[41] By 0645 hours, Major Dana reported that 15 tanks accompanied by numerous infantry were closing on Kommerscheidt.[42] Second Lieutenant Richard Payne, a tanker, counted nearly 10 tanks.[43] This German armor worked its way in on the right of American positions, moving so cautiously that many did not see any tanks until they began firing. "They proceeded to work over our tanks and destroyers," Sergeant Ripperdam said. "A lot of them burned—at least five tanks and tank destroyers. There was a hellish amount of noise and confusion and everyone was pretty nervous. I was feeling pretty low."[44]

Hurting as they were, many GIs still had a great deal of fight left in them. Lieutenant Payne was one such. "I spotted a German tank coming around the western end of Kommerscheidt. Shell fragments the previous day had damaged the elevating mechanism of my gun. I was unable to depress it sufficiently to hit the hull of the German tank. We did register two hits on his turret but the tank kept on coming. I hollered to the TDs which hadn't yet seen this tank to 'get on him.' They spotted it and each placed two rounds right into it. It backed out and we saw it no more."[45]

As it grew light, PFC Clarence Skains could see a large group of German infantry moving toward Kommerscheidt out of a small patch of woods. He also saw a lone enemy soldier nearby, apparently an artillery observer. Skains took careful aim and shot the man. An enemy tank saw Skains and opened fire, first with its machine guns, then with its turret cannon. The shells missed Skains and he scuttled for the safety of his water-filled foxhole and pulled a mattress over it. Soon there was a thud. Skains looked out and saw a German on top of his mattress trying to throw a "potato masher" grenade into his hole. The two men wrestled as Skains grabbed for the grenade. He managed to yank it away and throw it. Skains then killed the enemy soldier. A frightened Skains was comforted to hear a buddy, PFC Nathaniel Quentin, firing his BAR at "Jerries" as Germans advanced through the morning rain and fog. The heavy popping of the BAR was nearly continuous.[46]

Tanks stood off out of bazooka range as Germans pressed their attack on

Kommerscheidt from the southeast, deliberately firing at American foxholes until they killed those in them, systematically eradicating men in each hole. "This was hell," Major Dana recalled, "and after seeing a number of nearby holes shot up, some men took off for the rear and others followed, streaming back."[47]

Colonel Ripple saw infantry lines crumbling, men no longer able to hold their weak positions. "The men were in an absolute daze incapable of taking or carrying out orders," he said. "I attempted to lead them forward, but they would not go." At one point, he and Colonel Peterson saw an enemy self-propelled assault gun poking its nose around a nearby building. "We ran like hell," Ripple admitted.[48]

Sergeant Tony Kudiak and PFC John Kerwacki had hidden in a stone barn during the night. At daybreak they looked outside when the artillery barrage began and saw tanks and enemy infantry moving toward Kommerscheidt through the rain. Three shells hit the old barn, shattering holes in its walls. "All hell was breaking loose," Kudiak said. Peering out regularly through windows and shell holes, Kudiak and Kerwacki saw GIs in nearby foxholes break and run, with "quite a number taking off over the hill to the rear, withdrawing in haste."

Then Kudiak and Kerwacki saw the reason for the rout: a Mark V rumbled forward through light-arms fire, straddled the American forward command post, and sat there, shooting those who tried to flee. "Survivors," wrote Cy Peterman, "say they still can vision that tank squatting on the dugout like a prehistoric monster, spitting slugs through our men." They then saw "a large group of our Joes," most of them personnel from the command post, "going up to it with their hands up, surrendering." A white flag stood nearby.

Kudiak and Kerwacki had seen enough. They climbed through a hole in the rear wall of the barn and ran 200 yards through the open before they reached cover while enemy infantry fired at them. They made their way north out of town to Kommerscheidt Hill, past C Company lines to positions held by 110th Regiment infantrymen and dug in with them. "We didn't want to get captured out there," Kudiak said.[49]

Sergeant Ripperdam also saw the surrender. "There was a big tank right on top of the battalion CP. . . . It was in a position to cover the entrance. American soldiers in front of the CP had their hands raised in surrender and a white flag was showing."[50] Captain Jack Walker also observed the incident. Watching from nearby, he saw a tank sitting almost on top of the CP. "I saw Staff and members of headquarters all with their hands upraised in surrender."[51] The time was late morning. The staffs of both 1st and 3rd battalions, 112th Regiment, all of whom were reported to be at the CP, were listed as missing in action by higher Headquarters. From these eyewitness accounts by Kudiak, Ripperdam, and Walker, it is reasonable to assume they were captured at that time. *Every* document of 1st Battalion—including logs, journals, special operating instructions, and personnel records—was seized at this time by German troops.[52]

Not far from the CP, Captain Walker was stopped by a "tall major" a few minutes after the surrender. The officer was Major Robert Christenson, acting commander of 3rd Battalion since the relief of Colonel Albert Flood. Christenson told Walker to pull his men back from town to Kommerscheidt Hill into the area held by C Company and men of the 110th Regiment. Their tenuous hold on the hamlet of Kommerscheidt was at an end. It was 1300 hours, 7 November.

"I saw him turn and head back into Kommerscheidt after he knew the Germans had taken it," Walker reported. "I conjecture he probably gave up himself, feeling strongly the stigma of defeat."[53] Sergeant Ripperdam also saw Christenson walk slowly away, bent with sorrow.[54]

Radio operators in the regimental command post on Kommerscheidt Hill broadcast desperate messages back to "Holiday 6," code name for General Cota, at the war bunker in Rott. At 1125 hours, 7 November, Carl Peterson, commander of the 112th Infantry Regiment, known as "Horseshoe 6," sent out a forlorn plea:

> Tanks expended, troops withdrawn from Kommerscheidt. Now forming line vic. Charley Co. Can't shell town because of wounded and captured men. Must have armor to attack or hold.

Only five minutes later, "Horseshoe 6" sent a second cry for help:

> Enemy Artillery firing—unbelievable—cannot pinpoint but believe bombing would help.[55]

The meager capabilities of the 28th Division Headquarters were demonstrated when General Davis asked First Lieutenant Leon Simon, assistant S-3 operations officer of 3rd Battalion, 112th Regiment, to organize a platoon and take it forward from the rear area to Kommerscheidt Hill to help defenders there. What could Davis have had in mind? In what way would *one* platoon of men have been able to help their desperate buddies on the encircled Kommerscheidt hill?*[56]

Despite the formation on paper of Task Force Davis, General Cota had no

---

*Simon agreed to help, but his efforts were unavailing. He went to the straggler line at Germeter and called for volunteers. Only two men stepped forward, a private and a second lieutenant. Simon declined to use them. He and one other man started for Kommerscheidt Hill but were forced to seek cover due to intense artillery fire ringing the area. In the process, Simon misplaced his map and got lost; then he huddled in a ditch until nightfall. The two men finally worked their way back through the woods to the rear regimental command post at 2300 hours that day, victims of another exercise in total futility.

way of helping those entrapped men south of the Kall. That did not lessen his determination for them to continue to battle against hopeless odds. Cota's radio broadcast orders for those on Kommerscheidt Hill to hold out at all costs.[57] Lieutenant Richard Payne summed it up. Forced back upon the regimental command post by enemy fire, Payne dismounted from his tank and spoke with his battalion commander. Colonel Ripple told him, "we would have to stay with our tanks and slug it out. He had been ordered to hold the position at ALL costs."[58]

Sometime during that frantic day of 7 November—estimates of the time vary from 0900 to 1500 hours[59]—divisional headquarters sent a radio message to the 112th regimental command post ordering Colonel Carl Peterson to report immediately to the CP at Rott.

Peterson, from Bradford, Pennsylvania, had formerly served as executive officer of the 109th Infantry Regiment. He took command of the 112th Regiment following the evacuation of Colonel Hodes. He thus returned to head a regiment in which he had served almost continuously since 1916.

Although it was a strange time to be recalled from the battlefield, Peterson left willingly enough. He wanted an opportunity to give firsthand testimony to divisional staff officers about conditions on Kommerscheidt Hill, and rumors had previously come to him that he was to be relieved for inefficiency and replaced by Colonel Gustin Nelson, a recently transferred officer from the 5th Armored Division. General Cota later insisted there were no plans to recall or replace Peterson, but the very presence in the division of Colonel Nelson confirmed the fact that Peterson was on his way out. Peterson departed, taking a jeep belonging to Captain Bruce Hostrup, a tanker, leaving Colonel Ripple as senior commander for all those trapped in the encircled pocket.

Two enlisted men went with Peterson—PFC Gus Seiler, and another man whose name the colonel never learned. They traveled only about 300 yards when German small-arms fire forced them to abandon the jeep and move on foot through the woods. As they intersected the Kall trail near the river, they saw American bodies strewn across its surface, crushed by vehicular traffic, and several abandoned Weasels. The three men pulled the bodies off the road and removed several corpses from the tracked cargo carriers before enemy rifle fire again forced them back into the trees.

Peterson and his two companions followed the riverbank, looking for a place shallow enough to cross. After they waded across they were once more fired on by German soldiers. They fled deeper into the forest as enemy mortar shells dropped around them. A few moments later they were forced into a fire fight and killed two Germans. Mortar rounds again exploded, one of which wounded Peterson in his left leg. Adrenalin pulsed through the colonel so thoroughly he thought only that he had irritated a fragment of metal still in his leg from an old World War I wound.

The unnamed man with Peterson offered to go on alone and bring back help. The colonel refused, but the man's pace quickened so much he soon outdistanced the other two and was seen no more. Hearing Germans talking in the woods around them, Peterson and Seiler dropped to the earth and crept forward on hands and knees. They were not sufficiently quiet. Enemy slugs ripped into Seiler and he collapsed, dead instantly. More mortar shells burst, and this time a steel fragment hit the colonel in the right leg, rendering it useless. With one leg injured and the other totally unusable, Peterson painfully dragged himself forward. He recrossed the Kall River, thinking he might find a safer way to the rear that would avoid contact with enemy soldiers.

Peterson crawled from the water nearly at the feet of three Germans, who quickly ran when he fired his submachine gun at them. The colonel was hardly conscious as he dragged himself among the trees. He then heard the blessed sound of Americans talking and the ring of a pick against stone. Mortar shells burst around him and he passed out.

When he awoke, still hearing GI voices, Peterson cried out for help. The talk abruptly stopped. More shells exploded. In a daze, the valiant officer dragged himself to the riverbank, crossed the Kall, then crossed still again. Lying in exhausted pain beside the river road, he watched as two enemy soldiers walked along it and sat down not far away. He lay quietly as two American soldiers appeared and captured the Germans. Peterson shouted and then fainted. They turned their rifles toward the sound of his voice, but hearing nothing, the men left with their prisoners.

Clawing his way back to consciousness, Peterson knew he could go no farther. Certain he was going to die but still unwilling to give up, he repeatedly shouted the words "General Cota . . . Colonel Peterson." Two engineers, perhaps the same ones who had earlier captured the Germans, heard and located him. They carried him to the rear on a stretcher after a corporal gave Peterson plasma and a shot of morphine.

Evacuated by jeep to the divisional command bunker at Rott, Peterson looked as if he had been through a war. Unshaven, eyes red-rimmed, covered with mud, exhausted, twice wounded by shell fragments, clothes torn beyond repair, he still insisted on seeing General Cota. When the division commander saw this man who had crossed the Kall four times and walked and crawled thousands of yards before his rescue, the sight was too much. "At the sight of him, Cota fainted."*

When Cota and Peterson later talked, the colonel told his commanding officer of his receipt of the recall message. Cota claimed never to have sent such an order and insisted Peterson's courage had failed him and, as a consequence, he deserted his command under hostile enemy fire. Only much later did Cota at last admit that *someone* from his headquarters might have

*General James M. Gavin described Cota's fainting spell in his book *On to Berlin*. No other reference to this strange behavior has been found. General Gavin knew full well the gravity of this charge which he levied against "Dutch" Cota.

recalled Peterson but *he* certainly had not done so. It was another example of a good officer in a crucial position who was wasted because of a foul-up in communications.[60]

While Peterson made his way to the rear, those he left behind in the Kommerscheidt pocket faced the continuing ferocity of German shells and attacking infantry. The few GIs left within the limits of the hamlet infiltrated toward the rear. Sergeant Ripperdam tried to stop those near him, "grabbing as many men as we could lay our hands on. The men hesitated for a few minutes . . . but they were so badly shaken that for as long as they could continue to get away they did. It was no use," Ripperdam admitted, "so we fell back on the 110th battalion to reorganize what was left of our two battalions."[61]

Captain Guy Piercey, commander of M Company, saw the lines around him breaking up as riflemen withdrew. He and his 50 men also pulled back, following and outpacing others until they found themselves near the bridge over the Kall. On the way a shell from an enemy tank blew one man straight up into the air before he dropped on the ground like a broken doll. They continued without stopping after passing the river, walking out to safety through the deadly Hürtgen Forest.[62]

No one told Clarence Skains or Nathaniel Quentin that a general withdrawal from Kommerscheidt had been ordered, nor could they see their buddies pull out, for buildings and hedgerows blocked their line of sight. So they remained in town while around them other members of their squad lay dead in their foxholes, killed by point-blank fire.

A dark man of half-Cherokee, half-Irish ancestry, Quentin was a pleasant, easy-mannered man whose soft speech carried a slight drawl. His next actions revealed extraordinary talent for close combat.

At 1300 hours, Quentin noticed a platoon of enemy soldiers crawling toward him, their uniforms blending with the saturated ground now covered by falling snow. He allowed them to advance within 25 yards and then opened fire with his BAR, killing 20 and forcing the others to retreat. A few moments later, 15 Germans rushed him, some armed with machine pistols. They twice tried to overrun Quentin but both times he drove them back with deadly fire from his BAR.

About 1445 hours, the Germans attacked again, in one- and two-man rushes, running through a turnip patch toward Quentin and Skains. They held their ground, firing steadily. The enemy advance faltered and stopped and then the Germans retreated frantically. Quentin shot several in the back as they tried to get away. Only two escaped. Quentin and Skains had repelled the third attack on their position in less than two hours.

At 1545 hours, the two American soldiers saw enemy tanks grinding toward them. They slipped to their right and came under fire from a nearby sniper. Quentin killed the gunman with a grenade. They crept up to a hedge, from which they saw a column of German infantry filing through the ruins of

Kommerscheidt. As the enemy soldiers drew closer, Quentin checked his ammunition, alarmed that he had only eight clips of shells left for his BAR. Slapping a new clip into his heavy weapon, he lay on his stomach and opened fire, using up all eight clips. Most of the men in the column fell dead or wounded, the rest scattering, scrambling for dubious safety.

An enemy tank took Quentin and Skains under fire, missed, and hit an apple tree beside them. Behind the tank were two others and an armored reconnaissance car. All four vehicles ground toward them. Quentin and Skains decided it was time to pull out. They crawled toward cover in a nearby patch of woods and made their way safely back to their own tank destroyer positions on Kommerscheidt Hill. Germans in the woods that night were so close Quentin and Skains could hear them talking with one another. In their two-man stand they had killed nearly 60 Germans and wounded dozens more.[63]

Those who drifted back into C Company positions on Kommerscheidt Hill that day were so shattered that reorganization was purely makeshift. There were so few men left in the 112th Regiment it was no longer possible for them to retain individual company identities.[64] Major Dana recommended to Colonel Ripple that all riflemen from the scattered companies be placed under the control of "Howdy" Rumbaugh. Ripple concurred and Rumbaugh formed them all into "Provisional Company A," setting up a defense of sorts against German infantry, tanks, artillery, and mortars.[65] Many men hadn't eaten for three days and some tried to retrieve ten-in-one rations from knocked-out tanks. Enemy fire drove them back, inflicting still more casualties. "All we could do," Joe Perll said, "was put them in foxholes. As a result a lot died."[66]

Tightening the circle, German forces moved high-velocity, self-propelled assault guns toward the American pocket "and knocked hell out of our tanks. The tank battle went on all day," Perll recalled.[67]

By 1500 hours, 7 November, the entire U.S. command in the pocket consisted of combat-shocked remnants of 1st and 3rd battalions, 112th Regiment, plus a decimated group of men from 3rd Battalion, 110th Regiment. For armor they had only two M-10 tank destroyers, one of which had a bad engine, and one tank without ammunition, as well as three towed antitank guns which had been pulled onto Kommerscheidt Hill the previous night by a Weasel convoy. It was an understatement to describe the situation as grave.[68]

They refused, however, simply to sit and await the end. They fired on approaches from Kommerscheidt, loath to fire on the town itself, since in their disorganized withdrawal they left many wounded behind and were afraid they might kill their own men. In a moment of bravado, Major Dana sent a message to divisional headquarters that they would need armor replacements if they were going to retake and hold Kommerscheidt and

Schmidt.[69] Their own armored vehicles destroyed, tankers and destroyer crews stayed in foxholes and fought as infantry.[70]

The enemy was not yet finished for the day. At about dusk German infantry and one Mark V advanced toward the Kommerscheidt pocket. American artillery knocked out the tank less than 100 yards from foxholes of its own men and also shelled in the woods west and southwest of Kommerscheidt. Courageous GIs even continued to take prisoners. Two PWs captured that night told how their battalion, reinforced with panzers, was to have attacked until American artillery knocked out one panzer. As the others milled around and backed away, their treads crushed 15 riflemen assembling for the attack order. In the resulting confusion, the attack was postponed.[71] Americans in the pocket would live to see still another day.

PFC Joe Perll shared in the low ebb of morale around him. "When we were surrounded and cut off on Kommerscheidt Hill, with capture essential," he said, "I tried to hammer the 'H' [for 'Hebrew'] off my dogtags with a rock, for I was deathly afraid of what the Germans might do to me as a Jew."[72]

German records were full of self-congratulations on 7 November. They described the steel ring closing around the encircled American pocket. From the east came infantry troops of *Wolf, Wilshewsky* and *Schindler* battalions. Assault guns and tanks moved toward Kommerscheidt from the south. *Battalion Onnen* advanced from the west. Those records spoke of a 3,000 round artillery barrage by German artillery batteries as they blasted away at "Ami" positions. German commanders knew of orders sent by Cota to Peterson and Ripple "to hold at all costs until relieved by reserves." They also saw how American positions crumbled "under concentrated fire of our weapons and the fanatical will of our grenadiers and tank men."

"Near MESTRENGER MUEHLE," an enemy writer recorded, "a few courageous men engage three enemy tanks with close combat antitank weapons. One is destroyed and the other two, undamaged, are the booty of Sergeant SUEDHAUSEN and his tank destroyer section. . . . The second-highest decoration for bravery for this courageous action and a well-deserved 'Tank Cracker' furlough immediately follow."

At 1500 hours, while Quentin and Skains were valiantly fighting on, German forces sent a message from *39th Infantry Division* to *Seventh Army* headquarters: "The battle of KOMMERSCHEIDT has ended successfully." Only a few small groups of American soldiers still clung to Kommerscheidt, and cleaning-up operations continued against those few resisters. They would not last long, crowed the writer, for Colonel Bayer with tanks and grenadiers "who for days and nights have hardly an hour's sleep and who have fought continuously, are pursuing the enemy to destroy the last remnant and to once more establish the defensive line."[73]

LXXIV Corps, one German officer recalled, had now nearly destroyed those American forces which, on 2 November, launched themselves from Germeter toward Schmidt. "After heavy fighting in both Schmidt and Kommerscheidt," he said, "the American tanks had been destroyed and the infantry could only pass individually back through the woods to Vossenack." There were, he believed, three overriding reasons for this successful German defense: (1) the steepness of the supply route from Vossenack to Kommerscheidt, (2) roads available to Germans south of the Kall capable of supporting an armored counterattack, and (3) effective massing of German artillery fire.[74]

On 7 November, Germans trumpeted the capture of 260 American prisoners in the area of the Kommerscheidt pocket. Battlefield body counts included over 100 dead soldiers of the 28th Infantry Division, with more still to be tallied.[75]

For the Germans there was but one sour note that day: Forces of the *116th Panzer Division* did not recapture Vossenack. Although they pushed as far west as the village church, "they could neither capitalize on nor retain this advantage. Without armored support, operating on open ground which left us at the mercy of aircraft and artillery, lacking reserves, and facing an excellent, spirited defense, our attack could go no further. In spite of heavy artillery support, repeated assaults achieved no success. When we saw that our attack to cut off the [American] penetration [in Vossenack] had no chance of completion, we ordered that the troops establish a defense along the edge of the woods" to the east, in the draw between Vossenack and the Brandenberg–Bergstein ridge.[76]

Late on 7 November, General Cota finally admitted to himself that this was one battle impossible for him to win. Kommerscheidt was once again in German hands, and his men now held only a small area on the hill to the north. Unwilling to rely on his own judgment, Cota turned to General Davis, who had seen battlefield conditions firsthand. He asked his assistant divisional commander if he had any recommendations. Davis' response was terse. To retake Schmidt would require a "full strength force with plenty of tanks." Having already seen Task Force Davis fall by the wayside that day, both generals knew there was no possibility of procuring infantrymen and tanks in sufficient numbers to drive through the German-held Kall Valley, link up with "Bloody Bucket" survivors on Kommerscheidt Hill, and forge south to capture Schmidt.

Cota plied Davis with questions. Should he leave his troops encircled on Kommerscheidt Hill? Should he send the rest of the 109th Regiment to reinforce them? "Or should we bring that force back?"

Any attempt at reinforcing troops south of the Kall would be difficult, Davis reminded his commander, adding, "Developments tonight in connection with [the] ridge indicate that we can't use that supply route."

Cota agreed the Kall trail was so infested with Germans that "it is not open."

For any reinforcement to succeed, said Davis, "we have got to have [a] road of supply." The Kall trail was already lost to them. "Fire is keeping up and is right across it and below it. Besides, it comes from every direction."

Under such conditions no reinforcement was possible. Cota bowed to the inevitable. "I recommend that we pull in."

General Davis agreed. "I Concur. The Germans are undoubtedly reinforced by all sorts of fire power. [We] Will have to clean up [the] tank situation and open up a supply route."

"Can I tell Gen[eral] Hodges that?" asked Cota.

"You can tell him that," replied Davis.

"If [this] recommendation is approved, we will have to get those people under way," Cota said, thinking of the difficulties his trapped men would face in extricating themselves from the pocket.[77] Cota spoke with General Hodges by telephone about the situation of American troops south of the Kall.

At 2310 hours, double daylight savings time, General Leonard Gerow, V Corps commander, called Cota. Hodges and Gerow had discussed the predicament of the 28th Infantry Division. Gerow warned Cota that Hodges "was very dissatisfied with [the] way things are going—All we seem to be doing is lose ground." At first, Gerow recalled, Hodges had insisted "he didn't want any withdrawal there and at the end of [the] conversation he said he would leave it to you. I don't want to leave you out on a limb. Now if you think it is best to pull back I will authorize you to do it. Pull those people back tonight or as soon as you can tomorrow."

Ever an unrealistic optimist, Gerow hoped something might still be salvaged from the divisional effort. "Be sure [the] VOSSENACK Ridge is secure and leave something in [the] draw," he said. "Get [the] rest of your outfit back in some area and get them re-constituted. Once you get that done you can hold VOSSENACK Ridge with one Reg[imen]t; you can have one Reg[imen]t to work South and I will take [the] other Reg[imen]t to put with [Major General Lunsford E.] Oliver's [5th Armored Division] force and work on STECKENBORN. I suggest you clean out [the] draws and ridge with 109 Inf[antry]. How long will it take to re-constitute [the] 112 Inf[antry]?"

Trying desperately to tell his superior what he wanted to hear, Cota assured Gerow that the devastated units of the 28th Infantry Division could again be combat-ready in "About 3 days if replacements come thru satisfactorily." This was, of course, utter nonsense. It would take more than three days to reconstitute regiments as blasted by combat casualties as were those of Cota's 28th Division.

The 12th Regiment, 4th Infantry Division "that came to you last night," Gerow assured Cota, "will continue to operate under your control. Give them [the] job of closing [the] gap [around the town of Hürtgen, on the divisional left flank] and connecting up with VII Corps and improving that situation up there. Give [the commander of the 12th Regiment] those instructions and get him on that tomorrow. Give [Colonel Theodore] Seely his [3rd] B[attalio]n, [110th Infantry Regiment,] back and get it in shape and work South to ROLLESBROICH. Get 112th Inf[antry] Reg[imen]t re-constituted or use your own judgment and get the one fixed up that can be done quickest."[78]

True visionaries, we are told, are young men, while their elders are consumed by dreams. General Leonard Gerow, V Corps commander, bore primary responsibility for the disastrous deployment of the 28th Infantry Division in its three-way attack into the depths of the Hürtgen Forest on 2 November. The ensuing week of unremitting combat drenched men of the "Bloody Bucket" with "blood, and fire, and vapor of smoke." Unfavorable weather during those days turned the sun "into darkness and the moon into blood." Thousands of those who, in the agony of their death throes, called "on the name of the Lord"[78] had not been saved at all. Yet Gerow still could not relinquish the folly of his unsubstantial reveries. He continued to conjure up phantasmagoric assaults against the German army with total disregard for the actual condition of his divisional forces.

11

"Fight your way out"

8 November 1944

On this day a constellation of stars fell on the war room of the 28th Infantry Division at Rott, Germany. Major General Norman D. "Dutch" Cota and his assistant division commander, Brigadier General George A. Davis, may have been understandably nervous when they awakened, for they were about to play host to some of the European theater's grandest illuminaries. They came from everywhere. General Dwight David Eisenhower, Supreme Commander, Supreme Headquarters, Allied Expeditionary Force, Europe, came forward with his escorts from SHAEF headquarters in Versailles. His famous smile may well have been strained that day as he sought to learn what had caused the calamity to his soldiers in the Hürtgen. Lieutenant General Omar Bradley, former commander of the 28th Infantry Division, arrived at Rott from his headquarters at 12th Army Group. Lieutenant General Courtney H. Hodges, commander of First Army, came to the meeting accompanied by his chief of staff, Major General William Kean. Present also was Lieutenant General Leonard T. Gerow, commander of V Corps.[1]

Cota knew he was in for an unhappy day. The conference that day would bring him no laurels and might even cost him his command. Nearly everyone present was under a pecking-order system of pressure. "Ike" was concerned about this difficulty within the boundary of his 12th Army Group. Bradley was dissatisfied with the performance of his First Army commander. Hodges plainly revealed his own disappointment with the lack of success by his corps commander. Gerow could not understand why his brilliant planning for the assault on Schmidt had been so badly botched by his subordinate. Cota—low man on the totem pole—could only listen and try to explain that failure was not his fault.

We have no record of what Eisenhower or Bradley said that day, only that they attended the conference. Nor is there much information about the role played by General Gerow other than the bare outline in the divisional G-3 journal that he "discussed [the] situation and plans for future operations with Gen[eral] Cota and staff."[2] There is no reason to believe he bared his conscience to reveal himself as the author of the war plan followed by the 28th Division. There is rather every reason to assume he let "Dutch" Cota bear the brunt of Hodges' wrath.

Throughout the preceding days of battle, General Hodges had endeavored to stay in touch with the tactical situation in the Hürtgen. Only the preceding Sunday, 5 November, Hodges and Kean, in company with Gerow and General Collins, visited Cota's war room to check on the reason for the loss of Schmidt and to inform him that Collins' VII Corps drive for the Rhine would be indefinitely postponed until the weather cleared. At other times the commander of First Army spoke by telephone with both Cota and Gerow. He had spoken with both only the previous day.

Until Tuesday, 7 November, when Cota conferred by telephone with Gerow and Hodges, it is quite possible that neither the corps nor army commanders were aware of the full extent of the disaster facing the 28th Division. Only then did Cota seek permission to pull his troops back from the pocket on Kommerscheidt Hill. Even on Wednesday, 8 November, if the assessment by Lieutenant Colonel James White, executive officer for the 1171st Engineer Combat Group, was correct, Cota had still not informed General Gerow that he had engineers fighting as infantry in efforts to hold Vossenack.[3]

Neither Gerow nor Hodges could have realized from perusal of Cota's G-3 operational periodic reports, which were sent to higher Headquarters, just how badly the battle was progressing. The effect of those reports was to cover up repeated reverses and transform them into victories. Panicky routs became "withdrawals" for the purpose of "reorganization." False entries insisted that "original positions" were quickly regained. Men hopelessly trapped in minefields were only "adjusting unit boundaries." "Combat efficiency" was inevitably described as "excellent" no matter what its true state might be.

On the day before the conference, Hodges was suddenly confronted by a request from Cota to be allowed to withdraw his men from south of the Kall. In Hodges' mind, such a disastrous situation could only be Cota's fault. In telephone conversations with Gerow on 7 November, Hodges gave his preliminary approval to Cota's petition. That did not prevent the First Army commander from expressing his wrath when, on Wednesday, 8 November, he came face-to-face with Cota at the conference. In a sharp exchange, he told the commander of the 28th Division that he was "extremely disappointed" in his performance. He was also incensed because "division headquarters appeared to have no precise knowledge of the location of its units and was doing nothing to obtain the information." Hodges later indicated to General Gerow that he should "examine the possibility of command changes within the division."[4]

After considerable discussion, Hodges finally agreed to allow Cota to withdraw his men from south of the Kall. For that smidgen of humanity, however, Hodges demanded a *quid pro quo.* Cota would have to retain his hold on the southern slope of the Vossenack ridge. There would be no surrendering of that ground. There was more. Hodges demanded that Cota supply the 12th Infantry Regiment of the 4th Division with sufficient troops to ensure that it procured an alternate attack site around the town of Hürtgen for a drive to the Rur River.*

Hodges had not yet listed all his demands. Cota must continue to press south from the flank of the Vossenack ridge toward the rear of the town of Monschau. He would also detach one regiment and send it to join Major General Lunsford Oliver's 5th Armored Division in a frontal assault on Monschau.[5]

Hodges' demands were severe, yet Cota could think of no alternatives. Asking to be relieved or reassigned in protest never seems to have entered his mind. He would do his best to carry out Hodges' orders.

Heavy, drenching rain heralded the beginning of that Wednesday, 8 November, the last day south of the Kall for exhausted and frightened American survivors in the Kommerscheidt pocket. They were not the only ones who suffered, although their suffering was the greatest. German records revealed that their men also had received "no food for several days and just a few hours of sleep."[6] Yet the suffering was not comparable, and no one, friend or foe, had doubts as to which side would prevail. As if sensing the weakness of their enemies, German forces softened for a few hours the pressure they had been focusing on their American adversaries.

When PFC Joe Perll looked around him that morning there were six dead men within 20 yards, four of them in two foxholes.[7] Sergeant Tony Kudiak wearily watched from his hole, four scrounged rifles pointing in the four directions of the compass so he could be ready to repel any attack on a moment's notice.[8] Captain Marion Pugh, a tank destroyer company commander, was grateful there was so little enemy activity during the early hours of the day.[9] Sergeant Frank Ripperdam recalled that, unlike all previous days since the German counterattack against Schmidt on 4 November, only an occasional artillery shell exploded around them.[10] When lonely defenders in

---

*Cota assigned three companies of 1st Battalion, 109th Infantry Regiment, to support efforts of the 12th Infantry Regiment, 4th Infantry Division. Those companies had only 62, 55, and 73 men, respectively. Just one company reached its assigned objective, and it was cut off for three days. It ended the action with but 33 men! See Weigley, *Eisenhower's Lieutenants,* p. 368.

the pocket looked south they could see Kommerscheidt filled with smoke and flame as its buildings burned. Then it began to hail.[11]

Sometime after daylight, Captain "Howdy" Rumbaugh, commander of all infantry troops surrounded in the German trap, learned that three Sherman tanks not far away had white surrender flags flying near them. He ordered a 15-man patrol to investigate. As the men gathered to start out, two German artillery rounds landed, wounding 12 of them. Rumbaugh organized another patrol and sent it out under the command of First Lieutenant James Waters. As this group approached the tanks, a crewman of one M-4 shot Waters in the right leg. The patrol retreated in hasty dismay. The Shermans were occupied by German soldiers dressed in American coveralls. Worse, they were located in a position to dominate completely the road to the bridge and any nearby troop movements.

Rumbaugh radioed divisional headquarters for help, but it was incapable of responding. He then called for artillery fire, but the fire direction center responded at 1000 hours that it could not shell on the coordinates given by Rumbaugh inasmuch as "Holland Blue"—code name for 3rd Battalion, 109th Infantry Regiment—was moving into that area. This was Rumbaugh's first indication that relief of any kind might be near. Another radio message, at 1200 hours, confirmed the location of 3rd Battalion.[12]

3rd Battalion, the "lost battalion" commanded by Major Howard Topping, was the unit that missed its way during movement orders the night of 7/8 November and ended up south of Germeter rather than on the southern slope of the Vossenack ridge near the Kall trail, as was intended. Located at 0700 hours, 8 November by Captain William Rogers and General Davis, 3rd Battalion, 109th Regiment, was now moving into its proper location, under orders to strengthen the American hold on the Vossenack slope and to regain at least some control of the Kall trail, which by now was nearly a German *Autobahn.*

For those in the pocket on Kommerscheidt Hill the nearness of 3rd Battalion was of little practical use. Even as troops of 3rd Battalion settled into place, Colonel Ripple was forced to radio a plaintive message to the rear command post of the 112th Infantry Regiment:

> Urgently need rations, water, armour, casualties heavy. No means of evacuation. Receiving intermittently heavy fire, position will soon become untenable. No contact with Holland Blue. Their arrival will not improve situation.[13]

The tempo of battle increased. An artillery barrage fell on Kommerscheidt Hill. Behind its exploding rounds, three German tanks moved forward. Captain Clifford Hackard, commander of B Company, 1st Battalion, 112th Regiment, saw them grind ever closer. With three of his men, he crept toward the clanking behemoths, carrying a bazooka and one shell. They allowed the tanks to get within 50 yards before Hackard fired his only round through the shoulder-held weapon. With a burst of flame, the bazooka shell spat forward, knocking out one tank. Its crew leaped from the burning panzer and assumed defensive firing positions. Hackard was armed only with his issue .45 automatic pistol. He grabbed an M-1 rifle laying on the ground nearby and killed or wounded six tank crewmen. The other two tanks vengefully fired their machine guns at Hackard. His men crabbed their way up to him with more bazooka ammunition they had found. Hackard loaded the weapon and scored several hits on the two tanks, causing them to withdraw.

On their way back within their own lines, Hackard and his men saw an enemy machine gun inflicting heavy casualties. Crawling toward it under a "vicious hail of machine gun fire with a terrific amount of artillery landing," Hackard killed the three-man crew of the automatic weapon with his M-1, captured the gun, and carried it back within American lines.[14]

For many hours, Colonel Gustin Nelson, newly designated commander of the 112th Infantry Regiment and replacement for the now wounded and evacuated Carl Peterson, tried to make his way through German lines to join his command in the pocket on Kommerscheidt Hill. Previously assigned as a trains commander for the 5th Armored Division, the brisk and ambitious Nelson wanted a more active combat assignment. On 3 November he submitted a request for transfer to General Oliver, who quickly gave his approval, reassigning Nelson to the 28th Division.

Colonel Nelson arrived at Rott at 1200 hours, 7 November. General Davis welcomed him and told the colonel he would take command of the 112th Infantry Regiment. He pointed on a map to the location of the encircled soldiers of the 112th on Kommerscheidt Hill, 1,000 yards north of the village. Davis also told Nelson he could reach his men by accompanying 3rd Battalion, 109th Regiment, which that evening was to move into position on the southern slope of the Vossenack ridge near the Kall trail. Davis ordered a guide to take Colonel Nelson to the 3rd Battalion.

The guide was understandably perplexed when he could not find the unit. No one, not even Major Topping, its commander, knew where it was as the unit meandered along the south wood line of the Vossenack ridge, totally lost and out of position. After a fruitless search, a frustrated Nelson returned to divisional headquarters.

General Davis then suggested he might get through to his command by joining a supply column that was to move down the Kall trail after dark. Unfortunately, those vehicles were unable to advance beyond the Germeter road due to heavy artillery and mortar fire. Nelson twice tried to go on alone, but both times artillery barrages drove him back. Once again he returned to headquarters to inform General Davis of his quandary. Nelson spent the night of 7/8 November at Rott.[15]

On the morning of 8 November, after Captain Rogers and General Davis located the "lost battalion" in a draw south of Germeter, the general called for volunteers from it to take Colonel Nelson to Kommerscheidt Hill. Second Lieutenant Edmund Tropp, Technical Sergeant Robert McMillan, Sergeant Alexander Bretal, and PFC Lester Sunburg—all members of 3rd Battalion's K Company—stepped forward and agreed to escort the colonel.[16]

The group started out at 1445 hours in diamond formation, with Colonel Nelson in the center. Lieutenant Tropp walked point. They had moved only about 30 yards into the forest when they encountered a six-man enemy patrol. Tropp opened fire with his carbine, Sergeant Bretal joining in with his M-1, firing it from the hip. They wounded one man and the Germans fled, dragging their injured comrade with them.

Moving on down the slope, they reached and forded the Kall and crawled up a steep cliff into dense trees. Their pace was rapid until Colonel Nelson warned his escorts not to be so aggressive. As they came upon some fallen trees, the men sat down to rest. They heard sounds of axes chopping wood, and Lieutenant Tropp moved carefully forward to investigate the noises. Colonel Nelson tried to attract the lieutenant's attention to tell him he should not leave because it would spread out his escorts too much. Tropp ignored the colonel's fears and disappeared into the trees. He soon came upon an American tank, saw its crew digging foxholes, and ran up to them. The men told Tropp that they were one of the few remaining M-4 crews and that he was now within the perimeter of American forces on Kommerscheidt Hill. They pointed him in the direction of Colonel Ripple's command post. Tropp retrieved his companions and they delivered Colonel Nelson to the men of his new command. The lieutenant and his three squad members faded into the woods on their way back to safety.*[17]

Upon reaching his new command at 1600 hours, Nelson asked Colonel Ripple how many soldiers were available.

"About 350 effectives and 50 wounded, 20 of which are walking wounded," Ripple replied.

As they spoke, an artillery round exploded, killing instantly a man in a nearby foxhole.[18]

Nelson conferred with Ripple, Rumbaugh, and Dana at the regimental forward command post on the hill. He told them about the newly formed Task Force Davis, conceived the morning of the previous day by General Cota and his assistant division commander as a successor to Task Force Ripple. Nelson's knowledge of its components was sketchy, but it was to include both infantry and armor. It would not, however, be able to help them. Although designed to come to their rescue it "could not get across the draw because Germans had infiltrated in strength."[19]

---

*Colonel Nelson submitted Tropp for the Bronze Star, writing that the lieutenant's "conduct reflexs [sic] great credit upon himself and the military service."

Since the units of Task Force Davis would never form for an attack, 3rd Battalion, 109th Regiment, was to help those on Kommerscheidt Hill withdraw from their trap. Men of that battalion were to hold the southern Vossenack slope and try to keep the Kall trail open. Nelson's listeners were aware that they might soon be able to infiltrate out of the Kommerscheidt pocket. A radio message received from divisional headquarters at 1530 hours, just prior to Colonel Nelson's arrival, approved just such a breakout.[20]

Nelson gave orders for his command to prepare to leave. Everyone would, he said, pull out after dark. He would lead them back.[21]

Nelson surveyed his men on the hill. Men still on their feet suffered from pneumonia, influenza, colds, trench foot, frostbite, and combat exhaustion. All had lost friends and companions to death, injury, or sickness. Hundreds were now captives of encircling German forces. Not one group—not even squads—was capable of mounting a sustained fire fight. As they moved about in intermittent hail, rain, and snow, they looked like ragged zombies. Emptied mentally and physically by the drain of combat since 2 November, nearly all would already have been evacuated for medical treatment or rest under more "normal" battlefield circumstances.

General Davis tried to help. About 1515 hours he told Lieutenant Colonel Truman Setliffe that his 1340th Battalion of engineers would continue their role as infantrymen to cover the withdrawal that night of forces from Kommerscheidt. They would also open the road from Vossenack to the bridge in the Kall gorge so wounded men could be evacuated.[22]

Continued enemy activity in the draw did not make the engineer task easy. Although fighting in built-up areas is a reasonable engineer mission, maneuvering in heavily wooded areas and defiles is not. Engineers lack communication equipment and small-unit combined arms team training. They have no forward observers and cannot communicate with either infantry or artillery outfits or liaison with close air support. They are on their own.

Some men on Kommerscheidt Hill felt no obligation to wait for nightfall to leave. Despite efforts of officers and noncoms to keep their soldiers in place, they were not entirely successful. Occasional riflemen slipped to the rear, claiming the "front lines" had surrendered as they fell back along the road to the north down the hill. Many did not even bother to carry their rifles with them. They felt they had suffered enough and were, in the words of Sergeant Tom Hunter, "pretty whipped." Making use of tree cover, they managed to reach the Kall and waded the cold, waist-deep water of the river while it was still broad daylight, hours before the time Colonel Nelson had set for withdrawal.[23]

But the majority remained as German units increased pressure on them "in superb cooperation" between the *1056th Infantry Regiment* and the *1st Battalion, 189th Artillery Regiment.* Enemy infantry drew ever closer using mortars, hand grenades, and machine pistols. Two German assault guns began firing at targets on Kommerscheidt Hill. The "proud result of the strenuous mopping up operation" and the "stubborn and bitter fighting" of German soldiers were 133 Americans taken captive.[24]

Colonel Nelson supervised preparations for the breakout. By nightfall, 8 November, said Captain Don Kelly, a tanker, "we were really sweating the situation out." Nelson told Kelly to disable or destroy any equipment still in working condition. There was not much to do. Only Ray Fleig's tank could still function. Of the original nine tank destroyers, seven had fallen victim to German fire. At 1730 hours, without lights and trying to make as little noise as possible, Kelly and a work crew disabled Fleig's M-4, the remaining M-10s, and the last jeep still capable of operating.[25] Captain Marion Pugh tallied his remaining crew members. Forty-five enlisted men and four officers had originally crossed the Kall with tank destroyers. Only 22 now stood waiting in the darkness to attempt the breakout.[26]

Survivors of the long days of hell milled about impatiently in the dark—Tony Kudiak, Frank Ripperdam, Marion Pugh, Richard Ripple, "Howdy" Rumbaugh, Ray Fleig, Bruce Hostrup, Jack Walker, Nathaniel Quentin, Clarence Skains, Joe Perll, and all the others. Colonel Nelson tried to enforce order and discipline.

The regimental commander delegated able-bodied men to act as litter bearers. They would carry wounded comrades down the road one half hour before the remainder departed cross-country. Nelson did not want the two groups to mix.

The colonel ordered only the lightest gear to be taken by his men. Nothing should be carried which would slow anyone down. Withdrawal was to be quiet and covered by darkness so the Germans would not realize what was happening. Despite his best efforts, confusion and pandemonium reigned among the motley assembly of tankers, engineers, destroyer crews, medics, and infantrymen from assorted companies and battalions.[27]

Then Captain Jack Walker, appointed earlier by Rumbaugh as commander of "Provisional Company A," got his men out on the road, all but blocking it because he didn't want to chance their being left behind. The roadway was packed with men four abreast. They were in terrible danger should enemy artillery open up on them. It would have been butchery, a slaughter.[28]

The litter party set forth. Tony Kudiak was one of those who carried wounded comrades. Most bearers had thrown their rifles away in order to carry their loads more efficiently.[29] They had to leave some injured men behind; there simply were not enough makeshift litters available to carry all those unable to make it on their own.[30] Carrying their burden of stretchers, they wended their way down the road, around the double switchbacks, and up to the bridge. Four Germans guarded the span. The column of bearers set down their load of 50 to 60 wounded men and waited in the cold rain. The

German guards were willing to let the injured be carried to the dugout aid station but insisted the litters be handled by no more than two men each. An unidentified medical officer from the bunker came down and arranged with the guards for everyone to pass, even those infantry littermen who still carried rifles.[31]

Second Lieutenant Alfred Muglia, a medical officer at the aid station, grew weary when he saw the number of new arrivals. Litter patients arrived until the bunker could hold no more. Additional patients were placed outside on the trail, protected by guards holding Red Cross flags. The continuing rain added to the misery of the injured men. Medics took blankets from those inside and spread them over shivering men lying on the trail.[32]

Captains Paschal Linguiti and Michael DeMarco, surgeons for 1st and 3rd battalions of the 112th, worked ceaselessly with their overload of patients. The night was, they agreed, a real nightmare as a minimum of 65 new litter cases accumulated at the log aid station. They appreciated the cooperation given them by German soldiers. "German medics guided and in some cases carried our wounded to us," they said. "Even German riflemen threw aside their rifles to give us a hand. Artillery shells from both sides fell all over the place but none hit the aid station." Both surgeons believed the Germans took special precautions to avoid hitting it.[33]

At some point during the night of 8/9 November, the aid station door opened and in walked General George Davis, who seemed to lead a charmed life during the entire action, crisscrossing the battlefield at will without injury. Captain DeMarco pleaded the medical situation with him, explaining how desperately the casualties needed to be evacuated. Davis listened impassively, said only "Thank you," and left, to make his way back to American lines.[34]

Tony Kudiak was surprised that none of the Germans tried to interfere with those infantrymen litter bearers who kept their rifles, but "they didn't bother us at all. It was dark but they could probably see us," he said. A couple of hours passed as he and other litter bearers waited at the aid station after depositing their companions there. At one point a medic told him the Germans intended to send in a patrol to check the wounded; anyone with only slight injuries would be taken prisoner. Kudiak and some others moved back into the trees across from the bunker out of sight. "We had no arms," he said. "Threw them away. It was pitch black." They lay on the ground until morning, when they saw a group of men they recognized from Kommerscheidt Hill. "Some Colonel Nelson led us out . . . to our kitchen area. That was it."[35]

That was not quite it. For those who started the breakout in the second group, it was a hellish night for them as they moved cross-crountry. Colonel Nelson led the column out a half hour after litter bearers disappeared down the hill with their load of injured men. An engineer unit acted as point for Nelson's column, followed by tankers and destroyer crews led by Colonel

Ripple. Behind them came the infantry.[36] All were supposed to hold onto the shoulder or belt of the man ahead, maintaining a human chain moving single file.[37]

The trip cross-country was a horror. The sloping, rough terrain, fallen treetops, roots—all made movement through the darkness very hazardous. At best visibility was three yards; at worst they could not see the man beside them. They began to lose contact with one another.

Then at 1900 hours, an artillery and mortar barrage exploded around them. During the next 15 minutes, 50 rounds shrieked through the night sky to burst by the column of frightened refugees from the Kommerscheidt pocket.[38] With the first explosion the men scattered for cover, breaking up into small units, most of which never again located one another. There was no way for officers or noncoms to give orders or retain control.[39] The rest of the breakout became a kaleidoscope of individuals and small groups struggling desperately toward safety.

When the shelling stopped, Marion Pugh had only eight men around him. He instructed them to guide on the light of a fire burning in Vossenack, keeping to its left at all times. They slipped down a steep hill, waded the icy Kall River, and reached the aid station. Seven of them remained there; the eighth man disappeared. "I met two medical officers and two chaplains who said it had been captured but was still operating," Pugh said. "They warned me to take off my gun or I'd be captured or killed." He did. Medics offered to make the captain a litter bearer, but the idea was less than appealing. Pugh and the others finally crawled into some foxholes inside the tree line beside the trail to wait out the night. They set forth once again the following morning, 9 November, reaching Germeter at 1010 hours.[40]

Tanker Captain Don Kelly peered through the darkness as the barrage lifted. He finally located eleven other men and they struck out for Germeter. The slope they traversed was so steep that one misstep would cause a 15-to-20-foot slide in the darkness. They found the river, waded across through hip-deep water and up the other side of the slope, avoiding the German-held Kall trail. Individuals and small groups of stragglers joined them along the way. Kelly led 75 men into Vossenack at 0200 hours, 9 November.[41]

Bruce Hostrup and Ray Fleig retained contact with 50 men. They moved north, keeping a two-yard interval between one another, and forded the river 300 yards from the bridge. It was foggy when they entered Vossenack at 2300 hours and, after all their sufferings, they came under friendly small-arms fire as they entered the town. They reached Germeter at 0030 hours, 9 November.[42]

First Sergeant Robert Toner of Item Company, 3rd Battalion, 112th Regiment, and six other men from his outfit* struggled to their feet as the shelling lifted. They continued on through the darkness, waded the Kall, and

*Sergeant Roger J. Plattes, Technical Sergeant Louis Mizak, Sergeant Ralph J. Voelker, PFC George Zerbey, PFC Carmel Risenhoover, and PFC Edward McLendon.

moved up the north slope. "In my group," noted an amused Toner, were "a couple of Jerries who apparently had gotten into the wrong column, but who were discovered and turned over to the 109th in Vossenack." Tired, worn, and hungry, GIs eagerly wolfed down K rations given them at the 109th Regiment's command post. An MP there arranged a Weasel ride for them to their own rear CP from which they went to Item Company's kitchen area, where cooks gave them hot coffee and more to eat. They arrived at 0445 hours, 9 November.[43]

Joe Perll managed to cross the bridge over the Kall at 0530 hours, 9 November, under cover of an early-morning mist. As he drew nearer to American lines, "our own artillery hit us."[44]

When Captain Jack Walker reached Germeter, he tried to count all those in his L Company who had returned safely. The company had gone into battle with six officers and 187 men. A total of 106 were now missing in action.[45]

All of the scattered groups faced a difficult passage. When noise from the shell bursts faded away, Colonel Nelson raised his head and looked around. Somehow during the barrage he had lost his compass, no small loss in that black void in which his men moved. Now they could only stumble forward. Those with Nelson swung too far to the left. Telling them to wait, Nelson said he would locate the bridge and see if it was safe to cross there. With his head lowered, "using my helmet as a shield to keep from knocking out my eyes against tree limbs," he found forward progress almost impossible. The terrain had been intensely shelled; shattered tree trunks, branches, and debris were everywhere. The steep hill, the blackness, and his unfamiliarity with the area made movement even more difficult.

He decided to return to his group. "At one point on the return," he said, "I came suddenly to the edge of the fir woods . . . into what turned out to be a patch of deciduous trees, which I did not recognize. The area . . . had been so black that the contrast caused me to think I was about to step into a lake. I knew there was a dam near Schmidt and because I had lost my compass I thought we might have wandered to its edge. The illusion was so intense I actually took the first tentative step fully expecting to find myself in water. Only then did I discover that the 'lake' was simply sky-glow coming through branches of leafless trees."

Rejoining his group, Colonel Nelson led them northward. "I moved on to a point which appeared to be a big rock surface. I made a sideslip to the right to get around but discovered a sheer drop below me so I swung over to the other side and took the column along with me." Without warning, they came out on the Kall trail, and Nelson found himself in the middle of the group of wounded he had ordered forward half an hour before his own column set out. Passing through them, Nelson and his men finally reached an assembly area to the rear of the 109th. All his men were strained and exhausted. As if they had not suffered sufficiently, it began to rain, making life even more miserable in "an already muddy and sodden sector."

The Germans kept up a constant artillery and mortar barrage throughout the night. Shells landed all around the assembly area with a din that was nerve-shattering.*[46]

"Howdy" Rumbaugh, Colonel Ripple, and 80 other men waited 40 minutes after the barrage before they felt it was safe to move again. Captain Rumbaugh ordered the column to advance and called Colonel Ripple up to walk beside him. The night was like thick ink as they tried to intersect the Kall River some 300 yards from the bridge. As they approached the stream, Ripple suddenly stepped off into nothingness and plunged down a steep and rocky slope for 25 feet. Rumbaugh called out with alarm into the darkness, "Where are you?"

The colonel had landed on his neck, which made even his later recollections of that night hazy ones. After a few seconds of anxious silence, Ripple replied shakily, "Down here."

The small group forded the hip-deep water. Rumbaugh then told Ripple and the others to go ahead. He would wait by the river to collect stragglers. He ordered First Lieutenant Leo Seery to remain with him.

Ripple and those with him reached the assembly area at 2300 hours, still wet from crossing the Kall and miserable in the nearly freezing air as they endured intermittent enemy shelling. As a result of the days of battle, Ripple's battalion lost 15 tanks from A Company, seven from B Company, and eight of C Company's M-4s.[47]

Back on the bank of the Kall River, Captain Rumbaugh told Seery to recross the stream and comb the area for stragglers. The lieutenant returned later with eight men. Rumbaugh sent them on ahead with orders to guide on a building burning in Vossenack, the same fire used by Marion Pugh and his eight men as a beacon. Rumbaugh later found three more men and they struggled up the slope toward the Kall trail. As they reached it they were halted by a GI, who suddenly stepped out into the roadway, his weapon aimed toward them.

"Who are you? 110th?" asked the shadowy figure.

"Yes," a tired Captain Rumbaugh replied.

"Right up this road," the guide said, pointing. He was one of several men stationed along the route of retreat by 3rd Battalion, 109th Regiment, in its effort to aid the evacuation from Kommerscheidt Hill.

At full strength, Rumbaugh's 3rd Battalion, 110th Regiment, had numbered 871 men. When Colonel Tait led it onto Kommerscheidt Hill as part of Task Force Ripple, his men in I, K, L, and M companies numbered 316. Some 299 reached Kommerscheidt Hill, of whom perhaps as few as 30 to 60 could be described as "effective" fighting men, the remainder suffering from minor wounds or illness or simply fatigue. According to Rumbaugh, about 200 withdrew from the encirclement the night of 8 November. When they finally reached the rear assembly area about 0900 hours, 9 November, all were given

*Colonel Gustin M. Nelson was awarded the Bronze Star for his part in the breakout from the Kommerscheidt Hill pocket.

a quick but careful medical check. Of those 200 men, all but 75 were evacuated for combat exhaustion or because of trench foot. Only one K Company officer still survived, and he became the transportation officer for the 110th Regiment. The only officer to survive in Item Company was Lieutenant Leo Seery. Only one officer in Love Company still lived; he became 3rd Battalion transportation officer. Mike Company kept four of its six starting officers. Losses at battalion staff were tragic: the commanding officer, the executive officer, the S-2 intelligence officer, the S-3 operations officer, the battalion surgeon, and the battalion medical assistance officer. Two hundred replacement fillers assigned to 3rd Battalion the night of 9/10 November did not begin to bring the unit back to an appropriate strength level.[48]

When Captain Rumbaugh reached the assembly area, Colonel Nelson told him to have his men dig in for the night. In the morning they would resume their march to the rear. Soaked from the hips down from crossing the river, they spent a miserable night in nearly freezing temperatures. Toward morning it began to snow heavily. The records give no indication whether Rumbaugh that night thought of, and regretted, his impetuous confrontation with Colonel Theodore Seely, his regimental commander, which ended with orders sending Rumbaugh south of the Kall into the Kommerscheidt pocket. Worse yet, he was still a captain a month later when he was captured by the Germans in fierce fighting during the Battle of the Bulge.[49]

As word spread through rear areas north of the Kall that a breakout from Kommerscheidt Hill was in progress, men scurried to prepare a welcome return for them. The 893rd Tank Destroyer Battalion rear command post efforts were typical. Men there labored to arrange for replacement of lost equipment. They set up temporary shelters in pyramidal tents with heat, blankets, and with straw for bedding. Staff officers surrendered all private hoards of liquor so that those who returned might each get a dollop to drink. As weary soldiers arrived, aid men met them to tend their wounds and issue them their tiny liquor ration. Battalion maintenance crews went to work on a 24-hour basis to service and condition replacement vehicular equipment. Supply people requisitioned shelter halves, mess kits, and new clothing.[50]

Late as usual, General Cota sent a last message to Kommerscheidt Hill at 2115 hours:

> TO: TASK FORCE RIPPLE
>
> Fight your way out.
>
> CG
28th Div
2115 hrs.[51]

It is doubtful anyone waited at the regimental radio receiver on Kommerscheidt Hill's abandoned command post. Those men had begun their breakout at 1800 hours. By 1900, save for a few wounded soldiers left behind, they were all gone. Even in this, General Cota sent too little too late.

The Germans were ecstatic. "The last remaining remnants of the encircled enemy are annihilated or captured. The results of this stubborn and bitter fighting justified the losses we had to suffer. The enemy lost twice as many men, PWs and dead, as we had committed since the beginning of the operation. . . . The contemplated penetration of the enemy through the EIFEL into the open plains was prevented. . . . through the close cooperation of the units attached and assigned to the [*89th*] *Division.* Within the *Division* the spirit of the veteran of Falaise has united with the young men of the Luftwaffe, dashing and full of fighting initiative, and the battalions which have recently joined us in the Westwall."

German sources continued their self-congratulations. "Hardened through battle, united in dire emergency and danger, blood and sacrifice, our *89th Infantry Division* will also in the future repel the attacks of the enemy and will not rest till victory is ours." The Germans were fully aware that if they could continue to repel Allied attacks for only a few months; if they were allowed the opportunity to rebuild their armies and strengthen their defenses, then the much-heralded and long-awaited secret weapons promised by their leader would be ready to bring them ultimate victory over their foes.[52]

Those in Vossenack almost had time to lick their wounds. Lieutenant Colonel Joseph McSalka arrived as the new commander for 2nd Battalion, 112th Regiment, replacing the stricken Hatzfeld, who had been evacuated with combat exhaustion. Captain Pruden was glad to be relieved of his job as acting commander.[53] Reinforcements poured into line rapidly and in large numbers. 2nd Battalion received 529 replacements during the night of 8/9 November.[54]

Such new men were utterly essential. "The battalion," said Pruden, "came out of this action with fewer than fifty men, most of whom were battalion headquarters personnel and thus in a better position to withstand shattering artillery fire."[55] Weather conditions did not improve. "It was cold as hell and started to snow," Captain Nesbitt remembered.[56]

Colonel Jesse Gibney, formerly commander of the 60th Infantry, arrived to take command of the 109th Infantry Regiment. Its former commander, Lieutenant Colonel Daniel Strickler, became executive officer for the unit.[57]

Constant rumors floated through Vossenack of imminent enemy armored attacked. Colonel Sam Mays totted up such "sightings" for just the day of 8 November and totaled some 250 to 300 claims of "tanks spotted."[58] Some were real enough. Lieutenant Carl Anderson, a tanker in B Company, saw some six German tanks in column, moving about 10 miles per hour. He commenced firing at them, but the range was too great for his .75-caliber cannon. Anderson then radioed Captain Granger, asking for support from tank destroyers. Two M-10s arrived, accompanied by some towed antitank guns from the 630th Tank Destroyer Battalion. Anderson could not understand why none of the towed guns opened fire.

"It made me madder'n hell," he complained. He later learned that they were incapable of firing, suffering from such malfunctions as broken recoil cylinders, defective breach mechanisms, and scored barrels. "Yet with those defects," Anderson stormed, "they had nonetheless been emplaced in Vossenack as anti-tank defense!"[59]

On the evening of 8 November, General Cota called a meeting of his regimental and battalion commanders at his divisional command bunker at Rott. He wanted, he said, a minefield laid east of Vossenack between American and German positions. General Davis added that engineers could do the work, fighting from foxholes at night as infantry, laying mines during the day. Lieutenant Colonel James White, executive officer for the 1171st Engineer Combat Group, didn't like the idea. He asked for two more battalions of engineers to help out, knowing they were unavailable. He was not surprised when his request was turned down.[60] The next day engineers began laying 5,000 mines, protected in their work by men of 2nd Battalion, 109th Infantry Regiment.[61]

Men of 3rd Battalion, 109th Regiment, fought grimly to retain their hold on the southern slope of the Vossenack ridge near the Kall trail. German patrols repeatedly thrust against their lines, hitting them with small-arms fire and occasionally rolling hand grenades down the hill at them. Enemy artillery batteries blasted the 109th with shells ranging from mortars to 150mm cannons. German guns fired eight to 10 rounds a minute on a 24-hour-a-day basis. Despite the best efforts of GIs, German patrols moved freely up and down the Kall trail.[62]

It had stood firmly throughout the days of battle. It was a goal, an obstacle, a challenge. It had echoed to the sounds of both American and German feet and the threads of their vehicles. During the night of 8 November, German engineers finally blew the stone arch bridge over the Kall River, and its sturdy blocks crashed into the water below, severing once for all the no longer needed main supply route of the 28th Infantry Division.[63]

The low roof of snowy sky gradually pressed down on the land of western Germany, Wednesday, 8 November, as darkness extended its fingers along rocky summits of high Eifel ridges and into murky, pine-strewn clefts between them. Storm clouds, torn by wind, swirled across the heavens. The nordic god Wotan, in some dimly remembered time, gave his nine daughters the task of bringing from the world's battlefields the bodies of the bravest heroes. Transformed into immortals, those dead warriors would then serve as protectors of the gods. A believer in such myths who chanced to gaze across the battlefield in the *Hürtgenwald* might well have glimpsed those Valkyries laboring to transport thousands of both khaki- and gray-clad bodies to Walhalla.

12

"It is plenty hot down here"

9 November 1944–16 November 1944

Throughout Thursday, 9 November, stragglers from the groups which broke out from Kommerscheidt Hill continued to arrive at rear-area assembly points around Germeter as they made their way back from south of the Kall through enemy lines. One latecomer was First Sergeant Robert Toner, who mourned the fate of men in his unit. A member of Item Company, 3rd Battalion, 112th Regiment, Toner found only 15 men left in his 2nd Platoon, seven in 3rd Platoon. All the others were gone. "It was terrible," he said. "I wouldn't want to go through it again for any price. . . . That's hell."[1]

Men were not the only casualties of war. Even machines that escaped damage or destruction in combat were wearing out. Lieutenant Howard Davis noted that as the weather grew colder, M-10 tank destroyer batteries gave out. Drivers idled their vehicles even when not using them out of fear they would not restart if shut down. Destroyers that had been shut off had to be towed until their engines ignited. Even at best, motors ran sluggishly.[2]

Lieutenant Davis felt real satisfaction over the efforts of his destroyer crews. Infantrymen credited M-10s with stopping German assaults from overrunning them when riflemen were down to as few as 16 men per company. Most tank destroyer crews survived the November action in the Hürtgen, but they were not unmarked. Staff Sergeant Bill Gardner blamed most of their casualties on the weather, for the terrain was, he said, "a sea of mud and water," and consequently "many of our men contracted trench foot in varying degrees of severity."*[3]

---

*When Captain John Howe interviewed Sergeant Gardner on 23 November, it had been raining steadily for two weeks. Even at that late date, Howe noted, there were only seven pairs of galoshes for an entire tank destroyer company. Failure of the American logistics system to provide supply units with needed equipment must be accounted as an important reason for this failure in the Hürtgen.

Major Albert Berndt, surgeon in the 112th Regiment, felt deeply burdened by the number of wounded men strewn along the breakout route between Kommerscheidt Hill and the aid station in the gorge. The dugout itself remained packed with patients, all of whom needed to be evacuated. Regiment had earlier refused Berndt permission to request a truce with German forces. On the morning of 9 November, Berndt and Technician Fourth Class Wheeler Wolters, a German-speaking medical clerk, went ahead on their own.

At 0950 hours, the two men left Vossenack and moved down the Kall trail. Wolters carried a white flag of truce. It was snowing heavily, and visibility was limited. They reached the bridge site at the river and found the arch smashed into the water, which flowed tumbling over and around its remains. Someone had laid planking across broken supports, and the two Americans made their hazardous way across to the south bank.

They spoke there with a German lieutenant and five of his men. The Germans were courteous and made no effort to threaten or search Berndt and Wolters. The regimental surgeon stated his intentions as Wolters translated. He wanted to sweep Kommerscheidt and the area north of it for wounded men. The enemy officer replied that all such casualties had received treatment by a medical officer and enlisted personnel from the German Army Medical Department. Injured Americans, he said, had been evacuated only 20 minutes before Berndt and Wolters arrived at the river.

Major Berndt then told the lieutenant he would be removing patients to the rear from the Kall aid station. The German officer countered with an offer to conduct the evacuation himself. Berndt declined so as to give him no opportunity or excuse to seize aid station personnel as prisoners of war.

The lieutenant agreed to allow Americans to evacuate their wounded through German lines but pointed out that such actions could be dangerous. The German Army scrupulously observed the Red Cross, he said, and would not fire upon any person or vehicle clearly displaying it. He and his fellow soldiers in the woods would obviously let such vehicles pass. He had, however, no way to communicate with either his own superiors or with nearby artillery batteries. The heavy snowfall might obscure Red Cross markings, causing distant gun batteries to fire upon a convoy. Berndt indicated he would accept such risks. They exchanged salutes and Berndt and Wolters made their way up the hill to the aid station bunker.[3]

Entering the dugout, Berndt informed his two physicians, Linguiti and DeMarco, of his arrangements. Enemy line troops would not interfere, but German gun batteries could not be informed of any evacuation. The two surgeons were willing to risk the dangers, particularly since snow now fell so heavily there was little possibility that enemy forward observers would be able to see them through the thick white blanket that shrouded the trail.[4]

Berndt told Second Lieutenant Henry Morrison to arrange transportation for the evacuation. Morrison located two six-by-six trucks left behind by kitchen personnel 200 yards up the trail, and one serviceable Weasel cargo carrier with several holes in its gasoline tank. He could not, however, back the trucks down the slippery trail to the aid station, and the road ahead was blocked where German soldiers had felled trees across it. Morrison found some engineer troops who agreed to remove the trees and scour the trail for mines. He also found five cans of gasoline. The convoy was as ready as it would ever be. Medics carried patients up the trail, loading the Weasel and trucks with 44 men.[5]

Major Berndt and Wolters had already returned on foot to Vossenack. As the three vehicles moved off up the trail, Technician Third Class John Shedio walked alongside the Weasel pouring the contents of successive cans of gasoline into its badly holed fuel tank.[6]

The ambulance loading point at the top of the hill was cloaked from enemy observation by thickly falling snow. Lieutenant Loyd Johnson, ambulance platoon leader, waited at the top for the convoy. He had driven an ambulance out from Vossenack on Major Berndt's orders to pick up any successfully evacuated men. Debris and clutter on the top portion of the trail prevented the convoy from climbing all the way out of the draw. Patients were hand-carried the last few yards.

Johnson saw several German soldiers waiting with the convoy of wounded. In an attempt to make them more comfortable, the Germans had covered the injured men with their raincoats and extra blankets.[7] They helped him load as many patients as he could into his ambulance, and Johnson returned to Vossenack. He ordered seven other ambulances there to return with him to retrieve the rest of the casualties.[8]

Those helpful German soldiers were making more problems than Johnson knew. A *Wehrmacht* captain, a first sergeant, and nine enlisted men stepped out of the woods as the convoy drew near and demanded to see the doctor in charge. They knew nothing of Major Berndt's conversation with the German lieutenant at the river. Captain Mike DeMarco and Second Lieutenant Alfred Muglia, a Medical Assistance Corps officer, walked up from the dugout to talk with them. The two captains saluted one another. The German officer then insisted that only "seriously wounded and medical personnel" could be evacuated. "Line men and all those with light wounds would have to be prisoners."[9] All others would be "Kaput."[10]

Although they molested no one, the eleven German soldiers supervised the evacuation, carefully checking the seriously wounded men to determine the nature of their injuries and demanding to see the medics' Geneva Convention Red Cross cards.[11] American medical personnel eyed them warily and worried.

While DeMarco and others unloaded patients from the convoy onto waiting ambulances at the top of the hill, Captain Linguiti, Lieutenant Muglia, and the two chaplains, Madden and Maness, acted as litter bearers. They carried casualties from the dugout up the cold, slippery trail to the ambulance loading point at the crest of the hill. It was not long before they were exhausted. Lieutenant Johnson walked down to help them. He took one end of a litter while Muglia wearily lifted the other. As they staggered past the trucks, Muglia saw DeMarco conversing heatedly with the German captain. "It was muddy and slippery as I passed them," Muglia said. "At the top of the hill I slipped. A German soldier took my left hand and pulled until we were on the sod."[12]

The conversation was indeed heated. The German captain informed DeMarco that neither he nor Linguiti could leave. There were, he said, still other American troops surrounded in the immediate area who would soon need their assistance. In theory he was justified, for medical officers were in very short supply in the German Army.

The troops referred to by the enemy officer may have been men from companies K and L, 3rd Battalion, 112th Regiment, who fled into woods south and west of Schmidt on 4 November in the face of the German morning counterattack. Although some were immediately taken prisoner, others held out for some days, under constant artillery and mortar fire, without rations or water.[13] German records claimed capture of 133 men in that area the previous day.[14] The German officer who spoke with Captain DeMarco may have been unaware that they had already surrendered. He also placed the two chaplains, Maness and Madden, in "protective custody." His first sergeant told them the reason for doing so was that those same Americans would also need their services. The German officer agreed, however, to allow Lieutenant Muglia to leave with the ambulances.[15]

Johnson, at least, was impressed with the behavior of those enemy soldiers. He knew that during preceding days they and their fellows repeatedly offered drugs, water, and rations to personnel at the aid station. Captain DeMarco told Johnson how they were inevitably courteous, and several expressed to Johnson how they always tried to respect the "Geneva Cross." When Johnson arrived at the ambulance loading point, several enemy soldiers "even offered to fight off our men if an attack began and protect us in any way possible during the loading. . . . I believe them to be sincere."[16]

The loading completed, Johnson and the other ambulances drove away. Chaplain (Captain) Alan Madden shouted after them, "Come back for us tomorrow."[17]

Captain DeMarco noted that "after much prayer, anxiety and four hours," the German officer and his men departed. The two doctors, two chaplains, and a few other aid station personnel returned to the dugout to treat other wounded men who continued to straggle up to it.[18] The hours of the day and the following night fled by. Their patient load remained heavy as soldiers came on foot or were carried in by litter bearers. No longer trusting the safety of the Kall trail, Linguiti and DeMarco sent walking wounded and litter bearers on a roundabout path through the woods that stretched across nearly four miles of shattered pine forest tangles.[19]

On 10 November, Linguiti and DeMarco again walked up the Kall trail to the edge of the wood line and spoke with the hostile German captain, asking permission to evacuate more of their patients over this route. He insisted that any further evacuations would be impossible unless all Americans in the area surrendered. All slightly wounded German PWs, he said, would have to be returned to their own lines. Such conditions, the two doctors replied, were inconceivable. At that point an artillery barrage from one side or the other began falling around them. Ordering the two physicians to return to their bunker dugout, the Germans raced for their foxholes.[20]

The two medical officers tried again. On 11 November they spoke with a German medical officer near the Kall River. This man had not been influenced by the captain at the top of the trail. He asked for a truce so Germans might pick up their dead. At the same time, he said, Americans could evacuate their own wounded. This was, the doctors realized, a truce only among medics, since American artillery refused to recognize a lull and opened fire. German batteries responded by shelling Vossenack. In the midst of this barrage, medical personnel on both sides continued their work, determined to go through with their plan at all risks. Accompanying the last of their casualties, the two American doctors and two chaplains made their way safely out of the Kall gorge.[21]

Alone among American units involved in the Hürtgen Forest action, medical personnel later submitted extensive, analytic, and scathing criticisms of the attack on Schmidt. Their comments were pointed. Linguiti, 1st Battalion surgeon of the 112th Regiment, remembered violations of the Geneva Convention by Americans in Kommerscheidt.

Military units, Linguiti wrote, had absolute disregard for the proximity of an already established aid station site, thus jeopardizing the lives and safety of men unable to protect themselves. Tanks, mortars, and machine guns presented a definite hazard to adjacent areas. An aid station, he said, should not be used by combat personnel as a meeting place. Combat activities around such a site willfully placed in hazard those who were injured.[22]

Linguiti and DeMarco pointed out that medical evacuation was contingent upon the condition of the main supply route. Failure of the one made the other impossible. Further, they warned, tactical units should inform aid station personnel of the military situation. "We had no knowledge as to whether our troops had withdrawn from Schmidt, Kommerscheidt, or Vossenack," they said, "and had to guess at the best route to give to walking wounded." Battalion commanders, the two doctors added, should be reminded that the Fort Benning "School Solution" for handling an aid station was impractical. Establishment and maintenance of such installations should closely follow the advice of the battalion surgeon.[23]

Major Albert Berndt was even more scathing. Evacuation was, he said, impeded by difficult terrain, by a wretched road network worsened by daily rain, by an initial vehicle shortage made worse by German capture of medical vehicles, by frequent blockage of the main supply route up the Kall trail, by lack of communication, and by having to operate an aid station for three days behind enemy lines. Despite such difficulties, he pointed out, truce flags enabled every casualty and most medical personnel to return to their own lines.

"Let it be well noted to the credit of the Medical Department," Berndt wrote, that his personnel remained behind German lines for days, taking care of injured soldiers and making every effort possible to evacuate casualties. They remained at their posts for three days after every other man of the 112th Regiment withdrew behind the original line of departure.

Only one method of evacuation proved feasible, the regimental surgeon proclaimed. Truce flags worked. He had suggested this approach to the regimental staff in plenty of time to permit earlier evacuation of all wounded from the Schmidt–Kommerscheidt sector. His requests were denied until it was too late to reach south of the Kall. Consequently Germans captured American casualties there. Had his suggestion been adopted when he first made it, Berndt insisted, evacuation would have been far more efficient "with no detriment to the eventual tactical outcome of the operation." How could things have been worse? The division lost. Would that outcome have been changed if medics had been allowed to pick up wounded men under flags of truce? Obviously not. The only difference would have been the retrieval of dozens more wounded Americans before their capture by the enemy.[24]

The Germans seemed to show some level of consideration to American medical personnel throughout the battle area. The aid station for 3rd Battalion, 109th Infantry Regiment, was located in a cave on the south slope of the Vossenack ridge, and medics there tended both American and German wounded. Each morning, Private Henry Traszka recalled, an enemy patrol stopped at the cave with rations for aid men and to check on the condition of their injured. They also gave permission for ambulances to drive up to the mouth of the cave to load and remove patients. Both sides continued to respect truce flags under which they removed their dead. At such times, riflemen of both Germany and America lent their help to medics at work.[25] It was, however, the only mercy Germans showed to those who had invaded their forested sanctuary.

So viciously did German artillery batteries continue to pound American positions that replacements were often killed even before they reached their new company assignments. There was a consequent steady series of requests for still other replacements.[26]

All units of the 112th Regiment had been withdrawn from combat. For them the battle in the Hürtgen was at an end. The other two regiments of the division were not as fortunate. The 109th and 110th still faced more days of battle.

1st Battalion, 109th Regiment, moved onto high ground north of Vossenack to prevent German infiltration there. Its men were spread so thin "it was more like having outposts than company positions," said Lieutenant Potter. "The Germans were able to move between us at will."[27] They endured endless days of shelling. Explosions wreaked so much havoc in the woods that Lieutenant Tom Whitney observed that "trees looked like telephone poles." He found he could not recognize one position through which he had passed only four hours earlier, so thoroughly had shells blasted it.[28]

On 12 November, men of 2nd Battalion, 109th Regiment, captured three Germans. The PWs said they were part of two companies waiting to make a counterattack on Vossenack. To that end they had been provided with American uniforms, equipment, and arms. One PW had on an American raincoat over his uniform. An artillery barrage on the draw where those companies waited prevented the attack from materializing.[29]

Try as they would, mean of the 109th were unable to prevent German infiltrators from entering Vossenack. The Americans repeatedly blasted Germans out of houses on the east end of the village, only to see them slip back into place. The regiment simply no longer had the manpower to keep the little town secure.[30] GIs developed a numbed stasis as they endlessly reenacted previous actions: snatch a few hours of restless sleep, take cover from a barrage, eat a cold K-ration meal, assault a building suspected of harboring infiltrators. All the while ever greater numbers succumbed to wounds, illness, or combat exhaustion. It was no wonder many could not stand the strain as German artillery batteries regularly laid on barrages consisting of as many as 4,000 rounds.[31]

On 10 November, his German captors sent Father Alan Madden into the lines of 3rd Battalion, 109th Regiment, with a demand by the enemy commander that the unit should surrender. Major Howard Topping's answer was delivered by American artillery batteries—a concentration of time on target shelling in which 18 battalions of Corps artillery pounded German positions.[32] It was at least the equivalent of the reply by Brigadier General Anthony McAuliffe a month later when surrounded at Bastogne during the German Ardennes offensive. McAuliffe said simply "Nuts" when confronted with an ultimatum to surrender.

Lieutenant Colonel Truman Setliffe was at the site of the demolished Kall bridge on 10 November. When he told his engineers of the German ultimatum to surrender or be slaughtered, they said they would "stick it out." Heavy defensive artillery fire ringed American positions, Setliffe observed, neutralizing the planned enemy attack.[33]

The German commander sent Chaplain Madden back again on 11 November with a second ultimatum. It was treated with as much respect as the first.

On 13 November, General Hodges finally agreed to relieve the 28th Infantry Division from its front-line positions in the Hürtgen. Its replacement would be the 8th Infantry Division of VIII Corps. Over the next several days units of the "Bloody Bucket" would be pulled out of contact with the Germans and sent to some quiet sector of the front for rest and rehabilitation. Hodges' decision came none too soon.

By 14 November, many men in 1st Battalion, 109th Regiment, performed guard duty on their knees. They could no longer stand because of agonizing pains in their legs and toes caused by extensive tissue damage from trench foot. In many companies at least one third of the soldiers were diagnosed by medics as having foot immersion. Even some of those lucky enough to wear "arctic shoe packs" had to have them cut off by medics who sought to treat their gangrenous feet.[34]

From the evening of 16 November to the morning of 20 November, 8th Division troops arrived to replace the worn-out and haggard men of the 109th. They had spent their time in hell.[35]

The last days in the *Hürtgenwald* were as tragic for men of the 110th Regiment as for those of the 109th. They still contended with the enemy deep in the Kall gorge during their final week of combat. They were the 1st and 2nd battalions, units that had invested the tiny hamlet of Simonskall on 4 November. As early as 8 November, Colonel Theodore Seely, commander of the 110th, radioed divisional headquarters a succinct estimate of the situation of his troops: "No water. Little ammunition. High casualties. Pinned down. No tanks."[36] No help arrived. Men of those two battalions fought on alone.

Russell Arford of Company G remembered how concern for a job finally brought him to the Hürtgen. "I signed up in February 1941," he said, "figuring I would get my year of army service over with and get out. By 1942, I thought, jobs would be more plentiful. They were, but I didn't get any of them. I sure chose the wrong time to go in, for I was immediately federalized and in the army until the end of the war."[37] In the Kall Valley he often wondered if he would ever live long enough to work at any of those jobs.

Even in the midst of fierce combat there were sometimes moments of humor. Charles Hubner recalled some of them.* "We had a sergeant in our platoon who collected all the 'K' rations he could find and stuffed them into his shirt and field jacket. He looked like a walking supermarket. All anyone had to ask was 'What you got to eat, Sgt?' He'd pull out his groceries and you took your choice. He didn't eat much himself but loved to feed the boys. . . . If he was ever hit by a shell, he'd be so full of tin, scrambled eggs, hash, lousy biscuits, he would die of food poisoning."

---

*"Sure it was a terrible time," Hubner said, "but when I think back on those things, I always remember what was funny, what we laughed at." He added a telling comment. "I am a native New Yorker, and I love New York, but when I see the Keystone—even if it's on a can of Heinz Beans, I am proud to have served with the 28th Penna. Division."

During those days in the Kall gorge, recalled Hubner, "we were trapped in the dragon teeth of the Siegfried Line and enemy fire was ricocheting from one tooth to another. I thought we were going to get chopped up like hamburger. One soldier, about a couple of teeth away, suddenly spun up in the air and down on the ground. In a few seconds he was up amidst all the junk flying around, cursing and tearing at his cartridge belt. I met the soldier later and asked what happened. Was he hurt? He had just taken a Luger pistol from a German prisoner. A ricocheting shell fragment or bullet hit it and smashed the mechanism of his prized souvenir. He was so mad he heaved belt, pistol and all towards the enemy fire."

Hubner smiled at another recollection. "Whenever one of our men got nervous he would start whistling, no tune just tweet. We called him the Whistler. At first we were annoyed and tried to break his habit but couldn't. . . . Some of us were holed up in a captured seven foot thick reinforced concrete bunker, low ceiling, in which a normal size American soldier could just about stand up in. We got a . . . new shave tail out of O.C.S. from the States. The Whistler got nervous over something and let out a tweet. The poor 2nd Lt. jumped straight up, thinking it was a screeming mimie. He slammed into the ceiling and flattened the top of his helmet like a cooking pot. Needless to say he had one whopper of a headache."[38]

Late in the afternoon of 6 November, two Poles—deserters from the German Army—walked into the lines of 1st Battalion and surrendered. Officers of the 110th Regiment sent them back to battalion S-2 intelligence section for questioning. The Polish PWs returned to Simonskall the next morning and spent the day helping American artillery batteries register fire on German troop locations.[39]

At 1930 hours, 9 November—the day after the American breakout from Kommerscheidt Hill—Lieutenant Colonel Floyd Davison, commander of 1st Battalion, 110th Regiment, received new orders. American efforts against the Germans were not yet at an end. Spurred by divisional pressure, the 110th Regiment was to assault an enemy stronghold at Raffelsbrand, capture it, and continue the attack toward Monschau in the southwest. By initiating such orders, Cota was carrying out part of his "bargain" with General Hodges, who had insisted on certain prerequisites before he would approve any withdrawal of American forces from Kommerscheidt Hill. The assault on Raffelsbrand and Monschau would begin at 0700 hours, 10 November.

Colonel Davison conferred with his company officers at 2200 hours in his command post the night before the attack. He gave them their instructions. What they heard did not please them. So little time remained before the attack they had no opportunity to make a ground reconnaissance. There was not even time to work out company-level assault plans. It was a frustrating moment. Weather added to their difficulties. Heavy snow fell for the second night in a row. The snow, darkness, and the treacherous, splintered forest made it difficult for Davison's company officers to get back to their own commands in time to form up their men for the dawn attack. Bad weather also abetted previous rains and snows in creating a wave of trench foot problems for soldiers of the regiment.[40]

Sick and weary infantrymen moved out against their enemies on the morning of 10 November, the last gasp of a dying regiment. It was typical of all the vicious and costly fighting in the Kall gorge. Snow lay as much as one foot deep on the level, and men slogged through piled drifts. The wet and slushy snow increased their discomfort, filled their positions with water and ice, served to aid enemy observation of forward movements, and made even more difficult the problem of keeping weapons dry.[41]

They walked in silence toward their objectives, the strongpoint of Raffelsbrand and its protecting pillboxes. "We kept walking—and waiting—for that first alarm or shot from the 'jerries' indicating that our advance had been spotted," said Technical Sergeant Warren Dunlap of 2nd Battalion's Fox Company. As the skirmish line drew closer to the first "box," an enemy outpost raised the alarm and opened fire. This alerted other Germans, who also brought fire to bear on advancing American troops. "We hit the ground *fast,*" Dunlap remembered, "and began doing a little shooting ourselves."

They reached and captured the first pillbox. Sergeant Dunlap assumed command of his platoon when his lieutenant was wounded. They continued their advance using what Dunlap called "the old fire and movement," forging ahead against rifle grenades, small-arms fire, mortar rounds, and machine guns. Dunlap's platoon suffered so many casualties they were forced to pull back to the "box" they had captured earlier. By 1045 hours, only he and five others remained alive. Dunlap called his company command post over a landline telephone.

"We won't be able to hold out much longer. . . . It is plenty hot down here," Dunlap shouted into the mouthpiece. To illustrate his quandary, he held the receiver away from his ear. First Sergeant Steve Levering, who listened on the other end, was amazed at the noise level around Dunlap. "That damned fool," Levering thought. "He'll get his goddamned arm shot off holding the phone up like that."

First Sergeant Levering bellowed into the telephone, "Do what you deem best." Sergeant Dunlap and his five men abandoned the pillbox and "ran like hell" back along the route on which they had advanced only a few hours earlier. They were back in their original company positions by 1130 hours. Adjoining platoons did no better, also retreating from German fire "in disorganized haste."

Captain Lake Coleman, commander of Fox Company, saw another disaster in the making. His platoons were so shattered and disorganized that at 0830 hours he turned his command over to First Sergeant Levering and worked his way forward in an effort to help. Locating several stragglers,

Coleman ordered them to rejoin their platoons. Within less than five minutes they were again running back toward the company command post. "Most of them probably never went very far forward," Coleman said. "Their morale was at a very low ebb."

Coleman tried a second time, taking Staff Sergeant Edward Wold with him. Searching through foxholes, they rounded up nearly 20 men. With Coleman in the lead, they attacked a nearby pillbox. Crawling through snow and slush, they fought their way forward until small-arms and machine-gun fire pinned them down.

German soldiers yelled at Coleman and his men to surrender. For a moment the captain was confused, thinking it was the Germans who wanted to surrender. He shouted for them to come out with their hands up, to which they responded with a "razzberry-like burp" from a machine gun. Again the Germans shouted for them to surrender. Coleman repeated his demand for the second time. His foes called back that he and his men were outnumbered and outflanked. The captain refused to surrender. They fought on, able to see their enemies "sneaking and infiltrating" around them. At 1430 hours, worried that they might be cut off, Coleman signaled his men to pull back. "The withdrawal was slow. We lost several more men. [It] was not orderly. Some just got up and ran to the rear."

Back at his command post, Coleman and First Sergeant Levering took a nose count of survivors. Prior to the attack, 1st Platoon had 25 men. Now it had 10 privates. 2nd Platoon began with 25 men, and only six were left. 3rd Platoon started out with 27 men, of whom only six survived. Fox Company had by midafternoon only 35 "effectives" left available for combat. Over 50 percent of them suffered from severe cases of trench foot, and none had gotten much rest for more than eight days.[42]

For a time that day, things went better for Fox's sister company, George. Moving out promptly at 0700 hours in tight squad formation, leading men advanced no more than 40 yards when they all but stumbled into foxholes and bunkers occupied by sleeping Germans. Walking quietly, using bayonets to prod the "Jerries" awake, they persuaded their foes to come out of their shelters. Their surprise attack allowed them to capture 60 PWs.

Then George Company moved on toward the Raffelsbrand strongpoint, where it was forced to take cover from machine-gun and mortar fire some 100 yards short of the old stone forestry hut. Further advance was impossible. At the end of the day, Staff Sergeant Joseph Paczesna had only five "effectives" left in 2nd Platoon; Sergeant William Pennington and six others were the only survivors in 1st Platoon; Staff Sergeant Abraham Kumukau had only nine uninjured men left in 3rd Platoon.[43]

Easy Company had no better luck in its assault on Raffelsbrand. Its men crawled to within 25 yards of the objective. Private Leroy Carson, a BAR gunner, crept up almost to the protective wire around its perimeter. Standing carefully, he took one step forward and touched off a booby trap, which knocked him off balance. Trying to stay on his feet, he stepped on a mine, which blew away the lower half of his left leg and flung him into the wire. Private William Blatner ran forward to free Carson from the vicious barbs. A burst from a German burp gun felled Blatner with seven slugs through his head and upper body. Enemy fire kept the company at bay. By nightfall, few GIs in Easy Company were left.[44] 2nd Battalion failed to achieve anything in that attack on 10 November except to inflict savage casualties on its own men.

1st Battalion did no better. Progress through the woods after the jump-off hour of 0700 was slow. Fallen trees impeded visibility as well as movement. German resistance was fierce. By 0900 hours, the battalion was pinned down. It pulled back some distance and dug in, remaining there the remainder of the day. Colonel Theodore Seely, commander of the 110th Regiment, ordered 1st Battalion commander, Colonel Davison, to renew the attack during the night, and Davison duly passed the word along to his company officers.

Few men in those badly battered companies even stirred from their foxholes in the bitter night air. They had been under constant enemy fire for over a week, with no opportunity to relax or dry out. There was no fight left in them. They were so worn down they would have given anything to get out of the Kall Valley.* At least half the men in 1st Battalion were replacements with only hours or days of service in their units. New to the terrors of fighting in the Hürtgen, they sat waiting for the end.[45]

The night of 10/11 November was bitterly cold. Soldiers the next morning found two Signal Corps wiremen, attached to 1st Battalion, almost frozen to death. They had stopped to rest briefly while repairing breaks in the wire and were too exhausted to resume their work. In the morning they were covered with frost.

Colonel Seely ordered 1st Battalion to renew its attack on Raffelsbrand and toward Monschau. H Hour was to be 0630, 11 November. Such orders were a farce. C Company consisted of its commander, Captain Dini, three NCOs, and 19 exhausted enlisted men. They were attempting to eat their first meal in two days when they received orders to move out. In spite of their hunger, fatigue, and painful feet, "not one of the men offered any bitches or complaints." They picked up their M-1s and hobbled forward in a magnificent example of dedication and bravery. Both Able and Charlie companies advanced under consistently heavy and "damnably accurate" mortar fire. They continued a listless attack until 1500 hours and then once again dug in for another endless night.[46]

---

*Their condition may be seen in the actions of Captain William Dobbs, for a time commander of E Company, 2nd Battalion, 110th Regiment. During the night of 7/8 November, already driven to distraction, Captain Dobbs "mistook" a gasoline can for a water container, poured himself some, and drank a couple of swallows. Violently ill, he was then evacuated. See Dobbs interview.

Official reports on 11 November described the companies of 1st and 2nd battalions as engaged in actions "strengthening the lines." In actuality they did less than that. Men in those units were "so damned tired and weary at this point that they just stayed put in their foxholes."[47]

During the afternoon, Captain Lake Coleman, commander of Fox Company, received orders to attack once more the following day. The plan received by the captain passed the boundary of the absurd and plunged into insanity.

A composite platoon, Coleman learned, made up from I, K, and L companies and commanded by First Lieutenant Leo Seery of Item Company, would reinforce Coleman's Fox Company. Lieutenant Seery was the only remaining officer in Item Company. He had remained with "Howdy" Rumbaugh on the banks of the Kall River during the breakout from Kommerscheidt Hill on the night of 8 November. At Rumbaugh's request he recrossed the river to look for stragglers and then took the few he found on toward Vossenack, leaving Rumbaugh to search for still other missing men. Now he was back in action, sent by his commanders on a fool's errand.

Seery's composite platoon was to attack down a firebreak toward the southeast, supported by one tank destroyer. While the lieutenant's "unified command" pressed its assault, Coleman's Fox Company was to "protect the division right flank." By this time, Fox Company consisted of Lake Coleman, First Sergeant Steve Levering, Technical Sergeant Warren Dunlap, and *25* other men, all of whom were in such poor shape they needed to be withdrawn from battle. This was the force responsible for protecting what was left of a *divisional* flank![48]

Such orders could have been drawn up only by men who no longer knew or cared about reality. Like hurt and enraged scorpions trying to sting themselves to death, General Cota was determined to carry out the wishes of Hodges and Gerow no matter how thoroughly his actions might destroy surviving members of the 28th Infantry Division.

Seery's composite platoon arrived at Fox Company positions just before dark, at 1630 hours on 11 November. The entire group consisted of *eight* privates and *one* sergeant! Lieutenant Seery did not accompany them. The NCO explained to Captain Coleman that Seery, feeling totally exhausted, had stopped at an aid station as they were enroute, saying he would be along shortly.

Lieutenant Seery arrived some time later. Since it was now too dark for a reconnaissance on the ground, Captain Coleman gave him a map orientation and then listed existing problems. The force was obviously too small to be effective. Roads and the firebreak had not been swept by engineers for mines. Pole and satchel charges to be used to blow a path through enemy fortifications had not arrived. Exhausted and dispirited troops "didn't give a damn about moving" or anything else.

Seery agreed with Coleman that attack was impossible. Coleman radioed Lieutenant Colonel James Hughes, his battalion commander whose home was in Coral Gables, Florida. After listening to his company commander, Colonel Hughes concurred that the regimental orders could not be carried out. He told Coleman he would talk with Colonel Seely at regiment. Seely broached the issue with the divisional chief of staff, Colonel Charles Valentine, who took it up with Generals Davis and Cota. Finally, upon divisional order, the proposed attack was canceled at 2300 hours, 11 November. [49]

Thereafter 2nd Battalion sat quietly in place. On 13 November its men learned that General Hodges had ordered their relief. On 16 November, troops of the 13th Infantry Regiment, 8th Infantry Division, moved into the *Hürtgenwald* to take their place.[50]

Replacements filtered down the slope of the Vossenack ridge on 12 November toward 1st Battalion, 110th Regiment. They were quickly pressed into service as they reached company positions. At Able Company, the battalion S-1 personnel officer, Captain Wesley Rose, and an A Company runner, Private Lawrence "Alabama" Thomas, moved along the column of new men. Thomas counted them off: "1, 2, 3, 4; 1, 2, 3, 4 . . ." Rose followed behind him, telling those so counted, "You're in the 1st platoon, You're in the 2nd platoon, and so forth."

The hastily divided new men were sent forward to platoon positions. As they moved along they ran into small-arms and mortar fire and immediately began to take casualties. There had been no opportunity to brief them on how to react under enemy fire. The "main trouble" with such green troops was that they were "not battlewise." Captain Rose discussed what happened. "Instead of moving when artillery or mortar shells landed, even at ranges of 3-400 yards, they fell to the ground. Some would hide behind trees thinking they were safe there. . . . They just didn't know what it was all about."

Captain Rose found it necessary to force frightened new replacements forward into less dangerous positions away from the barrage zone. As he did so, he saw Captain Sidney Dini, commander of C Company, in his foxhole. Dini was so exhausted and nearly frozen he could not move. He was evacuated on the spot.[51]

At 1100 hours the following morning, 13 November, the omnipresent General Davis came forward into 1st Battalion area. Accompanied by Colonel Seely, commander of the 110th Regiment, Davis wanted to see for himself the condition of its troops. After a brief inspection, he ordered 1st Battalion to pull out of line. The move rearward began at 1500 hours.[52]

An hour before the troops left their positions, Captain James Burns, 1st Battalion S-3 operations officer, scoured the area to ensure that everyone had gotten the news to pull out. He discovered that very few knew anything about such orders. Burns found it necessary to go to each individual foxhole, alerting soldiers about the planned withdrawal.

Captain Burns remained behind as others left, still searching for those who might not have been told to leave. At the crest of a hill he suddenly found himself surrounded by Germans. "First there were two. Then there were four. I remember a huge heinie lunging at me with his bayonet saying 'halt-surrender-halt-surrender.' I said, 'Nuts to you' and ran like hell back down to a rock crevice and hid there until about 1550, then made it back o.k."[53]

As the men of 1st Battalion walked wearily back into a rear assembly area, Captain Wesley Rose made a nose count of their numbers. He tallied only 57 survivors of an entire rifle battalion that at full strength included 871 men.* These were all who remained of three rifle companies, including 95 replacements who had been sent forward the previous afternoon, and two attached heavy-machine-gun platoons. Most of the 57 men were evacuated with trench foot caused by continued exposure, continuous rain or snow, and the impossibility of keeping dry. Few had galoshes, and men often went four to five days without a chance to change either their socks or shoes.[54]

That night of 13/14 November, some 200 additional replacements were added to battalion strength reports. The unit went into regimental reserve for reorganization. On the night of 16/17 November it moved south into Luxembourg for rest and recuperation. A month later it sat directly on the route used by the German Army in its December Ardennes offensive. Once again those American soldiers were tried in the crucible of combat.[55] Some of the equipment used by German forces in the Battle of the Bulge had been captured in the *Hürtgenwald* and reconditioned.

The 12th Infantry Regiment of the 4th Infantry Division, attached to the 28th in order to relieve the 109th Regiment from its stalemate in the forest and minefields south of the town of Hürtgen, soon learned how devastating it was to fight in this sector. In five days of combat, the 12th Regiment suffered over 500 casualties.[56]

Those days of battle, General James Gavin later wrote, were "our Passchendaele."[57] Historian Charles MacDonald described the action as "one of the most costly U.S. division actions in the whole of World War II."[58] A British analyst, R. W. Thompson, believes that "in the final upshot," troops of the 28th Division marched into battle "in a state of innocence most terrible to contemplate" in the "irresponsible attack on" Schmidt, which caused the unit to suffer "the worst disaster on a divisional level to befall U.S. troops in the campaign in northwest Europe."[59]

---

*Despite the bravery and awesome casualties suffered by his troops, General Cota was tightfisted in approving awards for them. Through all their days of fighting in Europe, officers and men of the 28th Infantry Division received a grossly disproportionate low number of awards: only 359 silver stars, 15 soldier's medals, 2,627 bronze stars, 18 distinguished service crosses, and but one Congressional Medal of Honor. See Table of Awards, *Historical and Pictorial Review.*

It would have been very difficult for Cota or Gerow or Hodges to be proud of what they forced upon soldiers of the "Bloody Bucket" division. Its men suffered through 14 days of unalleviated combat while absorbing savage numbers of casualties in order to gain *no* key features and only some 1,000 yards of useless, unimportant land amid a broken and splintered forest.

Headquarters
First United States Army
Office of the Commanding General
Fort Bragg, North Carolina

TO THE OFFICERS AND MEN
OF THE 28th INFANTRY DIVISION:

You can well be proud of your service with the First Army in Europe. . . . and your valiant part in shattering the German Seventh Army will go down in history to your everlasting credit. I remember best, however, those bitter days in the Hurtgen Forest where the going was toughest and where your gallant division was pitted against cruel weather and a fanatic enemy. . . .

I am proud to have commanded you in battle. Each of you has strong reason to be proud of your division and of the individual part you each played in amassing the 28th's record of courage and fighting stamina.

/s/ Courtney H. Hodges
COURTNEY H. HODGES
General U.S.A.
Commanding[60]

TO THE OFFICERS AND MEN OF THE 28th DIVISION:

Now that the war is over and we are home again, I would like to express to you all my deep and lasting appreciation for the fine job you did while serving under my command, both during active hostilities and the occupation period.

None of us will ever forget the drive across the continent to the Siegfried Line; the stubborn battles to break through those defenses; and the bloody fighting in the Hurtgen Forest under the most adverse conditions of weather and terrain. In these tests of soul and body, the officers and men of the Division lived up to the finest traditions of the United States Army and added new and glorious pages to its history. To the families of those men who did not return,

I extend my sincere sympathy and console them with the thought that their loved ones gave their lives to preserve those principles we have always believed are more precious than life.

Best of luck and all good wishes to every member of the Division.

/s/ L. T. Gerow
L. T. GEROW
Lt Gen, U S A[61]

Headquarters
28th INFANTRY DIVISION
Camp Shelby, Mississippi

15 September 1945

TO THE MEN OF THE 28TH:

. . . you pushed the enemy back from every inch of ground he sought to hold. I am proud of the 28th Infantry Division. I am proud to have had the high honor to command the fine men who composed the Division. I say to all, "Well Done," "Roll On."

/s/ Norman D. Cota
NORMAN D. COTA
Major General, USA,
Commanding[62]

13

"They hated the Hürtgen Forest"

November Aftermath

Robert E. Lee, the great general of the American Confederacy during the Civil War, once said, "It is well that war is so terrible—we should [otherwise] grow too fond of it."[1] Survivors of the 28th Infantry Division's incursion into the *Hürtgenwald* knew full well the horrors of war. Death had been their constant companion for 14 days.

Cy Peterman, one of the war correspondents who covered the battle, described the feelings of those who endured that conflict. "If they never traveled its fragrant ravines or pitched another tent or [built a] new-hewn hut to ward off [shell] fragments and falling treetops, if they never saw a timbered slit trench or smelled the tangy odor of burning cones and felt springy . . . needles that carpeted the forest, they would not care. . . . If they never saw the Hürtgen Forest again, it would suit them. . . . They hated the Hürtgen Forest. . . ."[2]

They were gone now. No grunts and curses from frantic riflemen resounded across the battlefield. No longer did M-1s and Spandaus, machine guns and BARs shatter the air of the high Eifel with their reports. No artillery barrages exploded along the plateaus or among the grenadier ranks of stately Douglas firs, epauleted with snow. Silence lay over the battlefield and along the devastated length of the Kall trail, cluttered with wrecked jeeps and trucks, abandoned Weasels and broken tanks, discarded radio sets and rifles, felled trees and shattered branches. Still other equipment and vehicles lay strewn among broken trees as they sloped away from the trail, pushed from the road by laboring men in futile efforts to keep open that vital main supply route. Only foot soldiers could have made their way down that steep path past snow-filled rifle pits and among the detritus of war.

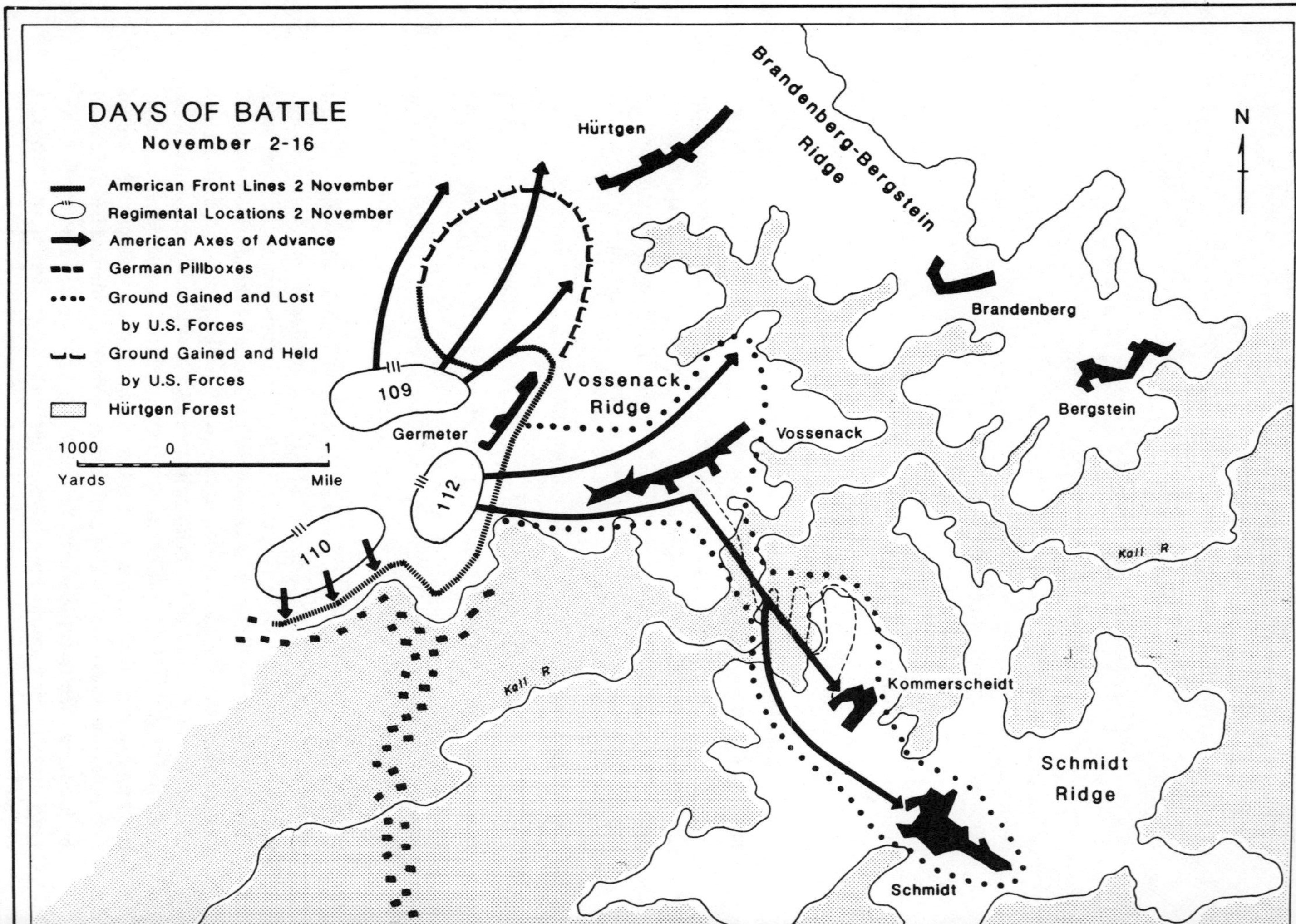
DAYS OF BATTLE
November 2-16
American Front Lines 2 November
Regimental Locations 2 November
American Axes of Advance
German Pillboxes
Ground Gained and Lost by U.S. Forces
Ground Gained and Held by U.S. Forces
Hürtgen Forest
1000
0
1
Yards
Mile
N
Hürtgen
Brandenberg-Bergstein Ridge
Brandenberg
Bergstein
Vossenack Ridge
Vossenack
Germeter
109
112
110
Kall R
Kommerscheidt
Schmidt Ridge
Schmidt

The Kall trail gave mute testimony to the savage combat that raged through the Hürtgen during the first half of November. The contours of stiff, frozen cadavers mutilated by the wounds of war were softened by the gentling touch of winter's snow. Rotting, mouldy uniforms still clung to corpses of American warriors, on some of which could still be seen the *Blutiger Eimer* keystone-shaped blood-red patch. Those bodies gave mute protest to the futility of the action that took their lives. Sprinkled among them were contorted forms of *Wehrmacht* troopers, sacrificed on behalf of *Vaterland und Führer*.

Near the old abandoned aid station the roadway was dotted with makeshift litters on some of which still lay the quieted bodies of American soldiers, dead from wounds or from freezing temperatures. Neither division nor corps nor Army removed those fallen warriors or recovered abandoned equipment. And so throughout the winter of 1944–1945, this gruesome tableau remained as a graphic illustration of the fruits of war.

Given the difficulties it faced, the 28th Infantry Division did magnificently against all odds. For 14 days its men struggled over steep hills and fought off infantry and tanks while enduring endless artillery barrages. They crossed between the ridges of Vossenack and Schmidt using no more than a narrow, twisting trail. They captured briefly the towns of Vossenack, Kommerscheidt, Schmidt, and Simonskall.

Private soldiers, noncommissioned officers, and company-grade officers who fought on those ridges were brave, courageous, and resourceful. Staff officers deserted their desks and rear-area command posts to participate in the fighting. Battalion commanders suffered an inordinate number of wounds and fatalities. Regimental commanders, such as Lieutenant Colonel Carl Peterson, deliberately shared every hardship endured by their subordinates. They deserve both honor and glory.

Orders sent those brave men into a combat situation that made little sense, into a maelstrom of mud, men, steel, and blood—a world gone insane. Although in November 1944 the Army could still not take victory for granted, there should have been no particular haste to throw away men's lives in a spate of frenzy. Italy's *Il Duce,* Benito Mussolini, once said, "War is to man what maternity is to woman."[3] Senior American general officers were midwives to a birthing in the Hürtgen which produced a monstrous, deformed creature slavering for the lives of their soldiers and which satiated itself with their blood.

Lieutenant General Leonard T. Gerow, commander of V Corps,* assigned

---

*Before the European campaign ended Gerow became commander of Fifteenth Army, the last American army to be organized in the European Theater; he commanded it in its participation in mopping up the Ruhr Pocket.

a group of his staff officers to study the Schmidt operation. They concluded that planning for the battle, given the circumstances faced, was tactically sound. Improvident weather, an inadequate supply route, savage German resistance, divergent regimental missions, insufficient divisional reserves, and continual German barrages launched from the sanctuary of the Brandenberg–Bergstein ridge line—all these combined to ensure defeat in a "gamble that failed."[4]

This conclusion was overcharitable to Cota, Gerow, and Hodges. A gamble implies a chance of winning. Soldiers of the 28th Division failed because they were placed in an impossible situation. They were never given a chance. They followed orders that were skewed by the fears and errors of their superiors. Despite "grave misgivings" about the operation, the generals in charge determined to go ahead with their plans. Everything that could go wrong seemingly did.

Prior to battle, American intelligence planners did not know that the German *272nd Volksgrenadier Division* was in the process of relieving the *89th Infantry Division* and consequently could quickly be thrown into any battle that might begin. Nor did they know how rapidly the *116th Panzer Division* could be brought to bear against them. There was no way planners could have predicted the fortuitous meeting of high-ranking German officers at *Schloss Schlenderhan* just at the time when the 28th Infantry Division launched its attack, which allowed enemy forces to give nearly immediately responses to the American thrust into the Hürtgen.

There was, further, no way American staff officers might have predicted the intended German Ardennes offensive scheduled for December. Yet warnings about the value of the sector were available, and First Army and V Corps staffs ought to have given more thought to the importance of the Rur dams and the steadfastness with which Germans planned to defend them. It should have been obvious that they would never surrender such a key position without a considerable fight.

From Eisenhower at SHAEF to Bradley of 12th Army Group; from Hodges at First Army to Cota of the 28th Division—all were lulled by the ease with which American forces had driven across France to the German border. They failed to appreciate how well Germans could fight when properly motivated. They never understood how determinedly their enemies would resist any intrusion into the Hürtgen.

Yet the foregoing were only unfortunate circumstances mitigating against an American success. Had they been the only obstacles, U.S. troops might well have won their way through to victory at Schmidt, as they already had in so many places. Other and needless obstacles prevented any possibility of success, most of which were crystal clear before the first man crossed the line of departure at Germeter on 2 November.

The generals knew the woods were full of German artillery but assumed they could blind those enemy fire batteries by interdicting the Brandenberg–

Bergstein ridge line with smoke shells. It was a mistake that was unnecessary. Aerial photos and maps revealed the inadequacy of the Kall trail as a main supply route. Patrols could have seen that it was incapable of handling tanks and other armored vehicles, but none was sent, and generals designated a nine-foot-wide, twisting path as the MSR for a division. It was a mistake that was unnecessary.

Adverse weather conditions were known to the lowliest private, yet the 28th Division was sent into battle at a time when IX TAC Air was unable to provide appropriate support. Poor weather conditions and bitterly cold temperatures meant that soldiers fought in clothing that provided them with little more protection from the cold than Washington's troops had at Valley Forge. It was a mistake that was unnecessary.

Even lieutenants know the importance of keeping sufficient reserve forces available to use when necessary, but generals allowed a division to go into combat with only a battalion in reserve, and even it was rapidly committed to battle. It was a mistake that was unnecessary. Military schools teach the folly of dividing one's forces and urge the importance of concentrating troops in sufficient massed strength to accomplish the mission. Generals at Schmidt ordered the regiments of the 28th to strike in three different directions. It was a mistake that was unnecessary.

Grievous leadership faults—not lack of bravery by individual soldiers—brought about the debacle in the Hürtgen. There were three objectives sought by the generals: (1) to give additional supply routes and maneuver space to VII Corps for its 5 November attack, (2) to protect the southern flank of VII Corps, and (3) to pull enemy reserve forces away from VII Corps, thus opening the way for its attack on 5 November.

Only one of those objectives was achieved. The attack by the 28th Infantry Division drew German units into its area with a vengeance. Yet even this single accomplishment was wasted when Hodges and Collins postponed the attack of VII Corps, leaving the doomed men of the 28th to fight on alone.

Of all the generals involved in this story, only Brigadier General George A. Davis saw fit to see firsthand the conditions under which their troops were fighting. General Davis repeatedly drove and walked through the entire battle zone. He saw brave men stand and die. He watched frightened men flee. Ambulances carted butchered men past him toward the rear, and he observed the glaze of combat exhaustion in the haunted eyes of those trapped in the forest. From 4 November on, he endured bombardments, slept in platoon command posts at Kommerscheidt, argued with Colonel Sam Mays, received radio situation reports from tankers, and even went behind enemy lines to inspect the Kall aid station. He ordered the 20th, 146th, and 1340th Engineers to fight as infantrymen in Vossenack and along the trail. He visited 3rd Battalion command post in Vossenack to order troops placed "out there." He was willing to command his own "task force" in a last-ditch effort to retake Schmidt. He was everywhere!

Many of his appearances did not make good sense, for generals do not properly expose themselves on a regular basis to dangers of capture, injury, or death. He interfered with chains of command, issuing orders to tankers, TD crews, infantrymen, and engineers, without regard for their superiors. But at least he sought to find out what was happening and was willing to put his own life on the line. Despite his experiences, he provided no palliative to Cota's approach to battle, and we do not know whether he advocated alternate approaches to the looming disaster in meetings with Cota, Gerow, Hodges, Kean, Collins, Bradley, and Eisenhower.

Cota, Gerow, and Hodges were less adept than Davis. Whatever Cota may have done before, whatever he became afterward, his mistakes in this battle are legion. He tried to present a successful front to his superiors while he knew full well that the battle was a disaster, that victory was an illusion, that his men were being massacred. His G-3 periodic reports portrayed such an unrealistic picture of the combat they can only have reflected three possible motives: the effort of a staff that wanted to hide from Cota what was occurring; or they reported what Cota thought was happening; or what he wanted Generals Gerow and Hodges to think was happening. If the first, he was an ineffective leader in this situation. If the second, he was out of touch with his own command. If the third, he was deliberately misrepresenting the action in the Hürtgen to his superiors in hopes of redeeming the situation by some last-minute accomplishment before they learned how close he had come to defeat. Much can be forgiven of one who brings news of victory.

Cota, Gerow, and Hodges weighted the battle against their own troops by ignoring the value of long-established tactical principals: objective, mass, maneuver, unity of command, security, simplicity, and economy of force. The only ones they followed were those of surprise and offensive action. The terms are technical, but their meanings are easily understood.

Although Cota made one trip into the battle zone of Vossenack and certainly was aware of the deplorable state of his soldiers, it seems not to have changed his approach. Cota never again had complete control of his division following the German counterattack against Schmidt on the morning of 4 November. Although he issued orders, his ideas often were not carried out, ignored by subordinate commanders on the spot who knew better.

Cota's tactical skills broke down when he forgot to create—or was not allowed to use—uncomplicated battle plans and clear, concise orders for his subordinate commanders. Instead, he ordered both the 110th and 112th regiments to advance, followed by a 90-degree change of direction, a maneuver difficult under the best of circumstances and one that violated the military principles of maneuver and simplicity.

Military units must achieve maximum military superiority at a decisive time and place. They must locate available resources so that they will be readily available. Cota compromised these principles of mass and maneuver when he pressed the attack knowing full well that his only available supply route was small, inadequate, and difficult. Cota should have ensured effective action to minimize hostile interference with his operation. Instead he seemed unaware that a single battalion would not comprise a sufficient reserve for a division, and he was unmindful of the German ability to move unopposed along the Kall River road, severing American lines whenever they wished.

With resolute determination, Cota tried to fling 300-man battalions—in which there were perhaps 100 "effectives"—against preponderant German forces, thus violating the principle of mass or concentration of force. He sent platoons to attack toward Monschau and allowed company remnants to "protect the flank" of the division. His daily summaries of activity were untouched by reality. He relieved Lieutenant Colonel Carl Peterson and then disclaimed responsibility. He may have fainted under the stress of battle. His unwillingness to take a stand on behalf of the welfare of his division against Gerow and Hodges condemned thousands of his own warriors to agonizing deaths long after there was any possibility of their success.

Cota's faults loom large in any analysis, yet perhaps his gravest mistake was his willingness to accede to demands of his superiors without protest when they gave him flawed orders. Lieutenant General Leonard Gerow, commander of V Corps, violated principles of war as surely as did Cota.

In battle all activity must be directed toward a single, clearly defined goal. Gerow gave Cota *three* objectives, one for each of his regiments: to secure a line of departure north of Germeter for a later attack, to strike south into the Siegfried Line to open a better supply route, and to capture Schmidt. Achieving the new line of departure and a more effective MSR were secondary goals, yet Gerow assigned two thirds of the division's forces to securing them. Far better for Gerow to have assigned first the capture of a new LD as a primary goal; after its acquisition, to assign seizure of an MSR as the next objective; and only then to have ordered the attack against Schmidt.

These disparate goals Gerow decreed for Cota so scattered the regiments of the 28th that the division no longer had the strength to hold Schmidt after occupying it. To split forces in this way minimized Cota's ability to provide unity of command—for it was Gerow, not he, who made such assignments—and as well violated the principles of objective, mass, maneuver, and simplicity. Had General Gerow kept his hands off divisional planning; had he allowed Cota more freedom in using his own unit, there might well have been a different ending.

General Courtney Hodges, commander of First Army, must also bear a burden for the slaughter at Schmidt. He was senior in command to both Gerow and Cota. He saw their plans; he pronounced himself satisfied. Their failures were his as well, for it is long-established military doctrine that the senior commander is *always* responsible—for both success and failure. Particularly is this true when a senior commander participates as much in the planning for a battle as did Hodges in this case. His were failures of commission.

The incursion into the Hürtgen came about because Hodges wanted it. It was he who feared that the *Hürtgenwald* of World War II was comparable to the Argonne Forest of World War I. It was he who required an unnecessary assault into those tangled depths—not once but *four* times, ordering repeated divisions into the yawning jaws of that "green hell" as if he had never heard of the military principle of mass or concentration of force.

Major General Louis Craig's 9th Infantry Division lost 4,500 men between 6-16 October 1944 in the Hürtgen. Hodges then sent the 28th in battle as a diversionary attack, and it fought desperately from 2-16 November. Even after bad weather forced an indefinite postponement of Collins' main attack, Hodges allowed the bloody battering of the 28th to continue. By the time he met with Cota on 8 November, the 28th was more battered than any other American unit in all the fighting across the face of Europe during the Second World War. It ultimately suffered a *minimum* of 6,184 casualties.

The 12th Infantry Regiment, 4th Infantry Division, went into battle south of the town of Hürtgen on 6 November. In only five days it absorbed more than 500 casualties, and by the time the division was withdrawn from battle, it had suffered 4,053 combat casualties plus 2,000 more from shell shock, foot immersion, and respiratory ailments. 2nd Battalion, 110th Regiment, 28th Division, was relieved by 13th Regiment, 8th Infantry Division on 16 November. Elements of 2nd Ranger Battalion and 5th Armored Division also participated in relief of the 28th Division. They sustained another 4,000 combat casualties and 1,200 nonbattle injuries. When the 78th Infantry Division attacked and finally captured Schmidt and the Schwammenauel Dam in February 1945, it suffered another 1,000 casualties. These rough figures reveal a *minimum* of nearly 23,000 casualties. If successful generals must be immune to the number of casualties suffered, then Hodges emerges as one of the greatest leaders of the war. Violations of fundamental principles paved the way for the endless, bitter days at Schmidt.

Even German commanders could not understand Hodges' fixation on the *Hürtgenwald*, particularly after the October failure there of the 9th Infantry Division. Even months after the end of the war, *Generalmajor* Rudolf Freiherr von Gersdorff, chief of staff of the German *Seventh Army,* remained amazed at how unnecessarily his American enemies had scarred themselves in those forested depths. "It would have been more favorable," Gersdorff wrote, "to secure the area in a sufficient manner and to mine [its approaches] effectively." That would have sealed Germans off in those woods without bloodying American divisions. Hodges chose otherwise. As a result, said Gersdorff, "The fighting caused them heavy losses, without bringing them any tactical or strategical success of decisive importance."

Nor did Gersdorff respect Hodges' military prowess. The thrust into the West Wall, Gersdorff believed, "was neither planned nor executed skillfully. It would have been necessary to use stronger forces. The execution of this attack was weak and inefficient, and, therefore, we were able to contain and later eliminate it by comparatively weak German forces."

In the German general's view, the attack by the 28th Division was counterproductive in many ways. "This enterprise caused the Americans heavy losses and greatly improved the morale of German troops, who had suffered a previous series of defeats. For the first time it had been possible to defeat American troops. The steadily increasing feeling of inferiority, on the German side, was reduced substantially by this fighting. Thus this operation was disadvantageous to the American command in every respect, even if it was meant to be only a scouting raid or a [diversionary] attempt."[5]

The approaches chosen by Hodges, Gerow, and Cota ignored military necessity and the reality endured by soldiers of the 28th Division. Divisional, Corps, and Army generals plotted the campaign with grease pencils on map overlays. The calamity that befell the "Bloody Bucket" was directly related to their commanders' lack of understanding for, as General James Gavin later wrote, "battles are not won on maps."[6]

How, General Gavin asked, could those senior commanders have fallen "into such a predicament"?[7] He wondered what got them "involved in attacking across the Kall River valley." He sought answers. "I raised this question with a Corps staff officer . . . , but he brushed it aside. I asked why in the world they had attacked through the Hürtgen Forest in the first place, but apparently that was a 'no-no' question." Cota, Gerow, and Hodges fought in such a way, Gavin believed, as to sacrifice their ground mobility, their armored capabilities, and their tactical air support. Worst of all, they did so on terrain that favored their enemies.

"Obviously," General Gavin wrote, "the attack on Schmidt should have been made straight down the ridge from Lammersdorf. Lammersdorf and Schmidt are connected by a paved road, the terrain was a mixture of woods and open farmland, good tank country, . . . a much simpler tactical undertaking than crossing the Kall river. . . . Why not stick to the high ground, bypassing the Germans in the valley, and then go on to the Roer River?"[8] In his view, it was tragically "*a battle that should not have been fought*. . . . I think it fair to say that little was learned from it and less understood."[9]

Gavin's plan was the most tactically sound. But Cota was not given the opportunity to choose the place and route of his attack. Given the location in the front lines into which the 28th Division was placed by higher authority, Cota might still have won through to victory.

Had units to the north and south of the 28th been ordered to protect its left and right flanks, there would have been no need for the 109th Regiment to attack toward the town of Hürtgen or for the 110th to strike into the Siegfried Line below Germeter. Cota could then have used all three of his regiments to best advantage, observing the principles of mass, maneuver, unity of command, simplicity, surprise, offensive action, and objective. He could have used one *regiment* to invest Vossenack rather than one *battalion.* Two other *regiments* could have crossed the Kall and gone on to Kommerscheidt and Schmidt rather than two *battalions.*

One regiment could have held Vossenack in strength; there would have been no rout. Two regiments could have protected the Kall trail from German incursions as they forged south; they could have widened and maintained it, interdicted the river road, cut German transits of that sector, and protected the bridge. One regiment could have remained in Kommerscheidt, ready to advance on notice to reinforce its sister unit in Schmidt. There would have been no rout from Schmidt on 4 November. Had these things been allowed, then Cota would indeed have had a "gambler's chance" of winning. Without them, he had no chance whatever.

Many Americans, first because of glowing wartime propaganda that portrayed them as capable of doing no wrong, and later due to fond memories and inattention by historians, still labor under the illusion that U.S. ground forces in Europe during the Second World War were always well led by incisive and competent general officers. That is not quite true. Sometimes those generals were unimaginative, plodding, inferior products who knew only how to throw masses of cannon fodder against the enemy. They depended more upon massive columns of men and inexhaustible piles of supplies than upon thoroughgoing knowledge of tactics and strategy. They lacked training, talent, and insight.

Obviously there were exceptions. But we had no MacArthur in Europe. One biographer has said of him that he "took more territory, with less loss of life, than any military commander since Darius the Great."[10] MacArthur maintained a 10-to-one kill ratio of Japanese to American dead as his troops fought their way west toward the Land of the Rising Sun. Seldom has there been a military leader of any nation who was as economical in shedding his soldiers' blood as was MacArthur.

In contrast, consider the casualties caused by some U.S. generals in single battles on the European landmass. In the single battle for Anzio, Italy, 72,306 GIs perished. In the battle for Normandy, General Eisenhower's soldiers suffered 28,366 dead. In the Hürtgen Forest, some 23,000 more young men became casualties. MacArthur's troops, by comparison, absorbed only 27,684 casualties in their island-hopping tactics from Australia to their reentry upon Philippine soil two years later,* including such bloodbaths as Buna on the coastal beaches of New Guinea.[11]

---

*There were, however, differences in the scale of fighting and the numbers of troops engaged between the Southwest Pacific area and Europe, and these casualty figures do not include those who fell during the reconquest of the Philippines with its dubious battles for bypassed islands and the even more questionable battles in Borneo where MacArthur slugged it out to capture everything, whether his targets had any strategic importance or not.

The difference can be summed up in a single word: leadership. Schmidt was just one, although the most serious, of the tactical blunders committed by American commanders in Europe. As such it deserves to be recalled to attention and stand as a memorial to the tactical futility and intellectual paucity of much that went under the wartime name of leadership. The lack of grasp of military principles of Cota, Gerow, and Hodges produced the war's most costly and useless attack. It changed nothing save the grisly number of filled body bags.

Note on the Sources

The men who did the battlefield interviews were Captain John S. Howe and Captain William J. Fox and Technician Third Class José M. Topete, of the 2nd Information and Historical Service. They were later joined by First Lieutenant Harry Jackson. These men did a magnificent job of covering the action around Schmidt in the Hürtgen Forest area.

Even before the start of the action, they talked with staff members at each regimental headquarters and obtained, from official reports and field orders, a complete picture of the plan of attack from corps level to regiment; thus they were able to place the 28th Infantry Division within the larger view planned by First United States Army.

In conferences with Corps' G-2 and G-3 staff, they obtained a concise statement of difficulties confronting the operation—that is, that the road net was inadequate, that Germans held commanding ground on three sides of the area of intended penetration; letters from Gerow to Hodges written between 15-31 October stressing the difficult terrain, which was unsuitable for armor operations.

Armed with such knowledge, interviewers visited the command post of the 28th Infantry Division, arriving 31 October at its location at Rott, Germany. There they discussed the upcoming battle with Lieutenant Colonel Thomas E. Briggs, the divisional G-3, who discussed battle plans and who stressed his own (and Major General Cota's) misgivings about having to attack enemy-dominated terrain over roads inadequate for armored vehicles, which stretched through dense forest. "None of the officers to whom we talked regarding this operation was in the least bit optimistic. Many were almost certain that if the operation succeeded it would be a miracle." Later, in

December, when Howe, Fox, and Jackson were able to interview Cota, he recalled he had been ordered where and how to dispose his troops, and his objections to attacking the Germans at a point where they "looked right down the throat of the attacking force" were overruled.

The historians met with the air liaison officer for the 28th Infantry Division, Major Edwin M. Howison, who informed them that the plan for air operations "provided for strong and concentrated air blows against specific targets in the initial stages, to assist the artillery in blasting enemy positions, and to prevent, during the latter stages of the operations, the movement of enemy reinforcements into the area in sufficient numbers to alter the situation in favor of the Germans." During the course of the battle, Howison kept the interviewers informed of the extent and estimated effect of daily air operations and, at the end of the battle, "listed the reasons for the almost negligible amount of air support given" to the ground forces.

The men notified each regiment that they would be dropping in for briefings and interviews. Fox went to the 109th Infantry Regiment, Howe to the 110th, Topete to the 112th. They remained there during the first four days of the attack, noting changes of plans, reasons for such changes, and any results. During lulls in battle, they conducted interviews with individuals coming back off the line, with key staff officers, and with members of major supporting units such as engineers, tanks, and tank destroyers.

By 5 November, Fox and Howe were dissatisfied because they were not making as much progress as they desired, and so they pulled Topete back from the 112th Infantry Regiment's advance command post in Kommerscheidt. Almost immediately it was surrounded and cut off for three days. Had he stayed, he might well not have gotten out. The men returned to the divisional command post at Rott where, during a lull in operations, they discussed the developing battle with staff officers there. The combat became so heavy and sustained that further interviewing was impossible. The historians returned to Corps to check decisions and actions there and to write up rough notes already made.

There they stayed until 10 November by which time the attack on Schmidt had already failed. They began interviewing support units; Fox spoke with men of the engineer outfits, and Howe worked with members of the tank and tank destroyer units.

On 14 November, First Army decided to pull the 28th Infantry Division out of line, replacing it with the rested 8th Infantry Division. The historians now faced a dilemma. They planned to cover the entire operation by interviews, yet those they needed to see were being sent into another corps zone while supporting units were to remain in V Corps' area to support the 8th Infantry Division's attack on the towns of Hürtgen and Kleinhau. So Fox and Howe decided to complete interviews with attached units first; men in those outfits would have less free time than would soldiers of the 28th Infantry Division, who were moving to a "quiet" area in Luxembourg.

After completing their interviews of support units, Fox and Howe returned to their quarters at corps to change clothes and pick up additional maps and equipment. Another member of their section, Master Sergeant Forrest Pogue, had just returned from leave in Paris, so the two officers sent Pogue and Topete to cover the action of the 8th Infantry Division's attack while they traveled to Wiltz in Luxembourg to begin interviewing survivors of the 28th Infantry Division's actions around Schmidt. At that point, First Lieutenant Harry Jackson, from VIII Corps historical section, joined them. Jackson worked with the 109th Infantry Regiment; Howe with the 110th; Fox with the 112th. They had nearly completed their interviews when elements of the German Army launched the Ardennes counterattack known as the Battle of the Bulge.

Fox, Howe, and Jackson met at the command post of the 110th Infantry Regiment in Clerveaux, Luxembourg, on 17 December. From there they ran the gauntlet through St.-Vith and Malmédy to safety without incident and finally reached their haven at corps headquarters. There they set to work on their notes. "I believe," wrote one of the interviewers, "that the material we have obtained on this action, when finished, will constitute the most complete coverage of any single operation in this war. It covers the Infantry action, *by interview,* from Division right down through regiment, battalion and . . . most of the companies involved." Captain Howe, writing those words some months after the fact, went on to state his belief that he and Fox agreed that "the Hürtgen Forest campaign will and should be made the subject of an exhaustive study." Although it has taken many years for his hope to be realized, his reasons are still valid. Several American divisions—the 9th, 28th, 4th, 8th, and a combat command of the 5th Armored Division—"were chewed to pieces and greatly reduced, so reduced in fighting strength that they had to be pulled out of line . . . . This action was a costly, bloody failure. It is typical of the deadly, back-breaking, soul-killing fighting that characterized the entire Hurtgen Forest Campaign." Howe was clear that proper study of it would reveal many lessons that the military ought to learn to avoid similar devastating mistakes in the future.

It must, wrote Captain Howe, be emphasized "*and strongly,*" that when the 28th Infantry Division launched its attack "the entire western front was quiet. . . . it was the *ONLY* unit attacking on the entire sector from southern Luxembourg to the British sector." As a result, Germans were unrestricted in their ability to bring reserves of infantry, armor, and artillery into play against it.

The main First Army attack toward the Rhine by Lawton Collins' forces was delayed from day to day while the diversionary thrust of the 28th Division fought on alone. Initially scheduled to begin on or about 5 November, Collins' hammer blow was delayed until the 10th and then day by day until 16 November by which time the decimated 28th Infantry Division was being replaced by the 8th Infantry Division. As Captain Howe wrote, "*Any* benefits from the 28th's efforts had been lost." Further, no effort was made to help those involved understand the importance of the role they were to play. "Based upon the testimony of regimental, battalion and company officers whom I interviewed, the lower units were not aware of the place in the overall plan which their particular actions were to play. The morale of the men and officers in the Division took a distinct drop. I saw it happen." Consequently, Captain Howe observed, "The Division was destroyed as an effective fighting machine."

There were, he noted, several overriding reasons for the disaster:

1. *Weather.* During most of the action, rain, mist, and snow filled the skies and covered the ground. Low-hanging clouds prevented effective employment of the air support allocated to the division. Inadequate in themselves to serve as supply roads, narrow firebreak trails through the forest were turned by rain and snow into rutted, slippery quagmires. Even jeeps and Weasels became stuck. Unbelievably bad weather made it impossible for underequipped troops to protect themselves against the ravages of trench foot. On an average, only about 10 to 15 men in each company were equipped with galoshes. The rest endured the wet and cold without them. "Foxholes, by my own knowledge, turned into veritable artesian wells during the latter part of the action," and the ground became so soaked it was impossible for American troops to keep dry. A glance at the divisional surgeon's report of casualties shows approximately 750 cases of trench foot.
2. *Terrain.* In the dense pines of the Hürtgen Forest, visibility regularly narrowed to about 150 yards. In many places, soldiers had a difficult time seeing more than 25 feet ahead of them. As the attack progressed, constant artillery and mortar fire knocked out tops of trees, blew others down, and choked the ground with debris so thoroughly that both visibility and movement were dangerously impeded. The attack of the 28th Infantry Division was made into and through land dominated by enemy-held high ground. This factor put attacking troops out in the open "like a fly in a saucer" in areas where Germans could pour observed, and in many cases direct, artillery fire upon them from an arc of 180 degrees. Colonel Thomas E. Briggs, divisional G-3, believed this factor to be one of the greatest single causes for the failure of American soldiers to achieve combat success in the Hürtgen. Further, the road net was limited and inadequate for use by supporting armor. The Kall trail, selected by the divisional staff to serve as the unit's main supply route, was chosen "initially from *MAP STUDY ONLY*. . . . Commanders of all units I interviewed considered it to be *the* greatest single factor bringing about failure of the entire operation."
3. *Communications.* Communication in wartime is inevitably essential

and always difficult, but in the Hürtgen it was never adequate. Heavy artillery and mortar barrages knocked out communication lines with deadly regularity from battalions to companies and periodically for prolonged periods of time from regiments to battalions. Despite exhausting and futile struggles of communications wire-team personnel to keep lines repaired and communications open, they were unable to keep pace with the rate at which the Germans could destroy their work. This lack of communication greatly affected the entire battle. Lack of knowledge regarding specific situations across the battlefield hampered quick and effective command decisions and increased the demoralization of those exposed to the savagery of combat. They had nowhere to turn, no one to rely upon, no help to call upon. The only means of communication which worked at all was radio, and even this was done only with great difficulty. Hilly, densely wooded terrain features frequently blocked radio transmissions. Batteries quickly wore out due to frequent and prolonged use, or deteriorated as they drew moisture in the steady, drizzling rains. Supply people were never able to bring up new batteries as often as they were needed to replace worn-out ones. Like telephones, many radios were also damaged or destroyed by enemy artillery fire. Terrain in the Hürtgen made soldiers blind; failing communication equipment made them deaf and mute. They could only thrash ineffectively and in agony.

4. *Inexperienced personnel.* After its disastrous attempts to penetrate the Siegfried Line during September, the 28th Infantry Division moved back to a quiet sector near Elsenborn to receive and train replacements throughout October. Not many of those it received were infantrymen. Rifle company officers and, particularly, noncommissioned officers were too often siphoned out of the personnel pipeline from antitank companies, antiaircraft units, and Air Force ground crews. During the time of comparative quiet at Camp Elsenborn, Belgium, there was little opportunity to correct such deficiencies or retrain such men into effective infantrymen. As a result, when the attack against Schmidt began on 2 November and casualties began to occur, loss of experienced and well-trained men immediately became apparent in the performances of engaged units. This helps to explain the repeated routs of American soldiers at Schmidt, Kommerscheidt, and Vossenack. More replacements poured into the lines. Reinforcements were brought forward so rapidly and in such large numbers that proper unit organization became impossible. On 8 November, for example, 515 new men were assigned to the 2nd Battalion, 112th Infantry Regiment and, on 9 November, the divisional G-3 *Journal* recorded that "there have been instances of firing by friendly troops on elements of the 112th Inf. during withdrawal, believed to be done by new replacements." As the operation continued, rapid attrition of companies, loss of the few remaining well-trained and

experienced officers and noncoms, and complete lack of trained replacements virtually ensured failure for the mission of the 28th Infantry Division.

5. *The German defense.* Prior to the attack, units of the 28th Infantry Division failed to probe enemy lines and positions sufficiently. They lacked extensive knowledge of German defenses and dispositions prior to and during the attack. Patrols had not penetrated the tangled forest to seek such information. When they did go out, they drew unusually heavy fire, often from both sides. Thus the 110th Infantry Regiment attacked frontally into strong, deadly defenses; strongpoints, wire, and ground-level log bunkers protected by automatic weapons. Thus the 109th Infantry Regiment's advance bogged down when its men moved into a previously unknown minefield. Further, the Germans were free for a prolonged period to concentrate their efforts on repulsing the attack. Why not? The delay in VII Corps' drive for the Rhine meant that there was no activity elsewhere and the Germans could, with impunity, channel men and equipment into the battle to stop the 28th Division. Those who wore the patch of the Bloody Bucket, due to their dispersed formations and missions, were unable to concentrate their efforts effectively. The terrain was completely familiar to the Germans, and on it they had prepared their defenses in depth. The Hürtgen was ideal for defense, unfavorable for attacking forces. The area, one of the strongest in the Siegfried Line, was a battleground the Germans chose wisely, for it combined natural factors of commanding terrain covered by almost impenetrable pine forests, which hid their defenses. The ground across which Americans attacked had an inadequate road net; the German defensive arc was supplied by good, all-weather roads over which they could move men and equipment rapidly and well. The Germans fought viciously, gave up ground when necessary, counterattacked frequently, suffered heavy losses, and won. They halted and cut to pieces the men of the 28th Infantry Division in a "costly, tragic failure" called by General James Gavin a battle that "had been our Passchendaele."

Notes

1.
"Jerry seemed to know exactly where we were at all times"

1. Throughout this story all times for sunrise, sunset, moonrise and moonset are drawn from the 28th Infantry Division G-2 Periodic Report for 292400 October to 302400 October 1944, Number 94. In "date-time groups" such as 292400 October, the first two digits refer to the date; the last four give the time of day. All times given herein follow the military practice of using a twenty-four hour clock. U.S. forces and other Allies in Europe during World War II were on double-daylight saving time.

   References to weather conditions during this battle have been drawn either from official reports and forecasts or have been gleaned from German records and interviews held with American participants in the fighting. Those interviews were conducted by 1LT Harry G. Jackson, CPT John S. Howe and CPT William J. Fox. They were assisted by Technician Third Class Jose M. Topete, and Master Sergeant Forrest Pogue.

   Transcripts and worksheets of these men and various other materials they gathered may be consulted under this reference: Combat Interviews, 28th Division Hurtgen Forest Campaign, Record Group Number 407, Records of the Adjutant General's Office, World War II Operations Reports, 1940-1948, The National Archives, Washington, D.C.

   The actual materials are housed at the National Archives' facility in Suitland, Maryland. Except where otherwise noted, citations in this book are based upon these documents.

2. General Dwight Eisenhower, *Report by the Supreme Commander to the Combined Chiefs of Staff on the Operations in Europe of the Allied Expeditionary Force,* 6 June 1944 to 8 May 1945 (London: His Majesty's Stationery Office, 1946), pp. 86–87.
3. Field Order Number 14, Headquarters, 109th Infantry Regiment, 30 October 1944.
4. See interview by 1LT Harry G. Jackson with LTC Daniel B. Strickler, commander, 109th Infantry Regiment, and MAJ William J. Moraney, regimental S-3 at the time of the battle, at the regimental command post in the vicinity of Ettelbruck, Luxembourg, held on 8 December 1944. Hereafter cited as Strickler interview.
5. Quoted from a pamphlet produced by the U.S. Army Command and General Staff College as an instructional aid for classes in "Fundamentals of Combined Arms Warfare," and designated by the numbers M3121-2/R3121-2. The pamphlet is entitled *The Battle of Schmidt* and is a compilation of three works by Charles B. MacDonald; *The Siegfried Line Campaign* (Washington, D.C.: Office of the Chief of Military History, 1963); *Three Battles: Arnaville, Altuzzo, and Schmidt* (Washington, D.C.: Office of the Chief of Military History, 1952); and *The Last Offensive* (Washington, D.C.: Office of the Chief of Military History, 1973). This citation is drawn from page P2-I-1 of the pamphlet which hereafter will be cited as MacDonald, *Schmidt.*
6. See interview by 1LT Harry G. Jackson with 1LT Edward L. Peer; 2LT Carl J. Emrick; T/SGT Thomas Budd; 1/SGT Robert D. Francis; S/SGT Hobert Kirk; SGT Alexander Zaltsburg, L Company, 3rd Battalion, 109th Infantry Regiment at company command post, Diekirch, Germany, 10 December 1944. Hereafter cited as Peer interview.
7. MacDonald, *Schmidt,* P2-I-15 and Joseph J. Chmiola, "History of the 109th Artillery" (privately printed, 19 May 1969). Chmiola, an LTC in the Pennsylvania Army National Guard and commander of 1st Battalion, 109th Field Artillery, was a forward observer at the time of this battle and was wounded in Vossenack.
8. See interview by 1LT Harry G. Jackson with CPT Max R. Whitetree, commander; 1LT Samuel J. Leo, 1st Platoon leader; T/SGT Charles E. Frawley, 2d platoon; T/SGT Leo D. Balleger, 3d Platoon; A Company, 1st Battalion, 109th Infantry Regiment at company command post, Diekirch, Germany, 9 December 1944. Hereafter cited as Whitetree interview.
9. Whitetree interview.
10. Based on untitled sheets produced by the 28th Infantry Division G-2 intelligence section.
11. See interview by 1LT Harry G. Jackson with 2LT Thomas H. Whitney, B Company, at company command post, Diekirch, Germany, 9 December 1944. Hereafter cited as Whitney interview.

12. *Ibid.*
13. Peer interview.
14. See interview by 1LT Harry G. Jackson with 1LT Francis Sheehan, S/SGT Aiken Still; T/SGT Robert McMillan; S/SGT Harold A. Jenkins; K Company, at company command post, Diekirch, Germany, 10 December 1944. Hereafter cited as Sheehan interview.
15. Sheehan interview.
16. See interview by 1LT Harry G. Jackson with 1/SGT Leonard E. Konsaer; S/SGT Robert G. Wolf; SGT Glen Bice and CPL Melvin W. Kaufmann, at 2nd Battalion command post, Beaufort, 8 December 1944.
17. Peer interview.
18. See interview by 1LT Harry G. Jackson with CPT William T. Rogers at 3rd Battalion headquarters, Diekirch, Germany, 10 December 1944. Hereafter cited as Rogers interview.
19. See interview by 1LT Harry G. Jackson with 1LT Bruce W. Paul, commander; 1LT William Pina; T/SGT Thomas F. Blair; T/SGT Norman D. Payne; 1/SGT William W. Johnston; S/SGT Frank F. Stunar; S/SGT Edward W. Parks; S/SGT Steven G. Raferty; S/SGT James L. Baker; SGT Dagly D. Collett and SGT Gerald Bowbly, I Company, at company command post, Diekirch, Germany, 8 December 1944. Hereafter cited as Paul interview.
20. Paul interview.
21. Whitney interview.
22. See interview by 1LT Harry G. Jackson with 1LT Donald P. Clark, S/SGT Martin A. Slaughter, S/SGT Ralph A. Galiso, SGT Herbert W. Hawksley, PFC Earl W. Olsen, at 2nd Battalion command post, Beaufort, 8 December 1944. Hereafter cited as Clark interview.
23. Whitetree interview.
24. See interview by 1LT Harry G. Jackson with 1LT Charles E. Potter, 1st Battalion S-2, at battalion command post, Diekirch, Germany, 9 December 1944. Hereafter cited as Potter interview.
25. Whitetree interview.
26. See interview by 1LT Harry G. Jackson with S/SGT Cleo C. Barrett, S/SGT William C. Horan, S/SGT Erwin S. Mucha, PVT James A. McCutchen, Jr, at 2nd Battalion command post, Diekirch, Germany, 7 December 1944. Hereafter cited as Barrett interview.
27. Whitetree interview.
28. Whitetree interview.
29. MacDonald, *Schmidt,* P2-I-15.
30. Strickler interview.
31. Peer interview.
32. Rogers and Potter interviews.
33. Rogers interview.
34. Peer interview.

35. G-2 "Summary of Activity from Regiments," 28th Infantry Division, 3 November 1944.
36. Whitetree interview.
37. Potter interview.
38. Whitney interview.
39. *Ibid.*
40. Peer interview.
41. Paul interview.
42. Rogers interview.
43. Whitetree interview.
44. German planes were sighted by one of the interviewers. See note on interview work sheets for 3 November 1944 by Captain William J. Fox.
45. MacDonald, *Schmidt,* P2-I-15.
46. See "IX TAC Air Summary," 3 November 1944 and combat interview with MAJ E. M. Howison, the air liaison officer. See also MacDonald, *Three Battles,* p. 292.
47. Peer interview.
48. Whitney interview.
49. Peer interview.
50. Potter interview.
51. Peer interview.
52. Whitney interview.
53. Potter interview.
54. See interview by 1LT Harry G. Jackson with 2LT Frank McFeaters, T/SGT Edward H. Serafin, T/SGT Hugh T. Sharp, S/SGT B. J. D'Amico, S/SGT Toivo E. Pihlagh, and SGT Arthur E. McGrew, G Company, Second Battalion, 109th Infantry Regiment, at battalion command post, Diekirch, Germany, 8 December 1944. Hereafter cited as McFeaters interview.
55. An excellent discussion of manpower tables may be found in Russell F. Weigley, *Eisenhower's Lieutenants: The Campaign of France and Germany, 1944–1945* (Bloomington: Indiana University Press, 1981), p. 24.
56. Whitney interview.
57. Paul interview.
58. Clark interview.
59. Whitetree interview.
60. Whitney interview.
61. Potter interview.
62. Paul interview.
63. McFeaters interview.
64. Clark interview.
65. Peer interview.
66. McFeaters interview.

67. Weigley, *Eisenhower's Lieutenants,* p. 24.
68. Peer interview.
69. Barrett, McFeaters, Clark, Whitetree, Whitney, Potter and Sheehan interviews.
70. I have benefited in some ways from the work of Ralph Geiger, "The 109th Infantry Regiment Attack on Huertgen" (seminar paper, University of South Florida, March 1979).

2.
"A bloody finger pointing into Germany"

1. This discussion of General Hodges is drawn from James M. Gavin, *On to Berlin: Battles of an Airborne Commander, 1943–1946* (New York: Bantam Books, 1978), p. 227, and Weigley, *Eisenhower's Lieutenants,* pp. 84–85, 297, 602, 672 and *passim.*
2. MacDonald, *Three Battles,* p. 251n.
3. Gavin, *On to Berlin,* p. 290.
4. Much of this discussion has been based upon MacDonald, *Schmidt,* P2-I-1.
5. See Field Order Number 30, Headquarters, V Corps, 212000 October 1944 and Letter of Instructions from V Corps to Commanding Generals of 4th Infantry Division, 9th Infantry Division, 28th Infantry Division, 5th Armored Division and V Corps Artillery, 232000 October 1944. See also interview by CPT William J. Fox with Major General Norman D. Cota, commanding general, 28th Infantry Division, and Brigadier George A. Davis, assistant division commander, 28th Infantry Division, at divisional command post, Wiltz, Luxembourg, 13 December 1944. Hereafter cited as Cota/Davis interview.
6. These comments have been based on Weigley, *Eisenhower's Lieutenants,* pp. 325, 365, 366.
7. *Ibid.,* p. 286.
8. Gavin, *On to Berlin,* p. 294.
9. Weigley, *Eisenhower's Lieutenants,* p. 432.
10. *Ibid.,* p. 471.
11. Russell F. Weigley, "Shaping the American Army of World War II: Mobility versus Power," *Parameters, Journal of the U.S. Army War College,* XI, 3 (Sept. 1981), pp. 18–19.
12. For a similar discussion, see Cincinnatus, *Self-Destruction: the Disintegration and Decay of the United States Army During the Vietnam Era* (New York: W. W. Norton, 1981), pp. 183–85.
13. These comments were based upon an unnamed, undated, unpaginated typescript, with addenda in the handwriting of CPT William J. Fox,

which contains initial impressions and items to be later investigated by the interviewers as they worked up their account of the struggle for Schmidt.

14. The foregoing discussion has drawn heavily from a booklet issued by the Orientation Section, Information and Education Division, European Theater of Operations, United States Army, produced in cooperation with and basic material supplied by the staff of the 28th Infantry Division. No publisher is listed, nor is there any indicated date of publication, but it was probably in 1945. The title of the booklet is "28th, Roll On: The Story of the 28th Infantry Division." See also James Jones, *The History of American Infantry Divisions* (New York, 1981), p. 34.
15. L. K. Jackson, *U.S. Military Commanders in World War II* (New York, 1981), p. 358.
16. Field Order Number 30, HQ, V Corps, 212000 October 1944; Letter of Instructions from V Corps to Commanding Generals of 4th, 9th, 28th Infantry divisions and 5th Armored Division and V Corps Artillery, supplement to Field Order Number 30, dated 232000 October 1944; Cota/Davis interview.
17. Jack Colbaugh, *The Bloody Patch: A True Story of the Daring 28th Infantry Division* (New York: Vantage Press, 1973), p. 83.
18. G-3 Journal, Headquarters, 28th Infantry Division, 310001 October 1944 to 312400 October 1944.
19. Cota/Davis interview.
20. *Ibid.*
21. This discussion of terrain is based upon an article by COL John C. Gazlay, U.S.A. (Ret.), "An Open Book," *Military Review* LVIII 10 (Oct. 1978), 47–49.
22. Procedural and summary statement of their investigations by interviewers CPT John S. Howe, CPT William J. Fox, and T/3 José M. Topete, V Corps, and 1LT Harry Jackson, VIII Corps. Undated. Hereafter cited as Procedural and summary statement.
23. A note in CPT John S. Howe's handwriting on interviewers' worksheets, p. 2.
24. Procedural and summary statement. See also MacDonald, *Schmidt,* P2-I-8 and MacDonald, *Three Battles,* pp. 251–52.
25. MacDonald, *Schmidt,* P2-I-9.
26. *Ibid.,* P2-I-8.
27. *Ibid.,* P2-I-2, 3.
28. *Ibid.,* P2-I-3, 4.
29. *Ibid.,* P2-I-3.
30. *Ibid.,* P2-I-4.
31. *Ibid.*
32. *Ibid.,* P2-I-9.
32. *Ibid.,* P2-I-8.

34. *Ibid.,* P2-I-9.
35. *Ibid.*
36 *Ibid.,* P2-I-4.
37. Comments by Generalmajor Rudolf Freiherr von Gersdorff, chief of staff, German Seventh Army, European Theater Historical Interview, translated from General Gersdorff's German text in the presence of CPT N. B. Sigband and CPT F. C. Mahin, USFET historical officers and approved by General Gersdorff, 12 December 1945; contained in a publication by the U.S. Army Command and General Staff College, Fort Leavenworth, Kansas, entitled "The Battle of Schmidt, R3121/7 Fundamentals of Combined Arms Warfare, Tactics." Hereafter cited as Gersdorff interview.
38. MacDonald, *Three Battles,* pp. 253, 418–19.
39. Procedural and summary statement.
40. Cota/Davis interview.
41. *Ibid.*
42. *Ibid.*
43. Message from the Commanding General to the Officers and Men of the 28th Infantry Division and Attached Units, 20 November 1944.
44. Field Order Number 14, 109th Regimental Combat Team, 30 October 1944.
45. Statement of Methodology used by the combat interviewers, written by CPT John S. Howe. Hereafter cited as Howe statement. See also an unnamed, undated, unpaginated typescript, with addenda in the handwriting of CPT William J. Fox, which contains initial impressions and items to be investigated later by the interviewers. Hereafter cited as Fox statement.
46. MacDonald, *Three Battles,* p. 255.
47. Colbaugh, *Bloody Patch,* p. 84.
48. Procedural and summary statement.
49. *Ibid.*
50. Colbaugh, *Bloody Patch,* p. 83.

3.
"Battered remnants"

1. B. H. Liddell Hart, *The German Generals Talk* (New York: William Morrow & Company, 1979), pp. 68–70; John Keegan and Andrew Wheatcroft (eds.), *Who's Who in Military History* (New York: William Morrow & Company, 1976), p. 223; Weigley, *Eisenhower's Lieutenants,* p. 215.
2. Information on the 89th Infantry Division is drawn from the G-2 Periodic Report, Headquarters, 28th Infantry Division, 292400 October to

302400 October 1944, Number 94; from Frank Frey, "A History of the 89th Infantry Division" (seminar paper, University of South Florida, 1980); and from Georg Tessin, *Verbände und Truppen der Deutschen Wehrmacht und Waffen-SS im Zweiten Weltkrieg, 1939–1945* (Vol. VI (Osnabruck: Biblio Verlag, 1972).

3. Most material in this chapter has been drawn from the recollections of *Generalmajor* Rudolf Freiherr von Gersdorff, chief of staff of *Seventh Army* before and during the action of the 28th Infantry Division in the Hürtgen Forest. Like many other German officers, Gersdorff was questioned extensively by the American military after the war and in response wrote lengthy answers to supply the material asked of him. See Gersdorff interview.

4.
"We left a hell of a lot of our best men up there"

1. Quoted from Ivan H. Peterman, "Pennsylvanians on the Western Front" (no date, no place of publication, no publisher), p. 3. This is a collection of dispatches from the war zone reprinted from *The Philadelphia Inquirer*. The dateline on this one is "Hurtgen Forest, Germany, Nov. 16, 1944 (Delayed)." Hereafter cited as Peterman, "Pennsylvanians." Also of interest is *History of the 110th Infantry of the 28th Division, United States Army, World War II, 1941–1945* (Atlanta: Albert Love Enterprises, 1946), an unpaginated work with no listed author.
2. Weigley, *Eisenhower's Lieutenants,* p. 24.
3. CPT John S. Howe, "Summary of action," 2-16 November 1944, 110th Infantry Regiment, 28th Infantry Division, Vossenack–Kommerscheidt–Schmidt. Hereafter cited as Howe, "Summary of Action."
4. Division Review of the *89th Division*: the Battles of Schmidt and Kommerscheidt. 9 November 1944. "*For the information of the troops.* This document must not fall into enemy hands." This report is included in the Command and General Staff College publication "Fundamentals of Combined Arms Warfare, Tactics: The Battle of Schmidt." R3121/7. Hereafter cited as *89th Division Review.*
5. CPT Stanley H. French, Medical Assistance Corps, Office of the Surgeon, 28th Infantry Division. SUBJECT: Battle Casualties, 7 December 1944.
6. Howe, "Summary of Action."
7. See interview by CPT John S. Howe with CPT George H. Rumbaugh (regimental anti-tank company commander until 4 November; regimental assistant S-3 operations officer until night of 6/7 November; acting battalion commander until relief on 16 November by 13th Infantry Regiment, 8th Infantry Division); and S/SGT Martin J. Joyce, battalion

intelligence sergeant; plus information obtained at regiment CP, Hürtgen Forest, 2-5 November, from LTC Theodore A. Seely, commander, 110th Infantry Regiment; MAJ Harold R. Yeager, Regiment S-3; and CPT William S. Linning, Regiment S-2; conducted at 3rd Battalion command post, Consthum, Luxembourg, 15-16 December 1944. Hereafter cited as Rumbaugh interview.

8. From a written statement on 2nd Battalion by CPT John S. Howe on the circumstances of that unit. Hereafter cited as Howe statement.

   Material also drawn from interviews conducted by CPT John S. Howe with CPT William C. Dobbs, company commander; 1LT Frank J. Deptula, executive officer; 1/SGT Lonnie C. Bland, E Company, 2nd Battalion, held at company command post, Neiderfeulen, Luxembourg, 4 December 1944. Hereafter cited as Dobbs interview.

   And see interview by Howe with CPT Lake Coleman, commander; 2LT Edward J. Matheny, 1st Platoon leader; 2LT J. D. King, 4th Platoon leader; 1/SGT Steve N. Levering, 1/SGT; 1/SGT George W. Fetzer, surplus 1/SGT; T/SGT Warren H. Dunlap, 2nd Platoon sergeant, F Company, at company command post, Neiderfeulen, Luxembourg, 3-4 December 1944. Hereafter cited as Coleman interview.

   Also see interview by Howe with 2LT Frank R. Nation; SGT Avery Lanning, mortar squad LDR, 4th PLN; S/SGT Joseph K. Paczesna, (rifleman and later assistant squad LDR, 2nd squad, 1st PLN); SGT William M. Pennington (rifleman and platoon runner, later PLN SGT, 1st PLN); S/SGT Abraham Kumukau, 1st squad LDR, 3rd PLN; S/SGT Manuel C. Suarez, 1st squad LDR, 1st PLN; S/SGT Morris G. Sykes, assistant 1/SGT; of G Company, 2nd Battalion, held at company command post, Neiderfeulen, Luxembourg, 6 December 1944. Hereafter cited as Nation interview.

9. See interview by CPT John S. Howe with CPT James H. Burns, battalion S-3; CPT Wesley J. Rose, S-1; CPT Joseph L. Minter, 109th FA BN liaison officer attached to 1st Battalion; 1LT Francis P. Diamond, S-4; 1LT Francis K. Richwine, battalion communications officer; 2LT Harold E. Miller (a PLN SGT at the start of the battle who received a battlefield commission); 1st Battalion, 110th Infantry Regiment, held at battalion command post, Urspelt, Luxembourg, 12-13-14 December 1944. Hereafter cited as Burns interview.
10. *Ibid.*
11. Chattaway, *Gentlemen From Hell,* p. 33.
12. Howe, "Summary of Action."
13. Interview by the author at reunion of members of the 110th Infantry Regiment, Washington, Pennsylvania, 8 September 1979, with Mr. Robert Craff, Louisville, Kentucky.

14. Letter, Earl Fuller, Jr., to the author, 10 August 1979.
15. Interview by the author at reunion of members of the 110th Infantry Regiment, Washington, Pennsylvania, 8 September 1979, with Ed "Red" Guthrie, Vernon, New Jersey. Guthrie was a member of Company E, 2nd Battalion.
16. Interview by the author at reunion of members of the 110th Infantry Regiment, Washington, Pennsylvania, 9 September 1979, with Fred G. Cope, Bloomton, New Jersey. Cope was message center chief, headquarters, 3rd Battalion, 110th Infantry Regiment.
17. Interview by the author at reunion of members of the 110th Infantry Regiment, Washington, Pennsylvania, 8 September 1979, with M. C. Schreffler, Lisbon, Ohio. Schreffler served as acting platoon leader with 3rd Platoon, K Company, 3d Battalion.
18. Cope interview.
19. Letter, Harry Geary, Jr., to the author, 28 September 1979.
20. Cope interview.
21. Letter, Harry Geary, Jr., to the author, 28 September 1979.
22. Cope interview.
23. Earl Fuller, Jr., letter.
24. Interview by the author at reunion of members of the 110th Infantry Regiment, Washington, Pennsylvania, 9 September 1979, with Mr. Daniel DeFail, Greensburg, Pennsylvania.
25. Interview by the author at reunion of members of the 110th Infantry Regiment, Washington, Pennsylvania, 8 September 1979, with Robert C. Wells, Logan, Ohio.
26. Interview by the author at reunion of members of the 110th Infantry Regiment, Washington, Pennsylvania, 8 September 1979, with Earl Fuller, Jr., Washington, Pennsylvania.
27. Howe, "Summary of Action."
28. Interview by the author at reunion of members of the 110th Infantry Regiment, Washington, Pennsylvania, 9 September 1979, with Russell Arford, Co G, 2nd Battalion.
29. Howe, "Summary of Action," and Divisional Operation Plan and Divisional Field Order Number 25.
30. Howe, "Summary of Action."
31. *Ibid.*
32. See Rumbaugh and Burns interviews and Howe statement.
33. Rumbaugh interview.
34. Howe statement.
35. Earl Fuller, Jr., letter.
36. Rumbaugh interview.
37. Letter, COL Albert G. Kuhn, Pennsylvania Army National Guard, Hershey, Pennsylvania, to the author, 5 December 1978.

38. Geary letter.
39. Coleman interview.
40. *Ibid.*
41. Nation interview.
42. Dobbs interview.
43. Letter, Charles Hubner, to the author, 25 September 1979.
44. Craff interview.
45. See interview by CPT John S. Howe with CPT George S. Granger, commander; 1LT Carl A. Anderson, 1st Platoon LDR; S/SGT Letford W. Walling, 3d Platoon SGT; S/SGT John B. Cook, 2nd Platoon SGT; B Company, 707th Tank Battalion, at company command post at Pintsch, Luxembourg, 1 December 1944. Hereafter cited as Granger interview. See also Colbaugh, *Bloody Patch,* pp. 85–86, and G-2 Journal, Headquarters, 28th Infantry Division, 3 November 1944.
46. Coleman interview.
47. Nation interview.
48. Rumbaugh interview.
49. Hubner letter.
50. Burns interview.
51. See Burns and Dobbs interviews. Also see the unpaginated *History of the 110th Infantry of the 28th Division, United States Army, World War II, 1941–1945,* Chapter V.
52. Dobbs interview.
53. Rumbaugh interview.

5.
"Into the Valley of Death"

1. Of help in all discussions of tank destroyer doctrine and use has been COL Richard Ehrhardt, USAR (Ret.), "The 893rd Tank Destroyer Battalion in 'The Forest Frolics'" (seminar paper, University of South Florida, Mar. 1979). See also Kent Roberts Greenfield, Robert R. Palmer, et. al., *The United States Army in World War II: The Organization of the Ground Combat Troops* (Washington, D.C.: Office of the Chief of Military History, 1947), pp. 83, 400, 425–27; and Weigley, *Eisenhower's Lieutenants,* p. 10.
2. An interview conducted by CPT John S. Howe with LTC Samuel E. Mays, commander, 893rd Tank Destroyer Battalion; MAJ John J. Lavin, battalion S-3; MAJ Henry C. Merlin, executive officer; held at battalion command post, Müllarschütte, Germany, on 17 November 1944. Hereafter cited as Mays interview.
3. *Ibid.*

4. See Field Order Number 2, Headquarters, 2nd Battalion, 112th Infantry Regiment, 301830 October 1944.
5. An interview conducted by CPT John S. Howe with LTC Richard W. Ripple, commander, 707th Tank Battalion, held at battalion command post, Müllarschütte, Germany, 14 November 1944. Hereafter cited as Ripple interview.
6. An interview conducted by CPT John S. Howe with 1LT James J. Leming (initially C Company acting executive officer and 2nd Platoon LDR. When C Company commander, CPT George W. West, was killed, Leming took command); 2LT William D. Quarrie, 1st Platoon LDR; 1LT James J. Ryan, C Company maintenance officer; S/SGT Paul F. Jenkins, Platoon SGT (and acting platoon LDR after the evacuation of 2LT Joseph S. Novak); held at C Company command post, Heidescheid, Luxembourg, 2–3 December 1944. Hereafter cited as Leming interview.
7. *Ibid.*
8. Ripple interview. Of some help has been Bruce Whittemore, "The Battle of Schmidt: 707th Tank Battalion" (seminar paper, University of South Florida, Mar. 1979).
9. Fuller interview.
10. An interview conducted by CPT William J. Fox with 1LT Clyde R. Johnson, weapons platoon leader, G Company, held at company command post near Lieler, Belgium, 15 December 1944. Hereafter cited as Johnson interview.
11. An interview conducted by CPT William J. Fox with CPT John Pruden, 2nd Battalion executive officer, held at the battalion command post in a house at Leiler, Belgium, 8 December 1944. Pruden took over and ran the battalion throughout most of the action when the commander broke down from combat exhaustion and became unable to function. Hereafter cited as Pruden interview.

    See also an interview conducted by CPT William J. Fox with CPT James T. Nesbitt, 2nd Battalion S-1 personnel officer, at Leiler, Belgium, on 8 December 1944. Hereafter cited as Nesbitt interview.
12. An interview conducted by CPT William J. Fox with 1LT James A. Condon, acting E Company commander, held at company command post in Malusmühle, Luxembourg, 14 December 1944. Hereafter cited as Condon interview.
13. John B. Allard, "A Replacement and the 'Bloody Bucket'" (typed, undated, and mimeographed reminiscence) When he wrote this, Allard was superintendent of the Stanislaus County Department of Education in Modesto, California. Hereafter cited as Allard reminiscence.
14. Colbaugh, *Bloody Patch,* p. 85.
15. Condon interview.
16. *Ibid.* See also an interview conducted by CPT William J. Fox with

T/SGT Donald Nelson, 1st Platoon SGT; E Company, held at company command post at Leiler, Belgium, 9 December 1944. Hereafter cited as Donald Nelson interview.

17. From citation of 1LT John B. Wine, F Company, 2nd Battalion, for the Distinguished Service Cross; signed by 1LT Eldeen H. Kauffman, commander, F Company.
18. An interview conducted by CPT William J. Fox with 1LT Eldeen H. Kauffman, commander, F Company, 2nd Battalion; held at company command post at Leiler, Belgium, 8 December 1944. Hereafter cited as Kauffman interview.
19. Kauffman and Condon interviews.
20. An interview conducted by CPT William J. Fox with 1LT Clifton W. Beggs, 2nd Platoon leader, E Company; held at the platoon command post, Leiler, Belgium, 9 December 1944. Hereafter cited as Beggs interview. See also Peterman, *Western Front,* p. 4.
21. Condon, Beggs, and Donald Nelson interviews. See also an interview conducted by CPT William J. Fox with S/SGT Charles W. Cascarano, 2nd Squad, 1st Platoon, F Company; at company command post in Malusmühle, Luxembourg, 15 December 1944. Hereafter cited as Cascarano interview.
22. An interview conducted by CPT William J. Fox with CPT Charles Crain, commander, H Company; held at company command post, Leiler, Belgium, 9 December 1944. Hereafter cited as Crain interview.
23. Nesbitt interview.
24. From citation of PFC John W. Smedberg, Medical Detachment, for the Distinguished Service Cross; signed by 1LT Eldeen H. Kauffman, commander, F Company, 2nd Battalion.
25. Leming interview.
26. An interview by CPT William J. Fox with MAJ Richard S. Dana, S-3, 112th Infantry Regiment; held at regimental command post in a house at Ouren, Belgium, on the German border, 1 December 1944. Hereafter cited as Dana interview.

    See also an interview by CPT William J. Fox with S/SGT Nathaniel Quentin, 3rd Squad, 3rd Platoon, Company A (he was a BAR man and a PFC at the time of the battle); 1/SGT Harvey Hausman; T/SGT George A. Lockwood, weapons platoon SGT (he was sent back to the United States on temporary duty during the time of the interview); S/SGT Stephen J. Kertes, platoon guide for 3rd Platoon; and SGT Travis C. Norton, assistant 2nd Squad LDR; Company A, held at company command post in the Siegfried Line, 7 December 1944. Hereafter cited as Quentin interview.
27. Letter from Raymond G. Carpenter, Seminole, Florida, to the author, 3 September 1978.

28. An interview by CPT William J. Fox with SGT Eugene Holden, operations sergeant, 1st Battalion, at battalion command post in the Siegfried Line, 6 December 1944. Hereafter cited as Holden interview.

    See also an interview by CPT William J. Fox with S/SGT Joseph Perll, operations sergeant, C Company (who started the action in the Hürtgen Forest as a PFC radio operator and messenger in C Company and by the end of the battle was an acting platoon leader), at battalion headquarters, 7 December 1944. Hereafter cited as Perll interview.

    See also an interview by CPT William J. Fox with SGT Thomas G. Hunter, reconnaissance sergeant, D Company, and 1LT Jack E. Kelly, executive officer, D Company, at the company command post in the Siegfried Line, 4 December 1944. Hereafter cited as Hunter interview.

    See also an interview by CPT William J. Fox with CPT Richard Gooley, S-1, held at 1st Battalion command post, 4 December 1944. Hereafter cited as Gooley interview.

    See also an interview by CPT William J. Fox with T/SGT Roy Littlehales, 2nd Platoon guide; SGT (then PFC) Clarence J. Skains, assistant squad leader, 2nd Platoon; B Company, held at company command post in the Siegfried Line, 7 December 1944. Hereafter cited as Littlehales interview.
29. See 28th Infantry Division Air Support Party VHF Performance Log. Also see interview by CPT John S. Howe with MAJ Edwin M. Howison, air liaison officer of IX Tactical Air Command with the 28th Infantry Division; held at divisional command post at Rott, Germany, 1 November 1944.
30. Peterman, *Western Front,* p. 6.
31. See interview by CPT William J. Fox with CPT Jack W. Walker, commander, L Company, 3rd Battalion, in the company CP in a Siegfried Line pillbox near Ouren, Belgium, 2 December 1944. Fox wrote in his transcript of this interview that he believed Walker to be a glib-tongued and evasive spokesman. Fox had the feeling that Walker was holding out more than he told, since the part he played in the later rout from Schmidt was so prominent and personal. Like others, Fox said, Walker always shied away from direct statements that would give a true picture of the completely demoralized and frightened infantrymen who fled the scene of battle when the German counterattack began. This interview is hereafter cited as Walker interview.
32. An interview by CPT William J. Fox with 1/SGT Robert C. Toner, I Company, 2rd Battalion, at company command post in frontline positions in the Seveniger Wald, near Sevenig, Germany, 10 December 1944. CPT Fox noted that those positions at the time of the interview were covered with midwinter snow and constantly subjected to harassing

mortar fire throughout his interview, which he conducted by flashlight. Conditions in the command post, he noted, were fair, though a grim sense of waiting pervaded the atmosphere. Men at the command post had been subjected to a severe psychological experience in earlier fighting and felt little desire to talk about the Schmidt action, an attitude Fox found prevalent in other regimental units during his days of interviewing.

Fox included in his report the fact that three men, wounded by a shell burst just outside I Company command post, were brought into the cramped space for emergency treatment just before the start of this interview, thus disrupting and delaying it. This interview is hereafter cited as Toner interview.

See also Dana interview.

33. An interview by CPT John S. Howe with CPT Bruce M. Hostrup, commander; 1LT Raymond E. Fleig, 1st Platoon leader; 2LT Richard H. Payne, 3rd Platoon leader; A Company, 707th Tank Battalion, at company command post, Roetgen, Germany, 14 November 1944. Hereafter cited as Hostrup interview.
34. An interview by CPT William J. Fox with 1LT William George, motor officer, 3rd Battalion, 112th Infantry Regiment, at battalion command post, Lieler, Belgium, 6 December 1941. Hereafter cited as George interview.
35. An interview by CPT William J. Fox with SGT Frank Ripperdam, 1/SGT, L Company, 3rd Battalion, 112th Infantry Regiment, at company command post near Ouren, Belgium, on the German border, 2 December 1944. Hereafter cited as Ripperdam interview.
36. An interview by CPT William J. Fox with 2LT Richard Tyo, 1st Platoon leader; SGT Carl E. Stadelbacher, assistant communications sergeant; and PVT [no first name given] Dorn; K. Company, 3rd Battalion, 112th Infantry Regiment, at company command post near Sevenig, Germany, 3 December 1944. Hereafter cited as Tyo interview.
37. Toner interview.
38. See Tyo interview.
39. Ripperdam interview.
40. Perll interview.
41. Peterman, *Western Front,* p. 5.
42. An interview by CPT William J. Fox with SGT Tony Kudiak, A&P platoon, at 1st Battalion headquarters in the Siegfried Line, 5 December 1944. Hereafter cited as Kudiak interview.
43. Holden, Hunter, Perll and Quentin interviews.
44. Tyo interview.
45. Riperdam interview.
46. Tyo interview. See also Toner interview.
47. Cota's comment is quoted from MacDonald, *Schmidt,* P2-I-19.

48. Dana interview. See also an interview by CPT William J. Fox with 1LT Leon Simon, 3rd Battalion assistant S-3, 112th Infantry Regiment, at battalion command post in a pillbox in the Siegfried Line near Lieler, Belgium, 6 December 1944. Hereafter cited as Simon interview.
49. Walker interview.
50. *Ibid.*
51. George interview. Simon interview.
52. An interview by CPT William J. Fox with LTC Carl J. Isley, commander, 146th Engineer Combat Battalion, at battalion command post in the woods between Eupen and Monschau, 27 November 1944. Hereafter cited as Isley interview.
53. Statement of COL Edmund K. Daley, commander, 1171st Engineer Combat Group, on operations, 2-8 November. Hereafter cited as Daley statement. See also Engineer Plan of 1171st Engineer Combat Group for Operation "X" dated 30 October 1944 and Amendment Number 1 to Engineer Plan for Operation "X," dated 1 November 1944. See also interview by CPT William J. Fox with COL Edmund K. Daley to complement a previous statement made by him, held at group command post in the Hürtgen Forest, 18 November 1944. Hereafter cited as Daley interview. Also of use has been the essay of COL Richard Ehrhardt, USAR (Ret.), "Engineers in the Hürtgen Forest" (seminar paper, University of South Florida, March 1978).
54. Statement of LTC Jonathan E. Sonnefield relative to the operation of the engineer plan, 6–10 November 1944.
55. Daley statement.
56. An interview by CPT William J. Fox with CPT Henry R. Doherty, commander, A Company, 20th Engineer Combat Battalion, at company command post in the Hürtgen Forest, 22 November 1944. Hereafter cited as Doherty interview.
57. An interview by CPT William J. Fox with CPT Edwin M. Lutz, commander, B Company, 20th Engineer Combat Battalion, at company command post in the Hürtgen Forest, 22 November 1944. Hereafter cited as Lutz interview.
58. See Hostrup and Lutz interviews.
59. Daley statement.
60. *Ibid.*
61. Hostrup and Ripple interviews.
62. *89th Division Review.*
63. Statement by Generalleutnant Hans Schmidt, commanding general, *275th Infantry Division,* "Attacks Without Artillery Preparations," made for the Prisoner of War Interrogation Board at Camp Number 19, Foucarville, France. Originator: Lieutenant Mahin, Siegfried Line Section, MS Number B-804. This is a selection contained in M/3121/7,

Fundamentals of Combined Arms Warfare, the Command and General Staff College, Ft. Leavenworth, Kansas.

64. *89th Division Review.*
65. Gersdorff interview.
66. Fuller interview.
67. Nesbitt interview. Also of help has been Charles Crabtree, "The 112th Infantry Regiment at the Battle of Schmidt" (seminar paper, University of South Florida, Apr. 1982).
68. Beggs interview.
69. An interview by CPT William J. Fox with 1LT Melvin J. Barrilleaux, commander, E Company (at the time of the action); held in I Company command post near Sevenig, Germany, 10 December 1944. Hereafter cited as Barrilleaux interview.

6.
"I'll do what I can, boys"

1. Engineer Plan of 1171st Engineer Combat Group for Operation "X" dated 30 October 1944.
2. Of some help has been Lawrence A. Gardner, "Operation 'X': The Engineers' Battle for Schmidt" (seminar paper, University of South Florida, Apr. 1982).
3. Statement of CPT Edwin M. Lutz, commander, B Company, 20th Engineer Combat Battalion, relative to operation of the Engineer Plan for the Assault on Schmidt. Undated. Hereafter cited as Lutz statement. Also see an interview by CPT William J. Fox with CPT Edwin M. Lutz at company command post in the Hürtgen Forest, 22 November 1944. Hereafter cited as Lutz interview.
4. Lutz statement. Also see Daley statement.
5. Hostrup interview.
6. Peterman, *Western Front,* p. 5.
7. Hostrup interview.
8. Lutz interview.
9. Daley statement.
10. *Ibid.*
11. An interview by CPT John S. Howe with CPT William H. Pinchon, S-4 707th Tank Battalion and 1LT Howard S. Rogers, RCN PLN LDR, Headquarters Company, 707th Tank Battalion, at battalion command post, Müllarschütte, Germany, 14 November 1944. Hereafter cited as Pinchon interview.
12. This account of the difficulties of tankers on the Kall trail has been reconstructed from the Pinchon, Hostrup, and Ripple interviews.

13. Tyo interview.
14. Toner interview.
15. Tyo interview.
16. Ripperdam interview.
17. Ripperdam interview.
18. *Ibid.*
19. Walker and Tyo interviews.
20. Tyo interview.
21. Ripperdam interview.
22. Walker and Dana interviews.
23. Tyo interview.
24. Dana and Cota/Davis interviews.
25. Cota/Davis interview.
26. Toner interview.
27. Piercey and Toner interviews. An interview by CPT William J. Fox with CPT Guy Piercey, commander, and Lt. John P. McInnes, executive officer, M Company, 3rd Battalion, 112th Infantry Regiment, at battalion command post in a pillbox in the Siegfried Line near Lieler, Belgium, 6 December 1944. Hereafter cited as Piercey interview.
28. Piercey interview.
29. Ripperdam interview.
30. Simon interview.
31. Toner interview.
32. *Ibid.*
33. Tyo interview.
34. Simon interview.
35. Ripperdam interview.
36. *Ibid.*
37. Walker and Tyo interviews.
38. Tyo interview.
39. Peterman, *Western Front,* p. 6. See also Perll interview and his recommendation for a Distinguished Service Cross written by 1LT Francis G. Smysor.
40. Dana interview.
41. Ripple interview.
42. Hostrup interview. See also Peterman, *Western Front,* p. 5.
43. *Ibid.*
44. Cota/Davis interview. Also see Simon interview.
45. George interview.
46. Quentin and Littlehales interviews.
47. Quentin interview.
48. Hunter-Kelly interview.
49. Of help has been Susan Decker, "The Battle of Schmidt: Evacuation and

Treatment of the Wounded" (seminar paper, University of South Florida, March 1982).

50. Report on Medical Evacuation, dated 10 November 1944, by MAJ Albert L. Berndt, regimental surgeon, 112th Infantry Regiment, sent to division surgeon, 28th Infantry Division. Hereafter cited as Berndt Report.
51. Report on Medical Evacuation, dated 11 November 1944, by 2LT Alfred J. Muglia, Medical Assistance Corps, surgeon's assistant, 3rd Battalion, 112th Infantry Regiment, sent to division surgeon, 28th Infantry Division. Hereafter cited as Muglia Report.
52. Pinchon interview.
53. Misuse of Aid Station Site, dated 16 November 1944, by CPT Paschal A. Linguiti, surgeon, 1st Battalion, 112th Infantry Regiment, sent to MAJ Albert L. Berndt, regimental surgeon, 112th Infantry Regiment. Hereafter cited as Linguiti report.
54. Crain and Condon interviews.
55. Condon interview.
56. *Ibid.*
57. Allard reminiscences.
58. Peterman, *Western Front,* pp. 6–7.
59. Condon interview.
60. Condon interview.
61. Nesbitt interview.
62. Crain interview.
63. *Ibid.*
64. *Ibid.*
65. Dana interview. Also see PW interrogation report, G-2, 28th Infantry Division, 5 November 1944.
66. *89th Division Review.*

7.
"We were in very bad straits"

1. G-3 Journal, Headquarters, 28th Infantry Division, 5 November 1944. See also *Historical and Pictorial Review of the 28th Infantry Division in World War II* (Nashville, Tenn.: The Battery Press, 1944), p. 91, and R. W. Thompson, *The Battle for the Rhineland* (London: Hutchinson & Co., Ltd., 1958), p. 58.
2. An interview by CPT William J. Fox with LTC James F. White, executive officer, 1171st Engineer Combat Group, 18 November 1944. Hereafter cited as White interview.
3. Johnson interview.

4. Condon interview.
5. Kauffman interview.
6. Barrilleaux interview.
7. See note about Hatzfeld's condition by CPT William J. Fox in his Condon interview.
8. An interview by CPT John S. Howe with 1LT Howard C. Davis, 1st PLN LDR; SGT Hammet E. Murphy, 2nd Section LDR; S/SGT William D. Gardner, 3rd PLN SGT, Company B, 893rd Tank Destroyer Battalion, at company indirect firing positions in the Hürtgen Forest, 23 November 1944. Hereafter cited as Howard Davis interview.
9. See Howard Davis interview. Also see an interview by CPT John S. Howe with CPT Marion C. Pugh, commander, C Company, 893rd Tank Destroyer Battalion, at company fire direction center in a water-soaked log bunker in the Hürtgen Forest at the time of which all personnel were engaged in fire missions in support of the 121st Infantry Regiment and, except for Pugh, were unavailable for questioning, 22 November 1944. Hereafter cited as Pugh interview.
10. Howard Davis interview.
11. *Ibid.*
12. An interview by CPT John S. Howe with CPT Sidney C. Cole, commander, Reconnaissance Company, 893rd Tank Destroyer Battalion, at Müllarschütte, Germany, 17 November 1944. Hereafter cited as Cole interview.
13. An interview by CPT John S. Howe with 1LT Jack W. Fuller, platoon leader, Reconnaissance Company, 893rd Tank Destroyer Battalion, attached to C Company from 4-7 November 1944; held at battalion command post, Müllarschütte, Germany, 17 November 1944. Hereafter cited as Jack Fuller interview.
14. Pugh interview.
15. Howard Davis interview.
16. Pugh interview.
17. Ripple interview. See also an interview by CPT John S. Howe with CPT Donald C. Kelly, commander, Headquarters Company, 707th Tank Battalion, at Müllarschütte, Germany, 14 November 1944. Hereafter cited as Kelly interview.
18. Pinchon and Rogers interviews.
19. Kelly and Pinchon interviews.
20. George interview.
21. Linguiti report.
22. Berndt report.
23. Report of Medical Evacuation, dated 11 November 1944, by 2LT Henry W. Morrison, Medical Assistance Corps officer, 112th Infantry Regiment, sent to division surgeon, 28th Infantry Division. Hereafter cited as Morrison report.

24. Muglia report.
25. *Ibid.*
26. Evacuation of wounded from Vossenack, Kommerscheidt, and Schmidt Area, 2-11 November 1944, by CPT Paschal A. Linguiti, surgeon, 1st Battalion, and CPT Michael DeMarco, surgeon, 3rd Battalion, 112th Infantry Regiment; sent to division surgeon, 28th Infantry Division. Hereafter cited as Linguiti-Demarco report.
27. Doherty interview.
28. Tyo interview.
29. Walker interview.
30. Toner interview.
31. Citation for S/SGT Paul Kerekes, M Company, 3rd Battalion, 112th Infantry Regiment.
32. Citation for S/SGT Arthur Johnson, K Company, 3rd Battalion, 112th Infantry Regiment.
33. Hunter interview.
34. Holden interview.
35. Perll interview.
36. Piercey interview.
37. Dana and Simon interviews.
38. Littlehales interview.
39. Quentin interview.
40. Walker interview.
41. Simon interview.
42. Ripple interview.
43. Quentin and Dana interviews.
44. Statement of Technician Fourth Class James A. Krieder, 3rd Platoon, A Company, 20th Engineer Combat Battalion.
45. Statement of CPL Marion Martone, 3rd PLN, B Company, 20th Engineer Combat Batalion.
46. Statement of Sergeant William F. O'Neal, 3rd PLN, C Company, 20th Engineer Combat Battalion. Also see an interview by CPT William J. Fox with Sergeant William F. O'Neal at company command post in the Hürtgen Forest, 23 November 1944. See further an interview by CPT William J. Fox with Major Bernard P. McDonnell, S-3, 20th Engineer Combat Battalion, in battalion command post in theHürtgen Forest, 22 November 1944.
47. See personal operation report on battalion activities from 29 October to 10 November 1944, dated 14 November 1944, by LTC Jonathan E. Sonnefield, Commander, 20th Engineer Combat Battalion; and see statement of LTC Jonathan E. Sonnefield, commander, 20th Engineer Combat Battalion, relative to the operation of the engineer plan, 6-10 November 1944; and report of battalion activity from 29 October to 9 November by Major Bernard P. McDonnell, S-3, 20th Engineer Combat

Battalion, dated 14 November 1944. I am indebted to Ehrhardt, "Engineers in the Hürtgen Forest," for his analysis of engineering operations along the Kall trail.

48. An interview by CPT William J. Fox with 1LT Clarence White, 1st PLN LDR, C Company, 20th Engineer Combat Battalion, at the company command post in the Hungarian [sic] Forest, 23 November 1944.
49. *89th Division Review.*

8.
"The Saddest sight I have ever seen"

1. Johnson interview.
2. An interview by CPT William J. Fox with CPL Joe E. Philpot, G Company clerk, at the company command post near Lieler, Belgium, 15 December 1944. Hereafter cited as Philpot interview.
3. *Ibid.*
4. Howard Davis interview.
5. Pruden interview.
6. Lutz interview.
7. Kauffman interview.
8. Cascarano interview.
9. Crain interview.
10. Nesbitt interview.
11. Condon interview.
12. Nesbitt interview.
13. Condon interview.
14. *Ibid.*
15. Beggs interview.
16. Johnson interview.
17. Pruden interview.
18. Barrilleaux interview.
19. Kauffman interview.
20. Beggs interview.
21. Barrilleaux interview.
22. An interview by CPT William J. Fox with T/SGT Donald Nelson, 1st PLN SGT, E Company, at the platoon forward command post, Lieler, Belgium, 9 December 1944. Hereafter cited as Nelson interview.
23. Beggs interview.
24. Cascarano interview.
25. Condon interview.
26. Kauffman interview.
27. Pruden interview.
28. Philpot interview.

29. Mays after-action report. After-action narrative prepared by LTC Samuel E. Mays, commander, 893rd Tank Destroyer Battalion (SP), dated 18 November 1944.
30. Howard Davis interview.
31. Leming interview.
32. Granger interview.
33. *Ibid.*
34. Condon interview.
35. Nesbitt interview.
36. Condon interview.
37. Nesbitt interview.
38. Condon interview.
39. W. J. Fox note in Condon interview.
40. An interview by the author with Baptiste Palme, bürgomeister of Vossenack, Germany, August 1979.
41. Howard Davis interview.
42. Mays after-action report.
43. Condon and Nesbitt interviews.
44. Pruden interview.
45. Isley interview. See also journal of the 146th Engineer Combat Battalion, LTC Carl J. Isley commanding. Hereafter cited as Isley journal.
46. Isley interview and Isley journal.
47. *Ibid.* See also notes taken by LTC Pratt, G-3 section, V Corps, on Statements of LTC Sonnefield, commander, 20th Engineer Combat Battalion, and LTC E. K. Daley, commander, 1171st Engineer Combat Group, on engineer part in defense, loss, and recapture of Vossenack, 3 November–8 November 1944.
48. Isley interview and Isley journal.
49. An interview by CPT William J. Fox with CPT Sam H. Ball, Jr., commander, A Company, 146th Engineer Combat Battalion, in woods between Eupen and Monschau, 27 November 1944. Hereafter cited as Ball interview.
50. Isley journal and Isley interview.
51. See LTC Carl J. Isley, commander, 146th Engineer Combat Battalion, "Notes on Operations of 146th Engineer (C) BN in the Recapture and Defense of Vossenack." Undated.
52. Ball interview.
53. See Major Robert L. Argus, S-3, 1171st Engineer Combat Group, "Notes on Operations Against the Enemy on 6 Nov." Dated 13 November.
54. Isley interview and Isley journal.
55. Ball interview.
56. Isley interview and Isley journal.
57. Ball and Isley interviews and Isley journal.
58. Isley and White interviews and Isley journal.

59. Ball and Isley interviews and Isley journal.
60. Leming interview.
61. Isley interview and Isley journal.
62. *Ibid.*
63. Condon interview.
64. *Ibid.*
65. Ball and Isley interviews and Isley journal.
66. A series of written answers to questions put to Generalmajor Siegfried von Waldenburg, commander, *116th Panzer Division,* Command and General Staff College pamphlet, *Fundamentals of Combined Arms Warfare,* R3121/7; MS A-905, Historical Division, Headquarters, United States Army, Europe, 1954, pp. LP-5-3ff. Hereafter cited as Von Waldenburg answers.
67. Palme interview.
68. MacDonald, *Three Battles,* pp. 362–63. See also G-3 Periodic Report Number 112, and G-2 and G-3 journals for 2–9 November 1944.

9.
"I'm dying right here"

1. Berndt report.
2. *Ibid.*
3. Muglia report.
4. Morrison report.
5. Muglia report.
6. Berndt and Muglia reports.
7. Statement of 1LT Lunur T. Makousky, senior officer now present with B Company, 1340th Engineer Combat Battalion, on Operations, 6–10 November. Hereafter cited as Makousky statement. See also an interview by CPT William J. Fox with 1LT Lunur T. Makousky, executive officer, C Company, 1340th Engineer Combat Battalion, 24 November 1944. Hereafter cited as Makousky interview.
8. An interview by CPT William J. Fox with S/SGT Benjamin A. P. Cipra, Jr., 1st Platoon, C Company, 1340th Engineer Combat Battalion, at battalion command post in the Hürtgen Forest, 25 November 1944. Hereafter cited as Cipra interview.
9. Statement by 1LT Carl B. Setterberg, platoon leader, B Company, 1340th Engineer Combat Battalion, dated 11 November 1944. Hereafter cited as Setterberg statement. See also an interview by CPT William J. Fox with CPT Thomas F. Creegan, commander, B Company, and 1LT Carl B. Setterberg, executive officer, B Company, 1340th Engineer Combat Battalion, at company command post in the Hürtgen Forest, 24 November 1944. Hereafter cited as Creegan interview.

10. Statement by CPT Frank P. Bane, "Operations 'A' Company, 1340th Engineer Combat Battalion on 7 November," dated 14 November. See also an interview by CPT William J. Fox with CPT Frank P. Bane, commander, A Company, 1340th Engineer Combat Battalion, in the Hürtgen Forest, 24 November 1944. Hereafter cited as Bane interview. Also see Makousky interview and an interview by CPT William J. Fox with S/SGT Earlis S. Gillespie, 2nd Platoon, C Company, and MAJ Bruce Renfroe, S-3, 1340th Engineer Combat Battalion, in battalion command post truck in the Hürtgen Forest, 24 November 1944. Hereafter cited as Gillespie interview.
11. Cipra and Gillespie interviews.
12. Makousky interview and Makousky statement. Also see statement by MAJ John G. Auld, executive officer, 1340th Engineer Combat Battalion, "OPERATIONS, 6–10 Nov 44," dated 16 November 1944.
13. Pugh and Fuller interviews.
14. Ripple interview.
15. *Ibid.* See also Burns interview.
16. Ripple interview.
17. Pugh interview.
18. Dana interview.
19. Fuller and Howard Davis interviews.
20. Ripple interview.
21. Hostrup interview.
22. *Ibid.*
23. "Report of Tank Company Commander on Counterattack to Retake Kommerscheidt," 6 November 1944. No name or unit identification is given. Command and General Staff College pamphlet, *Fundamentals of Combined Arms Warfare,* R3121/7, pp. LP-6-1ff.
24. Hostrup interview.
25. *Ibid.*
26. Kudiak interview.
27. George interview.
28. Kudiak interview.
29. Ripperdam and Tyo interviews.
30. Peterman, *Western Front,* pp. 5–6.
31. Kudiak interview.
32. George interview.
33. Hunter interview.
34. Perll interview.
35. *Ibid.*
36. Kelly interview.
37. Walker interview.
38. Ripperdam interview.
39. Quentin interview.
40. Holden interview.

41. Ripperdam interview.
42. Tyo interview.
43. Perll interview.
44. Riperdam interview.
45. Dana interview.
46. Perll interview.
47. George interview.
48. *Ibid.*
49. Kudiak interview.
50. Tyo interview.
51. Kudiak interview.
52. *89th Division Review* and Von Waldenburg answers.

10.
"All hell was breaking loose"

1. Isley interview and Isley journal.
2. Granger interview.
3. Pruden interview.
4. Nesbitt interview.
5. Granger interview.
6. Condon interview.
7. Nesbitt interview.
8. Isley interview and Isley journal.
9. Condon interview.
10. Isley interview and Isley journal.
11. Condon interview.
12. Nesbitt interview.
13. Philpot interview.
14. Beggs interview.
15. Beggs and Condon interviews.
16. Kauffman interview.
17. Daley interview and statement, Isley interview and journal.
18. Peer interview.
19. Whitetree, Sheehan, Whitney, Peer, Paul, Clark, and Rogers interviews.
20. Strickler interview.
21. Clark and McFeaters interviews.
22. Strickler and Rogers interviews.
23. Rogers interview.
24. Mays after-action report, Cota/Davis interview, Howard Davis interview.
25. Tyo interview.
26. George interview.

27. Creegan interview.
28. *Ibid.*
29. Gillespie interview.
30. Cipra interview.
31. Morrison report.
32. 1LT Loyd C. Johnson, "Casualty Evacuation Report" (undated), C Company, 103rd Medical Battalion, 112th Infantry Regiment. Hereafter cited as Johnson casualty report.
33. Berndt report.
34. Field Order Number 26, 070830 November 1944, Headquarters, 28th Infantry Division.
35. Mays after-action report; G-3 Journal, Headquarters, 28th Infantry Division, 7 November 1944.
36. Several men with whom I spoke at a reunion of members of the 110th Infantry Regiment, Washington, Pennsylvania, 8–9 September 1979, recalled seeing such occurrences.
37. Toner interview.
38. Dana interview.
39. Ripple interview.
40. Quentin and Littlehales interviews.
41. Hostrup interview.
42. Dana interview.
43. Hostrup interview.
44. Ripperdam interview.
45. Hostrup interview.
46. Littlehales and Quentin interviews.
47. Dana interview.
48. Ripple interview.
49. Kudiak interview. See also Peterman, *Western Front,* p. 4.
50. Ripperdam interview.
51. Walker interview.
52. Gooley interview.
53. Walker interview.
54. Ripperdam interview.
55. See divisional message traffic logs.
56. Simon interview.
57. Ripple and Quentin interviews.
58. Hostrup interview.
59. In the Rumbaugh interview, the time is given as between 0900 and 1000 hours; the Ripple interview states the message came a little after 1000 hours; and the Dana interview claims the order was received at about 1500 hours.
60. This episode was reconstructed from interviews with Ripple, Rumbaugh, and Dana; from *Historical and Pictorial Review,* p. 75; from Gavin, *On*

to Berlin, p. 298; and from MacDonald, *Three Battles,* pp. 375, 380–81, 389.
61. Ripperdam interview.
62. Piercey interview.
63. Quentin and Littlehales interviews, and see Quentin's citation for the Medal of Honor.
64. Ripperdam interview.
65. Rumbaugh interview.
66. Perll interview.
67. *Ibid.*
68. Dana interview.
69. *Ibid.*
70. Perll interview.
71. Dana interview.
72. Perll interview.
73. *89th Division* Review.
74. Gersdorff interview.
75. *89th Division* Review.
76. Gersdorff interview.
77. Telephone conversation, General Cota to General Davis, 072200A November 1944, typescript among divisional papers.
78. Telephone conversation, General Gerow, CG, V Corps, to General Cota, 072310A November 1944, typescript among divisional papers.
79. ACTS 2: 17, 19, 20.

11.
"Fight your way out"

1. G-3 Journal, 080001-082400 November 1944, Headquarters, 28th Infantry Division. See also *Historical and Pictorial,* p. 92.
2. *Ibid.*
3. White interview.
4. Quotes are drawn from MacDonald, *Schmidt,* P2-I-37.
5. Weigley, *Eisenhower's Lieutenants,* p. 368.
6. *89th Division* Review.
7. Perll interview.
8. Peterman, *Western Front,* p. 4.
9. Pugh interview.
10. Ripperdam interview.
11. Hunter interview.
12. Rumbaugh interview.
13. Ripple to 112th Infantry rear command post, 1140 hours, 8 November 1944, message traffic logs.

14. Citation for CPT Clifford T. Hackard, commanding officer, Company B, 1st Battalion, 112th Infantry Regiment, for the Distinguished Service Cross.
15. This portion of the story is reconstructed from "Report of Colonel Gustin M. Nelson to the Assistant Division Commander, 28th Infantry Division." Undated. See also Rogers interview.
16. Sheehan interview.
17. *Ibid.* See also citation by COL Gustin M. Nelson for 2LT Edmund W. Tropp for Bronze Star. Undated.
18. *Historical and Pictorial Review,* p. 92.
19. Dana interview.
20. Rumbaugh interview.
21. Dana and Rumbaugh interviews.
22. After-action report dated 13 November 1944 by LTC Truman H. Setliffe, commander, 1340th Engineer Combat Battalion. See also statement relative to engineering aspects of operation, 2–6 November, by LTC Truman H. Setliffe, commander, 1340th Engineer Combat Battalion.
23. Hunter interview.
24. *89th Division* Review.
25. Kelly, Hostrup, and Pugh interviews.
26. Pugh interview.
27. Rumbaugh interview.
28. *Ibid.*
29. Kudiak interview.
30. Ripple interview.
31. Kudiak and Dana interviews, and report of COL Gustin M. Nelson to assistant division commander, 28th Infantry Division. Undated.
32. Muglia report.
33. Linguiti-DeMarco report.
34. Muglia report.
35. Kudiak interview.
36. An interview by CPT John S. Howe with CPT Donald C. Kelly, commander, Headquarters Company, 707th Tank Battalion, at Müllarschütte, Germany, 14 November 1944. Hereafter cited as Don Kelly interview.
37. Rumbaugh, Perll, and Don Kelly interviews.
38. Ripple interview.
39. Perll interview.
40. Pugh interview.
41. Don Kelly interview.
42. Hostrup interview.
43. Toner interview.
44. Perll interview.
45. Walker interview.

46. Nelson report.
47. Ripple and Rumbaugh interviews.
48. Rumbaugh interview.
49. *Ibid.*
50. Mays After-action report.
51. See divisional message traffic logs.
52. *89th Division* Review.
53. Nesbitt interview.
54. Pruden interview. See also *Historical and Pictorial Review,* p. 92.
55. Pruden interview.
56. Nesbitt interview.
57. *Historical and Pictorial Review,* p. 92.
58. Howard Davis interview.
59. Granger interview.
60. White interview.
61. Clark interview.
62. Peer interview.
63. *Ibid.*

12.
"It is plenty hot down here"

1. Toner interview.
2. Howard Davis interview.
3. Berndt report and Johnson casualty evacuation report.
4. Johnson casualty evacuation report.
5. Linguiti/DeMarco report and Muglia report.
6. Berndt report.
7. Johnson casualty evacuation report.
8. *Ibid.*
9. Muglia report.
10. Linguiti/DeMarco report.
11. *Ibid.*
12. Muglia report.
13. MacDonald, *Three Battles,* f411n.
14. *89th Division* Review.
15. Johnson casualty evacuation report and Muglia report.
16. Johnson casualty evacuation report.
17. Muglia report.
18. Linguiti/DeMarco report.
19. *Historical and Pictorial Review,* p. 92.
20. Linguiti/DeMarco report.

21. *Ibid.* See also MacDonald, *Three Battles,* p. 411.
22. Linguiti report.
23. Linguiti/DeMarco report.
24. Berndt report.
25. Sheehan and Paul interviews.
26. Clark and Paul interviews.
27. Potter interview.
28. Whitney and Potter interviews.
29. Garrett interview.
30. *Ibid.*
31. Garrett and McFeaters interviews.
32. Sheehan interview. Cf. *Historical and Pictorial Review,* p. 92.
33. Setliffe after-action report.
34. Whitney interview.
35. Clark, McFeaters, Potter, Whitney, and Whitetree interviews.
36. COL Theodore Seely to CG, 081122 November 1944, divisional message traffic logs.
37. Arford interview.
38. Hubner letter.
39. Rumbaugh interview; see also 110th Regimental summary of action.
40. See 110th Regimental summary of action and Burns interview.
41. Garrett interview.
42. Coleman interview.
43. Nation interview.
44. Dobbs interview.
45. Burns interview.
46. *Ibid.*
47. Dobbs and Nation interviews.
48. Coleman interview.
49. *Ibid.* See also Dobbs interview.
50. Rumbaugh, Nation, Coleman, and Dobbs interviews.
51. Burns interview.
52. *Ibid.* See also 110th Regiment summary of action.
53. Burns interview.
54. Howard Davis interview; see also Burns interview.
55. 110th Regiment summary of action.
56. MacDonald, *Schmidt,* P2-I-42.
57. Gavin, *On to Berlin,* p. 298.
58. MacDonald, *Schmidt,* P2-I-44.
59. Thompson, *Battle for the Rhineland,* p. 65, and p. 40.
60. *Historical and Pictorial Review,* p. 99.
61. *Ibid.,* p. 174.
62. *Ibid.,* p. 1.

13.
"They Hated the Hürtgen Forest"

1. Burke Davis, *The Gray Fox: Robert E. Lee and the Civil War* (New York: Holt, Rinehart & Company, 1956), p. 168.
2. Peterman, *Western Front,* p. 3.
3. Laura Fermi, *Mussolini* (Chicago: University of Chicago Press, 1961), p. 401.
4. MacDonald, *Three Battles,* p. 416.
5. Gersdorff interview.
6. Gavin, *On to Berlin,* p. 299n.
7. Gavin, *On to Berlin,* p. 297.
8. *Ibid.,* p. 294.
9. *Ibid.,* pp. 297–98.
10. William Manchester, *American Caesar: Douglas MacArthur, 1880–1964* (Boston, 1978), p. 280.
11. *Ibid.,* p. 339.

Selected Bibliography

Primary Materials

The following primary materials are catalogued as "Combat Interviews, 28th Division Hurtgen Forest Campaign, Record Group Number 407, Records of the Adjutant General's Office, World War II Operations Reports, 1940–1948, The National Archives, Washington, D.C."

109th Infantry Regiment

(Interviews with the 109th Infantry Regiment were conducted by 1LT Harry G. Jackson.)

1st Battalion

Headquarters Company: 1LT Charles E. Potter.

A Company: CPT Max R. Whitetree, 2LT Samuel J. Leo, T/SGT Charles E. Frawley, T/SGT Leo D. Balleger.

B Company: 1LT Thomas H. Whitney.

2nd Battalion

E Company: 1LT Donald P. Clark, S/SGT Martin A. Slaughter, S/SGT Ralph A. Galiso, SGT Herbert W. Hawksley, PFC Earl W. Olsen.

F Company: S/SGT Cleo C. Garrett, S/SGT William C. Horan, S/SGT Erwin S. Mucha, PVT James A. McCutchen, Jr.

G Company: 2LT Frank McFeaters, T/SGT Edward H. Serafin, T/SGT Hugh T. Sharp, S/SGT B. J. D'Amico, S/SGT Toivo E. Pihlagh, SGT Arthur E. McGrew.

H Company: 1/SGT Leonard E. Konsaer, S/SGT Robert G. Wolf, SGT Glen Bice, CPL Melvin W. Kaufmann.

3rd Battalion

I Company: 1LT Bruce W. Paul, 1LT William Pina, T/SGT Thomas F. Blair, T/SGT Norman D. Payne, 1/SGT William W. Johnston, S/SGT Frank F. Stunar, S/SGT Edward W. Parks, S/SGT Steven G. Raferty, S/SGT James L. Baker, SGT Dagly D. Collett, SGT Gerald Bowbly.

K Company: 1LT Francis Sheehan, S/SGT Aiken Still, T/SGT Robert McMillin, S/SGT Harold A. Jenkins.

L Company: 1LT Edward L. Peer, 2LT Carl J. Emrick, T/SGT Thomas Budd, 1/SGT Robert D. Francis, S/SGT Hobert Kirk, SGT Alexander Zaltsburg.

Headquarters Company: CPT William T. Rogers.

Regimental Headquarters: LTC Daniel B. Strickler, MAJ William Moraney.

110th Infantry Regiment

(Interviews with the 110th Infantry Regiment were conducted by CPT John S. Howe.)

1st Battalion

Headquarters Company: CPT James H. Burns, CPT Wesley J. Rose, CPT Joseph L. Minter, 1LT Francis P. Diamond, 1LT Francis K. Richwine, 2LT Harold E. Miller.

2nd Battalion

E Company: 1LT Frank J. Deptula, CPT William C. Dobbs, 1/SGT Lonnie C. Bland.

F Company: CPT Lake W. Coleman, 2LT Edward J. Matheny, 2LT J. D. King, 1/SGT Steve N. Levering, 1/SGT George W. Fetzer, T/SGT Warren H. Dunlap.

G Company: 2LT Frank R. Nation, SGT Avery Lanning, S/SGT Joseph K. Paczesna, SGT William M. Pennington, S/SGT Abraham Kumukau, S/SGT Manuel C. Suarez, S/SGT Morris G. Sykes.

3rd Battalion

Headquarters Company: COL Theodore A. Seely, MAJ Harold R. Yeager, CPT George H. Rumbaugh, CPT William S. Linning, S/SGT Martin J. Joyce.

CPT John S. Howe, "SUMMARY OF ACTION, 2–16 November 1944, 110th Infantry Regiment, 28th Infantry Division, Vossenack–Kommerscheidt–Schmidt."

112th Infantry Regiment

(The following interviews with 1st Battalion were conducted by CPT William J. Fox)

1st Battalion

Headquarters Company: CPT Richard Gooley, SGT Tony Kudiak, SGT Eugene Holden.

A Company: S/SGT Nathaniel Quentin, 1/SGT Harvey Hausman, T/SGT George A. Lockwood, S/SGT Stephen J. Kertes, SGT Travis C. Norton.

B Company: T/SGT Roy Littlehales, SGT Clarence J. Skains.

C Company: S/SGT Joseph Perll.

D Company: 1LT Jack E. Kelly, SGT Thomas G. Hunter.

The following interviews with First Battalion were conducted by COL Gustin M. Nelson.)

Headquarters Company: SGT Tony Kudiak and SGTs McCarl and Sibel.

A Company: T/SGT George A. Lockwood and SGT Gulden.

B Company: T/SGT Roy Littlehales, and SGTs Clark, Ostrowski and Sparling.

C Company: SGT Thomas G. Hunter and SGT Barbour.

2nd Battalion

(The following interviews were conducted by CPT William J. Fox.)

Headquarters Company: CPT John D. Pruden and CPT James T. Nesbitt.

E Company: 1LT James A. Condon, 1LT Clifton W. Beggs, 1LT Melvin J. Barrilleaux, T/SGT Donald Nelson.

F Company: 1LT Eldeen Kauffman, S/SGT Charles W. Cascarano.

G Company: 1LT Clyde R. Johnson, CPL Joe E. Philpot.

H Company: CPT Charles Crain.

3rd Battalion

Headquarters Company: 1LT Leon Simon, 1LT William George, 1LT Jack B. Greene.

I Company: 1/SGT Robert C. Toner.

K Company: 2LT Richard Tyo, SGT Carl E. Stadelbacher, PVT Dorn.

L Company: CPT Jack Walker, 1/SGT Frank Ripperdam.

M Company: CPT Guy Piercey, 2LT John P. McInnes.

Regimental Headquarters: COL Gustin M. Nelson, MAJ Richard S. Dana.

COL Gustin M. Nelson, "Report to Assistant Division Commander, 28th Infantry Division."

707th Tank Battalion

(The following interviews were conducted by CPT John S. Howe.)

Headquarters Company: LTC Richard W. Ripple, CPT Donald C. Kelly, CPT William H. Pinchon, 1LT Howard S. Rogers.

A Company: CPT Bruce M. Hostrup, 1LT Raymond E. Fleig, 2LT Richard H. Payne.

B Company: CPT George S. Granger, 1LT Carl A. Anderson, S/SGT Letford W. Walling, S/SGT John B. Cook.

C Company: 1LT James J. Leming, 1LT James J. Ryan, 2LT William D. Quarrie, S/SGT Paul F. Jenkins.

893rd Tank Destroyer Battalion

(The following interviews were conducted by CPT John S. Howe.)

Headquarters Company: LTC Samuel E. Mays, MAJ John J. Lavin, MAJ Henry C. Merlin.

Reconnaissance Company: CPT Sidney C. Cole.

B Company: 1LT Howard C. Davis, SGT Hammet E. Murphy, S/SGT William D. Gardner.

C Company: CPT Marion C. Pugh, 1LT Jack W. Fuller.

LTC Samuel E. Mays, "After-action narrative."

146th Engineer Combat Battalion

(The following interviews were conducted by CPT William J. Fox.)

Headquarters Company: LTC Carl J. Isley.

A Company: CPT Sam H. Ball, Jr.

C Company: 1LT Bernard E. Meier.

LTC Carl J. Isley, "Notes on Operations of 146th Engineer (C) BN in the Recapture and Defense of Vossenack."

Journal of the 146th Engineer Combat Battalion.

20th Engineer Combat Battalion

(Interviews of men in this battalion were conducted by CPT William J. Fox.)

A Company: CPT Henry R. Doherty.

B Company: CPT Edwin M. Lutz.

C Company: SGT William F. O'Neal.

MAJ Bernard P. McDonnell, "Report of Battalion Activity from 29 October to 9 November."

CPT Edwin M. Lutz, "Statement Relative to Operation of the Engineer Plan."

SGT William F. O'Neal, "Statement on the Action."

CPL Marion Martone, "Statement on the Action."

T/4 James A. Krieder, "Statement on the Action."

1340th Engineer Combat Battalion

(Interviews of men in this battalion were conducted by CPT William J. Fox.)

Headquarters Company: MAJ Bruce Renfroe.

A Company: CPT Frank P. Bane.

B Company: CPT Thomas F. Creegan, 1LT Carl B. Setterberg.

C Company: 1LT Lunur T. Makousky, S/SGT Benjamin A. P. Cipra, Jr., S/SGT Earlis S. Gillespie.

LTC Truman H. Setliffe, "After-action report."

_____, "Statement relative to Engineering aspects of operation, 2–6 November."
_____, "Operations, 6–10 November 1944."
MAJ John G. Auld, "Statement on Operations 6–10 November 1944."
CPT Frank P. Bane, "Statement on Operations of 'A' Company."
1LT Carl B. Setterberg, "Statement on B Company."
1LT Kelsey C. Mannin, "Statement on Operations for the Period 6–10 November 1944."
1LT Lunur T. Makousky, "Statement on Operations of C Company, 6–10 November 1944."

1171st Engineer Combat Group

(The following two interviews were conducted by CPT William J. Fox.)
COL Edmund K. Daley, LTC James F. White.
COL Edmund K. Daley, "Statement on operations, 2–8 November."
LTC Pratt, "Notes taken on statements of Lt. Col. Sonnefield, Commander, 20th Engineer (C) BN and Col Daley, Commander, 1171st Engineer (C) Grp, on engineer part in defense, loss and recapture of VOSSENACK, 3 Nov.–8 Nov. 1944."
MAJ Robert L. Argus, "Notes on Operations Against Enemy on 6 November."
Engineer Plan of 1171st Engineer (C) Group for Operation "X."
Amendment Number 1 to Engineer Plan for Operation "X."

28th Infantry Division

(The following two interviews were conducted by CPT William J. Fox.)
MG Norman D. Cota, commanding general, and BG George A. Davis, assistant division commander.
Air Support Party VHF Performance Log.
Divisional Field Orders and Operations Plans.
G-2 Intelligence Section Journal, Periodic Reports.
G-3 Operations Section Journal.

Medical Records

MAJ Albert L. Berndt, "Report on Medical Evacuation."
CPT Paschal A. Linguiti, "Mis-use of Aid Station Site."
_____ and CPT Michael DeMarco, "Evacuation of Wounded from Vossenack, Kommerscheidt, and Schmidt Area, 2–11 November 1944."
1LT Loyd C. Johnson, "Casualty Evacuation Report."
2LT Alfred J. Muglia, "Report on Medical Evacuation."
2LT Henry W. Morrison, "Report of Medical Evacuation."
CPT Stanley H. French, "SUBJECT: Battle Casualties."

Miscellaneous

CPT William J. Fox, An annotated typescript of items to be investigated by interviews.

CPT John S. Howe, "Procedural and summary statement of investigations of CPT John S. Howe, CPT William J. Fox, and 1LT Harry G. Jackson."

Citations for CPT Clifford T. Hackard, S/SGT Arthur Johnson, S/SGT Paul Kerekes, PFC Joseph R. Perll, PFC Nathaniel Quentin, PFC John W. Smedberg, 2LT Edmund W. Tropp, 1LT John B. Wine.

Secondary Materials

Privately Printed Materials

Allard, John B. "A Replacement and the 'Bloody Bucket.'" Typed and mimeographed reminiscence. Undated.

Chattaway, Charles. "'GENTLEMEN FROM HELL': The History of the 110th Infantry Regiment, 28th Division." Pamphlet. March 1979.

Chmiola, Joseph J. "History of the 109th Artillery." Pamphlet. 19 May 1969.

Colbaugh, Jack. *The Bloody Patch: A True Story of the Daring 28th Infantry Division.* New York: Vantage Press, 1973.

Command and General Staff College. *The Battle of Schmidt.* M3121-2/R3121-2. Pamphlet. Ft. Leavenworth, Kans., 1975.

Command and General Staff College. *The Battle of Schmidt.* R3121/7. Pamphlet. Ft. Leavenworth, Kans., 1976.

Books

Gavin, James M. *On to Berlin: Battles of an Airborne Commander, 1943–1946.* New York, 1978.

Jackson, L. K. *U.S. Military Commanders in World War II.* New York, 1981.

Keegan, John and Andrew Wheatcroft. eds. *Who's Who in Military History.* New York, 1976.

MacDonald, Charles B. *Three Battles: Arnaville, Altuzzo, and Schmidt.* Washington, D.C., 1952.

———. *The Siegfried Line Campaign.* Washington, D.C., 1963.

———. *The Last Offensive.* Washington, D.C., 1973.

Manchester, William. *American Caesar: Douglas MacArthur, 1880–1964.* Boston, 1978.

Thompson, R. W. *The Battle for the Rhineland.* London, 1958.

Weigley, Russell F. *Eisenhower's Lieutenants: The Campaign of France and Germany, 1944–1945.* Bloomington, Inc., 1981.

Index